$77.95

The Tempest

Recent Titles in
Greenwood Guides to Shakespeare

Henry V: A Guide to the Play
Joan Lord Hall

Macbeth: A Guide to the Play
H. R. Coursen

Hamlet: A Guide to the Play
W. Thomas MacCary

Julius Caesar: A Guide to the Play
Jo McMurtry

Romeo and Juliet: A Guide to the Play
Jay L. Halio

Othello: A Guide to the Play
Joan Lord Hall

THE TEMPEST

A Guide to the Play

H. R. COURSEN

Greenwood Guides to Shakespeare

Greenwood Press
Westport, Connecticut • London

Library of Congress Cataloging-in-Publication Data

Coursen, Herbert R.
    The tempest : a guide to the play / H. R. Coursen.
        p.   cm.—(Greenwood guides to Shakespeare)
    Includes bibliographical references and index.
    ISBN 0–313–31191–9 (alk. paper)
    1. Shakespeare, William, 1564–1616. Tempest.   2. Tragicomedy.   I. Title.   II. Series.
PR2833.C68   2000
    822.3'3—dc21   99–051320

British Library Cataloguing in Publication Data is available.

Library of Congress Catalog Card Number: 99–051320
ISBN: 0–313–31191–9

First published in 2000

Greenwood Press, 88 Post Road West, Westport, CT 06881
An imprint of Greenwood Publishing Group, Inc.
www.greenwood.com

Printed in the United States of America

The paper used in this book complies with the
Permanent Paper Standard issued by the National
Information Standards Organization (Z39.48–1984).

10 9 8 7 6 5 4 3 2 1

CONTENTS

Acknowledgments   ix

1. Textual History   1

2. Contexts and Sources   7

3. Dramatic Structure   45

4. Themes   63

5. Critical Approaches   79

6. The Play in Performance   141

    Bibliographical Essay   197

    Works Cited   201

    Index   225

1994 poster for the Stratford Festival, Stratford, Ontario.

ACKNOWLEDGMENTS

I want to thank my former colleague at Bowdoin College, William Collins Watterson, who is Edward Little Professor there, my present colleague at the University of Maine, Jill Rubinson Fenton, and Bookland of Brunswick for helping me find a couple of books that I could not provide "from mine own library." I also thank my former teachers of Shakespeare, John Shannon, Dorothy Dromeshauser, John Moore, C. L. Barber, Theodore Baird, Davis Harding, J.A.S. McPeak, Leonard Dean, and William Rosen, as well as Homer and Laura Swander and their wonderful Theatre in England program. The splendid Clemson Shakespeare Conference, conducted by Jim Andreas, Chip Egan, and Charlotte Holt, has been an inspiration for me over the years. I am grateful to Virginia Mason Vaughan of Clark University and Alden T. Vaughan for letting me look at the introduction to the Arden edition of *The Tempest* that they are editing. I am also grateful to Professor Susan Crowl of Ohio University for helping me with "Caliban on Setebos." I also thank George Butler of Greenwood Publishing Group for his encouragement and Maureen Melino of Greenwood for a meticulous job of handling permissions, and Elizabeth Meagher of Greenwood for her painstaking production editing of the manuscript. Finally, I want to thank Pamela Alwyn Mount for her support during the course of this project.

This book is for my mother, Mildred Huntoon Coursen, who would have sat right down and read it.

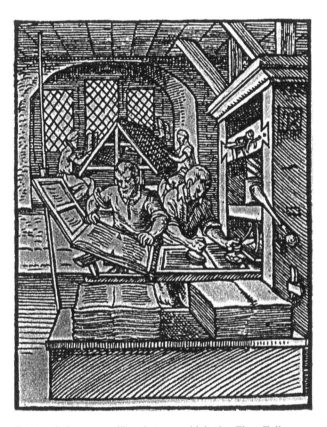

Early printing press like that on which the First Folio was printed.

1

TEXTUAL HISTORY

THE FIRST EDITION OF *THE TEMPEST*

The textual issues surrounding *The Tempest* are straightforward. The play was not printed during Shakespeare's lifetime. The only text is that of the First Folio (1623). Although *The Tempest* is the last play Shakespeare wrote by himself, it is the first play printed in the First Folio. There, the text is divided into five acts, with separate scenes clearly delineated, and with the Epilogue and a list of characters on the last page. The stage directions are unusually complete, even "literary," meaning that modifications like "tempestuous" and "quaint" seem more appropriate for a reader than for a stagehand. It may be that John Heminge and Henry Condell, who compiled the First Folio, decided that the play, which was popular and had never been published, should lead off their massive volume, and that the text should be especially prepared for a printed format.

John Jowett (1983) says that the stage directions in *The Tempest* tend to be "non-theatrical, and would be peculiarly ineffective in instructing the players" (107). The "transcript," Jowett says, "was [probably] prepared specifically in order to appear as the first play in F" (109). Its "literary quality . . . may be an impediment when the text is used in the theatre" (110).

A few scholars speculate that the Masque in Act 4 was added for a special performance: the wedding of Princess Elizabeth and Frederick, the Elector Palatine, on 14 February 1613. W. J. Lawrence argues that the Masque was interpolated shortly after Elizabeth's betrothal, in anticipation of a command performance (1920, 941–46). This is dubious, however, since the Masque serves within the play for the betrothed Ferdinand and Miranda, and since the play is already the second shortest in the canon, ahead only of *The Comedy of Errors*.

Irwin Smith, however, claims that "the masque was inserted in the play as an afterthought" (1970, 214). Ariel and Ceres are doubled because that boy actor had the "best soprano voice in the troupe," says Smith (215). Smith justifies his erasure of the "revels" speech by arguing that the play has not contained towers, palaces, and temples, and that the speech "is too majestic, too tranquil for its present context" (219). That is to interpret the speech in the direction of a thesis. For the play without the Masque, see Smith (220–21). In Smith's version, Prospero does tell Ariel that the "young couple . . . expect . . . Some vanity of" Prospero's art. Ariel responds with alacrity, and Prospero commands, "No tongue! All eyes! Be silent." Smith provides "soft music" and "a dance, towards the end whereof Prospero starts suddenly and speaks" (221). This is to promise and not deliver—to some extent as Shakespeare seems to keep promising an entrance for Edward the Confessor in *Macbeth* 4.3. But in Smith's editing, which cuts 113 lines from the play, we are left with an incomprehensible prelude—"Bring a corollary / Rather than want a spirit"—(4.1.57–58) to a series of movements that do not occur. If anything, the excision makes a case for the original inclusion. While some productions deal with the Masque more or less as Smith suggests the original text does, and while some productions mime it, overelaborate it, or drown it out with noise, Smith's approach would work more smoothly were the text to eliminate Prospero's calling of Ariel and Ariel's entrance. Why project a Masque that does not occur? "The masque is believed to be an addition for the wedding . . . in 1613" (Tobin 1984, 158). If so, the addition has been firmly embedded ex post facto.

One textual scholar, Jeanne Addison Roberts, having examined a number of First Folios in the Folger Library collection, suggests that Ferdinand says, "So rare a wonder'd father and a wife [not *wise*] / Makes this place Paradise" (4.1.123)—the line through the letter making it an "f," not an "s" (1978, 203–8). Older printing made the "f" and "s" almost indistinguishable. This is a doubtful reading, because it leaves Ferdinand with an awkward rhyme, even if his next line does not make a complete couplet.

Hallett Smith says that there is "no good reason to suppose the play has been abridged" (1969, 2), something that has often been speculated about *Macbeth*. Happily, *The Tempest* comes forward from its first appearance in 1623 relatively free of editing problems, emendations, added stage directions, and debate over alternative readings.

MODERN EDITIONS OF THE PLAY

With the exception of Horace Howard Furness's New Variorum edition, which is an 1892 hardbound edition, I deal here only with single-text, paperback editions published since World War Two. The definitive text is Frank Kermode's 1954 New Arden edition, reissued in paper in 1964. It will soon be supplanted by a yet newer Arden edition, a sparkling version compiled by Alden Vaughan and Virginia Vaughan (1999). I use Kermode's edition in quoting *The Tempest* in this book.

Kermode's edition defends the integrity of the First Folio and deals with theories of earlier versions. He treats the resonance of "the New World" in Jacobean England, the contrast between "nature" and "art," magic, genre, analogous literature, masque elements, verse, and criticism and has ample selections from possible sources, as well as notes on the background from which Ariel emerges, the play on the Jacobean stage, and music in the play. Any serious study of the play begins here. This edition was reissued in the 1990s with glue that holds the pages together and an amusing picture on the cover of Caliban playing peek-a-boo with the reader.

The Vaughans' edition is illustrated, while Kermode's is not, with versions and visions of the play from its early manifestation in Hogarth's idealized painting (circa 1735) onward. The Vaughans' edition emphasizes the history of the play in performance and the appropriation of its themes and characters at various times for various purposes, so that it becomes a useful document in an ongoing analysis of *The Tempest* as cultural force, as opposed to Kermode's more scholarly edition, which, in the manner of older editions, is a summary of "what is known." The Vaughans' edition assumes a teleology whose goals keep bringing others into view. They include a section on appropriations, featuring Robert Browning's "Caliban on Setebos," José Enrique Rodo's *Ariel*, and Dominique Octave Mannoni's *Prospero and Caliban*.

A third major edition is Stephen Orgel's Oxford edition (1987), which is particularly strong on the background of the play: political marriages, utopia and the New World, authority, epic and history, the masque, and so on. It is also usefully illustrated with historical material and with art deriving from the play.

The fourth major edition worth attention is H. H. Furness's New Variorum edition of 1892, which includes a compendium of eighteenth- and nineteenth-century criticism of the play. Much of this has dropped out of the discourse, but it is valuable nonetheless for its insight into how the play reflected itself to and through various moments in time. Also included are the Dryden-Davenant version and excerpts from Ernest Renan's *The Tempest* and from F. G. Waldron's *The Virgin Queen*, as well as a commentary on Browning's "Caliban on Setebos." I invariably find the nineteenth-century New Variorum editions valuable in showing a depth and complexity of prior response that modern criticism has discarded.

I refer to these editions in the discussions that follow, and to the introductions in many of the paperback editions I mention later. Many of the individual editions are incorporated into various volumes of the complete works. It may be that Norton will bring out its recent edition (1997), based on the Oxford edition, in separate paperbacks before long. All of these editions, with the exception of the Everyman edition, follow the First Folio text (1623), with the usual modernizations of spelling and standardization of punctuation. Almost all of them have sound essays on sources, information on Shakespeare's stage, and useful critical introductions. Teachers should read the note on editorial practices so that students can be aware of the remarkable amount of editing that has gone on since 1623, even with as "clean" an original as *The Tempest*. The place where notes appear and the amount and detail of the notes vary from edition to edition. A teacher should look at several editions to determine which one best suits the level at which his or her students encounter the play (a variable, of course, even within the same class), the size of the class, and the teacher's approach to Shakespeare. Some of these editions may have disappeared by now, and others may have been updated and reissued.

The Crofts Classics edition (1946) has a brief but wide-ranging introduction by Alfred Harbage. Notes are placed at the bottom of each page of text.

The Yale Shakespeare, originally edited by Chauncey Brewster Tinker and Tucker Brooke in the early 1910s and 1920s and reissued in paperback in the 1940s and 1950s under Helge Kokeritz and Charles T. Prouty, is a compact and convenient edition, "printed on good paper," as the jacket says, with notes at the bottom of the page and brief summaries of the sources. The original, edited by Tinker in 1918, has a blank page opposite each page of text, reflecting the lecture approach to Shakespeare made famous by George Lyman Kittredge of Harvard, who went through the text line by line, commenting on odd words and irregular metrics and pausing to delectate over an elegant turn of phrase.

The Pelican edition (1959, revised 1970) has a note on Shakespeare's stage and an elegant introduction by Northrop Frye, emphasizing, as one would expect, nature and its rhythms in the play and including a lucid summary of classical and contemporary sources. Notes are at the bottom of the page.

The Kittredge version (1939), revised by Irving Ribner (1966), is an attractive edition, valuable chiefly for the introduction and notes by that great scholar of a previous generation, George Lyman Kittredge. The introduction succinctly covers the topics of sources, themes, genre, and magic.

The New Penguin edition (1968) has a crystalline introduction by Anne Righter Barton on the language of the play, particularly the compound words (like "sea-sorrow"). Notes are placed at the end of the edition.

The BBC edition (1980), designed to accompany the BBC-TV production with Michael Hordern, has a brief and useful introduction by John Wilders and a note on the production by Henry Fenwick. In the notes, Fenwick describes the design of the production, based on the illustrations of Gustave Doré. Trees from a dying apple orchard were carried into the studio to become part of the set. The text shows where deletions have been made for production (4.1.60–105 of the Wedding Masque, for example). The edition contains many still photographs that help recall the imagery of the production itself, which will be discussed in chapter 6.

The Barron's "Shakespeare Made Easy" edition (1984) has the text on the left-hand page and the modern version, by Alan Durband, on the right-hand page. The edition demonstrates that—as Robert Frost once said—"poetry is what evaporates from all translations." Why must "sicklemen" (4.1.134) become "harvesters"? We lose words from the language all the time, but some words are needlessly forced out. "Here, kiss the book" (2.2.131) becomes "Here. Take a swig!" so that the metaphor and its resonances are lost. Durband does show some ingenuity and grace in rerhyming the songs and the Masque. The best use to which this edition can be put is to show the quality and resonance of Shakespeare's language. A good exercise with students at the high-school or college level is to ask them to translate ten lines of a Shakespeare play into their own idiom.

The University Press of America's Contemporary Shakespeare edition, edited by A. L. Rowse (1984), changes the text very little. Rowse claims that his modernizations meet the challenge of Shakespeare's being dropped from the curriculum (3). He gives his rationale in his opening essay. One notices "salt-hake" for "Poor-John," but the other changes are unobtrusive. The text has no notes.

Pocket Classics, which "bring great literature to life," is an illustrated modernization (1984). "What is that red juice? It tasted good!" The illustrations are elegant, in the Prince Valiant mode. Again, the book is useful as a contrast to the depth and suggestiveness of the verse in the play. In this instance, the "visualization" of the script may help some students.

The Bantam Classic edition (1988) has a foreword by Joseph Papp (who never directed the play) and a graceful introduction by David Bevington. He discusses major elements of the play in a balanced way that tends to see the play as ultimately positive and optimistic. The edition includes a sound performance history by Bevington and David Scott Kastan, selections from the sources, and an annotated bibliography that calls attention to some of the best work done in the period immediately prior to the ascendancy of the cultural-materialist/New Historicist mode of criticism.

The Wordsworth Classics edition (1994) uses the Quiller-Couch, Dover Wilson Cambridge New Shakespeare text, which incorporates many interpretative stage directions: "[I.2] The Island. A green plat of undercliff, approached by a path descending through a grove of lime-trees alongside the upper cliff, in the face of which is the entrance of a tall cave, curtained" (6). Such detail may help students visualize the play, or it may be a distraction.

The Everyman edition, edited by John Andrews (1994), has a somewhat anti-Prospero introduction, a useful "old-spelling" text that removes the editorial flavor that contaminates so many editions, and a copious selection of criticism from Samuel Johnson to Stephen Greenblatt that provides a solid sense of how the play has changed in the minds of its beholders through more than two centuries.

The New Folger edition (1994), revised and edited by Barbara Mowat and Paul Werstine, has the familiar notes and illustrations on the left-hand page facing the text, longer notes at the end, solid introductory materials on Shakespeare's language (aimed at those who conveniently claim that they "can't understand the language"), times, and theater, an excellent essay by Mowat that demonstrates how time is conceptualized in the play and how the image of colonizer is complicated in the person of Prospero, and a descriptive bibliography. The latter should be used with caution, though. Meredith Anne Skura's essay on *The Tempest* does not, as the description says, deal with *Hamlet*.

The Cambridge School edition, edited by Rex Gibson (1995), contains some wonderful exercises designed to vivify the issues of the play ("Resentful Servants," "Travellers' Tales," and so on), good summaries of magic, the colonial element, and the characters of Prospero, Ariel, and Caliban, and splendid photographs of productions. The latter, though, are maddeningly unidentified. This is a wonderful edition for students from middle school through first year in college. The text is complete, and the activities and questions will carry over into further Shakespearean experience.

The Applause edition, edited by John Russell Brown (1996), has a running commentary on the right-hand page opposite the text on staging and modulations in character. This book should be indispensable to actors and directors and to people attempting to imagine the text as script as they read. Brown's comments are invariably sane and do not insist upon agreement. They offer options for performance. This edition would be a logical next step from the Cambridge School edition a few years later in a student's experience. Brown's introduction, which deals with the play on stage, is excellent, but suffers from woefully imprecise citations of quoted reviews.

The Oxford School edition, edited by Roma Gill (1998), has notes on the left one-third of each page of text, spritely illustrations by Martin Cottam, brief excerpts from sources and critics, and a section on classwork and examinations that is far less comprehensive or imaginative than the exercises in Gibson's edition. Northrop Frye's name is misspelled on page 120.

The Signet Classic edition (revised 1998) contains useful introductory material, including notes on cross-dressing and the boy actor, language, costuming, and staging, a selection of criticism, an excellent introduction by Robert Langbaum that provides a jargon-free overview of the issues of the play, excerpts from the sources, a group of critical essays (Samuel Taylor Coleridge, E.M.W. Tillyard, Bernard Knox, Lorrie Jerrell Leininger, and Stephen Greenblatt), and a brief survey of the play on stage and screen by Sylvan Barnet. Reuben Brower's superb New Critical study of the play has been dropped from the Signet Classic edition since its inception in this format in 1987 in favor of Greenblatt's "Use of Salutary Anxiety" essay. That is unfortunate, since Brower's essay is a far more persuasive version of its genre of criticism than either the strident Leininger essay or the strained Greenblatt argument.

2

CONTEXTS AND SOURCES

No source for *The Tempest* has been found. As Robert Wiltenburg says, "More than most of the plays, it seems to be a rich confluence of elements drawn from Shakespeare's diverse reading, conversation, and theatrical experience" (1987, 159).

Clearly, however, Shakespeare was influenced by the "Bermuda Pamphlets," which include Sylvester Jourdain's *Discovery of the Barmudas* (1610), the Council of Virginia's *True Declaration of the state of the Colonie in Virginia with a confutation of such scandalous reports as have tended to the disgrace of so worthy an enterprise* (1610), and a letter by William Strachey, the *True Reportory of the Wracke*, dated 15 July 1610, but not published until 1625. That Shakespeare saw the letter is highly probable. His patron, the earl of Southampton, was an officer of the Virginia Company.

In May 1609, nine ships with five hundred colonists aboard set out from Plymouth under the command of Sir Thomas Gates and Sir George Summers to join John Smith's beleaguered colony at Jamestown. The *Sea-Adventure*, with Gates and Summers aboard, was separated from the rest of the fleet in a storm and driven toward Bermuda. While the ship was lost, all on board came safely to shore. The story of the storm reached England in late 1609, but it was not until the autumn of 1610 that news of the arrival of the colonists in Jamestown—after they had built boats on Bermuda—got to England. We can assume that it was an anxious interval, and that the good news brought great relief. Strachey's letter describes the storm and subsequent shipwreck on Bermuda:

A dreadfull storme . . . did beate all light from heaven; which like an hell of darkness turned blacke upon us. . . . Prayers might well be in the heart and lips, but drowned in

A ship at sea (1587).

the outcries of the Officers. . . . the Sea swelled above the Clouds, and gave battel unto Heaven . . . and overmastered the sences of all, which (taken up with amazement) the eares lay so sensible to the terrible cries, and murmurs of the windes, and distraction of our Company, as who was most armed, and best prepared, was not a little shaken. . . . During all this time, the heavens look'd so blacke upon us, that it was not possible the elevation of the Pole might be observed: nor a Starre by night, nor Sunne beame by day was to be observed. Onely upon the Thursday night Sir George Summers being upon the watch, had an apparition of a little round light, like a faint Starre, trembling, and streaming along with a sparkeling blaze, halfe the height upon the Maine Mast, and shooting sometimes from Shroud to Shroud, tempting to settle as it were upon any of the foure Shrouds: and for three or foure houres together, or rather more, halfe the night it kept with us; running sometimes along the Maine-yard to the very end, and then returning. (Kermode 1964, 135–37)

The description of Saint Elmo's fire could also come from Richard Hakluyt's earlier *Voyages* (1598):

I do remember that in the great and boistrous storme of this foule weather, in the night, there came upon the toppe of our maine yarde and maine maste, a certain little light, much like unto the light of a little candle, which the *Spaniards* call the *Cuerpo santo*, and saide it was *S. Elmo*, whom they take to be the advocate of sailors. . . . This light continued aboard our ship about three houres, flying from maste to maste, and from top to top; and sometimes it would be in two or three places at once. (Furness 1892, 51).

This passage is close to Ariel's description of his activity aboard the King's ship: "sometime I'd divide, / And burn in many places; on the topmast; / The yards and boresprit, would I flame distinctly, / Then meet and join" (1.2.198–201).

The shipwreck in *The Tempest* is also indebted to the story of Paul's arrival on Melita (Malta), as described in Acts 27. "Howbeit," Paul tells the men on the ship, "we must be cast into a certeine yland" (Berry 1969, 26). He promises, however, "there shal not an heere fall from the head of anie of you" (34). This is glossed as "they shoulde be in all points safe and sounde." Prospero tells Miranda that "there is . . . not so much perdition as an hair / Betid to any creature on the vessel" which she has seen "sink" (1.2.30–32). Some of the soldiers on Paul's ship want to kill the prisoners, including Paul. The gloss to verse 42 says, "This declareth the great and barbarous ingratitude of the wicked, & can not be wone by no benevolence." The boat is damaged, "and the hinder parte was broken with the violence of the waves" (41), but Paul is spared. "And the other, some on boardes, & some on certein pieces of the ship . . . it came to passe, that thei came all safe to land" (44). The response of the inhabitants of Melita to the party once they arrived on shore is worth noting: "And the Barbarians shewed us no litle kindnes" (28.2).

While Leonardo da Vinci can hardly be seen as a "source" for *The Tempest*, his description of a storm like that with which the play begins shares many

A magic storm (1555).

details with Shakespeare's (and with that experienced by the *Sea-Adventure* and many sailors who survived to tell their story):

To represent this tempest you must first show the clouds riven and torn and flying with the wind, together with storms of sand blown up from the sea-shores. . . . Let the sea be wild and tempestuous, and full of foam whirled between the big waves, and the wind should carry the finer spray through the stormy air resembling a dense and all-enveloping mist. Of the ships that are there, some should be shown with sails rent and the shreds fluttering in the air in company with the broken ropes and some of the masts split and falle, and the vessel itself lying disabled and broken by the fury of the waves, and the men shrieking and clinging to the fragments of the wreck. (1994, 15)

Jourdain's *Discovery* describes the ship's being wedged "betweene two rockes, where shee was fast lodged and locked, for further budging," and goes on to say that "our delivery was not more strange in falling so opportunely, and happily upon the land, as our feeding and preservation, was beyond our hopes, and all mens expectations most admirable." The land, "ever esteemed, and reputed, a most prodigious and inchanted place affoording nothing but gusts, stormes, and foule weather," proved to have "ayre so temperate and the Country so aboundantly fruitful of all fit necessaries for the sustenation and preservation of mans life" (Kermode 1964, 141).

So good was the life on Bermuda that some refused to continue on to Virginia, where, as was well known, conditions were far harsher. One member of the party, Henry Paine, was shot by Governor Sir Thomas Gates for insurrection. Stephen Greenblatt makes much of this as "a triumphant affirmation of absolute control linked to the manipulation of anxiety and to a departure from the island" (Barnet 1998, 169). He relates the episode to Prospero's control in the play: both document and play give evidence of "an institutional circulation of culturally significant narratives" that have as their "central concern the public management of anxiety" (164).

That the same documents can mean very different things depending on the emphasis is suggested by George Slover. He quotes the goal of the Virginia Colony as stated in the *Declaration* (page 26) and draws a more pious conclusion than Greenblatt's political interpretation: " 'to propagate the Gospell of Jesus Christ.' . . . Not nature alone but the events of history are sacramental. . . . [T]he deepest meaning of the Virginia plantation lies in its reenactment of the apostolic action" (qtd. in Battenhouse 1994, 258–59).

I will deal with the historicist and the Christian approaches to the play in chapter 5. The compiler of the sources of Shakespeare's plays, Geoffrey Bullough, would say to those who find single meanings in *The Tempest* that "all these ideas came into Shakespeare's mind and affected the characterization and texture of his play. He is not writing a didactic work" (1975, 245). David Hirst says that "it is the deeper ethical implications of this experience which were to inspire the most fundamental paradoxes of Shakespeare's drama" (1984a, 11). If, in *Macbeth*, it is hard to tell where an idea comes from because, as Stephen Booth says, "every new idea seems already there when presented to us" (1983, 94), the reason is that the depth structure of the play is a given from which language flows inevitably. All ideas are the same idea: this is God's universe, as defiance of that fact keeps proving. In *The Tempest*, Shakespeare's imagination combines opposing ideas so fluently that it is impossible to separate them—are they Christian or pagan, merely political or evidence of something far more deeply interfused?

Moments of the play are informed by Montaigne and Ovid, as translated by Golding. Gonzalo's Utopia draws on Montaigne's "Of the Caniballes," translated by John Florio in 1604. "It is a nation . . . that hath no kind of traffike, no knowledge of Letters, no intelligence of numbers, no name of magistrate, nor of politike superioritie; no use of service, of riches or of povertie; no contracts, no successions, no partitions, no occupation but idle; no respect of kindred, but common, no apparel but common, no manuring of lands, no use of wine, corne, or mettle. The very words that import lying, falsehood, dissimulation, covetousnes, envie, distraction, and pardon were never heard among them" (qtd. in Kermode 1964, 146–47).

Montaigne's description was not the only version of life among the savages circulating in the Jacobean culture, as Amerigo Vespucci's account demonstrates: "Everything being in common. They live amongst themselves without a king or ruler, each man being his own master, and having as many wives as they please. . . . They live according to nature, and are more inclined to be Epicurean than Stoic. They have no commerce among each other" (1894, 46–47).

Prospero's expression of "the rarer action" also may derive from Montaigne ("Of Cruelty"), as Eleanor Prosser argues (1965):

He that through a natural facility and genuine mildness should neglect or contemn injuries received should no doubt perform a rare action, and worthy commendations. But he who, being touched and stung to the quick with any wrong or offence received, should arm himself with reason against this furiously-blind desire of revenge, and in the end, after a great conflict, yield himself master over it, should doubtless do much more. The first should do well, the other virtuously: the one action might be termed goodness, the other virtue. For it seemeth the very name of virtue presupposeth difficulty, and infereth resistance, and cannot well exercise itself without an enemy. (133)

Prospero's abandonment of his magic in Act 5 is a paraphrase of Medea's speech in Golding's translation of *The Metamorphoses* (1567):

> Ye Ayres and windes: ye Elves of Hilles, of Brookes, of Woods alone,
> Of standing Lakes, and of the Night. . . .
> By charmes I make the calme Seas rough, and make the rough seas
>   plain. . . .
> I call up dead men from their graves: and thee O lightsome Moone
> I darken oft. . . .
> Our Sorcerie dimmes the Morning faire, and darkes the Sun at Noone.
>   (Kermode 1964, 149)

I will deal later with how this borrowing affects our view of Prospero and with the complex question of witchcraft and magic as a context for *The Tempest*.

Jonathan Bate makes a more complete case for Ovid. The entire play is "a kind of collaboration with Ovid," he says (in Vaughan and Vaughan 1998, 39). In *The Tempest*, "transformation [is] of a matter and manner learnt from the *Metamorphoses*" (39).

Jeanne Addison Roberts argues Shakespeare's indebtedness to Ovid at the deepest levels of *The Tempest*. Ovid does not distinguish between humans and animals, even if his transformations are mostly painful. "The insistence on a rigid hierarchy with a crucial chasm fixed between man and animal is foreign to him. Such a vision of living things is a legacy of the Christian tradition," a product of the "early church fathers, anxious to destroy primitive nature worship" (1991, 110). Shakespeare's play, then, challenges hierarchy and the "natural" divisions it defines.

Samuel Johnson suggests that Shakespeare may imitate Anacreon "when *Caliban*, after a pleasing dream, says, *I cry'd to dream again*." Johnson appeals to the universal in that moment. Anacreon "had, like every other man, the same wish on the same occasion" (1951, 508). If Anacreon is at all present in Shakespeare's imagination as he writes *The Tempest*, the Greek poet's "Insect" may contribute to Ariel:

Dewe of dawning is thy wine.
Strands of sunlight be thy vine.
Fields echoe with thy wing.
Woodlands with thy musick sing.
Blossomes hold their cups up still,
Fill againe for thee to fill.
Winter findes thee never there.
Summer sees thee ever here. (Anon. trans. 1554)

Kermode rejects K. M. Lea's thesis (*Italian Popular Comedy*, 1934) that *The Tempest* is indebted to the commedia dell'arte (1964, 1xvi–1xix): "Shakespeare had other and more suggestive materials for speculation. He did not need a jocose pantomime to teach him how to think about it" (lxviii). Kermode goes on to say that "the transformations wrought by Prospero and Ariel are of the common stock of magic lore" (lxviii). The Vaughans, in their Arden introduction, give Lea a fuller hearing, even if they state that "the extent of Shakespeare's indebtedness to this continental scenario is uncertain" (1999, 12).

A reference to Sycorax's "god Setebos" (1.2.375) appears in Richard Eden's translation of Pietro Martier d'Anghiera, *The Decades of the Newe Worlde or West India*, in 1577, as the "greate devyll *Setebos*."

Another suggested source for *The Tempest* is King James I himself. According to David Bergeron, "James and his family are represented in *The Tempest* through the issues of peaceful succession, royal genealogy . . . and the union of kingdoms" (1985, 181). Prospero's confessed dereliction from his duty as Duke of Milan (even if he was "for the liberal Arts / Without a parallel") would seem to reflect James's advice to his son in *Basilicon Doron*: "As for the study of the other liberal arts and sciences [as opposed to history] I would have you reasonably versed in them, but not pressing to be a pass-master in any of them: for that cannot but distract you from the points of your calling" (1918, 40). Even within the time frame of *The Tempest*, the "magician loses his awareness of the play's continuing action," as Stephen Orgel points out (1987, 50), almost repeating the neglect that had cost him his dukedom some twelve years before.

According to Richard Garnett and Edmund Gosse, Prospero is James: "A wise, humane, pacific prince, gaining his ends not by violence but by policy; devoted to far-off purposes which none but himself can realise, much less fathom: independent of counsellors, safely contemptuous of foes, and controlling all about him by his superior wisdom; keeping in the background until the decisive hour has struck and then interfering effectually; devoted to lawful knowledge, but the sworn enemy of black magic—such was James to James's eyes, and such is Prospero" (1904, 252–53).

According to J.E.M. Latham, James even provides imagery for the play, as in these instances from *Daemonologie*: James talks of magicians who "please Princes, by faire banquets and daintie dishes, carryed in short spaces from the farthest part of the worlde," and who imprint "impressions in the aire [of] castels and fortes" (qtd. in Latham 1975, 217). For Richard Wilson, however, Prospero is modelled on Sir Robert Dudley (1574–1649) (1997, 333–57). Dudley wrote a treatise on navigation. He lived as in exile in Italy for the last half of his life and died near Florence.

Garnett and Gosse promote a 1609 Spanish tale as a source. In Antonio de Eslava's *Noches de Invierno*, Dardanus, King of Bulgaria, dethroned by Nichiphorus, Emperor of Greece, flees with his daughter on a little ship. He causes a submarine palace to arise. Disguised as a fisherman, he kidnaps Nichiphorus's son. The young man falls in love with Seraphina. The young couple return to reign. Dardanus retires to a life of contemplation (1904, 251).

The Tempest's alleged indebtedness to the early-seventeenth-century German play *Die Schöne Sidea* is, says Kermode, "a tribute to the persistence of German scholarship rather than a measure of its real importance" (1964, xvi). By Jacob Ayrer, it is about a magician-prince who has a familiar spirit and a daughter. But, asks Arthur Quiller-Couch, "what fairy-tale or folk-tale is commoner, the world over, than that which combines a witch, or wizard, an only daughter, an adventurous prince bound to carry logs, etc.?" (qtd. in Hallett Smith 1969, 15). As Hazelton Spencer says, "The storm and the island are not in Ayrer's play, which is fundamentally unlike *The Tempest* and certainly no source. The common features were doubtless picked up independently by the two dramatists from some old tale or fable. None, however, has been discovered" (1940, 416 n. 10).

The Aeneid, however, has been a recent contender as a primary source. "*The Tempest*," says Jan Kott, "repeats the sequence of the first four books of the *Aeneid*: the sinking of the royal ship, the saving of the shipwrecked men, the attack by the harpies, the ordeal of hunger and thirst, the interrupted wedding pageantry. The Virgilian code becomes the theater of Prospero's art" (1976, 440). According to Gary Schmidgall, *The Tempest* is "a highly compact version of Virgil's epic of a lost civilization rewon" (1981, 75). Donna B. Hamilton argues that "the *Aeneid* has been dismantled, reversed, and rewritten" (1989, in Vaughan and Vaughan 1998, 18). That may be, although it is just as easy to suggest that it is inconsistently in Shakespeare's mind as he writes. Hamilton engages in a complex analysis of *imitatio*, "Conceptualization being the mental operation on which successful imitation so often depended" (31). The "Virgilian patterns," she says, "become the chief means by which Shakespeare accomplishes a large and complex figuration" (23). She quotes "O dea certe" (*Aeneid* 1.328), when Aeneas sees Venus, and suggests that it comes into the play as "Most sure the goddess" (1.2.424). The storm becomes an allusion to the storm that struck Aeneas's ship after it left Troy, and "Caliban becomes an anti-Aeneas figure" (30), in that he wants to stay on the island instead of moving on to Italy. Within this configuration, "Ferdinand becomes the new Aeneas," Nigel Smith claims (1988, 99). According to Wiltenburg, Shakespeare's " 'given' [is] the Virgilian situation characterized by tempests, defiled banquets, and 'widowhood' " (1987, 161). The island, he says, represents the "underworld" (165), in that the past is a kind of underworld. It seems to me, though, that Prospero's underworld is his own psyche, a "darkness" peopled by Caliban. If Shakespeare reworks the story of Aeneas, it is as a psychological drama. (See also Miola 1986, Hamilton 1990, and Tudeau-Clayton 1998 on Virgil and Shakespeare).

The major parallel is that in Book 3 of *The Aeneid*. After Aeneas and his men have slaughtered the cattle belonging to the Harpies, they are denied their meal. The Harpies take the meat from them and defile it. Celaeno, their leader, imposes "guilt for what you have murdered here" (253), as Ariel does in 3.3 of the play. Another possible echo is Aeneas's effort to embrace his father, Anchises, in the underworld: "ter frustra comprensa manus effugit imago, par levibus ventis volucrique simillima somno" (three times his clasp failed and the image escaped, like airy winds or the melting of a dream) (BK. 6.697–700), an event that might find its way into Prospero's "revels" speech ("the baseless fabric of this vision" [4.1.151]).

Don Cameron Allen suggests the influence of the earlier voyages of Odysseus. "The hero crosses watery wastes impelled by power beyond his will; he arrives on islands or strands beyond the reach of the real; and there he finds a perfection of soul that makes actuality, when he returns to it, endurable" (Hallett Smith 1969, 71). Allen argues the variety of contexts available for the play: "Earlier interpretations generally placed the play and its immediate source in the context of voyaging discourse in general, which stressed the romance and exoticism of discoveries in the Old as well as the New World" (1960, 43).

Certainly English history provided Shakespeare with multiple examples of neglected rule. In the first play to be written in blank verse, Thomas Norton and Thomas Sackville's *Gorboduc* (1561), Eubulus, the king's advisor, warns against Gorboduc's division of his kingdom between his two sons:

> To parte your realme unto my lordes yur sonnes
> I think not good for you, nor yet for them,
> But worste of all for this our native lande.
> Within one land one single rule is best:
> Divided reignes do make divided hartes,
> But peace preserves the countrey and the prince. (1.2.256–61)

This good counsel is rejected. The younger brother (Porrex) kills the elder (Ferrex). Queen Videna kills her son Porrex in revenge of Ferrex. The people rebel and kill king and queen. The kingdom falls "to civill warre . . . and the land for a long time [was] almost desolate and miserably wasted" ("Argument," Manly 1897, 214).

Not only the popular *Mirrour for Magistrates*, but Shakespeare's own plays demonstrate what happens to the body politic when the king neglects the politic segment of his dual persona (the plurality of rule, the "we" and "our"). Masculine energy flows from saintly Henry VI to his armored wife, Margaret. All that Henry V accomplished withers during the Wars of the Roses, but they have resulted from the weakness of Richard II, who used his kingdom like a credit card and elicited response from the ambitious Bolingbroke. Othello loses control in Cyprus, and knives rule the streets. Lear divides Britain and releases animals from within their human cages. *The Tempest* is a retelling of the fable of the failed ruler, but it gives him, through Prospero, a second chance.

A major "source" of *The Tempest*, then, is Shakespeare's own writing. Don Cameron Allen calls the play "a poetical summary of the poet's life" (1960, 68), and it can be that without having to be "autobiographical." Mark Van Doren says that *The Tempest* "is a mirror in which, if we hold it very still, we can gaze backward at all of the recent plays; and behind them will be glimpses of a past as old as the tragedies, the middle comedies, and even 'A Midsummer Night's Dream' " (1939, 280).

In his introduction to Jonson's "The Masque of Beauty," William B. Hunter, Jr., says, "The English development of [the masque] appears clearly in many of Shakespeare's plays, which frequently employ masques or materials similar to them" (1963, 411). Hunter mentions the scene in *Love's Labour's Lost* in which the masked ladies exchange tokens of identity to encourage the gentlemen to woo the wrong woman (5.2), the masked ball of the Capulets, at which Romeo sees Juliet, the song and dance at the end of *A Midsummer Night's Dream*, the "true masque . . . of Hymen" (412) at the end of *As You Like It*, and the masque of Ceres in *The Tempest*. Masques, Hunter says, "were almost always conceived as allegorical, being developed to suit the particular occasion for which the masque was performed" (412). Shakespeare includes such allegories within his plays, making the plays themselves much more than allegory, which has a simple one-to-one relationship between narrative and meaning. The Parable of the Talents is a good example. Some critics, of course, attempt to allegorize the entire play. That tendency, whether in the direction of Christian or colonialist readings, limits meaning at precisely the point when the rich suggestiveness of the play is attempting to resonate.

Shakespeare often incorporates plays within his plays to comment on drama, to frame his plays, or to contrast his style with that of, say, the short, rhyming lines of "Pyramus and Thisbe," which parody their tenor, or the sententious couplets of "Gonzago." Even in as highly stylized a play as *Love's Labour's Lost*, we get a bad play, as in Holofernes's mock-heroic description of Moth as little Hercules:

> Great Hercules is presented by this imp,
> Whose club kill'd Cerberus, that three-headed canus,
> And when he was a babe, a child, a shrimp
> There did he strangle serpents in his manus. (5.2.584–87)

Robert Langbaum says that "Shakespeare always uses a deliberately stilted style for a play within a play" (1987, xxii). Also, as in *Love's Labour's Lost*, Shakespeare could interrupt his inner plays with sudden changes in tone.

Stephen Greenblatt calls *The Tempest* an "echo chamber of Shakespearean motifs. . . . it resonates . . . with issues that haunted Shakespeare's imagination throughout his career" (1997, 3047). He lists the many elements that *The Tempest* picks up: a father surrendering a daughter, a ruler being betrayed, the hatred of one brother for another, the movement from court to wilderness, the wooing of a young woman in ignorance of her high position, the process of manipulating others by artistic constructs, the threat of loss of identity, the relationship of nature and nurture, and magic, among others. As in *King Lear*, "the tempest marks the point at which exalted titles are revealed to be absurd pretensions, substanceless in the face of the elemental forces of nature and the desperate struggle for survival" (3048). "Shakespeare returns to the dream [of Lear being with his daughter Cordelia, 5.3] in *The Tempest*" (3047).

Much of what Joan Hartwig says of *Pericles* applies to *The Tempest*: "A royal child is lost and rediscovered; sea journeys change men's lives; scenes occur in different countries, most of them remote; the main characters struggle against adversity and are rewarded in the end; characters thought dead are miraculously resurrected; and the final reconciliation is achieved through the agency of young people" (1972). The primary difference, of course, is the compression of *The Tempest* (its observation of "the unities"). The action occurs in one remote place, and Prospero's struggle against adversity is a narrated component of the past.

Bertrand Evans points out a difference between *The Tempest* and the romances that immediately precede it: "The replacement of incredible gods with a credible mortal of godlike powers marks . . . one profound distinction between the way of *The Tempest* and the way of the previous romances" (1960, 324). Other critics find similarities between *The Tempest* and earlier plays: its "originating action is constructed . . . on the pattern of *The Comedy of Errors* and *Twelfth Night* . . . wreck in tempest leads to separation of certain persons and their reunion on a strange shore," says G. Wilson Knight (1948, 131). It is an examination of revenge, as in *Hamlet* (with *The Tempest* giving us the "other ending"), of the murder of a king, as in *Richard II*, or of a sleeping king, as in *Hamlet* and *Macbeth*. As Coleridge says, "The scene of the intended assassination of Alonzo and Gonzalo is an exact counterpart of the scene between Macbeth and his lady, only pitched in a lower key. . . . By this kind of sophistry [associating the proposed crime with something ludicrous or out of place] the imagination and fancy are first bribed to contemplate the imagined act, and at length to become acquainted with it" (D. Nichol Smith 1916, 277–78). *The Tempest* also shows the abstention of a duke from his duties and his deputizing a replacement (as in *Measure for Measure*) and the reunion of father and child (as in *King Lear*). Bate points out that the play "shares with *Pericles*, sea-voyages and storm, lost children, magical transformations" (1989, 240).

In *The Winter's Tale*, the ship serves its purpose in handing a fragment of the future to Antigonus to place ashore. He serves by exiting away from where he has left Perdita. The ship sinks back into the sea, back into the unconscious, back away from the moment in which it has fulfilled its destiny. The ship in

The Tempest is the past and future landing on the zone in which the past will be recognized so that the sunken ship of the unconscious can rise anew in consciousness as a shining, taut example of an understood dream, an absorbed text of the unconscious. The ship becomes redeemed consciousness, but it has Antonio aboard. The living ego always creates shadows.

Parallels, of course, are easy to find. Martin Lings equates *The Tempest* and *As You Like It*: "In both a reigning duke is driven out of his duchy by a usurping brother; the plot of each turns around the love story of the rightful duke's daughter who also has been exiled; and the most striking resemblance of all is that each takes place in a setting which is beyond—and above—the confines of civilization" (1966, 110). James Driscoll contrasts Lear and Prospero: "Lear embodies the darker side of the Promethean archetype—possession of the spirit by suffering and defiance. Prospero . . . manifests its complementary brighter side—foresight, wisdom, and ability to utilize intelligence to tame nature" (1983, in Bloom 1988, 85). As with Richard II, political failure and deposition insist that they be understood (though how much Richard comes to understand in his long soliloquy is questionable). "Prospero," says Knight, "is a matured and fully self-conscious embodiment of those moments of fifth-act transcendental speculation to which earlier tragic heroes, including Macbeth, were unwillingly forced" (1948, 135). For Harold Goddard, *The Tempest* repeats the "theme of the King, Prince, Duke, or other person of high estate losing his place or inheritance only to recover it or its spiritual equivalent, after exile or suffering" (1951, 277–78). That pattern includes *Henry VI, Measure for Measure, King Lear, Timon of Athens, Coriolanus, Antony and Cleopatra, Pericles, Cymbeline, The Winter's Tale*, and, possibly, *Richard II*. For Jonathan Bate, "*The Tempest* comes closest to resembling . . . that other Ovidian comedy, *A Midsummer Night's Dream*" (1989, 243). For Kristiaan P. Aercke, *As You Like It* and *Cymbeline* "articulate and celebrate ideal, or exemplary, modes of conduct [and] versions of an ideal social order" (1992, 142). For Barbara Bono, "The character of Prospero in many ways summarizes all of Shakespeare's authorial figures, from the megalomaniacal Richard III, to the shifty Duke Vincentio, to the aging Lear" (1984, 222). Meredith Anne Skura discerns a configuration in *The Tempest* that hearkens back to *Measure for Measure*: "Vincentio's 'Caliban' is the libidinous and loose-tongued Lucio" (1989, 62).

The Tempest is a wonderful play to teach at the end of a Shakespeare course. It has its own uniqueness, of course, but it also serves as a superb summary of what has gone before. To use it merely as a summary, however, is to ignore what Keith Sturgess says: "It is both a summation of Shakespeare's writing career and a radically experimental new departure" (1987, in Vaughan and Vaughan 1998, 107).

MAGIC AND INTELLECTUAL BACKGROUND

One reason why *The Tempest* is so elusive is that magic is at the center of its imaginative structure. Magic, says Robert West, casts a "never eluded shadow of moral and metaphysical uncertainty" (1968, 87). The magician cannot say, with Banquo, "In the great hand of God I stand" (*Macbeth* 2.3.131). We cannot be sure where the magician stands. He cannot be sure.

Samuel Johnson wisely says that before "the Character and Conduct of *Prospero* may be understood, something must be known of the System of Enchantment which supplied all the Marvellous found in the Romances of the middle Ages" (1951, 530). "The system" was still alive a century and a half after the play's first performance, as Dryden attests in his 1679 Preface to *Troilus and Cressida*: Shakespeare makes Caliban unique: "a species of himself, begotten by an *Incubus* on a Witch. [This] is not wholly beyond the bounds of credibility, at least the vulgar stile believe it" (Furness 1892, 379). We cannot reconstitute ourselves as Shakespeare's audience or pretend that we are Dryden's "vulgar," who still believe in the possibility of demonic coupling with witches. We can read the play as a work of art within a world where magic existed for many of those who went to the Globe and Blackfriars. If a performance does justice to the script, it may reeducate our imaginations to that possibility.

Belief in evil spirits was doctrine in the reformed church: "Hee hath good Angels, hee hath evill angels," says the late-sixteenth-century sermon on Rogation Week (Part II 1623, in Rickey and Stroup 1968, 226). Writing some two decades after the first performance of *The Tempest*, the clergyman Thomas Browne suggests that one must believe in "instruments of darkness" in order to believe in the quality of spirit (the Holy Ghost): "There are Witches: they that doubt of these, do not onely deny *them*, but Spirits; and are obliquely and upon consequence a sort not of Infidels, but Atheists" (1885, 50). Browne goes on to discuss the theory of beneficent spirits: "I do think that many mysteries ascribed to our own inventions have been the courteous revelations of Spirits (for those noble essences in Heaven bear a friendly regard unto their fellow Natures on Earth) and therefore believe that these many prodigies and ominous prognostics, which fore-run the ruines of States, Princes, and private persons, are the charitable premonitions of good Angels, which more careless enquiries term but the effects of chance and nature" (51). Browne posits a Neoplatonic essentialism: "I am sure there is a common spirit that plays within us, yet makes no part of us, and that is, the Spirit of God, the fire and scintillation of that noble and mighty Essence, which is the life and radical heat of Spirits" (52). He argues the spiritual quality of the physical world: "Even in this material Fabrick the Spirits walk as freely exempt from the affection of time, place, and motion, as beyond the extreamest circumference" (56).

Hardin Craig (1936, 66) says that "the Renaissance had a vague, loose, less trustworthy body of knowledge [than we do] which gave far greater extension to the limits of the possible, the range of which was also increased by the theological sanction of the marvellous." James I, of course, curbed those sanctions, but it was still true that the syncretic blend of mixed religious traditions was more possible within a field of competing or contradictory systems of belief, and that the range of possibilities could encourage a wider spectrum out of which a work of art could be formulated and to which a work of art could respond—

something akin to postmodernism's "multiple signification"—than would be possible under a strict religious dispensation or an agreed-upon body of knowledge. New Historicism tends to deny that the Renaissance was a time and a place, not merely a process, a controlled environment, a circulation of documents. We tend to read certainty back into that time and place, rather than granting it the remarkable creativity that flowered under the lighting sent forth from its clashes of darknesses.

This "less trustworthy body of knowledge" easily entertained ancient ideas as they became available. James E. Phillips, for example, sees *The Tempest* as an allegory of distinctions made by Aristotle. Phillips notices a "striking similarity between the functions of Prospero, Ariel, and Caliban in the play and the functions of the three parts of the soul—Rational, Sensitive, and Vegetative—almost universally recognized and described in Renaissance literature on the nature of man" (1964, 148). Phillips goes on to say that "man since the Fall has faced a constant struggle to keep his vegetative and sensitive souls the servants of his rational soul, and above all to keep the passions subject to the control of his reason" (149–50).

Perhaps the most dominant concept of the history of ideas from Plato to Darwin was that of the great chain of being (Lovejoy 1936), which suggested that all life was organized within a gigantic hierarchy, beginning, for the Christian, with God and moving down through the ranks of the angelic host to man, animals, and the smallest stone in a peasant's field. Everything had its place. E.M.W. Tillyard is the spokesperson for this concept within Shakespeare: "With the general notion of order Shakespeare was always concerned, with man's position between beast and angel acutely during his tragic period; but only in *The Tempest* does he seem to consider the chain itself. . . . The whole play is alive with the sense of creation's flux and not blind to creation's limit" (1959, 34). "Caliban . . . shows himself incapable of the human power of education. Prospero too learns his own lesson. He cannot transcend the terms of his humanity . . . man for all his striving towards the angels can never be quit utterly of the bestial, of the Caliban within him" (34–35). Jeanne Addison Roberts says that "the merging and blurring of figures is characteristic of the entire play. The opposing qualities of stasis, paralysis and isolation are . . . played off against movement and transformation. The metaphorical shifts are activated by the yoking of surprising opposites, one of which is often animal . . . we are witnessing a dawning perception in Shakespeare of a possible kinship between Culture and the animal Wild" (1991, 112, 114).

Whatever was being constructed—plays or political doctrine—was not being formulated from a set of static concepts. Roberts argues that "the paradigm of the Chain was already dissolving. But such beliefs die slowly and inconclusively, as witness the survival of creationism in the post-Darwinian United States" (1991, 108), and witness the survival of the pagan gods into "Christian" Europe, even if they were marginalized as witches and conjurers (Seznec 1961).

Magic was not all bad. Francis Bacon could defend it: "We here understand magic in its ancient and honourable sense—among the Persians it stood for a sublimer wisdom, or a knowledge of the relations of universal nature, as may be observed in the title of those kings who came from the East to adore Christ" (1904, 145). Hiram Haydn (1950, 179ff.) distinguishes three areas of magic: divine (the mysteries of God), celestial (the heavenly bodies and their influence on the world—astrology and astronomy), and natural (the hidden virtues of objects and elements—alchemy and medicine). The Magi functioned within the first two of these categories. Prospero would seem to work in all three areas: he manipulates nature for his purposes, he reads the stars and interprets the time accordingly, and he treads on the edge of godlike powers, both pagan and Christian.

Magic was dangerous, of course. Haydn makes a distinction between magicians and empiricists in their approach to "power": "The magicians, believing nature to be full of miracles and mysteries, hope to be able to learn how to control these by a natural proper manipulation of natural sympathies and antipathies, and thus to exercise an almost godlike individualistic power . . . and glory" (177, 184). The issue is the individual, a concept that must be surrendered for other concerns—society, the future—if the risk of damnation is to be avoided. Prospero certainly places himself within and toward the top of the framework that Pico della Mirandola describes, which is the Neoplatonic zone equivalent to the "celestial" category listed earlier: "The world is a hierarchy of divine forces, a system of agencies forming an ascending and descending scale, in which the higher agencies command and the lower ones obey" (qtd. in Weber 1899, 266). As Gerald Pinciss and Roger Lockyer say, "White magic . . . operated in an area bound by natural science on the one hand and religion on the other" (1989, 88).

The Neoplatonic tradition is worth touching on because a "modern audience is more likely to receive the play in terms of its Christian pattern than . . . its neoplatonic one" (Neil H. Wright 1977, 243). I will deal with the Christian contexts of the play later. The Neoplatonic context not only fell away into the oblivion of outmoded theory, but it was not passed forward as a significant element of this play. As Palmer says, "Neo-classical critics of the later seventeenth and the eighteenth centuries showed little awareness of the philosophical themes" in the play (D. J. 1968, 18). It is not easy, says J. Anthony Burton, "to penetrate an alien mode of thought with modern attitudes" (1992, 42). Of the Neoplatonic quality of *The Tempest*, Burton says "man is a mediator between the physical world and that of ideas, redeeming the lower by transforming it into the higher . . . the central concept [is that of] the magus as a bridge between the two worlds" (42).

Walter Clyde Curry says that "Neo-Platonic philosophy known as sacerdotal science or theurgy . . . [is not] to be identified with that Black Magic developed during the Middle Ages and transmitted to the Renaissance" (1937, 166). He goes on to say that the "evil practitioner produced magic results by disordering the sympathetic relationships of nature" (167). The theurgist "must . . . identify himself spiritually with the superior divine natures and so render himself capable of controlling the lesser divinities who immediately govern nature" (171). The goetist, on the other hand, "transmutes [the emanations of a sympathetically ordered world] by abnormally commingling their energies, perverts, misdirects, transfers, and concentrates them to a purpose different from that for which they were imparted" (187).

The two magicians—white and black—were poised against each other in the Renaissance imagination. Sometimes, of course, they were impossible to tell apart. They represented the aspiring character we attribute to the Renaissance and the person tumbling down the chain of being toward damnation typical of a medieval allegory. Pico della Mirandola defines these opposite options of traffic in magic: "Thou shalt have the power to degenerate into the lower forms of life, which are brutish. Thou shalt have the power, out of thy soul's judgment, to be reborn into higher forms, which are divine" (qtd. in Garber 1980, 53). For Plotinus, "magic is the result of a disturbance in the natural harmony of the world" (Curry 1937, 178). That assumes harmony, of course, and we cannot be certain that Shakespeare, in *The Tempest*, so assumes. The chain of being—an ordered hierarchy that includes all created nature—was itself being challenged in the play, as Roberts argues (1991, 111–16). For Agrippa, "Magick is a faculty of wonderfull vertue. . . . [The] contemplation of most secret things, together with the nature, power, quality, substance, and vertues thereof, is also the knowledge of the whole nature, and it doth instruct us concerning the differing, and agreement of things amongst themselves, whence it produceth its wonderful effects" (1651, 2–3). For La Primaudaye, however, these wonderful effects must implicate their practitioners in damnation: "Some have been so wretched and miserable, as to give themselves to the Art of Necromancie, and to contract with the devill, that they might come to soveraigne power and authoritie" (1586, 230).

For King James, witches and magicians served the devil: "One master, although in diverse fashions" (1597, 32). James describes the Faustian ladder already defined by Pico and La Primaudaye:

For divers men having attained to a great perfection in learning . . . finding all naturall things common . . . they assaie to vendicate unto them a greater name, by not onlie knowing the course of things heavenlie, but likewise to climb to the knowledge of things to come thereby. Which, at the first face appearing lawfull unto them, in respect the ground thereof seemeth to proceed of naturall cause onlie; they are so allured thereby, that finding their practice to proove true in sundry things, they studie to know the cause thereof; and so mounting from degree to degree, upon the slipperie and uncertaine scale of curiositie; they are at last entised, that where lawful artes or sciences failes, to satisfie their restles mindes, even seek to that black and unlawfull science of Magic. (1597, 10)

Prospero's "renunciation is a standard feature in tales of spirit magic, and it appeals to the audience's sense of the dangers and insufficiencies of it," says Robert West (1968, 91).

One reason why magic and religion (or "truth") could conflict is that the magician operates by contrast and similitude, always reminding the viewer of what is "real" whereby to show him what appears unreal: references to dry land during tempests, perfect society among castaways, buildings among clouds. Prophets and apostles, on the other hand, function more directly and have "the wonderful power of God . . . without the cooperation of the middle causes" (West 1968, 193 n. 13).

Magic had to have an effect on religion and religion on it. The "simplicity of the Protestant service" (as opposed to the "color, mystique, and mystery of the old religion") encouraged it unwittingly, according to Pinciss and Lockyer (1989, 89). "The new directness and self-reliance of this religion, with its emphasis on the word in the Scriptures or from the pulpit, left a taste for mystery and magic that could only be satisfied by the local wizard, cunning man, or white magician" (89). Of course, the reformed religion also left space for the titillation provided by witch trials.

For Calvinist William Perkins, Roman Catholicism incorporated the "sinne [of] Magicke, sorcerie, or witchcraft, in the consecration of the host in which they make their Breadengod: in exorcismes over holy bread . . . in the casting out or driving away of devills, by the signe of the crosse. . . . For these things have not their supposed force, either by creation, or by any institution of God in his holy word: and therefore if any thing be done by them, it is from the secret operation of the devill himself" (1603, 744). The antimagic stance produced powerful arguments for the reformed sacraments: "The most part [of poperie] is meere Magique," said Perkins (36).

As always, theology could obstruct common sense. The witch of Endor in I Samuel raises Samuel to tell Saul of his destruction for not following the word of God ("Because thou obeiedst not the voyce of the Lord": 28.18). Since Protestant theology did not allow the souls of the saints to be disturbed by necromancy, this had to be an evil spirit. Transient doctrine changes the obvious meaning of the Bible. Samuel had not been sanctified by the time his own books were written, but the Geneva gloss insists that "Satan hathe no power over . . . the Saints after this life. . . . it was Satan, who to blinde his eyes toke upon him the forme of Samuel, as he can do of an Angel of light." Strangely, the message this evil spirit delivers is not deceptive, but accurate, so the witch has to be one of Banquo's "instruments of darkness [that] tell us truths . . . to betray's in deepest consequence" (*Macbeth* 1.3.124–26). The Weird Sisters are trolling for a soul. What the shade of Samuel is doing—other than delivering an accurate prophecy—is anyone's guess.

Agrippa's Neoplatonism emphasized "essence." John Dee's letter to the archbishop of Canterbury in defense of his magic (1604) talks of "proceeding and ascending . . . from things visible, to consider of things invisible; from things bodily, to conceive of things spiritual; from things transitorie, and momentarie, to meditate of things permanent; by things mortall . . . to have some perceiverance of immortality" (in Crossley 1851, 228). Dee cannily phrases his defense in the language of the Nicene Creed ("all thynges visible and invisible") and argues a spiritual progress to which the only objection might be the pride of the undertaker. Prospero's magic is not directed toward this version of individuation, but toward external ends. Those ends apparently achieved, he gives up his magic.

Richard Hooker, the great apologist for the reformed church of England, must account for the fall of the angels and for the presence of a pervasive spirit of evil in the world. Here he takes an Augustinian line:

It seemeth . . . that there was no other way for angels to sin but by reflex of their understanding upon themselves . . . whereupon their adoration, love, and imitation of God could not choose but be also interrupted. The fall of angels therefore was pride. Since their fall, their practices have been the clean contrary unto those before mentioned. For being dispersed, some in the air, some on the earth, some in the water, some among the minerals, dens, and caves that are under the earth, they have by all means laboured to effect in universal rebellion against the laws, and, as far as in them lieth, utter destruction of the works of God. These wicked spirits the heathens honoured instead of gods. (Hebel et al. 1953, 1032–33)

The angels, hurled headlong from the etherial sky, victims of a version of narcissism, become the pagan gods. These gods survive into *The Tempest*, both as negative forces and as positive resources.

Hooker argues against the thesis that "nature in working hath before her certain exemplary draughts or patterns, which subsisting in the bosom of the Highest, and being thence discovered, she fixeth her eye upon them, as travellers by sea upon the pole-star of the world." Hooker rejects a Platonic form ("an absolute shape or mirror") that guides the specific action. He argues that "no intellectual creature in the world were able by capacity to do that which nature doth without capacity and knowledge." It follows that "nature hath some director of infinite knowledge to guide her in all her ways. . . . These things which nature is said to do are by divine art performed, using nature as an instrument; nor is there any such art or knowledge divine in nature herself working, but in the Guide of nature's work." Divinity is not in nature—an important distinction for a reformed church that stresses the receipt of Communion by faith, by the inward man, and not by some magical transformation of the elements. Hooker goes on to suggest where Prospero may find himself at the opening of *The Tempest*: "The natural generation and process of all things receiveth order of proceeding from the settled stability of divine understanding. This appointeth unto them, their kinds of working; the disposition whereof in the purity of God's own knowledge and will is rightly termed by the name Providence. . . . Nature is nothing else but God's instrument." That includes human nature, of course, particularly when it is capable of intercepting or recognizing the workings of "Providence divine" (Hebel et al. 1953, 1027–31).

Why should King James, like elements of the church, see magic as the work of the devil? Partly, it would seem, because it was an alternative site of power. Maud Bodkin (1934) discusses how the devil archetype functions: devils "work their way toward consciousness, and if refused entrance they project themselves into the word, looks, and gestures of those around, arming these with a terrible power against the willed personality and its ideals . . . the devil is our tendency to represent in personal form the forces within and without us that threaten our supreme values" (223).

Two great minds inform the intellectual climate from which Shakespeare's plays emerged: Giordano Bruno and Francis Bacon. Bruno was a follower of Copernicus and had been in England in the 1580s, where he met Sir Philip Sidney. Bruno believed that "the true man of culture is defined [not by external signs or rituals, but by] the intimate nature of his soul and the refinement of his intellect" (qtd. in Gatti 1989, 27). The intimate nature of his soul, one assumes, is his contact with it. This view, of course, could be said to be "the Renaissance view of man." Bruno stressed achieving—as opposed to being given—special knowledge and the power deriving from it. For him, the prophets of history were Pythagoras, Moses, Christ, Ramon Llull, and Paracelsus. He perceived the impossibility of containing nature's fluidity within quantitative systems. For him, God was both transcendent and immanent. The universe is one, and that one is God. Nature is a going forth and a return of the divine nature—a movement into infinity and a return to the mind of man, who discovers changelessness, eternality, and unity in the changing scenes of finitude. That discovery marks the mind's return to God. In one of his dialogues, the Egyptian goddess Isis is quoted to the effect that "divinity reveals herself in all things, although by virtue of a universal and most excellent end, in all things, in great things and in general principles, and by proximate ends, convenient and necessary to diverse acts of human life, she is found and is seen in things said to be most abject, although everything . . . has Divinity latent within itself. For she enfolds and imparts herself even into the smallest beings, and from the smallest beings, according to their capacity" (Bruno 1964, 242). Bruno's mysticism did not—as mysticism does not—require the intercession of formal religion. He was burned at the stake in Rome on 17 February 1600.

William Morse suggests that the ending of Bacon's *Novum Organum* makes a "claim for the power of European culture's emergent model of rational, objective knowledge" but is also "shot through with a vocabulary of power, empire, and ambition so metaphorically charged that it decenters the speaker's claim to disinterestedness" (1992, 137). Bacon does commend "the latent process and latent conformations" of which we must be "good and faithful guardians, [so that] we may yield up their fortune to mankind, upon the emancipation and majority of their understanding; from which must necessarily follow an improvement of their estate, and an increase of their power over nature" (1904, 566–67). Science, says Bacon, can bring about a partial recovery "even in this life" of what was lost "by the fall" of man (567). We can sense that effort to redeem the fall in *King Lear* ("which redeems nature from the general curse / Which twain have brought her to" [4.6.206–7]), and in Shakespeare's final plays.

"Bacon," says Charles Davis,

is credited as the father of modern science, the man who cast out the demons of super-stition and instituted the inductive method of reasoning, the process by which primacy is given to the senses in conducting controlled and verifiable experiments, from which local, particular axioms are formulated and then elaborated upon to become more general axioms, which in turn prompts further experimentation. Ideally, the process continues until general, overriding axioms are formed. The method of controlled experimentation, of course, seems commonplace to the modern audience, but in the 17th century it rep-resented a radical departure from the established scientific method. Bacon opposed three trends that held the field in his time: scholasticism, which sought knowledge through perceived eternal truths, and which Bacon viewed as sterile disputation that produced no useful benefits; the humanistic approach, which cared more for pretty words than for substance; and coarse empiricism, which was dominated by magicians and alchemists. (1998, 22)

Bacon could attack the fallacy in magic: "The followers of natural magic, who explain everything by sympathy and antipathy, have assigned false powers and marvellous operations to things by gratuitous and idle conjectures: and if they have ever produced any effects, they are rather wonderful and novel than of any real benefit or utility" (Bacon 1904, 420). He did not, however, grasp the ne-cessity for selection and a control group in experiment, nor the ways in which a specific experiment conditioned the results by anticipation of it and by mea-surement. In other words, "the scientific method" awaited Newton.

The link between *The Tempest* and medieval "science" is suggested by John Mebane. "Tempest" for the alchemist was "a boiling process which removes impurities from base metal and facilitates its transmutation into gold" (1989, 181). Prospero can be seen, though, as negotiating not just between the medieval and Renaissance worlds, but between the Renaissance and the modern. He prac-tices a partial Galilean science, not seeking for cause, which has been science's purpose, but for relationships between time, of which he is so aware during the play, and other factors. That leads to description, not essence, and is a tendency that helps explain the variability of the descriptions of natural things in the play (Alfred North Whitehead 1925; Keith Devlin 1988). The link between the play and modern science is suggested by Brian Holloway, who says that Prospero is engaged in an "experiment, since the little island is a closed system into which Prospero puts certain ingredients to see what will happen" (1988, 87).

The world of Bacon did not understand what a scientific theory is. A theory "must accurately describe a large class of observations on the basis of a model that contains only a few arbitrary elements, and it must make definite predictions about the results of future observations" (Hawking 1988, 87). Hawking's ex-ample is gravity.

In Prospero, however, is embodied the contrast between the visionary Bruno of the Renaissance and the skeptical Bacon of Jacobean England. Prospero seems to glimpse magnificent imagery through and beyond mere things and, at the same time, to see nothing there at all. Depending on the emphasis a critic makes, Shakespeare's play might seem, then, to advocate either Renaissance or Jacobean values.

On "the nature of Nature"—specifically, "Caliban's terse and awful indictment of 'art' "—Hiram Haydn says, "In this matter, as in so many others, Shakespeare plays the great commentator, but his own point of view remains indeterminate" (1950, 513). What Shakespeare believed is virtually irrelevant except insofar as he questioned or undercut received opinion. To state it another way, the indeterminacy of his attitude creates an "absence" to be explored, responded to, and interpreted, with the result being a production—something that can be explored, responded to, and interpreted by an audience. Germaine Greer puts the issue this way: "In his theatrical teaching he did not aim at agreement with a position already taken but at understanding of what was involved in the issue" (1986, 39).

What things are ("what is is") in the plays is enticingly problematic. They are like the Communion elements of which Hooker says we must "meditate with silence what we have in the sacrament, and less to dispute of the matter how. What these elements are in themselves it skilleth not. It is enough to me which take them that they are the body and blood of Christ. The soul of man is the receptacle of Christ's presence" (1907, 542). In defending the new dispensation, Hooker had to elevate reason as coequal with the Bible and the church in determining "truth," but he also opened the door for the entrance of different "reasonable" approaches to "truth," including mysticism.

Kermode's discussion of Ariel argues that fairies were "the fallen angels" or "classical nymphs, fauns, hamadryads" (1964, 144), the latter being wood nymphs who lived in specific trees. A contemporary of Shakespeare, Robert Kirk, claimed that "fairies . . . are said to be of a middle Nature betuixt Man and Angel, as were Daemons thought to be of old" (qtd. in Curry 1937, 194). Curry suggests that a more neutral spirit than a fallen angel inhabits the region between earth and heaven. Ariel was "too delicate / To act [Sycorax's] earthy and abhorr'd commands" (1.2.272–73), not because Ariel was "good" but because, as Kittredge says, "Ariel has no moral nature, good or bad, being an elemental spirit of air. As such, his nature was physically pure, and he found it impossible to perform certain commands of Sycorax, which involved earthy stain or uncleanness" (1939, 16n). The morality of an action in this world resides not with the spirit but with the commander—witch or magus.

Any analysis of nature in the play becomes problematic—what it is remains unknown. By pulling up one or more strands of the vast network available to him, Shakespeare seems to imply the presence of the rest. He takes only what is artistically useful to him. Efficient cause—the playwright—does the sorting. But what does reach the surface insists on the assumption of correspondences underlying this or other plays. Critics and scholars pursue these assumptions. Part of final cause—the response to a work of art—is the effect of much more. On that assumption I will pursue "meanings" as if they do exist behind the words, recognizing that I am committing several fallacies as I do this. Curry's "philosophical pattern" is the model here—a depth structure out of which specifics emerge in a context called a play. At the same time, the philosophical pattern takes into account much that was going on around the creative action— the energies circulating through the culture as it attempted to understand and shape the philosophical pattern, which was only one among several, as Curry shows in contrasting *Macbeth* and *The Tempest*, the one with a Christian philosophical pattern, the other a syncretic work. Furthermore, "A theurgical system complete in all its ramifications is, of course, not exhibited in this drama. . . . [Shakespeare] has chosen only dramatically appropriate elements" of it (1937, 198).

A philosophical pattern is independent of the work of art; it is available in a culture as a set of premises out of which the work can emerge. Curry, for example, claims, correctly, I believe (see Coursen 1996, 51–59), that this pattern in *Macbeth* "is mediaeval, scholastic, and Christian" (1937, 198). In *"The Tempest*, with its Neo-Platonic concepts serving as artistic pattern [and] definitely under the influence of Renaissance thought . . . he creates an altogether different world, which is dominated by classical myth and integrated by a purely pagan philosophy" (198–99). Curry underestimates the syncretic nature of the play— that is, its mixture of religious traditions. He says, for example, that "if at times Christian conceptions seem to overlie the fundamental pattern, we shall find them inhering principally in the phraseology" (183–84). We find them also in plot configurations. The interrupted banquet goes back to the confrontation between Aeneas and the Harpies in *The Aeneid* (Book 3), but can also be seen as emerging from the archetype of Communion. It demonstrates the ways in which Shakespeare intentionally blurs distinctions, in this case, by using at least two sources for his scene. If we look at two other interrupted banquets, one in *Macbeth* and one in *Timon of Athens*, we can discern a distinct Christian analogue in the former and definite pagan resonances in the latter (see Knight 1947, in Palmer 1968, 144). In one an image of guilt denies the table to an evildoer (3.4.40ff.). In the other, a pagan prayer to a plurality of gods precedes a sterile feast (3.6.70ff.).

Curry argues that the "chaos of conflicting traditions—where the rigidity of old orders was shattered, ancient systems disintegrated and their debris prepared for absorption into startling combinations, and the shifting elements of knowledge themselves were in process of being fused or reduced to such fluidity as to facilitate assimilation and adaptation to the new—constituted the ideal milieu for artistic production . . . any idea, or concept of action, or story which [the poet-dramatist] might need was certain to be incredibly rich in associations acquired through a multiplicity of historical contacts" (1937, 155).

Curry's analysis helps with many of the play's imponderables. An interplay exists between things invisible, in which the "intelligible soul departs from the world of sense and energizes in mystic union with divine natures" (178). The "higher kingdom," he says, is the "realm of Providence. . . . the subordinate kingdom, which controls the sensible world alone, is the realm of Fate or Destiny" (174). Prospero claims to be the beneficiary of "Providence divine" (1.2.159), while Ariel and his company are "ministers of Fate" (3.3.61). In other words, a Neoplatonic chain of being works within the spiritual hierarchy of the play. Daemons, says Curry, are "servants of Fate" (175); "having neither reason nor principle of judgment of their own, they may be commanded by that rational creature, man" (179), or, in the case of this play, by the lieutenant general, Ariel. The "enchanter orders results, and the minister produces them by self-chosen methods and through the instrumentality of natural forces which he himself controls" (190). Prospero has no direct contact with the other spirits, or "rabble," and therefore "exactly resembles white magicians like Agrippa," as Kermode says (1964, 143). Furthermore, Prospero does not use his power for self-aggrandizement, but instead practices what D. P. Walker calls "transitive magic" (1958, 82).

Curry argues that some marvels are "a disorganization of the world of generated things," while others are "phantastic appearances" (1937, 179). We do not always know which is which in *The Tempest*. The Masque represents spirit engaged in organization and seems, in what it says, to be more than a fantastic appearance. Sycorax, however, can achieve her effects by infiltrating into the organizational structure. She " 'controlled' the moon only in the sense that she achieved effects . . . which nature intended only the moon to produce" (185). She "gained control of the moon's irrational ministers and through them created ebbs and flows when she pleased" (186). But Sycorax's power is subordinate to Nature's: she imprisons Ariel, but "having so disordered the corporeal world, which instantly righted itself into a new balance, she could not undo her charm" (188). Prospero "does not understand these signs and symbols; they are significant only to the gods who established them." He can "excite . . . the will of the gods, who recognize their own images" (189). This latter activity is what invocation is all about. The gods, apparently, must be summoned into recognition through the manipulation of signs and symbols. It is there that the magic is. Further action is the result of magic.

Karol Berger says that magus is "used in a technical sense" (1977, 211). A magus "wants to draw favorable planetary influences down from the heavens" (212). He combines medical skill with "Neoplatonic cosmic spirit" (213). Such magic "aims primarily at the imagination" (214). Prospero "uses spirit— . . . the instrument of imagination—as the medium of [his] operations" (214). In this implied allegory, Ariel becomes "Spirit," then, and Prospero is "Imagination." Berger argues that "only music can imitate and transmit affective and moral content" (213). It is true that music does seem to be the vehicle of the play's emotional meanings. It soothes Ferdinand, moves Alonso toward insight, and humanizes Caliban as he speaks of it.

According to Jerome Mandel, "The Renaissance experienced a universe in which spirits both malign and benign occupied a real and significant position. If part of this universe was benign, another part was [according to Curry 1937, 58] 'an objective realm of evil . . . peopled and controlled by the malignant wills of intelligences—evil spirits, devils, demons, Satan—who had the ability to project their power into the workings of nature and to influence the human spirit' " (1973, 63). Mandel suggests that man had control over the world's duplicity: "Whether [dreams] became delusory or not depended on the choice of response man made to them out of his own free will. In that choice, of course, character or desire is revealed" (63). The play may offer the same option: like a dream, "the play itself, as imaginative creation . . . may bespeak a higher revelation . . . to the audience" (66).

Robert H. West's excellent study (1968) concentrates on Prospero. West suggests that "the outer mystery [is] some ultimately unaccountable state of being that the dramatist may or may not conventionalize" (9). Shakespeare does not conventionalize it in *The Tempest*, but employs it as a way of interrogating its practitioner. In *The Tempest*, magic "appeals to an intellectual rather than a folk tradition" (81). "Ariel appeals to Renaissance pneumatology as Puck appeals to folklore" (81). In the play, "magic has standing in and for itself" (82), that is, it is not a symbol for "government, art, or science" (82). The question is, does Prospero's magic "countervail God" (92)? Prospero is "tense with doubts" on this point and also about whether his plan will succeed (85). He "must in the end, short of utter destruction, turn back to the world of pathos and the grave" (93).

Curry says that "theurgical practices . . . represent no more than a means of preparation for the intellectual soul in the upward progress; union with the intelligible gods is the theurgist's ultimate aim" (qtd. in Traister 1984; in Bloom 1988, 126). Prospero's goal, however, is social. He must step away from any goal of personal perfection, even if that were possible, and make "a choice to remain human" (Traister 1984, 126). Morse says that "to recognize in Prospero a type of the culture's emerging analytic individual . . . complicate[s] an original assumption of Prospero as a beneficent mage with a second perception preoccupied with his darker and more self-serving side" (1992, 137–38). As far as I can decode this approach, it is that the apparently disinterested nature of "rationality" is not disinterested. The claim that it is conceals its motives. An "idealized human rationality" (138) is to be suspected.

Kurt T. Von Rosador asks the Greenblattian question: "How can society distinguish between legitimate and illegitimate claims to sacred authority?" (1991, 2). *The Tempest* deals with "the half-latent, half-overt rivalry between the royal magic of the monarchy and the magician's art" (2). Prospero is torn between "the simultaneous existence and attractions of two charismatic powers" (3). He cannot appear simultaneously in magician's robes and ducal finery. That they are separate is something Prospero grasps. The ducal robes are part of his goal as magician. "To renounce magic is also . . . to renounce vindictiveness and vengeance," says Orgel (1987, 52). According to Von Rosador, "Magic and monarchy do not go together" (1991, 12), that is, unless magical powers are part of a monarch's gifts, as in the case of Edward the Confessor in *Macbeth*, and as in the case of James, who also claimed the healing power.

A discussion of magic illuminates certain specific aspects of the play. Of "superstitious magic," Bacon notes that "we cannot wonder that the false notion of plenty should have occasioned want" (1904, 382). Magic could betray its emptiness or be associated with emptiness—in a crucial way—via a feast-that-is-not, like the disappearing banquet in 3.3 of *The Tempest*. Agrippa, writing in 1527, describes a magician who was "wont to shew to straungers a very sump-tuouse banket, & when it pleased him to cause it vanishe awaie, all they which sate at the table beinge disappointed both of meate and drinke" (1651, 62–63). Faustus can conjure grapes into being even when out of season, but he is denied the Communion, as is Macbeth. Neither can enjoy the profound linkage between physical humanity and indwelling divinity that the "mystical incorporation" of the Eucharist renders to those who not only believe—perversely, like all sinners, Faustus and Macbeth have no choice but to know a truth they cannot evade—but who act on their beliefs.

A major issue in assessing Prospero is his statement that "graves at my com-mand / Have wak'd their sleepers, op'd and let 'em forth" (5.1.48–49). Some five years after the first performance of *The Tempest*, John Cotta said, "As touching the reall raising of the dead, it is impossible unto the limited power of the Divell, either in the substance of body or soule, to reduce or bring the dead back into this world, or life, or sense againe, because in death, by the unchange-able, and unalterable decree of God in His Holy Writ, the body returneth to dust, from whence it came, and the Soule to God who gave it." The devil, however, can "present . . . apparitions of the bodies and substances of dead men . . . if . . . only . . . the outward lively pourtraiture, and shapes of the substances of bodies, though the bodies themselves be away" (1616, 37–38). As with so much of the evidence, however, nothing in the play shows Prospero opening graves and letting their sleepers forth. King James, in *Daemonologie* (1597), discusses the "meane [whereby the Devil] borrowes a dead body and so visible, and as it seemes unto them naturallie as a man converses with them" (67).[1]

SOME ANALOGUES IN LITERATURE

Much pre-Shakespearean and Elizabethan-Jacobean literature demonstrates "Renaissance Europe's fascination with exotic tales of magicians, wizards, strange beasts, enchanted isles and romantic love" (Vaughan and Vaughan 1999, 56). With the beginning of the seventeenth century and the advent of King James, magic was deemed more damnable than before, though it had never been approved by the church, since it was an inroad on the church's versions of magic, a rising from the dead and transubstantiation (Pearson 1974, 255). The exorcism in *The Comedy of Errors*, for example, is a mock ritual, a parody. We know that Antipholus of Ephesus is not possessed, merely confused and enraged. In no way is the play or its author suggesting that exorcism is "real," either in the play or in the culture.

Often, magic is merely a vehicle toward acquisition, as opposed to a Neoplatonic avenue toward "higher form." It had no moral or spiritual value for Ben Jonson, who satirized it as charlatanism in his version of the Parable of the Talents, *The Alchemist*, and suggested that it was merely a means toward opulent material ends:

> My meat shall all come in, in Indian shells,
> Dishes of agate set in gold, and studded
> With emeralds, sapphires, hyacinths, and rubies. . . .
> And I will eat these broths with spoons of amber,
> Headed with diamond and carbuncle. (2.2.72–74, 78–79)

Here is an example of the nonexistent feast that figures so prominently in the literature of magic and witchcraft. Sir Epicure Mammon does not achieve any of this sybaritic dream, but he does not have to sell his soul either. He is merely bilked by the confidence game that Face and Subtle conduct. Sir Epicure is convinced that Subtle is

> a divine instructor! can extract
> The souls of all things by his art; call all
> The virtues and the miracles of the sun,
> Into a temperate furnace; teach dull nature
> What her own forces are. A man the emperor
> Hath courted. (4.1.86–91)

Sturgess points out that Richard Burbage (Prospero) would have played Subtle a year earlier in Jonson's *Alchemist*. Jonson's plays were performed by the King's Men. Subtle, of course, has to sneak out the back window at the end of the play when Face's master, Lovewit, returns. Unlike Prospero, Subtle is the "magician as charlatan . . . an illusionist whose art is cheating not charming and he is exiled from his little empire at the end of the play, not welcomed home in triumph" (1987, in Vaughan and Vaughan 1998, 109).

In his brilliant introduction to *The Alchemist*, Alvin Kernan says that "in none of [Jonson's] plays is the heroic subject matter [of Renaissance drama] converted to comic reality more obviously and successfully than in *The Alchemist*. Here the aspiration of the Renaissance as a whole to control and remake the world is imaged as a great swindle, alchemy, managed by an impudent servant and a cunning spiel-man, who are parodies of those Renaissance philosophers and scientists, such as Bruno and Kepler, to whom Marlowe had given tragic form as the great magician Doctor Faustus" (1974, 6).

Marlowe's Dr. Faustus (1592) does trade his soul for the power to startle the nobility with his tricks. The nobles are also culpable, according to King James. Princes who patronize magicians and who "delight to see them proove some of their practicques . . . sinne heavilie against their office in that poynt" (1597, 24–25). Faustus is denied marriage—a sacrament—and ends up yearning for annihilation rather than face damnation. In the Richard Burton film, Elizabeth Taylor played Faustus's demon lover. She waited for him, smiling amid the flames of hell at the end, and one achieved a chilling, existential sense of what damnation was all about.

Much of the intellectual background flows into *Dr. Faustus*. Divinity, for Faustus, is only an academic discipline. His selling of his soul to the devil occurs outside of the dull region inhabited by learned treatises based on a discredited cosmology. Faustus alludes to "cunning" Agrippa, a famous writer on occult subjects and reputedly a powerful magician. Agrippa, though, denied an interest in cabalism (a mystical interpretation of the Scriptures that did not require the mediation of the church or formal religion, and therefore a burning offense). Agrippa urged a return to primitive Christianity. Faustus, even as he is denied the sacraments in what he should recognize is a prelude to damnation, contents himself with the thought that he has time to repent. "Tush, Christ did call the thief upon the cross!" he says (4.5.26), adducing the last-minute salvation in the Gospel according to John. But he has been too long the scoffing other thief and so sinks downward with the gravity of his decisions—"A surfeit of deadly sin" (5.2.31).

That surfeit equates to emptiness, as Latham suggests. After Faustus feeds them, "the guests, having eaten and drunk to the full, go home thinking that they have had nothing" (1979, 216). Latham points out that the "hunger" of Faustus's guests "remains unsatisfied after the magic banquet is eaten" (1979, 217). The most frequent analogous banquet, she says, is "the mysterious table [of] the Grail myth" (219). Marjorie Garber likens the disappearing banquet to Tantalus, who could neither reach the grapes that dangled enticingly close nor touch the water that neared his chin until he bent down for it (1980, in Bloom 1988, 51). The ultimate example in Shakespeare is the banquet denied to Macbeth by the image of his guilt, Banquo.

The biblical Simon Magus was compared to Faustus. He understood faith intellectually, but lacked it spiritually. Belief without faith is a status more damnable than mere ignorance, because the options are available to the mind, as they are not to the pagan. As the Geneva Bible gloss to Acts 8.13 says, "The magestie of Gods worde forced him to confess the trueth: but yet was he not regenerat therefor." After being baptized, Simon offers Peter money for the power of laying on of hands. Peter rebukes him: "Thou has nether parte nor fellowship in this business: for thine heart is not right in the sight of God. . . . for I se that thou art . . . in the bond of iniquitie . . . so that now Satan hathe thee tied as captive in his bands" (8.21, 23).

Prospero uses magic for his purposes, not his pleasure, and does not make any bargains with whatever dark powers there be. To say that Prospero lacks the reckless abandon of Dr. Faustus is to put it mildly. The issue is to some extent the darkness within Prospero, which he must and does acknowledge. *The Tempest* is far less "Christian" than *Faustus* or *Macbeth*—"tragedies of damnation"—but it has Christian overtones and a deeply Christian rhythm, as I shall suggest later.

Garber equates Prospero with Daedalus, who could not teach his son Icarus and thus represents the "fable of failed education" (54). "All humane reason is but waxen wings," she says, and Prospero is "in danger of becoming Icarus" (56). Garber sees Daedalus as "unifying and extending the play's central concern with the necessary distinction between man and god" (59). The Minotaur "distinguish[es] between man and beast" (59). The "penning of the Minotaur in the labyrinth," the "monster within the maze," is the equivalent of the stying of Caliban in the rock (59). Barbara Mowat suggests that when Prospero is "looking down and commenting on the trapped figures below him, he [resembles] Daedalus. Throughout the play, he, like Daedalus, is almost trapped in his own intricate maze" (Mowat and Werstine 1994, 197). The equation begins to grow thin. It is Gonzalo and Alonso who refer to "a maze." For Garber, the play moves "out of the Old Testament into the New" (57) and thus out of older mythologies into its own *episteme*.

John Cutts discerns echoes of deep mythology in the music of the play. It is "equivalent to music of the spheres" (which Pericles hears at the end of his play), a "celestial harmony . . . the lawful counterpart of the Sirens" (Palmer 1968, 196). Prospero's island is a disjunctive counterpart to Circe's (197).

Ben Jonson, though skeptical about witchcraft, could use it when it suited his purposes, as in the "Third Charm" from *The Masque of Queens*:

> The owl is abroad, the bat, and the toad,
>   And so is the cat-a-mountain,
> The ant and the mole sit both in a hole,
>   And the frog peeps out o' the fountain;
> The dogs they do bay, and the timbrels play,
>   The spindle is now a-turning;
> The moon it is red, and the stars are fled,
>   But all the sky is a-burning.
> The ditch is made, and our nails the spade,
>   With pictures full of wax and of wool;
> their livers I stick, with needles quick;
>   There lacks but the blood, to make up the flood.
>   (in Judson 1927, 20)

Kermode argues that "the whole plot of *The Tempest* is based on two motifs used by Jonson in *The Masque of Beauty* . . . wandering and disenchantment" (1964, lxxii), but that is to ignore Shakespeare's use of "wandering" as early as *The Comedy of Errors* and of the concept of magic at the end of *As You Like It*, a play that easily predates *The Masque of Beauty*.

Bernard Knox argues Shakespeare's indebtedness to "the ancient comic tradition." Knox suggests that the "conjugations" of *The Tempest* conform to "the basic paradigms of classical comedy" (1955, in Barnet 1987, 166). He points to "the existence in ancient society of a dividing line stricter and more difficult to cross than any social barrier that has been since: the distinction between slave and free" (166). It "provided a fixed contrast of condition and standards on which comedy could be based" (167). In using this configuration "literally" (171), Shakespeare avails himself of "a dramatic design as old as European comedy" (175). Ariel, of course, can keep anticipating his freedom, while Caliban's "exchange [of] curses for Prospero's threats of punishment is a traditional feature of the comedy of master and slave" (177). The drunken butler is another stock character, the "slave in charge of his master's wine who drinks most of it himself" (178). Knox notes that "Caliban's meeting with Trinculo and Stephano is a servile parallel and parody of Miranda's meeting with Ferdinand" (178). In each, a mortal seems to confront a deity. Shakespeare takes risks with his "novel and fantastic effects" (164). A "defiance of the normal laws of cause and effect in the operation of nature is especially dangerous in comedy, for comedy's appeal, no matter how contrived the play may be, is to the audience's sense of the solid values of a real world, to a critical faculty which can recognize the inappropriate" (164–65). Shakespeare's awareness of his defiance of cause and effect may be reflected in the "normalization" of all events in Prospero's Epilogue. The stage is now a "bare island," and Prospero expresses what he has done within the ostensible value system of his audience.

Like many plays of Shakespeare, this last one hearkens back to his medieval heritage (Farnham 1936). Boas suggests that the final scene "recalls in certain aspects the 'pageant' of the Last Judgement," in that Prospero, like Christ, metes out rewards and punishments (1912, 538). The Wakefield "Judgement" is an appropriation of the York cycle of the early fifteenth century, incorporating Christ's indictment of the condemned for failing to observe the injunction to show charity as enjoined in Matthew 25.31–46: "And when the Sonne of man cometh in his glorie, and all the holie Angels with him, then shal he sit upon the throune of his glorie. / And before him shalbe gathered all nacions, and he shal separate them one from another, as a shepherde separateth the shepe from the goates" (Geneva Bible). God's opening invocation is missing, but the Wakefield Master surrounds the sober York play with a spirited topical discourse in which Tutivillus is a "Master Lollard in belief" and in which the Second Demon proves William James's thesis on the exercise of free will: "Let us go to our doom up Watling Street" (James's famous lecture of 1884 used his choice of streets as an example of his freedom from determinism [1965, 30–31]).

The Wakefield play includes, of course, a "porter at hell-gate . . . / in so sad a strait, / Up early and down late, / Rest has he never." The reminder of the late medieval emphasis on good works is probably clearer at the end of *Measure for Measure*, where the Duke makes sure he behaves "like power divine," than at the end of *The Tempest*, where Prospero is definitely not interested in being taken for a god. E. Martin Browne makes a crucial distinction when he says that "the Middle Ages was not a time of speculation about the nature of the world, but rather of things within a world" (1958, 12). *The Tempest*—Prospero, at least—speculates about both the world and the things within it. The interchange of energy between the total and the specific creates music heard and unheard; both are mysterious improvisations and notations of the deeper mystery of the unseen musician. The staging of *The Tempest* does not require "a stout staircase . . . built either inside or outside heaven's tower" (Martial Rose 1963, 551).

Mary Ellen Rickey says that Prospero's rewards and punishments have "recognizable precedents in Christian literature" (1965, 35). The banquet resembles Dante's treatment of the gluttons, while the game of chess has a resonance in George Herbert's "Providence," where God is the chess master balancing the seasons. The Dante analogy is tenuous. The gluttons, having gorged themselves, are empty, like bladders filled with air. They are half-sunk under a constant rain and serve as steps for Dante and Virgil. Ciacco calls to Dante, who does not recognize him. Ciacco predicts the victory of the Donati (or Black) party that has already exiled Dante and asks Dante to remember him to those in Florence. Virgil tells Dante that the punishment now experienced by those in the Inferno will be perfected after the Last Judgement. Virgil says, "Turn to thy science," which John Ciardi believes is Aristotle (1954, 70), Paolo Milano believes is Aquinas (1949, 35). The bodies are substanceless, having crammed themselves in life, so that the paradox of food and no food does relate to the disappearing banquet and to that tradition.

> And as we huddled under constant sleet,
>   from body to bloated body, down they sank,
> hollow as a cloud, beneath our passing feet. (6.34–36)

Jan Kott, in his influential *Shakespeare, Our Contemporary* (1964), links *The Tempest* with the morality play, a late medieval allegorical drama of which *Everyman* is the great example. The "morality play," Kott says, "has exposed the reasons of its failure; it repeats history without being able to alter it. It is essential that Prospero's magic mantle be thrown off his shoulders, together with bad theatrical tradition" (187). Kott twice quotes Prospero as saying, "My ending is despair" (166 and 205), and compares that statement with Cleopatra's "My desolation does begin to make / A better life" (*Antony and Cleopatra* 5.2.1–2). Prospero's statement about "ending" is hardly the same thing as Cleopatra's beginning to build from the single point of one's existence—the latter is existentialism. Furthermore, Kott's incomplete quotation obscures what Prospero is saying. However alone he is on his bare island, he asks to be made a member incorporate of a community that will express itself (or fail to express itself) in the instant after his last word. The context is the ending of *The Tempest*:

And my ending is despair,
Unless I be reliev'd by prayer,
Which pierces so, that it assaults
Mercy itself, and frees all faults.
   As you from crimes would pardon'd be,
   Let your indulgence set me free. (Epilogue, 15–20)

Richard Hillman develops a parallel between *The Tempest* and Chaucer's *Franklin's Tale*: "[T]he main magical event in the *Tale* . . . is nearly a mirror-image of Prospero's great trick—an illusion of protection from, rather than subjection to, shipwreck" (1983, 428). Chaucer's Dorigene would have the rocks that threaten her husband Arveragus's safe return "sonken into hell" (Chaucer 892). Miranda would have "sunk the sea within the earth" (1.2.11). Chaucer's magician is an "agent of release and forgiveness," says Hillman (431). Among Shakespeare's sources, "only in *The Franklin's Tale* do we find a precedent for his use of a magician's powers to effect a spiritual reformation, confirmed by an act of pardon and renunciation on the part of the magician himself" (431).

Dorigene promises that she will yield to Aurelius's importunity if he will cover the rocks that threaten her husband's return: "wolde God that alle thise rokkes blake / Were sonken into helle for his sake!" (891–92). Aurelius's brother knows a "bachelor of lawe" in "Orliens," who has studied "magyk natureel" (or astrology), "and swich folye, / As in oure dayes is not worth a flye; / For hooly chirches feith in oure bileve / Ne suffereth noon illusoun us to greve" (that is, the church will not permit us to come to grief by believing in that sort of dangerous nonsense: 1125–34). The magician has Prospero-like powers: To "every mannes sighte," he can create "a castel, al of lym and stoon; / And whan hem lyked, voyded it anoon" (1149–50). Arveragus does return safely, but Aurelius's magician has created the illusion that "the rokkes been aweye" (1337). That may be "agayns the proces of nature," as Dorigene complains, but what is she to do? She launches into one of the greatest of Chaucerian lists, this one of virtuous virgins and chaste wives: the daughters of "Phidoun [of] Atthenes" (1369), who drowned themselves in a well rather than submit to his murderers, the "fifty maydens" of "Lacedomye" (1380), who died rather than yield to the Messenians, "a mayden heet Stymphalides" (1388), who clung to Diana's statue to the death rather than surrender to Aristoclides, "Hasdrublales wyf" (1399), "Lucresse" (1405), "The sevene maydens of Melesie also" (1409), "Penalopee" (1443), "noble Porcia" (1448), Brutus's wife, and others—making Prospero positively laconic on the subject of chastity.

This tale, like Prospero's Masque as it deflects the venereal mischief of Venus and Cupid, has a chaste ending. While Arveragus says that Dorigene must fulfill her hateful bargain, Aurelius takes pity on her ("And in his hearte hadde greet compassion / Of hire and of hire lamentacioun" [1515–16]). His natural nobility emerges from his infatuation: "I have wel levere evere to suffre wo / Than I departe the love bitwix yow two" (1531–32). "Thus kan a quier doon a gentil

dede / As wel as kan a knyght, withouten drede" (1543–44). Aurelius has promised the magician a thousand pounds to hide the rocks—a sum that drains his
exchequer. The magician shows that he can "doon a gentil dede" (1543) and
releases Aurelius from his debt. The story ends with a question, as did many
medieval moral tales: "Which was the mooste fre, as thiyketh yow?" (1622).
"Fre" means "generous." The question includes Arveragus, who would not have
his wife make a false promise even at the cost of her chastity.

Apuleius's witch, Meroe, in *The Golden Asse*, a work with which Shakespeare
was well acquainted (Tobin 1984), had powers far beyond those Prospero attributes to himself. She had the ability "to rule the heavens, to bring down the
sky, to bear up the earth, to turn the waters into hills and the hills into running
waters, to lift up the terrestrial spirits into the air, and to pull the gods out of
the heavens, to extinguish the planets and to lighten the deep darkness of hell"
(qtd. in Mowat 1981, in Vaughan and Vaughan 1998, 197).

Alwin Thaler equates Caliban and the witch's son in Spenser's poem *The
Faerie Queene* Book 3, Canto 7 (cited in Kermode 1964, xliii). That is a dubious
parallel. Although the latter feels "brutish lust" for the fair fugitive, Florimell,
he woos her with "many kinde remembraunces . . . Girlonds of flowres. . . . All
of which she of him tooke with countenance meeke and mild." She flees not
just his potential "mischiefe," but that of his mother as well. Spenser does,
however, provide a forerunner to Prospero:

> For Merlin had in magick more insight
> Than ever him before or after living wight.
> For he by wordes could call out of the sky
> Both sunne and moone and make them him obay.
> The land to sea, and sea to maineland dry,
> And darksom night he eke could turne to day.
> Huge hostes of men he could alone dismay,
> And hostes of men of meanest things could frame,
> When so him list his enimies to fray:
> That to this day, for terror of his fame,
> The feends do quake, when any him to them does name. (*The Faerie
> Queene* 3.3.11–12)

(On Shakespeare and Spenser, see Watkins 1950.)

Dipsa, in John Lyly's *Endymion* (1594), claims, "I can darken the Sunne by
my skil, and remoove the Moone out of her course; I can restore youth to the
aged, and make hils without bottoms; there is nothing that I can not doe"
(1.4.28–32)—that is, except "rule hearts; for were it in my power to place affection by appointment, I would make such evil appetites, such inordinate lusts,
such cursed desires, as all the world should be filled both with superstitious
heats and extreme love" (36–38). This warning underlines Prospero's insistence
on chastity. But Cynthia (Queen Elizabeth) tells Dipsa, "Let all enchaunters
knowe, that *Cynthia*, being placed for light on earth, is also protected by the

powers of heaven" (5.3.27–28). Dipsa yields to this greater power: "Madam, I renounce both substance and shadow of that most horrible and hateful trade, vowing to the gods continual penance, and to your Highness obedience" (5.3.368–71). The play anticipates James's belief that "it is not in the Devilles power to defraude or bereave [the lawfull Magistrate] of the office, or effect of his powerfull and revenging Sceptre" (1597, 51).

Robert Greene's Friar Bacon, in *Friar Bacon and Friar Bungay* (circa 1589), would have a brazen head utter aphorisms and circle England with a wall of brass. His servant Miles, however, fails to wake Bacon during the head's moment of potency. The head is smashed by a heavenly, or perhaps hellish, hammer. "Time is past!" (11, 84). The effort to create an instant wonder of the world within a pause in time's movement goes by, with "Aristotle's stamp" (11, 70) upon it. Bacon bemoans the loss of the reputation of "a mortal man [who could] work so much. / Hell trembled at my deep-commanding spells, / Fiends frowned to see a man their overmatch" (11, 106–8). He repents: "I'll spend the remnant of my life / In pure devotion, praying to my God / That he would save what Bacon vainly lost" (13, 107–9). To him is granted that divination also accorded to Henry VI (in the case of Richmond) and Wolsey (in the instance of the infant Elizabeth). Bacon sees that "From forth the royal garden of a king / Shall flourish out so rich and fair a bud, / Whose brightness shall deface proud Phoebus flower, / And overshadow Albion with her leaves. . . . then the stormy threats of war shall cease" (16, 46–51). Nature's course will render brassy walls unnecessary—and Elizabeth will render Bacon's magic irrelevant as well.

One of Shakespeare's early witches is Marjorie Jourdain in *Henry VI Part II*. She is burned at the stake at Smithfield, but her prophecies come true, even if in a riddling way, like those of the Weird Sisters in *Macbeth*. Garry Wills compares Lady Macbeth to the woman who employed Jourdain, the repentant Duchess of Gloucester. Before her exile, she appears "in a White Sheet with a Taper burning in her hand" (stage direction 2.4) and says, "Dark shall be my light, and night my day. / To think upon my pomp shall be my hell" (2.4.40–41). Wills suggests that Lady Macbeth's entrance in 5.1, in nightgown and with candle, "said to Shakespeare's audience, repentant sorceress" (1995, 87). If so, repentance has come too late. Lady Macbeth, even in an unconscious state, senses her damnation: "Hell is murky."

Diane Purkiss's brilliant study *The Witch in History* (1996) suggests that for Shakespeare, the witch was still a classical construct—a Circe, a Medea. "*The Tempest* is haunted by a series of ghostly stories of encounters with foreign witches, including the soil of the New World. . . . Prospero's masque for Ferdinand and Miranda lacks an antimasque not because it is unfinished, but because the confrontation between rule and misrule has already been staged and misrule already banished, not by Prospero but by the same providential agency which ensures his arrival. Yet the shadowy form of the witch haunts the scene from which she has been removed" (251). Purkiss mentions Peter Hall's and Derek Jarman's visualizations of Sycorax—one an enormous monster-mother giving birth, the other an obese naked sorceress smoking a cigar—as untrue to her invisibility. The director does have to decide what Caliban looks like. Sycorax is left to the imagination, enticingly undisplayed. Her materialization "does no justice to the complexity and precision of the text's intertextuality" (251) or to its depiction of the "entanglement of Old and New World discourses" (251).

Caliban would have appealed to James as a denizen of "the wild parts of the world where the Devil finds greatest ignorance and barbarity [and thus] assails he grossliest," as James said in *Daemonologie* (1597, 76). As the eyes of monsters reflected the firelight of the eighth-century settlements huddled in tiny circles surrounded by ancient trees and lurking mountains, the wild man always stalked the edges of literature and language, an alien at once threatening and validating culture, making it a luxury that one enjoyed with a slight shudder. As Hayden White says of the wild man, "He is just out of sight, over the horizon, in the nearby forest, desert, mountains, or hills. He sleeps in crevices, under great trees, on the caves of wild animals" (1972, 121).

As Purkiss says, "The wilderness, where the ignorant and the barbarians live, is the devil's abode; as far away as possible conceptually and geographically from James, his books, his court, his city" (1996, 253). If, she continues, "the discourses of 'race' and imperialism were evolving together, [then] *The Tempest* stands at the earliest point of contact between literature and these discourses" (257). Purkiss argues back in time, rather than forward: "*The Tempest* represents the last moment of innocence in which the New World had yet to be interpreted and could be caught up in Mediterranean and demonological topographies without outraging the cultural and geographical difference. Sycorax represents not the first but the *last* moment at which a New World native woman, an Old World witch, and a classical world witch might be the same thing, the last moment at which vagueness about the New World could generate meaning" (257). The "new world could be seen in terms of the classics, and actually conflated with them" (258), so that the issue was not one world or another but "two interchangeable frames of reference" (258). *The Tempest* was "written in [a] hiatus between this moment of astounding vagueness and the moment of clarification" (258). This approach is useful because it refuses to locate what the play itself does not place in history or tradition, or to picture that for which no description exists. It does not exhibit the narrowing quality of so much criticism, recent and past, a quality false to the multiple suggestions and attitudes that this play flashes forth.

The play emerges against the background of Circe and Medea: "manslaying seductresses . . . embody[ing] a fear of miscegenation, emasculation, and the disruption of primogeniture" (258). One can understand Prospero's painstaking domestication of Miranda. "Medea is linked with the periphery wherever the centre locates itself" (259). Prospero represents "not simply an undoing of laboriously established differences between himself and Sycorax," but an erasure of "the spectre of his going native, a spectre inextricably linked with questions of desire and hence of gender" (259). He is in danger of becoming an "other" socially and damned theologically. "How does the play read if we see Sycorax as unknowable, or unreadable? What if her story exists to put out vagrant tendrils in many directions rather than to be tied to a particular point of origin?" (266). Sycorax becomes a grouping of ominous possibilities, a shadowy background that threatens Prospero, that Prospero threatens to become, that, in a sense, he does acknowledge in admitting that he is surrogate father to Caliban, that he also discards in casting off Medea in his renunciation of magic. The point of the likeness is that it ends as he paraphrases his classical counterpart.

Margreta de Grazia says of Sycorax and Prospero that "not only are their histories similar and their powers interchangeable, but both sorceress and magician are driven by the same passion—anger" (1981, 255). The parallel is primarily one of contrast, I would argue, as Shakespeare employs one of his favorite devices, the disjunctive analogue.

Purkiss's approach allows for a "metaphoric interchangeability between" worlds (1996, 266) and between personalities in a "polyvalent" environment (267). The "sweeter and more manageable figure of Miranda [is] the only female object of desire the play will allow. The dark lady is folded back into the Petrarchan object of desire. Circe transformed men into beasts; in *The Tempest*, this narrative is inverted as a (black) witch is displaced by the unambiguously virginal white girl" (267). Gender considerations slide into racial contexts here as well. The "opposition that Prospero tries to make . . . between himself and Sycorax is often too problematic to be sustained," Purkiss says (269). Prospero makes a "distinction . . . attributing the demonic power of magic to his enemy and alter ego, the witch Sycorax," according to Marjorie Garber (1980, in Bloom 1988, 56), and Stephen Greenblatt says something similar: "Necromancy—communing with the spirits of the dead—was the very essence of black magic, the hated practice from which Prospero is careful to distinguish himself" (1997, 3048). While Prospero talks of Sycorax's "earthy and abhorr'd commands" (1.2.273), he also talks of opening graves. It may be that he is not as certain of the distinction he would make as are some critics.

Caliban refuses to surrender "the gods, speech and customs of his mother," says Purkiss. "Yet Prospero taught him language" (1996, 269). Caliban refuses to give up the island. He couches his objection in language he learned from Prospero and in the concepts the new language has grown to incorporate. The island is "mine," says Caliban. Caliban is "mine," says Prospero in the "language of paternity . . . close to the language of the ownership of slaves" (270). "Once the other is acknowledged to be unchangeable, racism and fear of miscegenation can begin in earnest, unbridled, unchallenged by any missions to alter, amend, or convert" (271). If "things of darkness . . . are fully disarmed of" all that goes along with "the image of them as witches," it follows that "skepticism [makes] possible both contact and genocide, and both are foreshadowed in the play" (271).

This is an ominous reading, of course: Caliban has to be undemonized and humanized in order to be exterminated as undesirable. Prospero, though, is not skeptical. Purkiss reads a large cultural tendency into a character that will not sustain the interpretation, even if subsequent history shows benighted individuals and states acting on the thesis that nurture cannot alter nature. Prospero has known witchcraft and has discarded it. He promises pardon to Caliban. He asks for pardon from the audience. The type of Christ having dispelled pagan gods, including the Sycorax in himself, the threatening woman who threatens others (the unintegrated anima), and who acknowledges his shadow, the threatening male who threatens him, yields to a god of response, or to the response of a god—the audience.

In his splendid study of the geographical background of Shakespeare's work, John Gillies (1994) also pursues the intercultural implications of the script. Since cartography itself was a kind of fiction, projected from a point of view that insisted that the world be as belief or interest said it was, I include Gillies here, rather than under intellectual background. His book deserves, though, a wider application than my categories provide.

Gillies suggests that both Cleopatra and Caliban "seek some form of pollutive 'incorporation' with a host-city" (100). *The Tempest* has three narrative sectors: original or mythological, colonial or historical, and renewal or visionary. Sycorax reduced the island to wilderness (143). Caliban becomes implicated in the colonial activities of "reclamation, demarcation and territory-formation" (143). "Prospero and Miranda are inveterate line-drawers" (143). In the Masque of Ceres, however, "discord becomes concord" (144). Gillies might notice how the disruptive god, Cupid, is integrated into this concord, indeed accepts it on human terms ("And be a boy right out": 4.1.101), and thus erases significant conceptual boundaries. Cupid, though not depicted in the script, would become a boy actor, like the boy playing Miranda, threatened only by the maleness bound to overtake the voice and body that can, for a few years, impersonate womanhood.

Miranda's words on seeing Alonso and his party are "perhaps the most luminous statement of the 'renewal' theme in the play. [Shakespeare gives 'the other's'] lines to his European princess" (154). Of course, she has yet to become that princess in Europe. "Shakespeare privileges [the renewal topos] but hardly in the uncritical way of colonial apologists. . . . In celebrating . . . its beauty, he also exposes the dream-structure of the American colonial myth: its origins in the psychology of narcissism and utopian wish-dreaming" (154). In claiming that "Miranda and Caliban are brother and sister, children of ignorance" (155), Gillies might adduce Caliban's dream of riches (3.2.133–14). That speech, however, might clash with Gillies's insistence that, in making Caliban, "Shakespeare *chose* to represent the Amerindian as monstrous and to ignore more favorable character models" (151).

This reading would leave Caliban on the island, not permitted to intrude upon the new Neapolitan-Milanese hegemony. He will have what he wanted (we can hear Prospero telling him that with a magnanimous sneer), but the island will not be peopled. His bones may be discovered by the survivors of some future wreck. Nothing will tell them that this was the skull of a king denied the chance to people his little world.

NOTE

1. For suggestive comments on the ways in which "the magician has . . . remained one of the dominant images of the poet in the modern world" (in Goethe, Melville, Joyce, Yeats, Wilde, Kafka, Mann, Borges, and Hesse), see Alvin Kernan (1979, 146–59).

Nineteenth-century illustration.

3

DRAMATIC STRUCTURE

The text of *The Tempest* in the First Folio is neatly demarcated into acts and scenes. It has obviously been carefully "written," as opposed to being a "play-script" or a compilation of separate parts handed out to actors (as in *A Midsummer Night's Dream*). Here I merely outline what seem to me to be the major elements of the action, with an occasional pause for commentary, and with some emphasis on aspects to be explored later in more detail, like Prospero's Masque, his "revels" speech, and the game of chess at the end. I am using Kermode's New Arden edition for citations to *The Tempest*.

The play itself is not easy to describe. Not much happens, so the way events take place or do not take place is significant. If, as Kermode suggests, the play does not have much imagery (1964, lxxx)—language that appeals to the senses—the play's appeal lies elsewhere. While I disagree with Kermode, I think that he is right to call attention to a mode of perception deeper than just the sensory. The Chorus to *Henry V* tells us that we must deploy our "imaginary forces," we must "suppose" with "imaginary puissance," we must "think" that we "see" kingdoms and armies, hordes of horses and men struggling in battle. "For 'tis your thoughts that now must deck our kings" (Prologue, 18–28). "Minding true things by what their mockeries be" (4 Chorus, 53). In a sense, *The Tempest* makes that appeal to Ferdinand and Miranda as they observe the Masque, which represents deity via "rabble" (4.1.37). "May I be bold / To think these spirits?" Ferdinand asks (4.1.119–20). He is still thinking, even at the Masque's end. To us, the appeal of the larger play is not to thought, not just to sense, or even to imagination, nor is it as if we are dreaming. Dreams are not so coherent, so consistently characterized, so well phrased. It is as if we are being dreamed to, as if the dream's creator is collaborating with our own magnificent imagination, which we only recognize when we recall the ingenuity and invention that our dreaming selves show to us.

IF BY YOUR ART . . .

A "tempestuous noise of thunder and lightning heard," and the play opens on a ship at sea. The Master and the Boatswain shout back and forth, the Master afraid that the ship will "run . . . aground" (1.1.4). According to Kermode, the Boatswain's orders constitute "in proper sequence four of the things one was recommended to do in a gale at sea" (1964, 4). King Alonso and his party enter and demand to see the Master. The Boatswain tells them to get back to their cabins. They are getting in the way, or as the Boatswain says, "You mar our labour. . . . You do assist the storm" (1.1.13–14). In a precis of *King Lear*, the Boatswain makes the distinction between nature and political power: "What cares these roarers for the name of King?" (1.1.16–17) (Goddard 1951, 278). He mocks Gonzalo: "You are a counsellor; if you can command these elements to silence . . . we will not hand a rope more: use your authority" (1.1.22–23). Gonzalo predicts that the Boatswain will hang. His "complexion" (or makeup) "is perfect gallows" (1.1.29–30). The King and his party cry, "We split, we split!" and the ship apparently sinks. "It is as if [Shakespeare] had placed his whole tragic vision of life into one brief scene before bestowing his new vision upon us," says J. Dover Wilson (1932, 13).

The scene exhibits both natural and psychological storms. The Boatswain says, "A plague upon this howling! they are louder than the weather or our office" (1.1.35–37). That suggests that "the tempest in [the] mind" (to quote Lear, 3.4.12) is somehow more powerful than the sea and wind in which the ship founders. The scene also draws the distinction between rule on land and command at sea so often made in the fiction of Joseph Conrad. Since this is the first scene of the play, as opposed to the description of Antigonus's shipwreck in *The Winter's Tale*, we assume that we will see some of these characters again, including the King, Gonzalo, and the two younger men (Sebastian and Antonio) who have cursed the Boatswain. While Leo Marx says, rightly, "The rest of the action is colored by fantasy, but the storm is depicted in spare naturalistic tones" (1967, 52), we can doubt that Master Will Shakespeare has begun his new play by introducing these characters only to sink them forever out of sight. Some members of Shakespeare's audience may have remembered that they soon met the characters described in Egeon's shipwreck narrative at the beginning of *The Comedy of Errors*, some twenty years before the storm in *The Tempest*, and that Sebastian survived the sinking that Viola thinks has drowned him in *Twelfth Night*. Shakespeare liked to pull his characters out of the sea. Alfred Harbage says, "We are not too much concerned. The saltiness of the Boatswain and the whimsical garrulity of Gonzalo have taken the terror out of this storm" (1963, 462). Nigel Smith suggests that underlying the opening scene is the "familiar medieval image of the ship of state tossed in the stormy sea of fortune, fate, or Providence" (1988, 94).

The last page of *The Tempest* in the First Folio (page 19) tells us that "The Scene" is "an uninhabited Island." We discover two people there, however: Prospero and his daughter, Miranda. Shakespeare apparently has equated his island with his stage just before the first actor enters. Prospero will call it a "bare island" (Epilogue, 8) at the end. Miranda assumes that the storm is a product of Prospero's "art" and offers him the first of several examples of compassion in the play: "O, I have suffered / With those that I saw suffer!" (1.2.5–6). Prospero assures her that "There's no harm done" (1.2.15) and tells her that "'Tis time" (1.2.21) he should inform her of who they are. We will soon learn that the past has, in a sense, come to the island, making it at last relevant as an intersection with a suddenly available future. Stephen Greenblatt suggests, perversely, I think, that it is "as if Prospero believes that the revelation [of Miranda's identity] can be meaningful only in the wake of the amazement and pity he artfully arouses" (1988, Barnet 1998, 157). Greenblatt is anxious to prove that Prospero is a crafter of anxiety, but what seems much clearer is that the time for the story has come at last. Now the narrative can continue.

Miranda recalls her own past "rather like a dream" (1.2.45) Prospero tells her that he was the Duke of Milan, deposed by his brother, Antonio, who had allied with Alonso, King of Naples. Prospero had been busy studying and bettering his mind. Perhaps it takes a scholar to know one: "He had succumbed to the tyranny of his scholarly ambitions," says Leo Marx (1967, 70). "Prospero does not," says Walter Clyde Curry, "say that he neglected his duty; he says, rather, that he neglected 'worldly ends'—a virtue for the neo-Platonist and Christian alike" (1937, 196), but not a virtue for a duke in a Machiavellian Italian Renaissance. Prospero describes a collision of value systems.

Some of the people we saw fleetingly against the storm and heard above the wind are reintroduced in Prospero's long narrative. In an essay written in 1904, Lytton Strachey observes sourly that "a twelve years' monopoly of the conversation had developed into an inordinate propensity for talking" (1922, 412). David A. Zesmer suggests that Prospero "relives" the past as he tells his story (1976, 435), while David Hirst says that "as soon as he starts to describe Antonio . . . his syntax disintegrates under the strain of bitter emotional recollection" (1984a, 39). The Vaughans speak of "the emotions boiling beneath" Prospero's speech (1999, 21) and point to the ellipses and omissions that show that this is not a leisurely tale, but a compressed and urgent narrative within the flow of a suddenly available teleology and under the pressure of passion. Anne Righter Barton says that the "verse achieves an uncanny eloquence by way of what it omits or pares away" (1968, 13). Philip McGuire suggests that Prospero's interruptions of himself result from "the force of his feelings that the act of narrating, and therefore remembering the past, stirs in" him (1994, 207). Jay Halio argues that "Miranda may be more concerned with what is happening offshore than with events long since past" (1996, 222), and that her anxious glances draw Prospero's rebukes. Her words suggest otherwise. "To have Miranda gazing abstractedly out to sea, or yawning at her prosy father, is one of those cute buds that bloom in literal minds and throw modern productions off-key" (Harbage 1963, 464). Prospero's apparent impatience is born of his own urgency. It says nothing about Miranda's response. Of course she is interested in who she was and is.

Adrift in a rotten rowboat, Prospero and Miranda were conducted by winds "whose pity . . . Did us but loving wrong" (1.2.150–51), as he says, and by "Providence divine" (1.2.159). It is important to note that Prospero believes not only in a larger power, but in the presence of that power in nature itself. That belief does not mean that his own human agency can be dormant. "The play," says John Wilders, "begins at midday and Prospero's regular, anxious enquiries about the time imply that after six o'clock the stars will no longer be in his favor. Hence the play acquires a certain dramatic suspense from our knowledge that the plan must be completed promptly and that it may not actually succeed" (1980, 13).

James Walter says that the "initial evidence of [Prospero's] faith ['Providence divine'] suggests that he is not demonic, vengeful, or senilely irascible" at the outset (1983, in Battenhouse 1994, 271). Barbara Traister argues that "Prospero's benevolence towards his enemies has been obvious from the first act" (1984, 120). I agree, though the issue of whether Prospero has to again fight with his wish to revenge himself at the end will be debated later. In spite of his condemnation of his brother, Antonio, Prospero praises Gonzalo, who "Out of his charity [and] his gentleness" (1.2.162–65) provided the castaways with useful things, including Prospero's prized books. The stars are at their "most auspicious" (1.2.182), Prospero says, and "bountiful Fortune" (1.2.178) has delivered his "enemies . . . to this shore" (1.2.179–80). Having brought Miranda and his narrative up to date, he encourages Miranda to take a nap.

Aha! There is someone else here. Or is it a "someone"? Prospero summons Ariel, and the spirit appears. What it is is, of course, up to a director. While Ariel is a "he," he appears often in female roles (Nymph, Harpy, Ceres) and in the nineteenth century was often played by a woman. That practice is reappearing, for example, in productions at Ashland (1994), New York's Public Theater (1995–96), and Clemson University (1999). Ariel reports in detail his attack on the ship. It equalled "Jove's lightnings" (1.2.201) and "seem[ed] to besiege . . . the most mighty Neptune" (1.2.204–5), so that "his dread trident" shook. Neptune himself—god of the ocean—was frightened. That suggests Prospero's superiority over the pagan gods. Prince Ferdinand (someone we have not yet met) leaped from the ship, Ariel says, crying, " 'Hell is empty, / And all the devils are here!' " (1.2.214–15). The lines refer to the "flam[ing] amazement" that Ariel has spread "in many places" (1.2.196–97). Now that we have heard Prospero's narrative, the lines also point to some of those aboard the ship. Ferdinand is detaching himself from that negative context. Ariel complains about having to do anything more, and Prospero reminds him that he had been imprisoned in a pine by Sycorax, a witch and the island's former resident. Prospero threatens to put Ariel into an oak, "till / Thou hast howl'd away twelve winters" (2.2.295–96). Ariel promises to "do [his] spriting gently" (2.2.298). He exits. Prospero awakens Miranda and tells her that they will "visit Caliban" (2.2.310). We are about to meet another inhabitant of the island.

Miranda expresses repugnance, but Prospero reminds her of Caliban's utility: "he does make our fire / Fetch in our wood, and serves in offices / that profit us." Prospero calls Caliban, but the latter says that he has already lugged the daily quota of wood. What Caliban is is also a question for a director. The Vaughans make a convincing case for his being human (1991, 10–12), and regardless of his name, apparently an anagram for cannibal, he seems to be a vegetarian. Prospero, angry, calls him a "poisonous slave, got by the devil himself / Upon thy wicked dam," (2.2.322), Sycorax. Caliban enters cursing and complains that after he had shown Prospero "all the qualities o' th' isle" (2.2.339), the latter took the island from him, "Which first was mine own King." We have met one king. Now we hear of another. We will hear of more.

Prospero accuses Caliban of trying to rape Miranda, a charge Caliban does not deny. Had it been done, Caliban chortles, he "would have peopled. . . . / The isle with Calibans" (2.2.352–53). Miranda reminds Caliban that she had "pitied" him and "endow'd [his] purposes / With words that made them known" (2.2.355–59). Yes, Caliban replies, "You taught me language; and my profit on't / Is, I know how to curse" (2.2.365–66). Prospero orders Caliban to "Fetch us in fuel" (2.2.378), and Caliban admits that he "must obey." Prospero's power is "such . . . / It would control my dam's god, Setebos, / And make a vassal of him" (2.2.374–76). Whatever Caliban is, he is clearly a contrast to Ariel— "earth" versus "air," as some allegories have it. David William suggests shrewdly that Caliban exhibits "an aspiration towards human nature, whereas Ariel's is away from it" (1960, 151). Ariel's one approach to "human nature" will prove significant, however.

Ariel enters singing, "Come unto these yellow sands" (2.2.377), followed by Prince Ferdinand. The song is a prothalamion, or song before a marriage. "Although not 'about' bringing a groom to his bride, it is appropriate nonetheless," says Harbage (1963, 467). The music, says Ferdinand, has allayed both the "fury" (2.2.395) of the storm and his own grief for his father's apparent drowning "with its sweet air" (2.2.396). Ariel sings again of Alonso's transformation "Into something rich and strange" (2.2.404).

Seeing Ferdinand, Miranda thinks him "a spirit." Seeing her, Ferdinand believes that she is "the goddess / On whom these airs attend" (2.2.424–25). The young women of the romances are invariably compared to goddesses: Marina is a "goddess" (*Pericles* 5.3.6), Imogen is "more goddess-like than wife-like" (*Cymbeline* 3.2.8), and Florizel says to Perdita of the sheepshearing, "It is a meeting of the petty gods, / And you the queen on 't" (*The Winter's Tale* 4.4.4– 5). Without knowing Miranda's name, Ferdinand calls her a "wonder" (Miranda means "wonder"). So they fall in love, as Prospero's "soul prompts." Anne Righter Barton notices that "Miranda . . . shows no sign of connecting [Ferdi-

nand] with the story she has just heard" (1968, 11). Prospero claims that Ferdinand is a usurper sent "to win" (2.2.458) the island from him, "the lord on't."
Miranda defends Ferdinand, making the first necessary steps in her transition
from daughter to wife. Ferdinand complains that his "spirits, as in a dream, are
all bound up" (2.2.489), but discerns "liberty" in his ability to see Miranda from
his "prison" (2.2.496).

Critics chastise Prospero for his treatment of Ferdinand, but Prospero would
seem to be encouraging a "storge" (pronounced storgay) relationship, as John
Allan Lee calls it (1974). It "comes about with the passage of time and the
enjoyment of shared activities." It occurs "between people who grew up in rural
places" (which at least Miranda has done) and is based on "friendship and
companionship. This characteristic distinguishes storge from other types of
love. . . . The goals of storge . . . are marriage, home and children, avoiding all
the silly conflicts and entanglements of passion" (305).

The second scene emphasizes Prospero's power. At first glance, at least, his
use of his power seems justified. Those on the ship are his enemies. He needs
Ariel as an instrument for whatever it is he plans to do with those Ariel has
brought to shore. He tells Miranda that he will not harm them. He treats Caliban
harshly, of course, but Caliban seems compulsively to invite victimization. Prospero assists Miranda and Ferdinand in their love at first sight. As Harbage says,
it is a "manipulated miracle" (1963, 467). The only element that seems to challenge Prospero's control and his wise and defensible use of it is Caliban's claim
to the island. Caliban has learned language: not just the ability to curse, but the
concepts of ownership, inheritance, and sovereignty that grate against his condition as slave.

Keith Sturgess notices the dual nature of the play's music, an element, like
so much in the play, that can gracefully hold opposite meanings: "Music that
mourns Alonso's assumed death is also therapy that permits Ferdinand to go on
living" (1987, in Vaughn and Vaughn 1998, 122). It has eased his grief suffi-
ciently that his sudden transition is neither hypocritical nor laughable. Of course,
he fulfills the roles assigned to the adolescent in Peter Blos's great study of the
subject: "mourning and falling in love" (1962, 100).

Jean Paris suggests that Shakespeare's "*most extreme enigma* [is] 'Where
should this music be? i' the air, i' the earth?' " (1960, 180; his emphasis).
Shakespeare answers the question in *Antony and Cleopatra*, in the eerie scene
experienced by the soldiers as Hercules rumbles off to subterranean ("rock")
music (4.3), but the music in *The Tempest* remains a mystery. Does it require
a human ear—as sound does, by definition—or does it apprehend its own melody and provide the harmonies and counterpoints? Some "things" seem to rise
into being as if they are naming themselves as they make sounds and thus permit
themselves to be, to differentiate themselves from namelessness. Not only is the
language of the play itself subject to rhythmic control, but much of the play
comes at us as music, which reading cannot simulate, but which some modern
productions "postmodernize" into Schoenbergian or Bartókian dissonances.

Pierre Iselin links the play's music with its thematics: "Music is not only an agency; it operates in the play as a correlative of other discourses, those of desire and authority being the most prominent" (1995, 145).

I don't believe that we are told the source of the island's music. Was it there before Prospero arrived, as Caliban would seem to suggest ("the isle is full of noises, / Sounds and sweet airs" [3.2.133–34])? Is it a kind of residual effect of Prospero's magic, creeping along the waters, drifting under the leaves, awaiting a human ear to hear and interpret? The island reflects or is a product of the Pythagorean belief that the whole universe was harmony and that one of the basic aids to the purification of the soul was music. Prospero seems to be the conduit through which the insight becomes realized. For Pythagoras, a pre-Socratic whose influence on Plato and Neoplatonism was profound, "philosophy was the highest music" (Durant 1926, 6).

By the end of the first act, the dynamics of the island have been established: a commanding magician, a restless spirit, a sullen slave, and a space rising just over the sea that is saturated with music. The "romance" ending—two royal lovers of the younger generation—has already been traced in. Since one is the son of one of Prospero's enemies, it is doubtful that Prospero means to harm the father.

A sign of potential spiritual regeneration in the plays can be the "freshness and glosses" (2.1.60–61) of garments, which, in the case of the royal party, Gonzalo notices are "rather new-dyed than stained with salt water" (2.1.61–62). Antonio and Sebastian, of course, reject Gonzalo's discovery. "Give me fresh garments," Pericles says upon awakening (*Pericles* 5.1.218), and before Lear awakens, "fresh garments" have been placed on him (*King Lear* 4.7.22).

MY STRONG IMAGINATION SEES A CROWN . . .

The second act begins with the King's party. Gonzalo attempts to cheer a disconsolate Alonso. It would seem that the scene opens in the middle of a long and unsuccessful effort to persuade the King to be optimistic. Sebastian and Antonio exchange cynical comments and scoff at Gonzalo. The island yields different possibilities to different eyes and nostrils. Adrian finds that "the air breathes upon us here most sweetly" (2.1.46). Sebastian suggests that its "lungs" are "rotten" (2.1.46), and Antonio talks of the "perfume . . . [of] a fen" (2.1.47), or bog. Antonio is the educated malcontent to be found in so many of the plays of Shakespeare and his contemporaries (Vendice, Malevole, Jacques, Hamlet, Iago, Edmund, Iachimo, Bosola, and others). Gonzalo and the courtiers discuss Dido, Aeneas, and Carthage in what Kermode calls "a series of apparently trivial allusions" to the story of Aeneas's wanderings (1964, 46), but some scholars find strong correspondences between Virgil's *Aeneid* and the play, as I have shown. In his only speech of the play, aside from three words in Act 3, Francisco tries to convince Alonso that Ferdinand is alive. Sebastian, however, berates his brother, Alonso, for marrying Claribel to the King of Tunis—the reason for their voyage. To change the subject and to try to cheer the King, Gonzalo gives his speech about Utopia, which Sebastian and Antonio mock. Gonzalo would have no marrying among his subjects. Consequently, they would all be "whores and knaves" (2.1.162), as Antonio sneers. Ariel enters "playing solemn music" (stage direction), and the King's party grows sleepy.

A certain aimlessness does play across the first 180 or so lines of the scene. The party is lost, perhaps hopelessly marooned. The King's son has apparently drowned. Even the scalding wit of Sebastian and Antonio can be played as bravado, a defense against fear or despair. The "enchanted island [is] Life itself," says John Dover Wilson, "which seems so 'desert and uninhabitable' to the cynics and so green with 'lush and lusty' grass to the single-minded" (1932, 142). The scene demonstrates the subjectivity of any response to the natural world, as David Abram suggests: "The world and I reciprocate one another. The landscape as I directly experience it is hardly a determinate object; it is an ambiguous realm that responds to my emotions and calls forth feelings from me in turn" (1997, 74). Shakespeare can lull his audience when he wishes to, as in Horatio's disquisitions about external dangers to Denmark that are interrupted by the arrival of the Ghost in *Hamlet*.

The drowsy mood does not envelop two of the King's party. Antonio's "spirits are nimble" (2.1.197). He pretends to be reluctant to awaken ambition in Sebastian. "Thou let'st thy fortune sleep" (2.1.211). We are suddenly in the midst of a developing conspiracy, listening to what G. Wilson Knight calls "the *Macbeth* music" (1947, 212). As E.M.W. Tillyard says, "Antonio's transformation from the cynical and lazy badgerer of Gonzalo . . . to the brilliantly swift and unscrupulous man of action is a thrilling affair" (1938, 51). We have a moment resembling the tragedies—the murder of a sleeping king (Old Hamlet or Duncan). But as Antonio is about to assassinate Alonso (Antonio considerately takes on that task so that Sebastian will not be guilty of fratricide) and Sebastian is about to stab Gonzalo, Ariel rouses Gonzalo, who awakens the sleepers. The two would-be killers are caught with their swords out, claiming to have been defending against "bulls, or rather lions . . . a whole herd of lions" (2.1.307–11). "It was a din," says Antonio, "to fright a monster's ear" (2.1.309). Gonzalo agrees that he heard "a humming, / And that a strange one, too" (2.1.312–13). To this corroboration, Antonio and Sebastian agree with some relief.

The King and his party move on. Most of the scenes of this play end with a command to follow or to lead or with a suggestion of further movement. Ariel's closing line suggests Prospero's benevolent purpose: "So, King, go safely on to seek thy son" (2.1.322). The island is a space to be explored and to be understood in various ways. It is, like Spenser's "wand'ring wood," or the "green world" of Shakespeare's comedies, a zone where identity is to be lost and found, one half of the metaphor of being.

Caliban enters, proving that he has learned to curse. His are not shallow blasphemies, but invocations to those perfumed "bogs, fens, [and] flats" to drop "infection" (2.2.1–2) on Prospero. The self-defeating nature of his foul mouth is, however, the thrust of his speech. He knows that Prospero's "spirits hear" (2.2.3) him, and he speaks of punishment, of being pinched, pitched "i' th' mire" (2.2.5), being led astray at night, being chattered at by "apes" (2.2.9)—a mocking of Caliban by his near but distinct relatives—bitten by them, having hedgehogs "mount / Their pricks" (2.2.12) so that he steps on them with bare feet, and being twined about by adders, who "hiss [him] into madness" (2.2.14). While this is cruel punishment, Caliban admits that it is self-inflicted.

Trinculo enters, and, in a parody of the meeting of Ferdinand and Miranda, Caliban mistakes the jester for "a spirit" (2.2.15) of Prospero's. Trinculo fears "another storm brewing" (2.2.19), discovers Caliban, who "smells like a fish" (2.2.26), but has "fins like arms" (2.2.34–35). Trinculo could pause after "fins" since he is conditioned to expect fins. Were Trinculo only in England with Caliban, "there would this monster make a man" (2.2.30–31) by permitting the man to exhibit the monster under a sign like that with which Macduff taunts Macbeth: "Here may you see the tyrant" (*Macbeth*, 5.7.56). Thunder sends Trinculo under Caliban's "gaberdine": "misery acquaints a man with strange bed-fellows" (2.2.40–41).

Stephano arrives, drunk and still drinking, singing "a scurvy tune" (2.2.45). If Ariel sings soothing songs "at a man's funeral," songs of reconciliation and of transformation into beautiful, sea-stroked objects, of otherworldly miracles like those that occur in Yeats's Byzantium, Stephano sings bawdily of the bodily aspects of various unwashed women. Of Kate: "a tailor might scratch her where'er she did itch" (2.2.54). As J. L. Styan says, "The spirit of the comic action seems to be marked at key points by the style of the singing" (1988, 16). When Caliban cries out, Stephano repeats the lore of travellers: "Have we devils here? Do you put tricks upon's with salvages and men of Ind, ha?" (2.2.58–59). Stephano foreshadows his role as yet another "King o' th' isle" (5.1.287) by assuming a plurality. He stumbles across Trinculo and Caliban and wonders—as had Ferdinand of Miranda—"Where the devil should he learn our language?" (2.2.67–68). He hopes to tame this four-legged monster, give him as "a present for [an] emperor" (2.2.71), and thus make his fortune. He feeds the monster from his bottle of wine, but when Stephano hears two voices, his natural cowardice surfaces. "Mercy! Mercy! This is a devil and no monster" (2.2.98–99). Stephano pulls Trinculo out in an excremental parody of birth ("can he vent Trinculos?" [2.2.107–8]). Caliban, tasting alcohol for the first time—"celestial liquor" (2.2.118)—kneels to Stephano, who assumes the role of "the man i' th' moon," who has "dropp'd from heaven" (2.2.137–39). "I do adore thee," says Caliban, promising to show Stephano "the best springs," as he had once guided Prospero around the island. "Stephano's liquor [parallels] Prospero's magic [as] the basis of charismatic rule," says Kurt Von Rosador (1991, 12). Trinculo grows cynical, calling Caliban "ridiculous . . . to make a wonder of a poor drunkard!" (2.2.165–66). Stephano surrenders to his mounting megalomania and assumes the pose of a godlike white man stepping onto a foreign shore: "we will inherit here"

(2.2.175). Caliban sings drunkenly of his freedom, and Stephano cries, "O brave monster! lead the way" (2.2.188).

Here we have parody, though it will soon squirm out of its generic premises and turn serious: of the expectations of a voyager to a strange land—"salvages" or devils—of the way in which such voyagers were taken for gods by the native inhabitants and their acceptance of the designation, of the love at first sight of the royal children, Ferdinand and Miranda (the question of "our language" [2.2.68] and the "mak[ing of] a wonder" [2.2.165]), and of the Communion Service (the wine delivered by a surrogate of God is "not earthly" [2.2.127] either, having been transubstantiated or blessed and conferring "everlasting life" on its recipients). The scope of this parody is wide. In addition, the scene also suggests pretensions toward higher status on the part of the servants of nobility (Malvolio, for example). I would have my Stephano be a parody of Alonso, from whom Stephano has learned "royal behavior."

METHOUGHT THE BILLOWS SPOKE . . .

The first scene of Act 2 ended with Alonso moving on to seek his son. The second scene ended with Caliban happily giving up the "fetch[ing]" (2.2.181) of wood. Assuming that Caliban leads Stephano and Trinculo off stage left, Ferdinand might enter "bearing a log" (stage direction) from stage right. But while that circle completes itself, we hear no cursing. Ferdinand believes that "some kinds of baseness / Are nobly undergone" (3.1.2). His "sweet mistress / Weeps when she sees [him] work" (3.1.11)—another analogue of compassion working within the fabric of the play. Watched by an unseen Prospero, Miranda offers to carry the logs while Ferdinand rests. She suggests that attitude is significant: "my good will is to it, / And yours it is against" (3.1.30–31). Miranda tells Ferdinand her name—against Prospero's warning not to—and Ferdinand praises her as "the top of admiration . . . perfect and peerless" (3.1.38–47). He receives her reciprocating wish for no "companion in the world but" (3.1.55) him. They tell each other that they love each other, and they receive Prospero's blessing: "Heavens rain grace / On that which breeds between 'em!" (1.3.75–76)—that is, let their lives together be full of grace as well as the children that they produce. Miranda and Ferdinand exit, he presumably having shouldered the log again, and Prospero goes off to his "book" (3.1.94). He must do more conjuring, it seems, as a way of effecting "Much business" before "supper-time" (3.1.95–96). He is not "seen . . . as all-powerful," says Paul Brown (1985, 67), but, like Ferdinand, has work to do. Prospero does not take us into his cell. That is where his books are, where he crafts his spells. We see the results. That we do not see the cell permits us to believe in it. We see Shakespeare's play, but the mind behind these fleeting and variously interpreted words and images remains enticingly out of sight.

The scene between Ferdinand and Miranda can succeed if the actors playing the lovers show them moving toward an articulation of their love, with Ferdinand eager and courtly, Miranda tentative and vulnerable, perhaps unsure of what Ferdinand means by his elegant phrasing. "Do you love me?" (3.1.64) she asks. Her awkwardness can be amusing, but it need not, as John Russell Brown says, "confuse or mask the delicacy, strength, rapture, and transforming nature of their feelings" (1996, 81). This is their negotiation, not just something Prospero is coercing. It is often played sappily and thus unhappily, but it can be moving. In a sense it is the last scene of the "romance"—a betrothal approved by the father of the bride. "Nothing so far in the play has established such a sense of peace and fulfillment" (John Russell Brown 1996, 83). Ferdinand expresses one of the "themes" of the play, the New Testament paradox, that service equates to freedom: "for your sake / Am I this patient log-man" (1.3.66–67). He promises to be Miranda's "husband" "with a heart as willing / As bondage e're of freedom" (3.1.87–89)—that is, as willingly as any slave or laborer would embrace his freedom.

The three drunks enter, reeling. Stephano is becoming more autocratic, Trinculo is sniping at Caliban, and Caliban is growing angry with Trinculo. Gilbert Harrison notes that "Shakespeare had an acute knowledge of the effects of liquor. Stephano is suffering from illusions of grandeur; Trinculo is more cynical; Caliban more savage and revengeful" (1963, 231). As Roger Warren says, drink makes Trinculo "nastier but more craven, Stefano more anarchic and megalomaniac, Caliban more brutally violent" (1998, 171). Caliban repeats his complaint that Prospero "by his cunning hath cheated me of the island" (3.2.41–42). Ariel, invisible, says, "Thou liest" (3.2.44), and Trinculo is blamed. Caliban offers to "yield [Prospero] asleep" (3.2.59), where Stephano can choose his mode of assassination: a nail in the head, a braining, a battering with a log, stabbing with a stake, or cutting his windpipe with a knife. They begin to pursue the plot, and Ariel plays the tune they are singing. This terrifies Stephano. "Art *thou* afeard?" (3.2.131). Caliban might ask of his leader. Caliban recognizes that Stephano's denial ("No, monster, not I" [3.2.132]) is not true. "Be *not* afeard" (3.2.133). Caliban, beginning to assume leadership of the conspiracy, tells Stephano that "the isle is full of noises" (3.2.133). It is poetry—and high poetry at that—in which Caliban reveals his aspiration: "The clouds methought would open, and show riches / Ready to drop upon me; that, when I wak'd, / I cried to dream again" (3.2.139–41). Again, the scene ends with the suggestion of movement: "Lead," says Stephano, "We'll follow." "Wilt come? I'll follow, Stephano" (3.2.148–50) says Trinculo. Ariel, meanwhile, has left to "tell [his] master" (3.2.113) of this conspiracy. It may be that Prospero did not anticipate the arrival of Stephano and Trinculo to the island. They are irrelevant to his developing plan, but they pose a danger to him. As Greenblatt says, "Prospero, like all Renaissance princes, has a diligent spy network," the one-spirit operation of the ubiquitous Ariel (1997, 3052–53).

The King's party enters. The older men, Alonso and Gonzalo, are weary. The younger men, Antonio and Sebastian, continue to plot their coup. "Solemn and strange music" (stage direction) accompanies the entrance of a banquet. Alonso and Gonzalo hear the sounds—"What harmony is this?" "Marvelous sweet music!" (3.3.18–19)—before the "Shapes" (stage direction) enter with the food. The travellers are now willing to believe in unicorns and the phoenix. Even Alonso is pulled from his despair for a moment to "muse [on] / Such shapes, such gesture, and such sound" (3.3.36–37). The spirits depart, but the King and his party decide to partake of the food left behind. Alonso sees it as his last supper: "Although my last, no matter, since I feel / The best is past" (3.3.50–51). As they move toward the food, it disappears to angry sounds. "Thunder and lightning" (stage direction) echo the opening storm. Ariel enters as a Harpy, a mythological half-woman, a vehicle of vengeance and punishment. Ariel castigates the "three men of sin" (3.3.53) and promises "Ling'ring perdition—worse than any death / Can be at once" unless they achieve "heart-sorrow / And a clear life ensuing" (3.3.77–82).

Prospero praises Ariel's performance and exults that his "high charms work" (3.3.88). Alonso seems to have heard "The name of Prosper" in the thunder, "That deep and dreadful organ pipe" (3.3.98). He leaves the scene followed by a frantic Sebastian and Antonio, still fighting the invulnerable apparitions who brought in the banquet. Gonzalo asks the younger members of the party to "follow them swiftly" (3.3.107), and again a scene ends with a command to "Follow, I pray you" (3.3.109).

Prospero has repeated his experience for the King's party. They are pulled from the process of a wedding by a kind of Ancient Mariner to hear a story they have forgotten, although they dictated the first chapter. It is the story of Prospero and Miranda, a narrative of storm and sea that the King and his party have also experienced. Now Alonso hears its meaning as the billows speak.

The scene recapitulates the uneasy companionship of this group of aristocrats. Alonso, however, recognizes Gonzalo as a fellow sufferer and is, for an instant, transported by the music and the vision of the entering feast. His final speech, though suicidal in content, suggests that the "music" of the island has started to become an inner metaphor that will lead from annihilating sorrow to clarity. The banquet draws on the feast that the Harpies destroy on the island of the Strophades in *The Aeneid* (Book 3), and on the Communion, which must not be consumed by the unworthy, as the rubrics state: if any of the prospective communicants "be an open and notorious evil liver, so that the congregation by him is offended, or have done any wrong to hys neighbours by word or dede: the curate having knowledge therof, shal cal hym, and advertyse hym, in any wise not to presume to the Lordes table, until he have openly declared him self to have truely repented, and amended his former naughty lyfe" (*Queen Elizabeth's Prayer Book: 1559*). Kermode suggests other feasts: "Eve was tempted with an apple, and Christ with an illusory banquet" (1964, 86). In the latter case, a fasting Christ was tempted to make stones into bread (Matthew 4.3 and Luke 4.3), a selfish act when compared to his later miracle of loaves and fishes and one that, according to the Geneva Bible gloss, would show him devoid of faith: "Satan wolde have Christ to distrust God, and his worde and followe other strange and unlawful meanes" (Matthew 4.3). Christ recognizes that Satan is "but prince of the worlde by permission" (gloss to Luke 4.6) and that his promise, "all this power will I give thee," is, like those made to persons who would sell their souls, false. The language of the Bible rode the air of the late sixteenth and early seventeenth centuries. It is what a largely illiterate population heard in churches and if read to by a literate member of a pious household. The Bible was the age's television. The religious patterns underlying *The Tempest* will be discussed later.

Shakespeare's design is hardly random. From the second scene of the first act to the first scene of the fourth act, the "scenes arrange themselves symmetrically, concentrically (according to character groups) around a center scene, so that a triple-frame design accounts for almost the entire play," says Karen Flagstad (1986, 224–25). Mark Rose demonstrates this symmetry, showing that 1.2 has Prospero, Ferdinand, and Miranda, 2.1 has Alonso, Sebastian, and Antonio, 2.2 has Caliban, Stephano, and Trinculo, 3.1, Prospero, Ferdinand, and Miranda, 3.2, Caliban, Stephano, and Trinculo, 3.3, Alonso, Sebastian, and Antonio, and 4.1, Prospero, Ferdinand, and Miranda (1972, 173). The central scene in this patterning is Ferdinand's with Miranda, and their discussion of logs and love. One critic suggests that the play's "symmetrical structure of correspondence gives it the multiplicity of a hall of mirrors, in which everything reflects and re-reflects everything else" (Harold F. Brooks, qtd. in Vaughan and Vaughan 1999, 15). An infinite regress of mirrors provides no distortion, however. This play does: the distortion of analogy, which, by definition, is never precise, and the exaggeration on which parody depends. If mirror is the metaphor, the mirrors of this play often come from a fun house or from the darker imagery of nightmare.

SPRING COME TO YOU . . .

The fourth act is a single scene in which Prospero presents a Wedding Masque for Ferdinand and Miranda, but not before delivering a warning to Ferdinand about Miranda's chastity. In the Masque, the spirits that Ariel oversees play goddesses, with Ariel as Ceres. "On the actual stage the masque is executed by players pretending to be spirits, pretending to be real actors, pretending to be the real goddesses and rustics," says E.M.W. Tillyard (1938, 80), in yet another of the many transformations within the script. The Masque "is foreshadowed," says Francis Neilson, "in the speech of Gonzalo" (1956, 160)—a variation on the utopian theme. "To this marriage," says David Bevington, "the goddesses Iris, Ceres and Juno bring promises of bounteous harvest, 'refreshing showers,' celestial harmony, and a springtime brought back to the earth by Proserpina's return from Hades. . . . In Ferdinand and Miranda, 'nurture' is wedded to 'nature.' The bond unites spirit and flesh, legitimizing erotic pleasure by incorporating it within a cosmic moral order" (1980, xxi).

The Masque, however, is broken up abruptly by Prospero, who "had forgot the foul conspiracy / Of the beast Caliban and his confederates" (4.1.134–40). Prospero knows who is in charge. Along with the sudden withdrawal of the banquet by Ariel's associates, this is one of the few unexpected moments in the script. Hirst calls this "the most terrifying moment in the play" (1984a, 33). Prospero, however, is moved to comfort Ferdinand and gives his famous "revels" speech. The island is a function of point of view. It is not automatically sacramental. The doubleness of Prospero's vision—bitter and pessimistic, yet seeming to promise something beyond erasure—captures a duality that will be discussed later. Like the island, the "revels" speech can mean opposite things to different people. Prospero summons Ariel and "prepare[s] to meet with Caliban" (4.1.166). Prospero indicts Caliban as "A devil, a born devil, on whose nature / Nurture can never stick" (4.1.188–89). To claim, as Greenblatt does, that "Prospero's art has in effect created the conspiracy as well as the defense against conspiracy" and that "he himself brings these dangers to the center of his retreat" (1988, 145) is to lodge the objection so often made against *Paradise Lost*: that is, if God knows that evil will happen, why does he not prevent it? To be able to foresee an action is not to bring it about. A compulsively rebellious Caliban is evidence of the failure of Prospero's art, perhaps, but in no way can Prospero "in effect" be said to either interfere with or encourage the motion of Caliban's free will—that is, until he blocks the conspiracy at his very entrance. As Harbage says of Antonio and Sebastian, "The villainous ideas . . . are self-generated" (1963, 470).

Ariel places glittering clothes on a line outside Prospero's cell. Caliban, Stephano, and Trinculo have fallen into a "filthy-mantled pool" (4.1.182) and enter "all wet" (stage direction) and smelling bad. Furthermore, they are subject to the nasty, splitting-headache, dry-throated hangover that wine is said to induce. Stephano begins to posture like a parody Macbeth: "I do begin to have bloody thoughts" (4.1.119–20), but he and Trinculo are attracted by the clothes and begin to distribute them. Caliban is impatient: "Let it alone, thou fool; it is but trash" (4.1.222). Caliban is anxious to recapitulate the previous coup against Prospero: "All's hushed as midnight" (4.1.206). Twelve years before, Antonio's usurpation occurred at "midnight" (1.2.128). Caliban, being laden with stolen finery, continues to object, fearing that they will "All be turn'd to barnacles or to apes / With foreheads villainous low" (4.1.249–50). If Caliban is already an ape, his fear of being turned into one is strange, although if he is being played as a "missing link," his concern is justified. Before this latter-day plot can take place, Ariel and Prospero release spirit-dogs—a long way down the chain of being from the goddesses the spirits have just personated (from god to dog: Shakespeare must have savored the inversion)—upon the three would-be murderers. The dogs, Mountain, Silver, Fury, and Tyrant, chase Caliban and his confederates away. Prospero asks Ariel to "Follow, and do me service" (4.1.267).

Both the Masque and Prospero's speech at its conclusion are so central to the meanings that critics find in the play that I shall devote separate discussions to them in chapter 4. The scene does concentrate on transformation: Ferdinand from slave to beloved son-in-law-to-be, spirits to goddesses and then to dogs, and the would-be ruling party to stinking, hung-over fugitives.

IN THIS BARE ISLAND . . .

Act 5 begins with Prospero reiterating the outlines of his strategy and asking the time. Even if "Time / Goes upright with his carriage" (5.1.2–3) so far, the final crucial moments are yet to come. As Northrop Frye says, "Timing was important to a magician: everything depended on it when the alchemist's project gathered to a head; astrologers were exact observers of time" (1959, 20). Ariel reports the pitiable condition of "the King and's followers" (5.1.7): "if you now beheld them, your affections / Would become tender" (5.1.18–19). "Dost thou think so, spirit?" Prospero asks. "Mine would, sir, were I human" (5.1.20). Ariel is, in a sense, questioning Prospero's humanity. Will he revenge or forgive? Many critics see this as a crucial moment, but I think that his decision not to harm Alonso and his entourage has been announced long before. Prospero accedes to it now: "They being penitent, / The sole drift of my purpose doth extend / Not a frown further" (5.1.28–30). Ariel is sent to release the spell-stopped prisoners and takes Prospero's order a step further: "I'll fetch them, sir" (5.1.32).

Prospero then launches into a soliloquy, ominously borrowed from Ovid's *Medea*, in which he recounts his career and gives up his magic. Included in the speech is the controversial assertion that "graves at my command / Have wak'd their sleepers, op'd, and let 'em forth / By my so potent Art" (5.1.48–50). Such an act would put Prospero into the realm of black magic. Such feats, according to a 1632 commentary, "were not affected by the vertue of words, or skill of *Medea*: but rather by wicked Angels" (George Sandys, qtd. in Kermode 1964, appendix D, 149). It is, as Prospero says, "rough magic" and opens up a discussion of Prospero as magician and of the traditions he inherits and, in a sense, concludes. Bate says that "the parallel darkens the character of Prospero" (1993, in Vaughan and Vaughan 1998, 57), but Hirst points out that Medea in Ovid "was calling on her gods for assistance" (1984a, 40), and that, it follows, Shakespeare's intention is to contrast Prospero and Medea. Harry Berger, Jr., makes a similar argument. She, he says, wants to hold on to her magic for revenge (1969, 281, n. 18). The Vaughans say judiciously that the echo of Medea is "Shakespeare's signal that the magician's power is not really benign and must be rejected" (1999, 66). "As Prospero completes his speech," says Hirst, "we feel the energy draining out of him; the verbs change to 'break,' 'bury,' and 'drown,' sounding the heavy note of renunciation" (1984a, 40). The speech, of course, is taken as Shakespeare's farewell, but that confuses a number of issues and makes the play "easy" at precisely the moment when it is asking questions, not providing interpretations.

The personal climax for Prospero comes when he observes Gonzalo weeping over the plight of his companions. Until this moment, what Stephen Siddal says is accurate: Prospero "seems to find the *concept* of reconciliation easier to accept than its *feeling*" (1988, 88). Prospero has had presented to him examples of grief and compassion—Miranda's for the unknowns on the ship, Ferdinand's for his father's death, Alonso's for his son's death, Miranda's for Ferdinand's labors, Ariel's for the King and his party, and now Gonzalo's. As often happens, another's response to an event can trigger an emotional reaction that the event itself does not. Prospero weeps. The sea has given up its apparent dead. Now the sea within Prospero emerges—his rational plan is fulfilled by emotion at last—and with the same amount of salinity as the ocean. As he talks of "reason" (5.1.68) coming to his numbed enemies, emotion finally arrives within Prospero. This can only occur after he has given up his magic and reembraced his humanity.

Prospero sends Ariel to get his ducal garments and promises the spirit his freedom "ere long" (5.1.87). Ariel sings of his ahuman longings, flying "After summer merrily" (5.1.92) in a world of constant blossoming. The others awaken to Prospero as Duke of Milan, though Alonso is not sure whether Prospero is not just another "enchanted trifle" (5.1.112). Alonso immediately returns Prospero's dukedom to him and asks for "pardon" (5.1.119). He, at least, has gone through the process of "heart-sorrow" (3.3.31) and has begun to come up on the other side—"newenes of lyfe," as the Prayer Book's general confession says. Prospero tells Antonio and Sebastian that he "will tell no tales" (5.1.139), meaning that they remain at his mercy. Perhaps that is the only way that one like Antonio, who feels "not / This deity [conscience] in [his] bosom" (2.1.272–73), can be controlled. As Greenblatt says, "The generosity of the pardon [of Antonio] in this instance is inseparable from a demonstration of supreme force" (1988, 157). It cannot be otherwise. At the same time, as Greenblatt also says, "Audiences of Shakespeare's time would have had an all too clear image of how horrendous the vengeance of enraged princes usually was" (1997, 3049–50). The script does not show what Charles Lamb describes in his *Tales*: "Antonio with tears in his eyes, and sad words of sorrow and true repentance, implored his brother's forgiveness" (1807, 176)—though a production might mime this "happy ending." In Robin Phillips's 1976 Stratford, Ontario, version, "Antonio fell to his knees and Prospero, recognizing genuine repentance, took both of his hands" (Halio 1988, 67). Of Prospero's grudging pardon of Antonio, we might recall Montaigne's remark: "For it seemeth that the very name of Vertue presupposeth difficultie, and inferreth resistance, and cannot well exercise itself without an enemy" (1904, 2:11). Prospero tells Alonso that, as the latter has lost a son, he has lost a daughter. Alonso volunteers the wish "that they were living both in Naples, / The King and Queen there!" (5.1.149–50).

The exchange between Prospero and Alonso has been a negotiation about political power. Clearly, Prospero has won. He rewards Alonso by revealing Ferdinand and Miranda at chess. "At chess the sexes met on equal terms" (H.J.R. Murray 1913, qtd. in Kermode 1964, 123), and, as Kermode says, "We must suppose that Ferdinand and Miranda are discovered in a situation which suggests the context of high-born and romantic love" (1964, 123). The game of chess has been interpreted more darkly, as I will suggest in chapter 4. Alonso asks whether Miranda is "the goddess that hath sever'd us, / And brought us thus together?" (5.1.186–87). Sounding like Lear (4.7), Alonso says, "how oddly will it sound that I / Must ask my child forgiveness" (5.1.197–98). Miranda, seeing a group of humans for the first time, remarks their beauty and utters her famous line "O brave new world / That has such people in 't" (5.1.183–84). " 'Tis new to thee" (5.1.184), an older, perhaps cynical Prospero says. In some productions, Miranda, recognizing the family resemblance, can direct her line at Antonio, thus motivating Prospero's sour response.

The Boatswain enters to inform the "King, and company" (5.1.222) that the ship, seemingly "split / Is tight and yare [ready] and bravely rigg'd" (5.1.223–25). Ariel enters, "driving in Caliban, Stephano, and Trinculo, in their stolen apparel" (stage direction). Caliban admires Prospero, who is for the first time in twelve years wearing his robes of office. Antonio and Sebastian exchange cynical remarks about Caliban: "one of them," says Antonio, displaying the qualities of the calculator-villain, "Is a plain fish, and no doubt marketable" (5.1.265–66). Prospero points to Caliban and says, "this thing of darkness I / Acknowledge mine" (5.1.275–76). Is that acknowledgment merely that of master claiming ownership of a slave, or does it suggest that Caliban represents something in Prospero's psyche? The former reading fits the colonialist interpretation of the play, the latter a psychological thesis in which Caliban becomes a "shadow." Greenblatt says that "it is difficult not to hear in [the acknowledgment] some deeper recognition of affinity, some half-conscious acknowledgement of guilt" (1988, 158). Why must it be half-conscious? Jeanne Addison Roberts argues that the play's philosophical pattern erases the distinction between man and beast, suggesting "a possible kinship between Culture and the animal Wild" (1991, 114). At the very least, Prospero seems to be saying that he has the animal—repressed bestiality, or "an intractable element of shadow" (Robert Wilson 1988, 108) that he has heretofore refused to admit to his constructed persona—within his psyche. This recognition can come only after he has given up his magic and exposed himself to the feeling of his humanity. Maurice Charney says that Prospero is "forced to acknowledge that Caliban is a human being and not a monster or beast" (1993, 360). That is true and tells us something significant about Caliban that Prospero has resisted and something about Prospero that he has also resisted, that is, I am like this, too.

Sent off to "trim" (5.1.243) Prospero's cell, Caliban suggests that he has learned something: "I'll be wise hereafter, / And seek for grace. What a thrice-double ass / Was I, to take this drunkard for a god, / And worship this dull fool" (5.1.294–97)—both "drunkard" and "fool" being Stephano, since Caliban has never worshipped the fool Trinculo.

Prospero reminds Alonso that a dynastic marriage is scheduled—in "Naples" (5.1.307) he says, which may well put most of the expenses upon the father of the groom. Prospero will then "retire" to "Milan, where / Every third thought shall be my grave" (5.1.310–11). This need not be a morbid *memento mori*. Patrick Stewart's Prospero suggested that he would now think less about death than he had been doing. Prospero promises "calm seas, auspicious gales, / And sail so expeditious, that shall catch / Your royal fleet far off" (5.1.314—15). That is Ariel's final assignment. "Then to the elements / Be free, and fare thou well!" Philip McGuire says that "a *Tempest* that presents Ariel's silent departure after being granted freedom as a renunciation of Prospero differs significantly from one in which Ariel's silence suggests a mixture of joy and pain that Ariel himself feels as he and his master separate" (1985, 59). According to Anthony Dawson, Peter Brook's *La Tempête* Ariel "almost preferred staying with Prospero," as opposed to Mark Rylance, who "had already gone when Prospero spoke the words which were supposed to release him" (1988a, 236). In David Thacker's 1994 Royal Shakespeare Company (RSC) touring version, Bonnie Engstrom's Ariel "took a yearning step toward Prospero as he turned upstage and walked away from her. If a female Ariel seemed like a throwback to an old theater tradition long out of fashion, Engstrom at least made something significant of it, using her gender to create an additional layer to the master-servant relationship" (Holland 1997, 229).

Prospero then delivers his Epilogue, which, says Kermode, has "a weighty allusion to Christian mercy and the Lord's Prayer" (1964, 134): "As you from crimes would pardon'd be, / Let your indulgence set me free" (Epilogue 19–20). The final prayer, says Greenblatt, "implicates the prince as well as the player in the experience of anxiety and the need for pardon" (1988, 158). It must, of course, since it pursues the Christian rhythm that has also informed the movement of the larger play. The Epilogue implicates the audience as well. It is, as David Zesmer says, a "mysterious and deeply suggestive ritual" (1976, 443). Consensus has it that Caliban is left on the island. "He doesn't return to Milan with Prospero," says Charney, "but once more asserts his political rights over the island" (1993, 360). That is debatable.

Do the final moments of the play suggest harmony and reconciliation—with only one character left out of the ultimate taking of hands (Shylock, Jacques, Malvolio, and here, Antonio)—or do they show an arbitrary covering over of the inconsistencies and even criminality in Prospero's actions? These are questions to be asked, but not to be answered, because, as Brian Holloway says, "*The Tempest* is a play about a magician that is conjured up by an expert stage-magician himself—not only a profound enchanter with words but also a consummate stage-illusionist creating a play about wizardry that is at once traditional, iconoclastic, forward-looking, primitive, logical and mysterious—an illusion of unified contraries and suspended belief" (1999, 88).

4

THEMES

The thematic approach has been in disrepute since Richard Levin's devastating attack (1979). Levin demonstrated that critics were competing with increasing ingenuity and irrelevance to prove that "my theme is better than your theme." Levin chronicled the end of a paradigm and either cleared the way for new methodologies or insisted that different approaches flow into the roadbed he was blasting. Or Levin was insisting that "theme" be called "concerns of the play." The thematic approach has not gone away.

Levin characterizes the thematic approach to *The Tempest* as "showing how devastating it is to take a stand with Prospero, [who attempts] to [focus] attention away from himself to the evil power of Sycorax [when] the play deliberately parallels them" (1977, 133).

The Tempest incorporates themes that recur in various manifestations from first to last. It also benefits, in production, from a director's attention to the dynamics of the themes in the editing of the script and in the emphases of performance. I will make that argument in my discussion of the play in production, although my bias may be merely a reflection of my own upbringing in the friendly confines of the "New Criticism." There, the work of art was seen as self-contained and consciously crafted by the artist. It had its ironies, paradoxes, and ambiguities, to be discerned by the astute critic. Reuben Brower's analysis, discussed in chapter 5, is a superb example. More recent critical methods—deconstruction, cultural materialism, and New Historicism—have opened the text up by showing how it reflects unresolved tensions within its own construction and either expresses or suppresses issues that were carving faultlines under the late-sixteenth-century and early-seventeenth-century surface. These stimulat-

A magic storm (1553).

ing new approaches keep the works alive by insisting that they have something to say to our own skeptical, even pessimistic zeitgeist. Rather than "unity," the plays demonstrate a remarkable ability to conceal fissures and fractures below the "world picture," to slide subversion under apparent support of the dominant ideology. A Marxist critique combines with perceived weaknesses and hypocrisies in modern democracies to become a powerful instrument of interrogation of that ongoing phenomenon known as Shakespeare.

Any discussion of themes suggests self-containment. Themes do not communicate with other documents in a culture. A concern of the culture may show up as a concern of the play, but not as a theme in the sense that the New Critic uses the term, that is, as a consciously developed "central idea" within a discrete work of art. That is not to say that what the New Critic finds is not in the play. It is to say that it no longer interests the critic. But it can excite the imagination of the student reading the play or hearing it. If that process suppresses other cultural energies and commits what Robert Weimann calls the "autonomous fallacy" (1974, 166), it does argue that the work of art—the poem, play, painting, or sonata—is not the same thing as other documents circulating through the culture. Poetry that announces a theme and repeats it can, like music, appeal to the senses and, through those conduits, to the imagination. Poets know that, even if critics have developed a deafness to "literary values." A director reading or editing the text will also heed the poetry, so that the actors will have at their command the emphases the script provides. One of the great directors of this and other plays by Shakespeare, Peter Brook, says of *The Tempest*, "Shakespeare includes all the themes from his earlier work—kingship, inheritance, treachery, conscience, identity, love, music, God; he draws them together as if to find the key to it all, but there is no such key. There is no grand order and Prospero returns to Milan, not bathed in tranquility, but a wreck" (Trewin 1971, 135). Not all thematic analysis draws such a pessimistic conclusion, of course. Brook might use a word other than "theme" these many years later and still draw the same conclusion.

While few musicians or painters would agree with Richard Moulton's late-nineteenth-century criteria, those who craft with words are still committed to coherence: "The existence of some harmony binding together all varieties of detail is a fundamental conception of art: the only further question is whether, for any particular play, the unity can be formulated in words" (1901, 264). If Shakespeare wrote with some sense of "binding harmony" in mind, thematic criticism can still serve a purpose.

The Tempest seems to have been written very consciously, with an ear for every word of the script and its relationship to every other word. Shakespeare's plays do not always reflect a fragmented world or its insoluble problems, though such concerns are usually adumbrated even in the comedies through alienated characters who do not "take hands" at the end. The thematic approach may be the wrong way of looking at the play, but it can be brilliantly wrong. It can excite imaginations, which is more than can be said of much pedestrian current criticism.

Shakespeare deals with death, sex, love, revenge, and family—elements common to all cultures—but more than that, the script offers options for interpretation. Parts of Africa, for example, view Desdemona's fault as marrying outside of her tribe. That interpretation is present in the script, even if it is represented by the racism of Roderigo and Brabantio. The script may seem to be in sync with our cultural moment, and it may seem that our age somehow reflects Elizabethan-Jacobean England, but these optical illusions are engendered by scripts that can pick up and reflect particular zeitgeists and national moments, even as other parts of the same script fall away. We no longer see Hamlet as the victim of a romantic squeamishness, as Coleridge did. We no longer see Prospero as the wise colonist, as some Victorians did. We no longer see Henry V as all-conquering perfection. Our times find different and darker meanings as our own concerns flow into contexts—the plays—that, in turn, show our culture what it is. We learn what television is and is not through its confrontation with the plays (and learn how much more versatile Shakespeare's stage was than is television). Filmmakers are at last finding out that Shakespeare is an entertainer and not something to be approached as if a velvet rope stands between us and the object we are looking at.

One crucial difference between *The Tempest* and an essentialist play like *Macbeth* must be noted. *The Tempest* is not essentialist, as *Macbeth* is. If Shakespeare is to show how horrendous an event is the killing of a king, he must create a world that will be harmed by it, a cosmos that will respond to it (cf. Stallybrass 1982; Coursen 1997). *The Tempest* can place opposing ideas side by side; it can say that "nature is that which man spoils [and] nature is that which because it is defective, needs cultivation" (Hirst 1984a, 17). Every idea in *Macbeth* is the same idea—these actions occur "in the great hand of God" (*Macbeth* 2.4.130). *The Tempest* is syncretic in its use of religion; eclectic in its use of sources, formally more open-ended than "comedy" or "tragedy," and more capable of supporting radically opposed points of view than *Macbeth*, particularly about its chief characters, Prospero, Caliban, and Ariel.

Hiram Haydn says that the themes of *The Tempest* derive from the tension "between two highly confident and secure world-views" (1950, 229): religion and rationalism. Haydn says of the intellectual conflicts of the time that the "basic distinction, for men like Machiavelli, Guicciardini, Agrippa, Montaigne and Bacon [was] between men and things as they ought to be and as they are." This "theme, together with its sister one, the discrepancy between appearance and reality, appears in most of the major imaginative literature of the period" (228). If "one were to remove variations on these themes from [many of Shakespeare's plays, including *The Tempest*] there would be little left of the ideological structure of these plays" (229).

David Hirst says, "*The Tempest* is a play about power. [It is] the ultimate variation on one of the dramatist's favourite themes: the contrast between the pragmatic political realist and the philosophical idealist" (1984a, 9). Such "a confrontation is basic to the two cycles of history plays" (9). While no one would deny the play's politics, it is so much more than history or contest between theories of history that, as Levin would suggest, another critic is bound to leap in with an argument about "art" or "nature," "storm versus calm," or "dream."

The sea is seen as image and theme: "After erupting into violence in the first scene, the sea remains a haunting power, lying just under the play's language, imagery, and action, at times swelling into visibility to remind us of change" (Walter 1983, in Battenhouse 1994, 277). Marjorie Garber suggests that "the metaphor of dream achieves its fullest maturation and reveals itself, not as metaphor at all, but rather as metamorphosis—not as comparison, but as identity" in the play (1974, 220). She discerns a parallel between "the pattern of transmutation into art" and "the human pattern of resurrection" (152). That thesis touches elements like Ariel's "Full fathom five" song and Prospero's "revels" speech and allows aspects of the play as poem, as opposed to politics, to emerge. Garber points, of course, to one of the play's primary sources, Ovid's *Metamorphoses.*

Harold Bloom suggests "time" as theme: "Prospero forgives his enemies because he understands . . . the mystery of time. His magic reduces to what Nietzsche called the will's revenge against time, and against time's 'it was' " (1988, 7). Nietzsche's Zarathustra says, "To redeem what is past, and to transform every 'It was' into 'Thus would I have it!'—that only do I call redemption. . . . This, yea, this alone is *revenge* itself: the Will's antipathy to time, and its 'it was' " (1905, 149–50). The romance genre permits this version of "revenge."

The themes of the play seem to concentrate around three moments that pull a critic's imagination into their complexities: Prospero's Wedding Masque for Ferdinand and Miranda, his "revels" speech to Ferdinand after the Masque has been dismissed, and, at the end, the tableau of Ferdinand and Miranda playing at chess. A masque, says John Wilders, is "an early form of opera . . . distinguished by its elaborate and spectacular scenic effects, its combination of music, song and dance with spoken dialogue, and the inclusion of mythological and allegorical figures among its characters" (1980, 10). The Masque in *The Tempest*, says Keith Sturgess, "is a pastoral. The entertainment enacts through its ornate style [a] sense of civilized values. . . . Venus (physical love) and Cupid (erotic anarchy) are banished, so that 'ceremony' (a key Renaissance value) may have pride of place" (1987, in Vaughan and Vaughan 1998, 125). Its "drama" involves a recognition of positive nurture—the "proper ruling both of natural desires by intellect and of the kingdom by virtue," as Charles Moseley says (1988, 121). Its "central principle is the notion of gender in all things" (116). Iris celebrates the "covenant between God and man" (121). The departure of Venus and Cupid means that Ferdinand and Miranda "have mastered their desires. . . . virtue is the fruit only of . . . innocence being tested. . . . the rebellion of the baser nature would wreck the harmony of a marriage of true minds"

(123). The Masque, then, is completed, not interrupted, by the removal of Cupid, who is "associated with Fortune and Death" (Panofsky 1962, 112).

The Masque, say C. L. Barber and Richard Wheeler, is a "rite of passage [that] becomes a recognition by the older generation of the place of death in the great cycle of life beginning anew in marriage" (1986, 340). It is a "symbolic vision of married chastity and the fertility traditionally associated with it" (78). As Ann Thompson says, the Masque "explicitly banishes lust" (1991, in Vaughan and Vaughan 1998, 238). Its paradox lies in its expression of the "enormous power [of] female chastity and fertility." Lust produces weeds (239), as in Othello's bitter "O, thou weed!" to Desdemona (4.2.69). As Barbara Bono says, "Wanton Venus is dismissed while majestic Juno blesses the union" (1984, 223). Robert Langbaum suggests that the removal of the threat posed by Venus and Cupid means that "lawless passion [is] excluded from the natural force celebrated in the masque" (1987, xiii). Jonathan Bate agrees: "The commonplace Renaissance theme of the dangers of lust is a key motif in . . . *The Tempest*" (1993, in Vaughan and Vaughan 1998, 53). "When earth is seen as Ceres, it is no longer intractable, but productive and nurturing; when air is seen as Juno, it is no longer volatile, but universal and majestic" (48). The Masque communicates to "a theatre audience [a] sense of fruition . . . the harmony and the harvest, [a] harvest home" (55). Arthur Sewell puts the issue another way: "The harmony between what had once been seen as opposites—between the Reason which makes for order and those appetites which enable continuance—is the major reconciliation . . . in the Romances" (1961, 143). Karen Flagstad portrays the allegory in classical terms: the "loss of perpetual spring, [the] mythical counterpart of the Christian Fall of humankind, [is] effectively reversed" (1986, 209). Venus and Cupid would repeat the "plot [whereby] dusky Dis my daughter got," but do not. The "Rape of Proserpine, or Proserpine/Miranda [is] successfully averted" (211), and while spring is not perpetual, it follows immediately after autumn. James Walter extends the allegory to suggest God's promise to Noah: the Masque "speaks of a providential regularity in nature as the source of our daily bread and reminds us of God's continuing creation" (1983, in Battenhouse 1994, 275).

Karol Berger says that Ceres "represents the anti-erotic fertility divorced from death, the ideal of natural generation without corruption" (1977, 231). This is Prospero's elevated, idealized vision of his hopes for the next generation. It "exorcises death" (231). In doing that, however, and in turning barrenness into fecundity, the Masque "therefore has no viable connection with reality," says Robert Egan (1972, 178). The latter end forgets its beginning. "The masque is bound to fail. . . . it ignores the realities of post-Lapsarian existence . . . is incapable, as art, of comprehending or coping with the propensity for evil in fallen man" (179). The three goddesses, themselves "memories" of Miranda's attendants, give way to three would-be murderers. That vision—the Masque as obvious impossibility—leads to Prospero's negative "Our revels now are ended" speech to Ferdinand, or at least to a negative interpretation of it.

The negative view would argue that the Masque promises "foison plenty" (4.1.110), but it is really "baseless" (4.1.151). It becomes another empty banquet. Art is simultaneously overflowing and empty, as Prospero demonstrates in his magnificent poetry about dissolution. The most magnificent of art has behind it an imagination that can evoke the imagery of a bountiful paradise, where harvest time yields immediately to planting time again. But that imagination is part of a mortal, and, like the mortal in whom it lives, it must also die. That is one way to read the "revels" speech.

The speech is read by many as a central statement of "what the play means." It combines the aspects of "dream" and "time." It often becomes "what the critic means." It has been read along a spectrum ranging from nihilism to Christian optimism. One reason why it has attracted so much critical comment is suggested by Garber, who says that "we seem to have slept and dreamed all this before. . . . we are reacquainting ourselves with something we have long known or believed" (1980, in Bloom 1988, 47). Since our dreams are our own, however, our interpretation must also be our own.

The idea of the world's dissolving at some point just beyond the end of history is in the culture, as Spenser's Epilogue to "The Shepheard's Calendar" shows:

And, if I marked well the starres' revolution,
It shall continewe till the world's dissolution
To teach the ruder shepheard how to feede his sheepe. (Epilogue 3–5)

The speech's immediate context is anything but serene. Having momentarily forgotten the approach of Caliban and the murderous Stephano—a reenactment of Prospero's negligence some twelve years before—he dismisses the Masque, which rumbles off "to a strange, hollow, and confused noise" (stage direction). The moment is also the interruption of a wedding process, as was the storm that separated the King's ship sailing back from Claribel's wedding in Tunis. The speech is bracketed by Prospero's concern for Ferdinand ("You do look, my son, in a mov'd sort, / As if you were dismay'd: be cheerful, sir" [4.1.146]) and an apology ("Sir, I am vex'd; / Bear with my weakness; my old brain is troubled; / Be not disturb'd with my infirmity: / If you be pleas'd, retire into my cell, / And there repose: a turn or two I'll walk, / To still my beating mind" [4.1.158–63]). Prospero then makes plans with Ariel to deflect the conspiracy. It is worth noting, however, that after the Masque and the "revels" speech, Prospero trusts Ferdinand to be alone with Miranda.

In the 1996 RSC production, Caliban, Stephano, and Trinculo were actually disguised as "sun-burnt sicklemen" within the Masque's fiction. They masqueraded on the small proscenium on which the Masque was conducted. That was to permit the threat that Prospero has "forgot" to infiltrate his fantasy of productivity and to confront him directly with its danger, and, of course, to enrage him. His "revels" speech, then, was designed partly to calm himself—Ferdinand being his alter ego.

The speech reflects what the Vaughans call the "antithetical extremes and their many intermediate positions [that] exemplify *The Tempest*'s endlessly arguable nature" (1999, 1). It also reflects the nihilism of a bad mood, as Alvin Kernan says: it is not the "envisioning of the whole of human history as inconsequential, [merely] expressive of a momentary cynicism and despair" (1979, 141). It can be read as the calm certainty of a long-considered existentialist viewpoint, or the serenity of Christian optimism. It reflects, as Harold Bloom puts it, Plato's "recognition, fundamental to Shakespeare's own dream world, of the antinomy [opposition] of dream and reason" (1988, 5). The speech could be read as agreeing or disagreeing with Machiavelli's judgment that "the great majority of mankind are satisfied with appearances, as though they were realities, and are often even more influenced by the things that seem than by those that are" (1940, 1.25, 182). Alfred Harbage (1946, vii) compares the speech to Bishop George Berkeley's *Principles of Human Knowledge* (1710): "Some truths there are so near and obvious to the mind, that a man need only open his eyes to see them. Such I take the important ones to be, to wit, that all the choir of heaven and furniture of the earth, in a word all those bodies which compose the mighty frame of the world, have not any substance without a mind, that their being (esse) is to be perceived or known; that consequently as long as they are not actually perceived by me, or do not exist in my mind or that of any other created spirit, they must either have no existence at all, or else subsist in the mind of some eternal spirit." This is the thesis that Samuel Johnson's boot "refuted" by kicking a stone.

Speaking of Spenser, S. K. Heninger says that his "theory of metaphor permits [an] extrapolation from the human level to the heavenly. Though illusory, the human level is related to the real because the poet's metaphor shares validity with God's" (1974, 228). Heninger's observation extends to Shakespeare's theory of metaphor, or perhaps to Prospero's in the "revels" speech, where the bridge between mortal and divine apprehension is clearly felt, if impossible to phrase accurately. As Una Ellis-Fermor suggests in a brilliant comment, a "powerful and assured comprehension of some positive fact about the nature of the spiritual universe is at work, revealed no longer simply by the evidence of its presence in stability and serenity of mood, but by suggestions, often terrifying in their half-perceived significance, of an understanding so clear that it could, were men able to receive it, give positive and defined assurance. Shakespeare's utterance in this play is, I believe, like that of the mystics, definite but comprehensible only to the initiate" (1964, 269). I would amend that only by saying that Prospero's "revels" speech and *The Tempest* seem to be comprehensible, but flee to further levels of possibility as soon as one puts language to the apparent meanings.

Robert Langbaum says that Prospero "implies also that there is a reality behind life just as there is Prospero behind the masque" (1987, xxxiii). But that is to argue by analogy, which is never proof. What lies behind theater but bare bricks? And even bricks end up as the discoveries of future archeological digs.

Talking about architecture, the mother of the arts—that which encloses, protects, and gives background and context to a work of art—John Berger says, "Something painted or carved may be placed in a wilderness, far from any human habitation, but, when this happens, the image only works as an appeal to a superhuman power who exists outside time. No image can withstand natural or cosmic space alone: the draught extinguishes its flame. As soon as an image is addressed, at least partially to other people, it requires the mediation of the space proposed by a human habitation or a human tomb: it needs to be surrounded by other human work (this 'surrounding' was at the origin of architecture), it needs the assurance of an interior" (1985, 213). If towers, temples, palaces, and even the Globe itself disappear, so must art. The manifestation of timelessness is an illusion, but it loses even its mimetic quality when it loses its ability to inhabit interiors, its space in a gallery, along a staircase, in a theater. The speech points to the physical structure necessary for the "rounding" of works of art, whether on canvas, of clay, or in words. Architecture protects art "from endless space" (214), but that vacuum is all that will remain at the dissolution of the space/time continuum. That moment or event will swallow up art, as well as all other things.

Germaine Greer argues that "Shakespeare's nature and art are a continuum [not opposite and irreconcilable qualities]. *The Tempest* deals with good and bad art, useful and noxious, and takes an original position in conscious opposition to the schoolmen" (1986, 28). Our tendency to make art subject to binary oppositions, then, misses the point of what Shakespeare does in his art, which is to fuse rather than separate elements that lesser artists make distinct. The air in which Ariel wishes to swim unimpeded is known by its relationship with the place where Kate itches.

Benedetto Croce reads the speech in the direction of Prospero's wisdom: "Where others think they see firm foothold, he is aware of change and insecurity; where others find everything clear as day, he feels the presence of mystery, or the unsolved enigma" (1920, 262). For all of its apparent assurance, then, the speech is really a majestic statement of doubt, of ignorance about "truth."

Richard Hornby says that in "ceremony itself, the focus is never on the process, or 'plot' of the change, but rather on the eternal states of being that are seen as surrounding it. . . . Religious ritual . . . always relates its central event to this unchanging, eternal world. But even secular ceremony exists *to relate change to what is unchanging*" (1986, 53; his emphasis). Prospero's speech complicates the formula in that what should be unchanging—all that surrounds the "revels" or "pageant"—is felt to change, to become itself a baseless fabric.

The speech reflects the remarkable condensation of the play, as Harry Berger, Jr., says: "Compressed into the insistently noted limits of an afternoon and a small island, are not only twelve years of experience, but the beginning and the end of civilized man, the new world and the old, Africa and Europe, the travels of Aeneas and those of Sir Thomas Gates, the golden age and an earnest of apocalypse" (1969, 263).

Sixteenth-century scholar.

Some critics define the speech as a product of context. Don Cameron Allen sees the promise of the Masque confirmed in Prospero's response to it: "He accepts the promise of the masque, the benediction of Juno and the rewards of Ceres, [and therefore] can also accept the necessary condition that men and their worlds . . . are only visions and will dissolve like summer clouds. If the world that each man has made is a vision, then life as each man possesses it is a dream" (1960, in Hallett Smith 1969, 76).

From a purely practical standpoint, says Leo Marx, Prospero draws the "line that separates dream and reality. . . . He is not about to repeat [the] mistake" of twelve years before (1967, 64). It may be, however, that Prospero's own story, now nearing its conclusion, suggests its darker tonalities to him. The early narrative incorporated "Providence divine," a heavenly messenger, and an auspicious star. Perhaps it is not as easy for him to maintain a sacramental vision when he remembers Caliban and his murderous intention. Has the rest been a dream?

A. C. Bradley says that the past suddenly intrudes on a vision of the future and that the "repetition of his earlier experience of treachery and ingratitude . . .

troubles his old brain, makes his mind 'beat,' and forces on him the sense of unreality and evanescence in the world" (1904, 329–30). For John Middleton Murry, it is "not the plot against his life [but] the thought of what the plot means: the Nature on which Nurture will never stick" that disturbs Prospero (1936, 121). The speech and its moment, says Hirst, show that aspiration has fallen to disappointment: "Prospero is the representative of the world of nurture, of civilization, of art. His ethic is that of cultivating and improving the raw nature of which Caliban is the prime exemplar. . . . Caliban is the ungrateful, graceless savage who is incapable of appreciating the higher values of a nobler race" (1984a, 16–17). Harry Berger, Jr., makes a similar point. Prospero's vision runs into awareness of "the baseness of man's stock . . . of [the] darkness" that leaves the vision "more exposed, more susceptible, more disenchanted than before" (1969, 271). The pageant is insubstantial because it is threatened. Prospero expresses his "deeper sense of the futility" of dealing with evil "than his more humane intentions" can hope to achieve (272). In other words, why bother? Francis Neilson concurs: "This new manifestation of depravity makes him realize the perversity and disorder of the mind of man. The dreams of a better state of affairs are worthless" (1956, 165). The speech is "a discouraging picture of the future for a young lover, who, no doubt, is already building his castles in the air" (166).

Stephen Greenblatt agrees, saying that "Prospero offers this sublime vision of emptiness to make Ferdinand feel 'cheerful'—secure in the consciousness that life is a dream" (1988, in Barnet 1998, 159), but "like Duke Vincentio's religious consolations in *Measure for Measure*, they seem suited more to heighten anxiety than to allay it" (160). Greenblatt claims, of course, that Prospero's goal is to increase anxiety, so the "sublime vision" is reduced to political purpose.

Reuben Brower suggests that the speech pulls together the play's basic metaphors: "Within the metaphor of tempest-clearing and of cloudlike transformation, Shakespeare has included allusions to every important analogy of change in the play" (1951, in Barnet 1987, 198). "Shakespeare has gathered all the lights of analogy into a single metaphor which sums up the metaphorical design and the essential meaning of *The Tempest*" (198). When we encounter the speech, "We read first: that like the actors and scenery of the vision, earth's glories and man shall vanish into nothingness. Through a happy mistake we also read otherwise . . . [a] blending of states of being, of substantial and unsubstantial, or real and unreal, which is the essence of *The Tempest* metamorphosis" (198–99).

Barbara Bono says something similar: "From . . . this tempest in his mind . . . comes that speech which can be alternately read as a statement of most profound skepticism or implied hope. . . . From the recognition of his own creative limitations, his own mortality, Prospero hypothesizes either despair—his happy vision is but a dream—or cheer—these ideal visions that are in mortal life but a dream, are 'rounded' in eternal life into a reality" (1984, 223). Robert Speaight asks, "Is it man's essence, or merely his mortal experience, that has no more permanence than a dream? The question is left open" (1962, 182). But Speaight also finds that the speech suggests closure: "The symbolism of the storm is linked to the symbolism of the sea. The two are placed at the service of an overmastering idea—the idea of loss and recovery" (1962, 160).

If, however, the play were "an allegory, or a religious drama," Prospero's speech would say, "An eternal world takes their place" of those palaces, temples, and towers, according to Northrop Frye (1959, 17). He stops short of that easy formula, giving us instead a sense that we are made of dreams and that we return to dream—or sleep, at least—a sea of souls awaiting incarnation or re-incarnation.

John Russell Brown offers options for the actor. Prospero "is drawn into his explanation, so that he remembers all the glories of the world along with the 'baseless' fiction of his own most hopeful 'fancies.' [The speech] can be spoken in contrasting ways: Prospero may regret the loss of all that is 'gorgeous' and 'solemn,' wishing he could dream forever; or he can devalue these seductive notions because they are insubstantial vanities. The rhythms and versification are best suited to the former interpretation" (1996, 113).

Barbara Mowat links the speech to the issue of genre: "In choosing genre, style, mode, [Shakespeare] confronts a form with its opposite, using each form as a channel of perception; he thus forces us to question all representations of reality. . . . we are then led to question the reality of the empirical world itself. . . . and finally, illusion becomes equated with dream, magic, and those very stage representations of life which have already been revealed as fraudulent. At this point, lines separating substance and semblance begin to blur; that which seems to us most real (death, for instance) is revealed as illusory, and illusions (like Hermione's statue [or Ferdinand and Miranda at chess]) become warm and breathe" (1976, 111–12). "If the play were one in which dramatic intensity and coherence were paramount, such an aria might well be at best an ornamental flourish; here it is part of the very fabric of the play. Events happen, characters comment on them, the events fade and new events occur" (115).

Jerome Mandel goes further. The speech justifies drama itself: "The only way that Prospero's statement can be accepted as serious and revelatory is if the play is recognized as . . . an imaginative reality as profound and as relevant to their lives as . . . their own imaginative construct . . . their own dreams" (1973, 68).

Harbage can hear Prospero saying that "our lives are not the final reality, anymore than stage representations are our lives" (1963, 478), while F. E. Halliday says that he points to "the oblivion that lies beyond life's dream" (1964, 52). For Walter Kaufmann, the speech says that "man is thrown into the world, abandoned to a life that ends in death, with nothing after that" (1960, 3). Robert Egan adds an even darker tonality to that existential bleakness. The speech is "a bitter testament of nihilistic despair . . . antithetical to the sense of affirmation the play ultimately achieves . . . since his art-work has proved baseless . . . any attempt to order reality through art must ultimately fail, since reality itself is only a fading illusion" (1972, 179).

Some of the responses to the speech are themselves complicated, even metaphysical. D. G. James says, for example, "There is no need to assume that 'rounded' means 'finished off'; it may equally . . . mean 'encompassed by' and therefore 'occurring within' a 'sleep' " (1937, 241), meaning that life is a version of slumber. What, then, is sleep? Is it oblivion, loss of consciousness and human volition? Or is it the place where dreams deeper than consciousness tell us who we are—a place where identity is discovered? Leslie Fiedler says that "the world *does* decay, and only the individual, in his moment of discovery or passion or tragic insight, is forever. In this sense the apparent contradiction between our being immune to death . . . and yet 'such stuff as dreams are made on' is reconciled" (1949, 82). Stanley Wells also hears a tone "of acceptance rather than of mourning. . . . The dream is recognized for what it is, but is allowed the reality that belongs even to a dream, or to any product of the imagination—a play, poem, or romance" (1995, 368). Alvin Kernan says that "Prospero . . . qualif[ies] his contempt for the impermanence of his art by reminding his listeners that while reality may seem to take immediate precedence over such 'insubstantial pageants,' reality is itself, finally, an illusion too; for at some vast remove in time the great world will ultimately disappear, leaving not even a puff of cloud behind to mark the space it once had filled" (1979, 144). Neil H. Wright finds the speech equating the impermanence of nature and art: "Even the world of nature, which seems so stable and concrete, is like the very illusions that make up the world of art—a mere pageant, destined to fade away" (1977, 267). He posits an "awakening to a reality next to which the life we 'know' will appear as a dream" (260)—but that may be more than we know.

The speech is often placed against the paradox of time. As Curry says, it embraces the "Christian conception of the world as beginning and passing away in time" (1937, 244 n. 57). That vision of the world does not apply to the soul, of course. Arthur Sewell says that "time is accepted as the destroyer, because time is also the agent of renewal" (1961, 144). Time reduces the aspects of supernatural and temporal power to meaninglessness, as Nigel Smith says: "Magic, political theory and statecraft are the same thing when set against mortality" (1988, 98). Karol Berger says that "the stuff that dreams are made on is, technically, spirit" (1977, 233). Shakespeare likes to yoke "stuff"—material or fabric—with concept ("Youth's a stuff will not endure" [*Twelfth Night* 2.3.52]). "Life is not a dream, but its transience makes it similar to a dream," Berger says (233). It, too, is a stuff that will not endure in its material form. "Viewed in the light of eternity, for which human life is created," says James Walter, Prospero "foresees . . . a conclusion for all temporal being—specifically for all symbolic vessels of political power, religious worship, and artistic creation" (1983, in Battenhouse 1994, 276). Life is "not annihilated, but 'rounded' according to the cyclic progressions of nature 'with a sleep' that anticipates, the general tone and outlook of the play's conclusion imply, a consequent awakening" (276)—which resolves the paradox of time by erasing time itself.

Anne Barton says that the "shifting nature of reality on the island is not a universal condition. It is a special state of affairs created by Prospero. . . . What Prospero's fourth-act speech does is to annihilate precisely the world outside the island which has hitherto encouraged trust: the world to which the characters of *The Tempest* plan to return at the end of the play, and which the theatre audience instinctively identifies with its own reality" (1968, 15). That may be one reason why Prospero reminds the audience at the end of what world they— and he, the pleading actor—are in, where none "should 'scape whipping" (*Hamlet* 2.2.536) without the release of charity. Barton equates the "reality" of life beyond the confines of the island and of life outside the doors of the theater with the transitory existence of the play-within-the-play. It is no more solid than, no different from, that tissue of illusion that has just vanished so completely, dissolved into nothingness at the bidding of Prospero (15).

George Steiner says that the problem for Ludwig Wittgenstein, in responding to Shakespeare, is that he wants the artist to be a *Dichter*, "not only a matchless artificer and imaginer, but the beneficiary, the communicant with and communicator to his fellow-men of a high, articulate religious-moral-philosophical vision and criticism of life" (1996, 126). The Victorians could find Shakespeare to be thus, but their view was of an age. Wittgenstein, as Steiner rightly says, misreads "dramatic discourse . . . the principles of enacted truth in poetry" and denies "natural vitality . . . a lifelikeness more vivid than most of life itself in Shakespeare's men and women" (126–27). Wittgenstein's "aesthetic bridles at the quintessentially open-ended tragi-comic genius of Shakespeare's dramaturgy" (126). Characters in Shakespeare may give us a sense of "Jacob's wrestling with the presence or absence of the rival Creator" (127), but Shakespeare, as the great Victorian Matthew Arnold recognized, is "free" of that "question." Wittgenstein wanted the dream to be phrased as language and dream. He says that "if Shakespeare is great, his greatness is displayed only in the whole corpus of his plays, which create their own language and world. In other words, he is completely unrealistic (like a dream)" (quoted in Steiner 1996, 118). He is, then, as Steiner argues about giving language to dreams, a co-creator. Not God, but zeitgeist is the other source of energy. If Prospero is Wittgenstein's *Dichter* here, he would find the message frustratingly open-ended.

Neil H. Wright, Northrop Frye, and Ruth Nevo suggest that our own stance toward "reality" has been altered by the experience of the play and the Wedding Masque immediately preceding Prospero's "revels" speech. Thus what we hear there is not what we would hear if we heard the speech apart from the experience of the play. The "world of illusion impinges upon the world of normal expectation in such a profusion of ways that even the audience is bound to be uncertain at times of what is real and what is illusory. . . . the world of illusion is the established order, not the ordinary world of experience" (Neil H. Wright 1977, 243–44). The play occurs in a zone outside of experience "which has been there from the beginning, an order which takes on an increasingly religious cast and seems to be drawing away from human experience altogether" (Frye 1957, 185). "The embedding of play within play dissolves presentational boundaries so that the audience is required to suspend its attention, to negotiate a constant interchange between fictional reality and fictional illusion" (Nevo 1987, 147).

The speech's appeal to our *episteme* is suggested by John Berger: "Surrealist paintings conjure up the time of dreams[, which are] the only realm of the timeless left intact" (1985, 210). As far as time is concerned, Shakespeare seems to be ahead of it in Prospero's speech:

[T]he irreversible nature of time is asserted in cosmology and biology, but physics is based on a formulation of the laws of nature in which there is no distinction between past and future; in other words time is reversible and therefore illusory, as Einstein implied. The paradox is that the universe itself is full of irreversible transformations which imply an arrow of time (such as ourselves) and yet the basic laws of physics are said to be reversible. . . . Classical science emphasised stability and equilibrium. Now we discover fluctuations, instabilities and evolutionary patterns at all levels. This is not only true in science. . . . We are not at the end of physics, but rather at the end of predictability and certainty, which means that physics needs to include novelty and creativity. And a science in which creativity and participation in the construction of the world are intrinsic is a science [in which] probability will no longer be seen as ignorance nor science as equivalent to certainty. (Lorimer 1995, 18)

If the play dramatizes a clash of paradigms, it also adumbrates a new way of looking at things.

Prospero saves one of his best "illusions" for one of his last—the last being the "calm seas [and] auspicious gales" he promises Alonso. Prospero pulls back a curtain and "discovers" Ferdinand and Miranda playing at chess. Alonso does not want to believe what he sees. Conditioned to strange images by now, he fears it is "A vision of the island" (5.1.170). But now what seems a vision is reality, as planes of imagination become pulses that beat. Like Ferdinand before him, he wonders whether Miranda is a "goddess." The emphasis here is on Alonso's response. He is the king in the play and the chief agent of the politics that deposed Prospero and made Milan a client state of Naples.

The chess game itself reflects the politics of the play. "The territorial ambitions of their elders are transformed by Ferdinand and Miranda into the stratagems of chess," as Orgel says (1987, 197n). Loughrey and Taylor point out the "variety of thematic and architectonic significances in the chess episode" (1982, 113). Chess, they say, is a "war game." The "political marriage between them will ensure" the peace for which Prospero implicitly asks in unveiling the tableau (115). Prospero's manipulations "resemble . . . the progress of a game of chess. [They have] an almost mathematical precision" (116) that includes his opening of the curtain on Ferdinand and Miranda. Kings, says King James, can "make of their subjects like men at the Chesse" (James I 1918, 308), and so can magicians. Chess also relates to the conceptions of Utopia expressed by Gonzalo and by Prospero's Masque, in that chess in More's *Utopia* is a metaphor for an orderly society, as Michael Holquist points out (1968, 109).

Few would agree with Jan Kott that the two young lovers are an iconic arrangement that does not reflect the political arrangement that Prospero is announcing: "Ferdinand and Miranda [at chess] are outside history, outside the struggle for power and the crown" (1964, 204). It may be that Miranda's "you play me false" means that she is "certainly accusing him of cheating," as Orgel claims (1987, 30). I think that Orgel displays a tin ear, however, to claim that "her perfect complicity in the act" demonstrates "Italian *Realpolitik* . . . already established in the next generation" (30). Closer to the tone of their discourse is Sturgess, who says that the game of chess has "overtones of the power game . . . which starts up the story, but rendered in the lovers' affectionate teasing into the commerce of love and a kind of communication: love's kingdom is already lost and won; its battles are bloodless" (1987, in Vaughan and Vaughan 1998, 127). Chess also symbolizes sexuality, often with connotations of "illicit sexual overtures" (Orgel 1987, 197n), but here we find the lovers alone in a concealed space, engaged in a chaste variation on desire.

5

CRITICAL APPROACHES

The Tempest is seen as the epitome of Shakespeare's poetic genius and as a text complicit in England's evil colonizing—the beginnings of an empire on which, by the mid-nineteenth century, the sun never set—and as a manifestation of Shakespeare "at the height" or of Shakespeare as a crabby old man awaiting death. Some of these generalizations are better than others, some are based more solidly on the evidence than others, but it is amazing that so many of them can be convincingly argued. As it moves in time, the play lifts various facets to the light of criticism. It is, like the island, a function of its observation, of the "indeterminacy principle." It is also a function of the age that reads it or produces it. It is, perhaps, the supreme example of Keats's "negative capability," which "Shakespeare possessed so enormously." Keats defined it as "where a man is capable of being in uncertainties, mysteries, doubts, without any irritable reaching after fact and reason" (1962, 304). Nowadays, no one concurs with Barrett Wendell's gloomy late-nineteenth-century conclusion that in *The Tempest*, Shakespeare's "faculty of creating character, as distinguished from constructing it, is gone. All his power fails to make his poem spontaneous, easy, inevitable. . . . effort implies creative decadence—the fatal approach of growing age" (1894, 377).

The first commentary on *The Tempest* occurs in Ben Jonson's Induction to his 1614 *Bartholomew Fair*: "If there be never a *Servant-monster* i' the *Fayre*, who can help it, he sayes: nor a nest of *Antiques*? He is loth to make Nature afraid in his *Playes*, like those that beget *Tales, Tempests*, and such like *Drolleries*" (Spencer 1933, 416). This is a snide awareness of the power represented in plays like *The Winter's Tale* and *The Tempest*, plays that, for Jonson, overflow

Nineteenth-century illustration.

the boundaries of unified drama (Aristotle's unities of time and place) and pretend that the magic that Jonson scorns really does exist. Jonson's represents the first neoclassical attack on Shakespeare, one to be repeated for almost two hundred years.

Nicholas Rowe in 1709 called Caliban "one of the finest and most uncommon Grotesques that was ever seen" (qtd. in Palmer 1968, 15). One would like to ask Rowe what precisely he did see.

Samuel Johnson noted in his Preface to his 1765 edition of Shakespeare that "Shakespeare's mode of composition is . . . an interchange of seriousness and merriment, by which the mind is softened at one time, and exhilarated at another" (1951, 495), a principle of alterations of mood and tonality that Johnson felt vanquished "most of the criticisms of *Rhymer* and *Voltaire*" (495), and that challenges much criticism since.

The eighteenth century "underlined a neoclassical emphasis on human rationality and morality in Shakespeare's work" (Vaughan and Vaughan 1999, 83). Toward the middle of the century, however, the response of Joseph Wharton to *The Tempest* stands on the "verge of Romanticism" (1753, in Palmer 1968, 19). Wharton speaks of the play's "boundless imagination" and "pleasing extravagance" (1753, 37). "The poet is a more powerful magician than his own Prospero: we are transported into fairy land; we are rapt in a delicious dream, from which it is misery to be disturbed; all around is enchantment!" (41). The play, according to Wharton, is "an amazing wilderness of fancy" (1753).

The shift from the "extensive view" of the eighteenth century, which saw the plays as valid representations of a generalized and predictable nature, to a romantic sense of Shakespeare is signalled by Coleridge in a letter to Robert Southey (circa 1797): "I almost think that ideas *never* recall ideas . . . any more than leaves in a forest create each other's motion. The breeze it is that runs through them—it is the soul, the state of feeling" (qtd. in Stange 1959, 15), or, as he puts it in a version of "The Eolian Harp," "the mute still air / Is Music slumbering on her instrument." It is not surprising that Coleridge is one of *The Tempest*'s most sensitive critics. He senses in the play its "peculiar atmosphere of ontological suspension" (A. D. Nuttall 1967, in Hallett Smith, 83). The play does not define the nature of reality, and we sense that lack of definition. The play would obviously appeal to this master of the symbolic voyage as a supreme product of what Coleridge called "the secondary Imagination," which re-creates what the "primary Imagination" apprehends. The primary Imagination approximates perception. The secondary Imagination discerns archetypes (Richards, 1960, 57–60). It follows that Coleridge is wary of heavily scenic versions of Shakespeare: "The illusion may be assisted by the effect on the senses of the complicated scenery and decorations of modern times, yet this sort of assistance is dangerous. For the principal and only genuine excitement ought to come from within—from the moved and sympathetic imagination" (qtd. in Palmer 1968, 62). According to Terence Hawkes in his brilliant introduction to *Alternative*

Shakespeares II, in comparing Shakespeare's plays to "great trees," Coleridge insists on the organic unity underlying apparent irregularity and therefore "turns the Bard into a Romantic poet" (1996, 4).

The Vaughans (1999, 86) suggest that the split between text and performance, still wide today, begins in the romantic era. I suggest that it begins a hundred years earlier, with the publication of Shakespeare in versions that could be read in homes, as depicted in the novels of the eighteenth century and the early nineteenth century. These texts were not available on stage—even if one were close enough to a theater to attend—until the third decade of the nineteenth century.

We hear sober Victorianism in Edward Dowden's linkage of Prospero and his creator: the "grave harmony of his character, his self-mastery, his calm validity of will, his sensitiveness to wrong, his unfaltering justice, and, with these, a certain abandonment, a remoteness from the common joys and sorrows of the world, are characteristic of Shakspere" (1875, 371). Each is the apotheosis of all Victorian England thought itself to be—the superior and moral male (though ruled, like the Elizabethan male, by a female). Dowden sees in the play an allegory whereby Shakespeare (Prospero) instructs Fletcher, the young playwright of the King's Men (Ferdinand), that hard work is needed to succeed. Dowden is also responsible for reading the plays as signals of Shakespeare's psychological state and reflects the nineteenth-century concern with the chronology of the plays "to interpret Shakespeare's work as spiritual autobiography" (Palmer 1968, 21). Dowden pursues Keats's comment that "Shakespeare led a life of allegory, and his works are the comments on it." That is not to say that his works are allegories or that they are journals of his spiritual life. It is to say that Shakespeare saw at least one deeper meaning beneath all surfaces and that his works emerge from that constant sequence of insights.

The greatest of the early-twentieth-century Shakespearean critics, A. C. Bradley, does not treat *The Tempest* in any detail, a fact that argues a late-Victorian emphasis on the tragedies and, to a lesser extent, the histories. That does not diminish Bradley's importance to this discussion. His insistence on character, says Hawkes, "makes [the plays] over into Victorian novels" (1996, 4). But Bradley's "commitment to the almost palpable existence of single unitary individuals and the developing relations between them as the core of each play's interest" (1996, 5), and the "concern with individual personality fundamental to [Bradley's criticism] may ultimately reflect deep-lying dimensions of Western ideology, thus making it virtually 'invisible' " (5). That may be true. The construct of "individual personality" has been powerfully reinforced by some theories of the unconscious (Freud and Jung, for example) even if it has been undercut by the work that experimental psychologists have done on rats, worms, and pigeons. I would suggest further that some directors even today see the plays as Chekhovian workings out, or failures to work out, relationships. If we posit an Oedipal problem for Hamlet, it becomes impossible to avoid a "commitment to [a] single unitary individual" and to the results of his unperceived uniqueness. We also, probably, have a smack of Coleridge's unity at work—that is, the play emerges from a single theme (or acorn).

An argument that one puts forward these days with fear and trembling is that "personality" is not an invention of the nineteenth-century novelist, but that Shakespeare actually constructed characters—a Richard of Gloucester, for example, against "the comparatively colorless orators and warriors who populate the *Henry VI* plays," as E. Pearlman suggests (1992, 411). This point of view has been recently reiterated by Harold Bloom (1998). Such an argument carries with it the burden that Shakespeare, consciously and craftsmanlike, knew what he was doing as he wrote his plays. I will deal with characters as characters later in this chapter.

In a forgotten introduction to *The Tempest*, Henry James (1907) looks back on Victorian criticism of the play, which "abounds . . . in affirmed conclusions, complacencies of conviction, full apprehensions of the meaning and triumphant pointings of the moral" (Palmer 1968, 77). In the play, James finds "serenity . . . the subject itself intact and unconscious, seated as unwinking and inscrutable as a divinity in a temple, save for that vague flicker of derision, the only response to our interpretative head, which adds the last beauty to its face" (80). While the work mocks interpretations, "we feel behind it the immense procession of its predecessors" (81). He goes on to say that "nothing, surely, of equal length and variety lives so happily and radiantly as a whole: no poetic birth ever took place under a star appointed to blaze upon it so steadily" (83). It is "as if he had swum into our ken with [his power of speech] from another planet" (85). The artist, James says, works with "life itself, in its appealing, overwhelming crudity . . . in the very elements of experience; whereas we see Shakespeare working predominantly in the terms of expression, *all* in the terms of the artist's specific vision and genius" (86). The "author of *The Tempest* has no lesson for us" (86). The play is the perfect work of art—it has no flaw in its golden bowl. "It is by his expression of it as exactly as the expression stands that the particular thing is created, created as interesting, as beautiful, as strange, droll or terrible—as related, in short, to our understanding or our sensibility; in consequence of which we reduce it to naught when we begin to talk of either of its presented parts as matters by themselves" (86). Our own total psychology of perception takes it in as total. It is no coincidence that the novelist who used inference, varying points of view, and nuance as the stuff of his fictions should admire the indirect and message-free final play of Shakespeare's in the way he does. James's introduction has an elegiac tone, as if he knows that his own greatest work is receding into the time behind him. He may have realized through *The Tempest* that the sheer distance he imposed between his observers and an event had finally made it impossible for anything to happen, including his own superb fiction.

The movement from autobiographical criticism to thematic criticism is signalled by John Dover Wilson's rejoinder to Lytton Strachey. In response to Dowden's argument that Shakespeare's final plays show him "on the heights,"

Strachey suggests that Shakespeare was "half enchanted by visions of beauty and loveliness, and half bored to death; on the one side inspired by a soaring fancy to the singing of ethereal songs, and on the other urged by a general disgust to burst occasionally through his torpor into bitter and violent speech" (1922, 412). The final play may resemble *A Midsummer Night's Dream*, says Strachey, but "the gaiety of youth has been replaced by the disillusionment of middle age" (412). There is "no character in the play to whom, during some part of it, [Prospero] is not studiously disagreeable" (414).

Strachey perpetuates the thesis "that Shakespeare's work can be read as a direct expression of his personal state of mind, but Strachey's emphasis upon disillusion and cynicism announces a characteristically twentieth-century response to the play" (Palmer 1968, 21). "Strachey is the prophet of the anti-sentimental, anti-Romantic, 'realist' school of interpretation which has done so much to shape twentieth-century attitudes to Shakespeare" (21–22). An attempt to counter the gloomy vision is Arthur Quiller-Couch's in the early twentieth century: "The subject which constantly engaged his mind towards the close of life was *Reconciliation*" (1921, in Hallett Smith 1969, 15; Quiller-Couch's emphasis). But Strachey lives on, as in Clifford Leech's characterization of Shakespeare-Prospero as a sadistic puritan. The music of the verse shows "a glimpse of the purified world which Shakespeare the puritan might reach out to in his dreams. But the play as a whole shows also how the world looked to him awake" (1950, 158). Art, as in the Freudian formulation, becomes compensatory activity.

Responding specifically to Strachey, J. Dover Wilson calls *The Tempest* "the most consummate of all Shakespeare's masterpieces" (1932, 132). It reflects the benign fact that "Shakespeare fell in love with Stratford" (136). Wilson quotes *Tintern Abbey* ("We see into the life of things"). But Prospero would not say of his island, as Wordsworth does by the side of Grasmere Lake, "tranquility is here." Shakespeare did of New Place, according to Wilson. He closes with the ending of Keats's "Grecian Urn" (144), with its fusion of concept and sensuality, an appropriate oxymoron for the effect of *The Tempest*.

NEW CRITICISM

The New Critical approach involves a close reading of the work without reference to biographical or historical contexts. The critic applies a set of terms to the work, as if the artist moved within a critical vocabulary as he wrote and remained impervious to all other factors that might bear on what he wrote. It is to these assumptions that postmodernist modes respond. Irony, paradox, and ambiguity are what New Critics enjoy finding in literature, so it is not surprising that Donne is one of their favorites from a former age, while Eliot tends to be the preferred poet of the middle years of the twentieth century.

Hawkes mentions the work of G. Wilson Knight and L. C. Knights, who, in the New Critical mode, treated the plays as "long poems" (1996, 5). Knights is famous for his attack on A. C. Bradley's tendency to treat the characters in the plays as "real people" in "How Many Children Had Lady Macbeth?" (1933). He asserts that "the only profitable approach to Shakespeare is consideration of his plays as dramatic poems, of his use of language to obtain a complex emotional response" (1933, 20). The main thrust of Knights's critique of *The Tempest* is Prospero's movement toward the restoration of his soul and psyche (1974, 15–21).

For G. Wilson Knight, *The Tempest* "itself is an image" (qtd. in Hallett Smith 1969, 9). The "poetry is preeminently in the events themselves, which are intrinsically poetic. . . . the play itself is metaphor" (Knight 1947, 224) "Art," says Knight, "is an extraverted expression of the creative imagination which, when introverted, becomes religion" (20). In *The Tempest*, "Shakespeare looks inward and, projecting perfectly his own spiritual experience into symbols of objectivity, traces in a compact play the past progress of his own soul" (20). "Plato's two steeds of the soul, the noble and the hideous, twin potentialities of the human spirit," are Ariel and Caliban (21). Knight alludes to the *Phaedrus*, in which Plato divides every soul into three parts: a charioteer and two horses. One horse is wild and uncontrollable—appetite. The other is a lover of honor and responsive to command. The charioteer is wisdom. "If . . . the better part of the intelligence wins the victory and guides them to an orderly and philosophic way of life, their life on earth will be happy and harmonious since they have attained discipline and self-control: They have subdued the source of evil in the soul and set free the source of goodness" (1950, 256). Since the allegory describes Socrates' understanding of erotic love, it may help us understand Prospero's vehemence with Ferdinand regarding Miranda's chastity.

Reuben Brower's essay on *The Tempest* (1951) is a paradigm of New Criticism. Following lines set out by Knight and Knights, Brower says that "the harmony of the play lies in its metaphorical design. . . . It is hard to pick a speech at random without coming on an expression that brings us by analogy into direct contact with elements that seem [otherwise] remote" (182). The "recurrent analogies (or continuities) are linked through a key metaphor into a single metaphorical design" (183). "The . . . main continuities . . . are: 'strange-wondrous,' 'sleep-and-dream,' 'sea-tempest,' 'music-and-noise,' 'earth-air,' 'slavery-freedom,' and 'sovereignty-conspiracy' " (184). They are "varied and pervasive" (184). The scheme is slightly inconsistent in that some of the "continuities" incorporate the same concept, while others involve a contradiction. They help to explain the play's sense of artistic unity and compression, along with unity of time (184). "Recurrent expressions of 'sea and tempest,' like those of 'sleep and dream' . . . have a similar atmospheric value of not letting us forget the special quality of life on" the island (188). The "key metaphor is 'sea change' " (194). The repetitions of the metaphors have "a close relation to the main dramatic movement of the play" (199). Alonso's premonition of "harmony [in his speech after the banquet is removed] reveals . . . Shakespeare's exact sense of the movement of the drama, of the changing human relations and feelings he is presenting" (200). As Prospero awakens the conspirators, we hear in his words simultaneously both "the dramatic links and the analogical links" of the play (203). The "metaphorical design and dramatic design are perfectly integrated" (203). It follows that "metamorphosis is truly the key metaphor to the *drama*," not part of some "detachable design of decorative analogies" (204). In other words, metaphor follows plot, which follows intention.

The essentialist, often a "New Critic," sees the world of the plays as "of a piece," a conscious artifact crafted by the playwright. The essentialist critic approaches the play as if it were "a trans-historical phenomenon" (Bristol 1990, 151), free of the biography of the writer and the contexts of his time.

These obvious limitations do not obviate the value of a perceptive New Critical analysis. Brower's essay does not ignore the movement of the play as play. Rather, he shows how poetry reinforces that movement. He also shows how closely written the play is.

FEMINIST CRITICISM

Feminist criticism looks at gender issues, at marginalized characters, at the oppression that patriarchy can inflict upon its often-female victims, and at Shakespeare's sometimes subversive exploration of the role of women in a "man's world." In the hands of sensitive critics like Catherine Belsey, Anna Nardo, Carol Thomas Neely, Jeanne Addison Roberts, and others it vividly illuminates sections of the plays that have long lain in shadows. Its goal, as Kathleen McLuskie says, is to "both reveal . . . and subvert . . . the hold which such an ideology [of femininity] has for readers both female and male" (1985, 106). *The Tempest* has one female character, Miranda. Miranda's mother is mentioned, though not named, and Caliban's mother, Sycorax, is also mentioned, as is Alonso's daughter, Claribel. The play has not elicited much feminist criticism.

Hilda Doolittle calls Claribel "the figure of the exiled, alienated woman" (1949). Lorie Jerrell Leininger (1980) suggests that two members of the audience for *The Tempest* at court in 1613, Princess Elizabeth and Frederick, ruler of the Rhineland, were ill fated. They would fail as King and Queen of Bohemia. She would be an exile. He would die at thirty-six of the plague during the Thirty Years' War. Leininger claims that "it appears likely that [Elizabeth and Frederick] were influenced in their unrealistic expectations of their powers and rights as future rulers by the widespread Jacobean attempt to equate unaccountable aristocratic power with benevolent infallibility and possibly by the expression of that equation in *The Tempest*" (Barnet 1987, 213). Even if one assumes that equation to be embedded in the play, the influence of a "romance" on its audience may be overstated here. That the Jacobean formulation is "unrealistic" is probably true—most rationalizations of rule are just that. Does the play support the issuing of "the warrant to plunder, exploit and kill in the name of God— Virtue destroying Vice" (1987, 212)? Can we move from a play to history this easily? Plenty of happy ceremonies lead to acrimonious marriages, in which the participants "sink under being man and wife," as Robert Frost says in "The Investment."

Miranda, says Leininger, "is deprived of any possibility of human freedom, growth or thought. She need only *be* chaste" (213). "[A]ll virtue and vice [are schematically represented in the play] as chastity and lust" (211). Excluded "from the field of moral concern [is] the very domination and enslavement that the play vividly demonstrates" (211). Miranda is "forced into unwitting collusion with domination by appearing to be a beneficiary" (214). She should "join forces with Caliban . . . with all those who are exploited or oppressed" (214). She has been "given to understand ['What! I say, / My foot my tutor?' 1.2.469–70] that she is the foot in the family organization of which Prospero is the head" (209). Prospero, of course, "is acting out a role which he knows to be unjust" (209), but Miranda "has no way of knowing this" (209). That Prospero does have a goal in mind and that Miranda will accede to it should soften the obvious sexism and patriarchy of his reference to Miranda as "foot," but in Leininger's snide and strident treatment it does not. Still, she vividly describes the plight of the daughters of aristocrats. Had Elizabeth defied James and not "fallen dutifully in love with the bridegroom her father had chosen for her" (206), things would have turned out differently for her, no doubt. We are supposed to summon up sympathy for Miranda on the basis of a historical parallel that Shakespeare could not know.

We do not know how things turn out for Miranda or Ferdinand, of course. Shakespeare often leaves us with marriage at the end of courtship as his comedies close. He sometimes gives us a spectrum of possibilities within the play, as in *The Taming of the Shrew, As You Like It*, and *Much Ado about Nothing*. He occasionally gives us Macbeth and Lady Macbeth, Antony and Cleopatra. Leininger appeals to history for her ending and suggests that the play itself may have dictated a darker history to its aristocratic young audience than they would have experienced without it. Her aggressive essay insists that we not assume that present happiness will lead to future felicity. Miranda, though, seems happier at the end of the play than Leininger is willing to grant, but then, we assume that Princess Elizabeth was also happy at the end of that performance in 1613. Still, however, a shrill voice can claim that "*The Tempest* is arguably the most sexist and racist of all Shakespeare's plays" (Greene 1990, 178 n. 5).

Ann Thompson (1991, in Vaughan and Vaughan 1998) suggests that "Miranda . . . has fully internalised the patriarchal assumption that a woman's main function is to provide a legitimate succession" (235)—even if "Good wombs have borne bad sons." The story of "all white women in the colonial adventure [is] the nature of her subordination confirms her subordination to white men" (242). The same is also true for the imperial adventure. But what are the alternatives, given the political framework of 1610? Shakespeare questions and explores assumptions—they are there to shadow the happy ending, to qualify Gonzalo's overstatement. Too often in this politically saturated criticism, what is happening in the play has to be placed against critical theory spun from

Final scene, The Princess Theatre, 1857.

something external to the play—Freudian theory, postcolonial discourse, or the like. Miranda says that she is in love. Is this mere duty?

GENERIC CRITICISM

I agree with Gary Waller's statement that "today most Shakespeareans would recognize as unsatisfactory any criticism (or teaching) that dehistoricizes the Shakespearean script into a static monument. . . . We recognize perhaps that even in his own age, each time Shakespeare himself saw one of his own plays performed, he would have seen it in a new guise, modified by factors over which he had no control" (1992a, 103). It may be helpful, however, to explore certain generalizations or possibilities before they must be modified. Genre, or type of literature, is one question to raise. Shakespeare's plays are probably more unlike each other than similar, but asking the generic question can set limits on what can happen in the "world of the play." Genre is a Platonic form awaiting con-textualization. One of these contextualizations is, as Waller suggests, a play-in-history, subject to the pressures of changing times and of specific audiences, playing spaces, and zeitgeists. The question of genre can help define what these pressures are and what they cannot be. Indeed, the pressures of history and changes in modes of dissemination shape the trends within which genres rise or fall. Inexpensive means of printing helped the rise of the novel in the eighteenth century. Television has popularized the situation comedy.

Genre tells us what can happen within a given work. Poetry, according to Sir Philip Sidney, is "a speaking *Picture*, with this end, to teach and delight" (1595; 1926, 3.9). A play, of course, speaks and moves. The question is how its type conditions whatever it may be teaching and however it may be delighting. In *The Tempest*, the "darker themes of Shakespeare's tragedies—regicide, usurpation, and vengeance—are always near this comedy's surface" (Vaughan and Vaughan, 1999, 10). That terrible things may threaten, but finally do not occur, is one source of the play's pleasure. Another is the play's atmosphere, in which magic and music saturate a remote island.

Christopher Hardman isolates the simplest category within which the play functions: "Comedy [said the definition of dramatic form used in Elizabethan grammar schools] began with turbulence and ended with calm" (1988, 31). The two complex candidates, tragicomedy and romance, are not mutually exclusive. One points to the structure of the play, that is, a play in which tragic error is made, sometimes with tragic results. In *The Winter's Tale*, Leontes falsely accuses Hermione. As a result, Mamillius and Antigonus die, but, after sixteen years, reconciliation does occur. To isolate structure is to deal with formal cause and to suggest that "suspense and irony [are] implicit" in tragicomedy, as Russ McDonald says (1991, 26).

The reconciliation often comes about as a result of some supernatural power like magic or the intervention of the gods. The introduction of a metaphysical element, something beyond nature or normality, gives the final plays the quality of "romance." To make comedy out of tragedy or potential tragedy, some larger, surrounding power must be summoned. "It is required," as Paulina says in *The Winter's Tale*, "You do awake your faith (5.4.95). The romance, while it refers to what happens in the play, also includes final cause, that is, the effect of the play on us. We should experience something like the wonder we observe in Leontes and Alonso. The older we get, the more we have lost, and romance is "the literature of second chances" (Von Rosador 1991, 12). Structurally, *The Tempest* is an inversion of *King Lear*, with the tragedy (apparent death) in the subplot and the comedy (Ferdinand and Miranda) in the main plot. Both skeins—the story of King Alonso and his son and of Duke Prospero and his daughter—are resolved in the finale. Imaginatively, the play is a romance in that it intermingles the impossible and the empirical. Palmer points to the tonality of romance and "Some subtleties o' the isle" (5.1.124) when he says that "the 'meaning' [of the play] exists in [the ways in] which the poetry, spectacle, and music together create an evanescent world subject to swift transitions and transformations of mood, tempo, and poise . . . as much as in the metaphysical ideas and moral doctrines it draws upon" (1968, 23). Coleridge mentions "a grave beauty, a sweet serenity" as characteristic of the romances (Qtd. in Orgel 1987, 4). Orgel suggests persuasively that content and tone are inextricable: "The play is, in fact, as much concerned with tragic as with comic themes: the nature of authority and power; the conflicting claims of vengeance and forgiveness, of justice and mercy." This "rethinking of old issues [lends] a profoundly retrospective quality to the drama" (1987, 5).

According to Giambattista Guarini (1601, summarized in Hirst 1984a, 35–37), tragicomedy is a mixed form lacking unity of action. It incorporates one basic action, one denouement, and a communal happy ending. The coexistence of tragic and comic plots works out so that "the danger, not the death," is dramatized. As John Fletcher, Shakespeare's younger contemporary with the King's Men, explained in 1610: "A tragie-comedie is not so called in respect of mirth and killing, but in respect it wants deaths, which is inough to make it no tragedie, yet brings some neere it, which is inough to make it no comedie" (Vaughan and Vaughan, 1999, 10). As might be expected, such a combination of potentially antithetical materials demands a careful structure. The pattern Guarini sets out is this: the first act contrasts the tragic and the comic (in the case of *The Tempest*, the first act introduces the audience to the play's major contrast: the storm and our awareness that the storm is being controlled for a purpose). "Comic" is not meant as "something funny," but as an action that leads a character to greater self-awareness and reunion with society. The second act introduces new material (though Shakespeare has prepared us for much of it already by introducing the King's party on the ship). The third involves comic plotting. The fourth is the tragic movement, when characters are most threatened. The fifth act brings reconciliation and a weaving together of the various strands of the action.

If the play is a tragicomedy, it pursues a basic Christian rhythm. As Robert Langbaum says, "The essential message of tragicomedy [is] that we lose in order to recover something greater, that we die in order to be reborn into a better life" (1987, xxiv). Furthermore, if *The Tempest* is "pastoral tragicomedy," as Kermode argues (1964, lix–lxii), it links up generically with *As You Like It*: the debate between Corin and Touchstone, for example (3.2.11ff.). As Palmer says, "*The Tempest* expresses the traditional concern of pastoral with the antithesis of primitive and sophisticated planes of existence" (1968, 14).

Nathaniel Hawthorne calls the necessary atmosphere for his favorite genre of romance "the moonlight of romance" ("Roger Malvin's Burial"). In his introduction to *The Scarlet Letter*, "The Custom House," moonlight has a transforming quality: "The floor of our familiar room has become a neutral territory, somewhere between the real world and fairy-land, where the Actual and the Imaginary may meet, and each imbue itself with the nature of the other." Romance, then, involves a transaction in which reality and imagination exchange the corporeal and the diaphanous to make up a third state in which we might "discover a form beloved, but gone hence now sitting quietly in a streak of this magic moonshine, with an aspect that would make us doubt whether it had returned from afar, or had never once stirred from our fireside" (1991, 46). The firelight "mingles itself with the cold spirituality of the moonbeams, and communicates . . . a heart and sensibilities of human tenderness to the forms which fancy summons up." Here, the light in the room lends a human warmth to the cool shapings of imagination. "It converts them from snow-images to men and women" (1991, 46). The writer of a romance, says Hawthorne, must "dream strange things, and make them look like truth" (1991, 47). The romance is a fusion of the material world—too much with Hawthorne in the custom house—and that other place at which Hawthorne gazes: "my old native town . . . through the haze of memory, a mist brooding over and around it; as if it were no portion of the real earth, but an overgrown village in cloud-land, with only imaginary inhabitants to people its wooden houses, and walk its homely lanes. . . . I am a citizen of somewhere else" (1991, 52).

Hawthorne moves back into a past inhabited by the dour and unforgiving Calvinists in *The Scarlet Letter* (and in "The Minister's Black Veil," "Young Goodman Brown," and other works). Shakespeare's romances take us into the past as well, by creating it and leaving a gap of time, as, notoriously, in *The Winter's Tale*, or, as in the case of the "unified" *Tempest*, by including the past as a narrative intersecting with the present. The future, for the romances, involves pleasant retirement for the early protagonists and the movement of an evolved younger generation into an enlightened future. It is the dream of graduation speeches. The failure of Hawthorne's romantics is expressed in his comment on the dying Aylmer: in "rejecting the best the earth could offer . . . he failed to look beyond the shadowy scope of time, and, living once for all in eternity, to find the perfect future in the present."

Prospero recognizes the present and its bearing on the future:

> I find my zenith doth depend upon
> A most auspicious star, whose influence
> If now I court not, but omit, my fortunes
> Will ever after droop. (1.2.181–84)

Julian Patrick argues that romance deals "in the retrospective and prospective movement. . . . past and future are continually being woven together in the present space of narrative" (1983, in Bloom 1988, 69).

Howard Felperin says that romance is both genre and subject in that romance involves the struggle of the imagination against the brutalities of the political process (1972). Romance, says Robert Langbaum, "deals in marvelous events and solves its problems through metamorphoses and recognition scenes" (1987, xxxiii). "The recognized objects are transformed through the eyes of the beholders; so that more is restored than has been lost" (xxxiii). Furthermore, as the Vaughans suggest, the romance, for all of its fantastic features, is, in its way, true to life: "By yoking tragic themes and comic resolutions, realistic characterizations and exotic tales, the romances highlight the paradoxes of human experience" (1999, 17). One might add that the romance is true to the "dream life" of most people, which can dramatize all that seems impossible to consciousness. Shakespeare has prepared his audience, of course, by exposing it to tragedy and comedy and thus educating it to conventions and expectations that he can manipulate with the knowledge and participation of his audience. This kind of play is "metadrama," which means that we know that we are at a play that knows that it is a play. Charles Moseley claims that "no other play of Shakespeare's so consistently draws attention to itself as play" (1988, 114).

In her elegant study of the final romances, Barbara Mowat (1976) argues that "expectation patterns (generic, stylistic, tonal) are not so much ignored" in the final plays "as they are deliberately flouted. Tragic patterns collide with comic devices; presentational techniques [metadrama or straight narrative] mock representational style [where the action is actually shown]; narrative intrudes into mimetic action" (101). The final plays are "open form," meaning that they use the "unstable true/false world of Romance" (107) to create "theatrical experience which breaks through the aesthetic, deliberately destroying dramatic coherence and consistency in order to awaken us to new insights or disturbing truths, or to provide us with an experience sharply different from the experience of watching closed form drama" (100). Thus are the plays closer to "life" than those that function from strict, generic premises: "Few of us can see life consistently as tragic or as comic; few of us consistently suspend our disbelief in the face of created illusion; few can consistently give credence to a single knowable force which shapes our lives" (346).

The generic variableness of *The Tempest* insists that "the making of a consistent, meaningful artwork is put largely in the hands of the audience" (346)— hands asked to applaud at the end, but hands belonging to imaginations that no doubt have made a different work of art than the person to left or right (also applauding) has done. Prospero merely fits the shifting modes of the drama: "In him seems to be no attempt to achieve selfhood, to behave in a way befitting a preconceived self-image. Rather, he becomes easily what each situation demands, whether it be a magus, a loving father, a stage manager, or an actor begging for applause" (115). This "open form dramaturgy encourages concentration on story rather than on character." The "details of motivation . . . are tertiary" (117). Mowat explains the difficulties in examining Prospero's character. It is not there to be examined. Hers is a useful corrective to an overemphasis on character. She also may help an actor looking for a "through line" by showing that the "through line" is Prospero's assumption of several roles according to the shifting dictates of the script.

William Slights points out that the "intensely self-conscious narrativity"—the Jamesian quality—of the late plays "helps correct the too common notion that Shakespeare's modes of representation are dated, stagy, and unbelievable. . . . Shakespeare's plays, particularly the late ones," ask, "Can we really trust the teller *or* the tale anymore?" (103). Modern fictional techniques applied to the late plays suggest that they are exercises in point of view, selective memory, self-serving recollection, control of narrative, and the like, so that the "story" becomes a reflection of the teller, a product of narrative stance and bias. Or, to put it in the terms Slights provides from Patricia Waugh, "*Metafiction* is a term given to fictional writing which self-consciously draws attention to its status as an artefact in order to pose questions about the relationship between fiction and reality" (104).

Richard Hillman argues that *The Tempest* is, among other things, an interrogation of its own generic premises (1985–86, 141–60). Barbara Bono says that "Shakespeare's final plays are as much tragicomedies as romances" (1984, 149). Romances "share . . . young lovers, pastoral interludes, and disguises and regeneration, based on an underlying delight in the marvelous. *Tragicomedy* . . . is a more specific structural and generic term, implying that the premises of tragedy are fully present, and then deliberately reversed." Of romances, she says, "Their material is remote and improbable; there are many supernatural elements; and, while being in a predominantly tragic vein, they all have a happy ending" (149 n. 11). Michael Mooney argues that Shakespeare "enlist[s] . . . previous themes and conventions . . . in the service of a vision that moves beyond tragedy and loss to renewal and reconciliation" (1992, 49). The play deals with "what occurs after tragedy" (52), making it a tragicomedy, a *Hamlet* or a *King Lear* with the different ending, like *Wuthering Heights* in the next generation. The play eschews revenge and permits reconciliation.

Robert Egan constructs a potential tragedy along Aristotelian lines in which the hero must make a decision "which tips the scales for or against [him] in terms of the future action," as Fredson Bowers argues (1955, 742). Egan argues that as Prospero releases his hounds—"Fury" and "Tyrant"—on Caliban, Stephano, and Trinculo, he "threatens to become a satanic personification of revenge. Tragic chaos impends" (1972, 180). This makes the play very dramatic and gives the actor playing Prospero a useful subtext: "I am constantly fighting against my impulse toward absolute revenge." It makes the play potentially a tragedy of damnation, as the fourteenth-century Dominican Nicholas Trivet explains: "Although he recedes . . . from the order of the divine will in one way, he nevertheless falls into the order of the divine will in another; for in leaving the order of mercy, he falls into the order of justice" (qtd. in Robertson 1962, 26). Any decision against revenge, of course, makes the play a tragicomedy. Prospero must reverse the tragic decision—Hamlet to interrupt his play, Macbeth to murder Duncan—and thus avoid the "central and potentially tragic flaw. . . . He has . . . confused his role as an artist with that of a god, forgetting his humanity in the process" (Egan 1972, 177).

Having released his spirit-dogs, Prospero permits the reversal process to continue: "Let them be hunted soundly," he says, and withdraws, probably for an intermission, because he enters in the next scene in his magic robes and asks for a report from Ariel. Egan, however, argues that "Ariel checks the momentum of Prospero's passion by charging him with the central moral obligation he has hitherto ignored in his artistry" (180). Prospero's "elves of hills" speech "marks the point at which his art truly begins to function effectively," says Egan (181). "Prospero's conversion has all the theatrical force of the reversal of fortune and sudden recognition on the protagonist which Aristotle saw as basic to the functioning of tragic catharsis," says David Hirst (1984a, 37). Aristotle called that recognition *anagnorisis*.

The "specific tragic plot in the play," Tillyard says, is "the fall of Prospero" (1938, in Barnet 1987, 156). The "plot is entirely typical of Elizabethan revenge tragedy" (155). Tillyard implicitly cites *Hamlet*: "Allow Prospero to be put to death, give him a son instead of a daughter to live and to avenge him, and your tragic plot is complete" (155)—but this plot does not require the next generation or a reconfiguring of its gender. It is there.

In placing Prospero among the protagonists of the subgenre known as the "tragedy of revenge," Harry Keyishian says that Prospero achieves "personal restoration, public vindication, and justice" (1995, 162). We "enter imaginatively and straightforwardly into a pleasurable, vicarious vengeance, keyed very specifically to Prospero's wrongs and his personal feelings of injury" (163). He "uses [his power] to humiliate and expose those who have injured him" (164), applying what Kay Stockholder calls "punitive therapy" (1992, 164). "It is essential to Prospero's project that his enemies know the cause and source of their present troubles and feel the utmost guilt and remorse" (164).

The play does pursue a revenge pattern: a wronged person gains control over his enemies (through disguise or through a stratagem with which the evil person or people cooperate, or both) and then takes his revenge—or does not (as in *The Malcontent* or *Measure for Measure*). Whether Prospero intends merely to punish his enemies from the beginning of the play, or whether he has already decided to forgive them, is an issue I will examine under "Character."

Prospero's Wedding Masque raises specific generic questions. Writing of the Masque, Kristiaan P. Aercke suggests that it partakes of the ornate, ornamented, highly embellished characteristics of the baroque: "Prospero knows that the finale of a baroque spectacle often implies the destruction of the stage (the site of the illusion), as scenic action, fire, or water devours the scenic milieu. . . . Do the vanishing banquet (3.3) and the interrupted masque (4.1) provide encapsulated examples of this convention?" (1992, 147). They might, as might the opening scene. "Baroque plays . . . often sustain a certain openness or 'unclarity' in the movement of their design and content [and] unresolved questions" (149). "Since Ariel deceives sight and hearing, one does not know whether to trust one's eyes and ears" (150). "Is such art . . . merely useful to obliterate time?" Theseus, after all, asks, "what masques, what dances shall we have / To wear away this long age of three hours / Between our after-supper and bed-time? . . . / What revels are in hand? Is there no play / To ease the anguish of a torturing hour?" (5.1.32–37).

Prospero's Masque breaks up without a customary antimasque, in which lower-class characters, not the nobles who had acted in a typical masque, would carry on a parody, sometimes bawdy, of the serious themes of the masque. Bryan Loughrey and Neil Taylor suggest that "the buffoons, dressed in stolen fineries and chased by spirit dogs . . . provide the Jonsonian antimasque" (1982, 116). It is appropriate that this portion of the play, if it is an antimasque, feature low-born characters. Another possibility is that Shakespeare incorporates the antimasque within the baroque design of his Masque. Venus and Cupid threaten the young lovers with an attack of concupiscence, but are diverted. They represent "lawless passion, [but are] excluded from the natural force celebrated in the masque," says Robert Langbaum (1987, xiii). Barbara Bono adds, "Wanton Venus is dismissed while majestic Juno blesses the union" (1984, 223).

One of the "Bermuda Pamphlets," *True Declaration of the State of the Colonie in Virginia*, places the deliverance of the *Sea-Adventure* and its passengers and crew into a generic category: "What is there in all this tragicall Comaedie that should discourage us with the impossibilitie of the enterprise?" (11). Clearly, the advent of the tragicomedy gave the colonists a category into which to place their narrative. "Though the seas threaten, they are merciful" (5.1.179).

LINGUISTIC CRITICISM

Samuel Johnson credits Shakespeare with making English available in special ways to later poets: "To him we must ascribe the praise, unless *Spenser* may divide it with him, of having first discovered to how much smoothness and harmony the *English* language could be softened" (1951, 512). Spenser deserves the division of praise, since we can trace from him the line of development to Keats, Hopkins, and Thomas.

Emile Benveniste overstates the case when he says that "nothing can be understood . . . that has not been reduced to language. It follows that language is necessarily the right instrument for describing, conceptualizing, interpreting nature [and] the union of nature and experience that is called society. It is thanks to this transmuting experience into signs and of ordering things into categories that language can take as its object any order of givens, including its own nature" (1974, 97). Things can be "understood" as "there" even if they cannot be reduced to language. "Poetry is what evaporates from all translations," as Frost once said. To poetry could be added dreams and *The Tempest*. It can be argued that Shakespeare explores the "nature" of language early on, in *Love's Labour's Lost*. In *The Tempest*, he approaches, and perhaps goes beyond, the activities of describing, conceptualizing, and interpreting, giving us, in language, a sensation like that of dream. That is not to reduce, but to expand the possibilities of language. It is also to defeat our own efforts to accomplish the activities Benveniste outlines as we attempt to articulate the play. In many ways, *The Tempest* is like the "excellent dumb discourse" (3.3.38) of which Gonzalo speaks.

T. S. Eliot accurately describes how a poem comes into being. It begins with an "image," and since we experience images constantly, with "a feeling attached to an image . . . probably in suspension in the poet's mind until the proper combination arrived for it to add itself to" (qtd. in Schofield 1991, 122). That "combination" is a fusion of "objective correlatives"—images that carry an emotional or imaginative equivalent—into a poem. Eliot claims that "it was right and inevitable that Shakespeare in his last plays should proceed into regions into which the audience cannot follow him" (129). We follow Shakespeare in our own way, aware that our way is partial and that some melodies are unheard. As Stanley Wells says of the play, "The enchanted island reverberates with sounds hinting at tunes that never appear fully formed" (1966, 75).

We experience in the play the results of Caliban's recent acquisition of language. He has grown skillful in making distinctions: fresh springs, barren place and fertile, bigger and less, great'st and least. He has learned one of the first concepts of the child: "mine." Language may be innate, as Chomsky argues against Skinner, but the politics of possession would seem to develop during the earliest periods of language acquisition.

According to Anne Righter Barton, Shakespeare's language in the last plays serves "to distinguish the fictional from the 'real,' art from life, tales from truth. [It comes] in the Romances to replace the older, moral concern with identifying hypocrisy and deceit" (1980, 147)—and, one might add, to "educate" persons about the limits of language and the point at which something else must take its place.

For Barton, the play's language "seems to be driving towards some ultimate reduction of language, a mode of expression more meaningful in its very bareness than anything a more elaborate and conventional rhetoric could devise" (1968, 13). This condensation—it is the "pressure" on language that good poetry inevitably asserts—suggests that the play is "much bigger than it is" (14). Shakespeare is using language suggestively, of course, sending off several signals at once, sometimes in seeming conflict with each other. Shakespeare combines words to suggest new phrasings of imagination, but also goes back to old ways, so that the old and new fuse in our ears. In fact, he consistently employs the oldest method of English word formation, the Anglo-Saxon self-explaining compound (Baugh 1957, 75–76; Pyles 1964, 276–84). He has done this earlier, of course, but Barton points out the prevalence of the formulation in this play. Perhaps these combined words are inspired by the happily delivered ship, *Sea-Adventure*: sea-sorrow, thunder-claps, still-vex'd, brine-pits, Hag-seed, sea-change, fresh-brook, thunder-stroke, sea-swallow'd, urchin-shows, log-man, servant-monster, Moon-calf, fellow-ministers, heart-sorrow, virgin-knot, broom-groves, sea-marge, filthy-mantled, horse-piss, foot-licker, line-grove, weather-fends, spell-stopp'd, bully-monster, and so on. Not all of these are noun-noun combinations, of course, and no pattern of imagery seems to link them together, although one notices that several signify the sea and the power of storm and that several apply to that new thing, Caliban. Occasionally, a noun-verb combination compresses a sense of the action by combining act and actor.

Stanton B. Garner, Jr., argues that the play searches "for a way to make language an acceptable basis for social order" (1979, 177). "Language occupies only a middle ground in the range of sounds in this remote world. Above it hovers the enchantment of music for which Ariel serves as symbolic manifestation. Below it spreads the haunting and disturbing sub-stratum of the inarticulate—the 'hisses,' 'howls,' and 'roars' of Caliban's world" (177). Antonio and Sebastian are "sophists" (179)—those who use rhetoric for personal goals or for power divorced from principle, as exposed in Plato's *Gorgias*. Garner condemns the "anarchic misuse of words" in which Antonio and Caliban indulge (186). Antonio's "silence [at the end] is the most disturbing bit of language in the play," he says, because while unvoiced, Antonio's continued malevolence is communicated (186).

Jan Kott calls *The Tempest* "fugue like" (1987, 97), suggesting its counterpointed quality. F. E. Halliday says of Prospero's "elves of hills" speech that "the full beauty of a phrase is dependent on the passage as a whole, for each phrase is only a part of the Shakespearean counterpoint" (1954, 186–87). Russ McDonald says that "the tendency of words and phrases to repeat themselves may be linked to the play's profound concern with reproduction" (1991, 17). That strikes me as doubtful, since many of the plays have repeating words and phrases and many of the repetitions in *The Tempest* have nothing to do with reproduction.

Francis Berry notices that "Prospero's [opening] narrative is so charged with energy, not so much because of the frequency of verbs but because of the changes of tense that the verbs undergo" (1965, 161). From "a firm placing in the 'dark-backward,' " the verbs move to the present. "He *thinks* me now incapable. *Confederates*" (161, Berry's emphasis). The narrative is linked to the present with the present: "The very minute bids thee ope thine ear." Time in Prospero's narrative "gradually closes up on the audience until it mingles with, even supersedes, the stage picture physically exposed to them" (161). The verbs are pressing Miranda and Prospero into that present on which any future depends.

G. Wilson Knight offers an amusing echo of empire in his commentary on the names Prospero gives to his spirit-hounds: "The use of such names as 'Tyrant' and 'Fury' does not lower the animals' status, since the implied humanizing serves as an idealization; as with battleships, where the names H.M.S. *Furious* or H.M.S. *Venemous*, by attributing living status to a machine, witness a respect not usually offered to ill-temper and snakes" (qtd. in Palmer 1968, 152 n. 4). Like the unleashed dogs, sixteen-inch guns only seem angry or destructive.

PSYCHOLOGICAL CRITICISM

The psychological approach to the play concentrates on Prospero and, secondarily, on "family dynamics," both within and outside of Prospero. This approach inevitably slides toward the category of "character."

A useful response to the play via Freud's essay "Family Romances" is Gary Waller's: "Freud's concept of the family romance focuses on crucial, perhaps permanent, parts of our individual and collective lives" (1992, 57)—what Jung calls archetypes. "Students are aware, perhaps uncomfortably, of our century's major revaluations of how we understand ourselves as gendered beings" (58). Without "the struggle for differentiation between children and parents . . . there can be no viable self-identity, no later close and meaningful relations with others, no fulfilling sexual identity" (58). "The continued fascination of the late plays is, I suspect, based on the ways they elicit our most primal experiences" (62). "The utterances and conflicts of all the late plays present aspects of the family romance as we enact them today . . . generational tension . . . family ties and the need to break away from them, the delusions of omnipotence and fears of abandonment that we experience as children and project on our adult relationships" (61). "Such preoccupations [may] explain the remarkable popularity of the late plays in this century" (62).

Aware that he will be accused of being "essentialist" (which is as bad as being "nonhistorical"), Waller issues a disclaimer: "We call the romances 'great' not because they are somehow 'universal,' above the material or psychological details of our personal and collective histories, but because they are deeply embedded in those histories and have consequently been read in intriguingly different ways" (62–63). Precisely so. They are embedded in individual psyches, and the archetypes manifest themselves there in different ways, so that we can "individuate" and not merely replicate a stereotypic human experience. The kingdom of God is within, but, like Prospero's island, its temples and palaces, its brine-pits and freshlets, are illuminated in different ways by the lights and insights of different people.

In an often-persuasive analysis, Bernard J. Paris draws on the theories of Karen Horney and begins with the premise that *The Tempest* is, "more than any other play, a fantasy of Shakespeare's." He asks, "What . . . is it a fantasy of? What psychological needs are being met, what wishes being fulfilled?" (1989, 210). "Through his withdrawal into the study of magic, Prospero is pursuing a dream of glory far more grandiose than any available to him as Duke of Milan" (211)—but of course he does not think so. He "interprets his withdrawal as a commendable unworldliness and presents his behavior toward his brother in a way that is flattering to himself. . . . He seems to have no sense of how his own foolish behavior has contributed to his fate" (211). Horney's analysis operates on the simple model of a conscious/unconscious dichotomy, basically Freud's theory of repression. Jung might suggest that Prospero inevitably created a shadow figure in Antonio, an alter ego made up of precisely the elements Prospero rejected. This personality does represent an awakened "evil nature" that must be recognized and acknowledged. Caliban will be Prospero's shadow on the island. "Antonio's betrayal marks the failure of Prospero's self-effacing bargain," says Paris (212). "Prospero . . . craves a revenge that will assuage his anger and repair his idealized image . . . taking revenge and remaining innocent" (212). The "vindictive side of Prospero is embodied in the storm, his self-effacing side . . . in Miranda" (212). Ariel "has threatened his idealized image by making him seem unkind. . . . Prospero discharges onto [Caliban] all of the anger he feels toward the enemies back home" (215).

As in much psychological criticism, Prospero serves the plot and genre set forth by a particular theorist. The question is, how much of his character and how many of his actions fit the thesis? Paris suggests that Prospero puts Caliban in the classic "double-bind." Prospero treats Caliban as "subhuman, but he holds him morally responsible for his [attempted rape] and punishes him severely" (215). "Caliban provides Prospero with a splendid opportunity for justified aggression, for being vindictive without losing his nobility" (216). Prospero is involved in a complex negotiation between will and persona. "He could have used his magic more benignly if he had regarded Caliban as part of his moral community, but this would have . . . deprived him of his scapegoat" (217). One might suggest that early on, Prospero did regard Caliban as part of his community. "While he makes it seem that his only purpose has been to bring the men of sin to penitence, that is hardly the case. This is a play not only about renouncing revenge but also about getting it" (219).

The Christian approach, however, would suggest that damnation for the conspirators would be a consequence of Prospero's failure with them—and could still be. "Antonio's undeservingness contributes to Prospero's sense of moral grandeur" (219). But the way he deals with the "brace of lords" (or captured game) suggests that he knows otherwise. He is playing the game of realpolitik, not moral grandeur. It is not "inappropriate to the practical and moral realities of the situation" (220). It is, instead, craftily qualified, tailored to them. "He needs to see himself as a humane, benevolent, forgiving man, and also as a powerful, masterful, dangerous man who cannot be taken advantage of with impunity" (220). This apparent discrepancy is dictated by responses he gets, is it not? "Once he abandons his magic, he has no choice but to repress his arrogant-vindictive trends, for it was only through his magic that he was able to act them out innocently" (220). He seems to say otherwise: that danger, not innocence, lay in his role as magus. When he does abandon magic, his self-effacing tendencies do come through. As a person, he has a chance to recognize his shadow. As a person, he has a chance to recognize compassion in others. Often we respond not to an event but to others' response to it, as in Fielding's Partridge in *Tom Jones*, frightened because Garrick imitates fear so convincingly in his encounter with the Ghost in *Hamlet*.

Paris sees almost everything Prospero does as self-serving. "He gives up his magic because he needs to place himself in a humble position and to show that he has not used his power for personal aggrandizement but only to set things right, to bring about moral growth and reconciliation" (221). If he has done the latter, however, his magic has fulfilled the purposes he assigned to it. When does "a self-effacing response to his power" (221) become self-effacement, as opposed to a conscious and self-serving pose? It is as if demonstration and getting credit—even within himself—are more important than the results he has attained. At the end, "Prospero sees himself . . . not as the avenger but as the guilty party" (221), that is, as a human being, as one who has forgiven and now asks for the reciprocity from a kind of god for that action. "By forgiving others, he insures his own pardon. Giving up his magic serves a similar purpose: it counteracts his feelings of pride and places him in a submissive, dependent position" (221). He fulfills Christ's instructions on prayer. Prospero at least resolves a conflict in persona, that element of the personal unconscious with which Horney deals. In another sense, he seeks a deeper archetype. He acknowledges Caliban, his shadow, and the destructive aspects of the "maternal" embodied in his psychic alter ego, Sycorax. This is progress—individuation—not merely the self-justifying stance Paris attributes to Prospero. "The rhetoric of the play justifies the vindictive Prospero and glorifies the self-effacing one" (222). "In *The Tempest*, through Prospero's magic, he imagines a solution to Hamlet's problem" (223), as Hamlet himself did in planning "Gonzago."

Paris suggests that the play represents a psychological negotiation for Prospero (and for Shakespeare): "The fantasy is Shakespeare's, whose conflicting needs resemble those of his protagonist" (212). But what of the problem of evil, what of the issue of the unrepentant man? Prospero does not solve these problems, nor does he claim to do so, nor does the play. The problem with the resolution of issues that reside only in the ego, which is the outer zone of the structure of the psyche, is that such solutions only expand the edges of consciousness as it contacts an external world. They do not contact and energize deeper resources that, in turn, reinforce and encourage the education of consciousness.

It follows that Prospero "does not at the end seem to have attained psychological balance or to have discovered a viable way of living in the real world" (223–24). He "feels guilty with power, he feels helpless without it, as the Epilogue indicates" (224). When only the ego is accounted for, the psychological process becomes an endless series of repressions: "Like Prospero at the end of *The Tempest*, Shakespeare at the end of his career seems to have resolved his inner conflicts by repressing his aggressive impulses and becoming extremely self-effacing" (224–25). "At the end of *The Tempest* Shakespeare seems back where he started in the plays about Henry VI, with a nobly Christian ruler who cannot cope with the harsh realities of life" (224). That summation strikes me as nowhere near the truth. Prospero has taken on "the harsh realities" within himself and within his political sphere and can hardly be viewed as sitting on a molehill while others fight his battle for him.

Stephen Orgel discerns a very different result in a play that "has an obvious psychoanalytic shape" (1984, in Bloom 1988, 100). Orgel builds on the insights of Joel Fineman, who sees fratricidal rivalry as a recapitulation of the original differentiation from the mother and an essential preliminary to the Oedipal stage (1977, 409–53). Orgel suggests that "recent psychoanalytic theory has replaced Freud's central Oedipal myth with a drama in which the loss of the seducing mother is the crucial infant drama" (1984, in Bloom 1988, 101). Prospero "has been banished by his wicked, usurping, possibly illegitimate younger brother Antonio. This too has the shape of a Freudian fantasy: the younger brother *is* the usurper in the family, and the kingdom he usurps is the mother. On the island, Prospero undoes the usurpation, re-creating kingdom and family with himself in sole command" (103). Prospero's ostensible actions accord with a psychological subtext. His "giving away Miranda is a means of preserving his authority, not of relinquishing it" (112), because the marriage of Miranda to Ferdinand "exclud[es] Antonio from any future claim on the ducal throne" (111). Milan is reduced again to "a Neapolitan fiefdom" (111), but at Antonio's expense. Prospero's "grave is the ultimate triumph over his brother" (111). In a variation of this narrative, Karl M. Abenheimer suggests that Antonio became a surrogate parent, assuming control of the household before tossing Prospero out (1946, 399–415).

Coppelia Kahn suggests that revenge for Prospero would be merely a recapitulation of the past. He would "become mired . . . in a cycle of successive revenges" (1980, 240). He "breaks out of repetition, out of the revenge cycle, and out of his oedipal past" (240). "But he also fails to recreate in any mature

sexual relationship the lifegiving love experience first known with his mother"
(240). "The cost of [Prospero's] achievement . . . is sexual and social isolation. . . .
The Shakespearean family romance [as exemplified by *The Tempest*] remains
closer to the imperfect realities we live with than to the wishes we cherish"
(242).

According to Kay Stockholder, Prospero lives out a fantasy of sublimated
passion: He "has transformed his sexual desire into the magic by which he
restrains desire. His ideal is symbolized by, and made conditional on, the perfect
subordination of a pure woman to a man in whom lust has been supplanted by
affectionate appreciation of feminine spiritual radiance" (1992, 167). That radiance is something that Ferdinand seems to discern immediately, though he
does ask about purity.

William C. Watterson makes a compelling Freudian case for Prospero's rivalry with Ferdinand. Watterson sees "Ariel [as] the white horse of benign Eros
from Plato's chariot metaphor" and "Caliban [as] the black horse of primal
unchecked desire inimical to transcendence and a soul at peace" (forthcoming).
The Tempest is "a psycho-sexual drama of displaced patriarchal desire. [T]he
sadism born of homosexual repression . . . best explains Prospero's compulsion
to dominate." In the play, "sexual deviation [is] equated with the demonic."
Prospero has been "emasculated by his brother, Antonio," so "Ferdinand with
sword poised in mid-air is a dramatic icon of emasculated youth overmastered
by the Oedipal patriarch." "Ferdinand draws his sword against the patriarch only
to be disarmed . . . with a stick. Prospero then makes the young man's 'weapon
drop.' Posing as a fatherly discipline . . . Prospero's Oedipal aggression trans-
forms his not-too-patient 'log man' into a whipping boy calculated to enhance
Prospero's vulnerable self-image as deposed sovereign." "Prospero's injunction
against Ferdinand's premature breaking of his daughter's 'virgin knot' reflects
his fixation with phallic power." As Stockholder says, "Signs that Prospero's
sexual drives are neither extinct nor quiescent appear implicitly in his impris-
onment and humiliation of even the virtuous Ferdinand [and] the pinches with
which he torments Caliban" (1992, 165).

According to David Sundelson, Prospero achieves Lear's fantasy: "The departure from Milan is an escape from shame and weakness as much as an expulsion. . . . their exile is an ordeal to be endured, but in more important ways
it is a delicious idyll on an island which . . . unites them 'like birds i' th' cage' "
(1983, 36). The differences, of course, are manifold. Lear's speech as he and
Cordelia go off to prison ignores the terrible danger that he and his daughter
face. In erasing all political agendas, Lear makes a second huge "error in judgment." Prospero's political agenda—including his plan to have Miranda and
Ferdinand fall in love—is clear early in the play. His reluctance to surrender
Miranda may be signalled by his treatment of Ferdinand, of course, rationalized
into making the prize worth working for.

For Paul Brown, Prospero "demonstrates the crucial nexus of civil power and
sexuality in colonial discourse" (1985, 62–63). As Freud would have it, "Dream-

work [is a] contest between censorship and a latent drive" (66). Caliban's dream shows "a site beyond colonial appropriation [that] can only be represented through colonialist discourse . . . since Caliban's eloquence is after all 'your language' " (66). In that the dream is "free," not a response controlled by a fear of Prospero's pinching goblins of the night, it is beyond "colonialist discourse." But since that discourse is all Caliban has learned, the dream must be of the "riches" for which the colonist wishes. It is Prospero's dream, Brown suggests. The play does not show, however, that Prospero's wishes are those of the stereotypic colonizer. The play's visions and narratives "encode struggle and contradiction even as they, or *because* they, strive to insist on the legitimacy of colonialist narrative" (66). If a Freudian censor is at work—the superego invented because of repressive Viennese society or by Prospero's fears for Miranda's chastity—what do we make of Caliban's dream of riches? This would seem to be "direct discourse." What is being censored? What is being censored in Juno's "riches" (4.1.105) in the Masque? One assumes that Ceres' "foison plenty" (4.1.110) translates to illicit and rampant sexuality, in defiance of the ostensible content of the Masque. Everything in the play is saturated with the colonialist discourse.

Meredith Anne Skura, in her attack on the colonialist approach, develops a psychological counterargument against the thesis that "the emphasis now is on psychology as a product of culture" (1989, 46). The culture is to be blamed for individual lapses from the norm. This approach "eliminates what is characteristically 'Shakespearean' . . . to foreground what is 'colonialist' " (47). Caliban becomes "a walking screen for projection" (60). His sin becomes "Prospero's own repressed fantasies of omnipotence and lust" (60). "Shakespeare is dealing not just with power relations but also with the psychology of domination, with the complicated ways in which personal psychology interacts with political power" (61). Prospero does not manifest "a specifically colonialist strategy" but an "infantile need to control and dominate" (63). "Prospero treats Caliban as he would treat the willful child in himself" (65). Prospero "comes closer than anyone else in colonialist discourse . . . to acknowledging the otherness within" (66).

Kay Stockholder suggests that the play is an allegory of the struggle of good and evil, a conflict on which the future depends: "Only Prospero's commanding magic can protect the generative potency of a virtuous couple, necessary for a fertile kingdom, [from] the bad magic of [Sycorax's] opposing kingdom" (1992, 164). The island, according to Orgel, is "a space that is filled, for Prospero, with surrogates and a ghostly family: the witch Sycorax and her monster child Caliban, who is so often and so disturbingly like the other wicked child, the usurping younger brother, Antonio" (1987, 18). Jonathan Bate says that Sycorax "is his dark Other" and that "the darkness of Caliban is an inescapable part of Prospero" (1993, in Vaughan and Vaughan 1998, 51). Harry Berger, Jr., says that "Caliban is a platonist's black dream" (1969, 261). Prospero's acknowledgment of "this thing of darkness," Caliban, means only, according to Lorie Leininger, "It is as though, after a public disturbance, a slaveowner said, 'Those two men are yours, this darkie's mine' " (1980a, 127). Stephen Greenblatt, however, glimpses another dimension: "The words need only be a claim of ownership, but they seem to hint at a deeper, more disturbing link between father and monster, legitimate ruler and savage, judge and criminal . . . as Prospero leaves the island, it is he who begs for pardon" (1997, 3053).

Stockholder argues that Prospero suffers "the loneliness and burden of authority while resisting the enticement to misuse it in the service of self-interest" (1992, 162). His "most powerful antagonist [is] Sycorax" (162). His "magic derives from, and is composed of, both the good and evil powers of female figures" (163). The cruelty "of Sycorax and her forebears [and] their power to cast the spells that make others subject to them and to shape events that constitute reality for them" lives on (163). The island exists under her shadow, and Prospero will reinvoke her when he chooses to: "Hast thou forgot / The foul witch Sycorax?" (1.2.257–58). Balancing that darkness, however, "he aligns his magic with a cosmos that manifests its compassion in the winds and seas" (164). He experiences a struggle between two *anima* figures: the good witch Nature and the evil Sycorax.

It is obvious, as Karen Flagstad says, that "the ambitious endeavor of Prospero engenders its own antithesis, its own ultimate contradiction" (1986, 214). The contest of "quasi-deity versus 'beast' " (214) creates a Jungian shadow, a "dark counterpart of that Art which Prospero puts to such idealized purposes" (215). The Jungian approach might argue that the enlightened and educated man doing "the right thing" is bound to develop a personality that is brutishly devoted to doing the wrong thing. To deny a repressed desire for Miranda is to make it part of that dark persona—the Shadow, Caliban, sexual urges, irrational rage, and so on. If Prospero can bring those qualities to consciousness, they become an energy he can use. He can also empower other forces—compassion, for example, which can reinforce rationality at a level deeper than mere thought. Consciousness is forever manufacturing its shadows, which are always of the same gender as the dreamer. For Prospero, they are Antonio, then Caliban. Sycorax, the mother figure who must be propitiated, is a negative-anima, a threatening woman who is also acknowledged when Caliban is claimed by Prospero as "mine." As Orgel says, "The battle between Prospero and Sycorax is Prospero's battle with himself, and by the play's end he has accepted the witch's monstrous offspring as his own" (1987, 23).

The Jungian approach reaches beyond the play:

We watch as [Prospero] comes to experience at some level deeper than the rational what his mind has already worked out. The question for us, of course, is—has our experience of Prospero been more than merely observation? If we have merely observed, then we have not moved with Prospero from the rational to the feeling level. That would mean not that the play has failed us, but that we have failed the play. (Coursen 1986, 188)

The psychological approach, as conducted along Freudian lines, tends to ignore any "spiritual" content in the play, as we are reminded by David Horowitz:

"Compassion is a self-preserving force. It is putting oneself in the place of others, seeing oneself as one of their infirmity and imagining their sufferings as possible to oneself; it is the recognition of an essential humanity, despite all apparent differences, in which one shares" (1965, 82).

CHARACTER

Prospero

The issue of Prospero is basic to any discussion of *The Tempest*. His relationship to his magic, his attitude toward revenge, and the limitations of his power deserve specific discussion.

Orgel suggests the spectrum within which Prospero is placed: "a noble ruler and mage, a tyrant and megalomaniac, a necromancer, a Neoplatonic scientist, a colonial imperialist, a civilizer" (1987, 11). Sidney Homan says that for some, "Prospero is a powerful white magician, the consummate artist; for others he seems a puritanical, 'nasty' old man—an evangelist obsessed with a harsh moral code of which even he, not less than the island intruders, falls short" (1973, 69). Is he "distant, removed from the immediate concerns and lives of the audience. Or . . . as relevant to the human condition as anything Shakespeare had previously written" (70), an "artist . . . charlatan or . . . semidivine agent" (70 n. 5)?

Only a rare critic denies Prospero's power. John Andrews sees Toto pulling at the Wizard of Oz's curtain: "For all his magisterial aura, the wizard who orchestrates *The Tempest*'s culminating 'Pageant' is a self-confessed fraud: the vulnerable if ostensibly omnipotent human being beneath the persona of a domestic and political patriarch, the insecure, if stern principal of a 'Vanity' that repeatedly directs our attention to the nervous ventriloquist on the far side of the rear stage curtain" (1994, xvii). That opinion runs counter to that of John Middleton Murry, who says that the island has become the Utopia of the anarchists. It might be, were Murry's ideal person, Prospero, the "average citizen." The island "is what it would be if Humanity—the best in man—controlled the life of man. Prospero is a man in whom the best in man has won the victory" (1936, 322).

It is easy to see Prospero in the image of the "well-meaning liberal" suddenly surprised by the savagery of the right-wing response. Francesco Guicciardini, whose *History of Italy* was translated into English in 1578, is described as one "whose vertues were farre from all suspicion of parcialitie, favour, hatred, love, reward, or any other propertie of human affection which might have force to corrupt, or turne from the truth the minds of a writer" (Geffray Fenton's Dedicatory Epistle, qtd. in Haydn 1950, 226). That objectivity permitted Guicciardini to describe the discrepancy between men as they should be and men as they are. Prospero says that he "Awak'd an evil nature" (1.2.93) in Antonio. He certainly awakened Antonio's desire for more power than a deputy enjoys, but

Prospero is probably naïve to think that Antonio had been "virtuous" before he was deputized. In describing Hamlet, Claudius tells us who Prospero might have been before: Hamlet, says Claudius to Laertes, "being remiss, / Most generous, and free from all contriving, / Will not peruse the foils" (*Hamlet* 4.7.134–36). Prospero almost repeats Hamlet's and his own previous error of negligence with Caliban during the play.

To equate Prospero's renunciation of his magic with Shakespeare's abandonment of his writing of plays is to narrow *The Tempest* to a merely autobiographical dimension. To see Frost as the "cracker-barrel philosopher" he pretended to be at the end may make the man better than he was, but it certainly demeans the combination of bleakness and lyricism that inhabits his poetic line. The autobiographical obsession robs us of the detachment we need to respond to a work of art as art.

Those who emphasize Prospero's renunciation of his magic as the crux of his character provide what Harry Berger, Jr., calls the "sentimental reading" (1969, 254) as opposed to Berger's more "hard-nosed view" (279 n. 3). I find myself a sentimentalist.

Barbara Howard Traister, for example, sees Prospero positively: "The only unusual features of Prospero as dramatic magician are the success of his magic and his total domination of the play" (1984, in Bloom 1988, 113). At the end, the "lovers are real; magic has been abandoned," she says (118). The "future [is] to be shaped by them . . . without the assistance of magic" (118). Magic has done what it can, has even conditioned Alonso to expect it—"some enchanted trifle"—before he makes a transition back to the reality of "flesh and blood." We can be confused in a dream about whether it is real or not. Is it that easy in consciousness? Traister says that "we must recognize his [Prospero's] abjuration as a vital part of his overall plan" (119). His "magic," says Northrop Frye, "is an identification with nature . . . and is expressed only if he follows the rhythm of time" (qtd. in Traister, in Bloom 1988, 121).

Kenneth Muir claims that "when he has his enemies in his power Prospero has to overcome again the natural desire towards vengeance" (1961, 152). My own view is that the play suggests that Prospero has thought forgiveness all along. It is only much later that he feels what he means (Coursen 1968, 1986). If he represents what M. C. Bradbrook calls "a sublimated master of the revels" (qtd. in Traister, in Bloom 1988, 115), then he has thought the issue out and made his decision. Sublimation is the only defense mechanism that works. That he is still angry means that his sublimation retains some admixture of repression.

Miranda sets a mirror for magistrates before him right away: "Had I been any god of power, I would / Have sunk the sea within the earth, or 'ere / It should the good ship so have swallow'd, and / The fraughting souls within her" (1.2.10–14). In telling her that he intends "no harm . . . No harm" (1.2.15), he tells us that he has already acceded to her vision. Certainly Ariel's "So, King, go safely on to seek thy son" at the end of 2.1 does not signal any struggle within Prospero. That Alonso will suffer "heart-sorrow" is a punishment, and Prospero's awakening of Alonso's memory causes that grief. A "clear life ensuing," however, can result from the process. "At the end of the Harpy scene," says Barbara Mowat, "Prospero tells us that his enemies are now in his power but drops no hint about what he plans to do with them" (1976, 81). The text argues otherwise, but it is a matter of what the enemies do with themselves. Alonso repents. Antonio does not. Stanley Wells asks whether Prospero has "from the start . . . acted with the benevolent aim of bringing his enemies to a truer knowledge of themselves and then forgiving them, or [has] he acted with the intention rather of seeking a vengeance from which he is deflected only by surprised acknowledgement of Ariel's sympathy for them?" (1995, 367). Wells cites Michael Bryant's harshness as Prospero for Peter Hall in 1988 and says that Prospero's response to Ariel at the beginning of Act 5 ("my nobler reason . . . The rarer action [5.1.26–27]) "suggests meditation rather than crisis: Prospero is not an inverted Macbeth" (367). That strikes me as absolutely right.

Greenblatt says that "audiences in Shakespeare's time would have had an all too clear image of how horrendous the vengeance of enraged princes usually was. That Prospero restrains himself from the full exercise of his power to harm his enemies, that he breaks his magic staff and drowns his book, is his highest moral achievement, a triumphant display of self-mastery" (1997, 3049–50). Samuel Johnson says that Prospero "repents of his Art in the last scene" (1951, 531). Prospero's "renunciation of extraordinary powers and the return to the ordinary world" is "painful," says Orgel (1984, in Bloom 1988, 130), but that does not mean that he struggles against the decision. Curry may overstate the case for what Prospero gains when he says that in giving up his magic, Prospero's "soul is cleansed of his baser passions. [He] finds himself at the end of the play immeasurably nearer than before to the impassivity of the gods" (1937, 196). "In giving up his power, Prospero speaks as Medea," says Orgel. "[T]he distinction between black and white magic, Sycorax and Prospero, has disappeared" (1984, 110). It follows that Prospero recognizes that dangerous blurring of boundaries. Egan points out that " 'prospero' is the Italian word for 'faustus' " and suggests the fine, merely linguistic, line between them (1972, 175).

According to Bryan Loughrey and Neil Taylor, Ariel's show of feeling at the beginning of Act 5 "interrupts Prospero's 'project.' . . . [He] decides to abandon not only revenge but magic" (1982, 117). He does surrender his magic. Before that, however, his calm statement that "the rarer action is in / Virtue than in vengeance" (5.1.28) does not signal a decision, but a conclusion. Tillyard mentions, rightly, I think, Prospero's "already achieved regeneration from vengeance to mercy," though that "is put to the test" by Antonio (1938, 159). Tillyard is arguing against J. Dover Wilson's suggestion of "sudden conversion from a previously intended vengeance" (Tillyard, 158). In the play, Prospero announces his intention not to take revenge before he surrenders his magic. The two events are often conflated, however: "Prospero's own discovery of an ethic of forgiveness, and the renunciation of his magical power" (Doran 1964, 327). Hirst says that Prospero finds "the confrontation with his old enemies an experience very different from what he had planned" (1984a, 38). That is true, of course, but what had he planned? He has already confronted them via Ariel with an indictment, warning, and hope for the future. Nowhere has he planned a continued punishment. If the conspirators are unrepentant, "their inward pinches are therefor more strong," (5.1.77) but that is not something Prospero is doing to them. Croce's question "Will he punish?" (1920, 262) has already been answered. He has punished. They undergo what Stockholder calls "punitive therapy" (1992, 164). Punishment beyond these limits becomes self-punishment.

Early in the play, according to Egan, Prospero "cannot even cope with his memory" (1972, 176). An "acknowledgement of evil as part of the natural condition of man is unacceptable" to him (176). His acknowledgment of Caliban, then, and his recognition of his "wicked . . . brother" (5.1.130) signal one terminal point of his own education.

Interestingly, Prospero is sometimes blamed for the limits of his power, for his inability to regain the paradise his Wedding Masque briefly images. As with the temptation that Prospero places before Antonio and that Antonio then extends to Sebastian, Prospero cannot be held responsible for another's action or failure to act. He "can only provide an opportunity or occasion but not legislate or guarantee a result," as Arthur Kinney says (1992, 157). Orgel suggests that "Caliban represents a striking failure of Prospero's art" (1987, 23). Rose A. Zimbardo agrees: "What does . . . Prospero's art finally accomplish? . . . it had never been able to fix form on Caliban" (1963, 55). "Prospero's magic has not . . . been employed to bring about the reform of Antonio," says Orgel (1987, 51). But at what point—and all teachers have asked this question—is the "educator" no longer to blame? Kermode puts the answer succinctly: "A world without Antonio is a world without freedom" (1964, 1xii). "Prospero cannot," says Greenblatt, "reshape their inner lives and effect a moral transformation" (1997, 3050). Robert Egan expands on the point: "Antonio . . . remains ominously silent, but it is the very presence of his unreformed evil that underlines the triumphant order which has been achieved in its spite" (1972, 181). Robert G. Hunter says, "More than any other of Shakespeare's plays, *The Tempest* insists on the indestructibility of evil" (1965, 240–41). As Bacon says, "Though justice cannot extirpate vice, it keeps it under" (1904, 255). It would seem that Prospero has absorbed the lesson of Machiavelli's *Discorsi*: "Political society is not so much a part of virtue founded upon loyalty and service as a series of tensions between individuals and classes in which constraints interact with necessities to produce energetic achievement" (qtd. in Nigel Smith 1988, 96).

That is not all, however, that we take from the play, nor even its major meaning, assuming that we accept the way in which the Epilogue shifts meanings in a play full of shifting perceptions both within itself and in our perceptions of what is happening. At the very end, Egan argues, the audience is "invited to enter the play-world and assume a role, through their applause, as a moving force in its culmination" (1972, 173), to participate "in an act of prayer, which will bring down mercy and redemption on both the prayer and the prayed-for

. . . [a uniting] in a recognition, acceptance, and celebration of their shared humanity" (182). After the play, the audience returns to that last world the play holds up to us, that of the Epilogue, in a spiritual sense. Other worlds have existed in the construct of the play. Now, they have ended. Our own spiritual journey begins again, informed by our experience of the past two hours.

"Prospero's decision to forgive," says Douglas Peterson, "is exemplary, a utopian vision for governors in the world of the here and now to emulate" (1992, 144). The more cynical approach is that Prospero, like King James, pardons "for effect." No political decision has any heart in it, only a show of human compassion the better to demonstrate power. Prospero's tears for Gonzalo, however, are not calculated. They emerge from some zone deeper than politics. Egan says that "Prospero himself perceives [a] separation of his artistic function from his identity as a man . . . in putting off his garment . . . 'Lie there, my Art' " (1972, 173). His magic is not his essence, his body natural. Confusing them would be dangerous, Egan suggests. Prospero must "participate," says Egan, "in a cognate act of the love and recognition which are the essence of [his] art" (182). That should be rephrased, I think, to say "the essence of his humanity." Leo Marx says that "Prospero . . . learns compassion" (1967, 60). In a sense, compassion learns Prospero—it is larger, less voluntary than "education" in Prospero's sense of the word. It is a response from within, deeper than books or language. The lesson he would impose on others becomes his own.

I suggest that Prospero does not merely provide King James with congratulatory reinforcement for his political skills. He opens the channel between politics and the human heart that beats even in a king. Bacon talks of the limitations that humanity and godlike qualities place upon a king: "All precepts concerning kings are in effect comprehended in these two remembrances, 'Memento quod es homo,' and 'Memento quod es Deus,' or 'vice Dei'; the one bridleth their power, and the other their will" (1900, 94). King Lear learns the lesson, as does King Richard II. Prospero learns it sooner and in time to provide the muted "happy ending." According to James E. Phillips, "Prospero faces the choice of letting his passions or letting his reason direct and determine his action" (1964, 159). Prospero says that this is his choice at the beginning of Act 5, but in a tone that tells us it is already made. It is a conclusion, not an action imitated. Otherwise, passions would inevitably have controlled the decision. On the other hand, if "the reality of his compassion [has] yet to be tested," as Robert Wilson says (1988, 106), until Act 5, how can he be said to fail?

Germaine Greer says that "it is Prospero's tragedy that he must dote on Ariel, whom he must lose, and despise Caliban, the thing of darkness he is forced at the end of the play to acknowledge his" (1986, 30). While a production might depict Prospero's regret at parting from Ariel, that would not constitute tragedy, or if it is "tragic," it is so in that no human being can become a god. It is the tragedy of Adam and Eve. Theodore Spencer is more accurate, I think, to suggest what happens in the play: "Alonzo sinks *below* reason before returning to it; before Prospero returns to the rational human world, he has lived for a time *above* it. The important thing to notice is his return" (1961, 198). Clifford Leech, one of Harry Berger's "hard-nosed" critics (1969, 279 n. 3), warns, however, that Prospero may be merely a projection of a critic's unperceived megalomania: "the dream-figure of ourselves . . . able to chastise [and] to pardon" (qtd. in Hallett Smith 1969, 100).

Even with his last words, which are also the words of the actor, Burbage, hoping for applause, Prospero retains a sense of himself as artist. Michael Mooney says that "the play's determining dramatic technique [is a] pattern of projection and dissolution . . . found in each of *The Tempest*'s spectacles" (1992, 53). Even at the end, "bereft of his role, he still needs to dissolve the illusion," (56). He asks spectators to confirm the "truth" of the "illusion," in a sense, to agree to its sacramental component. As Hooker says of the elements of Communion, we ask not what the objects are but what we have by them. Final cause resides in the communicant or the spectator. Having commanded performances within his play and having responded to the aesthetics as well as to the results of his several productions, Prospero now turns to those who control him through their response to the entire work.

Caliban

Caliban is the product of "a witch and an incubus," says Kermode (1964, xl), following Dryden, while Curry confidently claims that Caliban's "father was an aquatic daemon" (1937, 184). He "was gendered between the earth and sea, in that part from which all life began," says Edith Sitwell, placing Caliban at that significant moment when the evolutionary process brought amphibians ashore (1961, 215). Shortly after Darwin's *On the Origin of Species* appeared in 1859, Dr. Daniel Wilson claimed Caliban for "the missing link, [an] intermediate being, between the true brute and man, which, if the new theory of descent from crudest animal organisms be true, was our predecessor and precursor in the inheritance of this world of humanity" (1873, in Furness 1892, 381).

Morton Luce says that "if all the suggestions as to Caliban's form and feature and endowments . . . are collected, it will be found that the one half renders the other half impossible" (1901, xxxv). "Perhaps Shakespeare himself had no settled ideas concerning the form of *Caliban*," says the preface to the Stevens edition of the plays in 1793 (158). If so, Caliban is an extreme example of what keeps the plays alive: the script's providing options for directors and actors that mean that the production is limited only by the imaginations of its practitioners. B. Ifor Evans says that in creating Caliban, Shakespeare "went outside man, and made a monster all of his own devising" (1940, 102). The Vaughans (1991), however, convincingly show that Caliban, although "salvage and deformed," is human. More and more, productions make him so.

Kermode says that "Caliban is the core of the play" (1964, xxiv), "the ground of the play" (xxv), "the natural man against whom the cultivated man is measured" (xxiv). He illuminates "by contrast the world of art, nurture, civility" (xxv). While Edward Tayler can remonstrate with Kermode on this point (1964, 127), Caliban has aroused enormous interest over the years.

According to the Vaughans, the late seventeenth century "deemed Caliban a pure monster, with emphasis on his vices, deformities, crudities, and beastl[iness]." In the eighteenth century, "a hint of potential virtue crept in." The romantics appreciated "his 'natural' qualities, and, after the publication of Darwin's *On the Origin of Species*, Caliban was seen as a missing link, "part beast, part human" (1991, xxii). The twentieth century has "embraced him for their own intellectual, social, and political reasons" (xxii). Few would argue with the Vaughans' qualification of Kermode: "Caliban is qualitatively more important to the play's dynamics than anyone but Prospero" (7).

The Vaughans provide an exhaustive guide to Caliban—what he is, what he looks like, the sources of his name, the heritage Shakespeare drew upon to shape him, and representations in productions and in art. No other characters in the canon have "undergone the extreme range of metamorphoses that have marked Caliban's tumultuous career" (1991, xiv). Caliban has become what Clifford Geertz calls an "expressive symbol" (1973, 144). The "varied uses to which succeeding generations and disparate cultures have put Caliban reveal a great deal about their changing attitudes toward . . . hierarchy, slavery, social progress, license, appetite, control, order, and power" (Vaughan and Vaughan 1991, xvii). Of course, if Caliban is a focal point for such discourse, so is the play, by implication and if twisted toward a specific interpretation. "Caliban has been widely appropriated by sociopolitical causes" (xv). "Caliban appeals to rebellious instincts because he challenges a dominant culture" (xv). "As an opposing force, the 'other' onto whom the dominant culture projects its fears of disorder, Caliban thus becomes a powerful symbol of resistance and transgression" (xv), "a recurring symbol for the victimization of Third World peoples" (3). He permits some pseudopolitical activists to appropriate him in the name of radicalism, but can remain at the service of a comfortable cuddling into the very hierarchy he defies. "His very opposition to Prospero's hegemony helps to define the appropriator's assumptions and values" (xv). Alden T. Vaughan demonstrates Caliban's appropriation for sociopolitical purposes, a flexible symbol that justifies the spectrum from harsh repression to uncompromising rebellion (1998, 247–66). It is remarkable that Caliban can be so plausible within so many contexts, and it is also healthy, not just for the survival of Shakespeare as a "relevant" force within our cultures, but also as a source of language for the voiceless, for those whose forebears could not read and write or were forbidden to do so, as were many slaves in America before the Civil War of the 1860s.

According to Brian Vickers, Caliban is "an anomalous category within the Great Chain of Being" (1993, 243), "between the human and the animal" (245). He represents Prospero's "failed experiment, the limit case of the civilising powers of language" (243). Shakespeare "is here challenging the humanists' . . . assumption that the gift of language necessarily endows speakers with reason" (243). Caliban "is resistant to nurture, impervious to reason, a creature that can only be counted on to follow its own desires, however violent" (244). Language is not only the medium of civilization, as Cicero and Sidney would have it, but a way of expressing what "civilization" denies: "I'll teach you to name what I am taking from you and preventing you from being." It also shows him what he is denied and gives him words for it—language is also the language of victimization. The question is not his lack of civilization, but the nature of his disentitlement: "I'll teach you to name what you are also losing as you gain language." Caliban is "capable [only] of practical education: moral principles are beyond him," according to Hallett Smith (1969, 5). E. E. Stoll suggests that Caliban has "the capacity of acquiring . . . the faculty of Common Sense" (in Hallett Smith 1969, 30). Does common sense include moral principles? Robert Speaight suggests that Caliban grasps education only as the opposite of what it espouses. Caliban is "worse than a wild animal; he is the incurable primitive who perverts the instruction he has received" (1962, 169). E. K. Chambers suggests that Caliban's name may derive from the gypsy "cauliban," meaning blackness (1923, 1:494). In a shrewd article that argues that Shakespeare is very conscious of the issues he raises in Caliban, Jean-Marie Maguin says that "what Caliban chiefly deplores is the step he was made to take into the human condition . . . the only profit he finds is a capacity to curse his fate" (1995, 150).

Only production can answer the question of Caliban's "redemption." Does his "I'll be wise hereafter, / And seek for grace" (5.1.294–95) signal an emergence from the "darkness" Prospero attributes to him? Julian Patrick says that Caliban recognizes that "nurture . . . has become necessary" (1983, in Bloom 1988, 83). Is his "inner core of viciousness deeper than the corruption induced by society and beyond the reach of society's mitigating nurture," as Barber and Wheeler suggest (1986, 339)? Is he really a devil, as Gilbert Harrison argues? Caliban "is no grotesque mockery, but real, dangerous beyond hope of reclamation, a devil, a born devil. [This] is a play of bright light and sinister darkness. We mistake its meaning if we regard Caliban and his confederates merely as comic accessories to a fairy tale" (1963, 233).

The Vaughans show that Prospero's phrase "not honored with / A human shape" does not apply to Caliban, and that "fins like arms" (2.2.34–35) suggests arms, not fins. Prospero's "tortoise" (1.2.318), they argue, "refers to Caliban's dilatoriness" (1991, 13). He creates, says Terence Hawkes, "an arena for the sifting of an immense issue: what makes a man?" (1974, 29).

Furthermore, if Caliban is not human, he cannot raise the possibility of "grace." If he is, as John E. Hankins says, "bestial man . . . less guilty but more hopeless than [those who can distinguish between good and evil] . . . he cannot be improved" (1947, 794); "grace" cannot even be within his vocabulary. Deborah Willis says that Caliban's plea for "grace" emphasizes the corruption of the "civilized" Antonio: "The play's true threatening 'other' is not Caliban, but Antonio" (1989, 280). If Caliban is not human, but a devil, then only Antonio raises the issue of human iniquity, and he is under a version of house arrest at the end.

Assuming Caliban's regeneration, Joseph Wharton also regrets it: "I always lament that our author has not preserved his fierce and implacable spirit in Calyban. . . . he has, I think, injudiciously put into his mouth, words that imply repentance and understanding" (1753).

According to Diana Devlin, Caliban "learns to recognize the superiority of his old master" (1988, 27). His negative experience means that "he has enlarged his idea of willing service [and] will be more careful to evaluate the object of his allegiance" (27). The word "grace," she says, means that "he has sensed something greater than a human master to aspire towards serving" (27). Devlin leaves Caliban on the island "abandoned by Prospero, isolated from the mood of harmony and relief of those who return to Milan, forced to remain in a world he has now learnt to recognize as lonely and loveless" (28). At the end, says Vickers, "it looks as if Caliban prefers to serve Prospero. . . . the island may well be uninhabited again" (1993, 246). Most believe that Caliban "will regain his liberty and his island" (Vaughan and Vaughan 1999, 9). The play does not answer the question of what happens to him, though productions may do so. If he stays, he is no longer an unconscious creature living in "symbolic harmony with the island's natural food resources" (Skura 1989, 51). He will have learned language only to mutter to himself. His procreative drive will fade away. But no Mrs. Caliban awaits him in Milan, nor any society of which he can be part. He will be in the position of the grotesquely disfigured Negro of Stephen Crane's great short story "The Monster." Shakespeare raises the questions of colonialization, assimilation, diversity, and the like by not answering them. They are unanswerable. Shakespeare leaves Caliban, to quote Matthew Arnold, "between two worlds, / One dead, the other powerless to be born" ("Stanzas from the Great Chartreuse," 85–86).

Ariel

What is Ariel? He is a "he," although he plays woman's roles—nymph of the sea, Harpy, possibly Ceres—and is often played by a woman. I have never seen a production where Ariel is only a voice, though he is visible to "no eyeball" but Prospero's.

Some critics see Ariel's manifestation in the play primarily as a function of Prospero. Ariel reacts and responds to Prospero and seldom, if ever, demonstrates any nature independent of Prospero's instructions—that is, until he manifests "a touch, a feeling" (5.1.21) of human affliction and holds up another analogue of compassion to Prospero. Robert H. West says of this moment that "Ariel's superiority to passion [is] matched with passion's superiority to Ariel" (1968, 94). Ariel, then, mirrors the intellectual grasp that Prospero has maintained throughout the play.

It may follow that Ariel's "imaginative power . . . finds liberty and integration in Prospero's own spiritual vision," as Derek Traversi says (1955, 229). Ariel "is a recreative and self-delighting spirit whose art and magic are forms of play

Thadd McQuade as Ariel in the Shenandoah Shakespeare Express
'95 WORD to the THIRD tour production of *The Tempest*. Photo-
graph by Julie Ainsworth.

[that find] an answering delight in Prospero" (255–56). To grant an "independent" form or shape to Ariel is, in a sense, to deny him his independence. We
can have no sense of what "freedom" means to Ariel. Our "freedom" is conditional, as Albert Camus suggests in "The Myth of Sisyphus" (1955). With
each seeming freedom comes a new responsibility that we do not necessarily
anticipate. It is not so for Ariel. In "the end the world of humanity bores" Ariel,
says D. G. James (1967, 68), and it may have been so from the beginning of
his association with witch or magician.

   Robert Speaight says that Ariel "is a personification of imprisoned grace, set
free at last, and now placed at the service of man, but always hungering for the
pure, unfettered liberty which is only to be found in Paradise" (1962, 166–67).
His freedom is consciousness without any further psychic structure (one element
that makes him strange, for human consciousness is never free within itself or
free of the weighty zones of the psychic structure below and prior to consciousness). No one has to know anything in Paradise.

   For the audience, Germaine Greer suggests, Ariel is "the power of the collective imagination, playwright's words working on audience's faculty ... descended from the image of winged thought used by the Chorus in *Henry V*" (1986, 29). If this is so, Ariel's appeal to the imagination is more direct than the Chorus's. The point is that we think we see him, but we don't. He has no identity that we would understand apart from his manifestation as Prospero's agent—except when he expresses a flicker of what we call conscience in prompting Prospero at the beginning of Act 5.

HISTORICIST CRITICISM

E.M.W. Tillyard was the chief among Old Historicists. His books "seemed initially to be definitive," says Hawkes, but were later seen to take "little account of the impulses to disorder that such ... a [supposedly] golden age of order, stability and established hierarchy ... contained and attempted to hold in balance" (1996, 6). "No longer, in the manner of *The Elizabethan World Picture*, would historical material be treated as a 'background' against which literary texts might be placed," says Hawkes (6). "A central focus of [New Historicism and cultural materialism] is the renegotiation in the name of a new use of history" (7). Hawkes reiterates his argument that "human actions, activities, the 'things' of this world, don't in themselves 'mean.' It is *we* who mean, *by* them" (8; Hawkes's emphasis). What "makes a different culture impenetrable to us is always, in Geertz's words, 'lack of familiarity with the imaginative universe within which their acts are signs' " (8). The task of current criticism, then, is to show how meaning, which "has no existence 'in itself,' ... operates as part of the meaning-making discourses by which [a] culture makes sense of the world it creates and inhabits" (9). Hawkes dismisses the totalizing mythology of "Shakespeare" as "all-wise, all-knowing genius [whose] plays present us with nothing less than the truth, the whole truth and nothing but the truth about the most fundamental matters of human existence: birth, death, and the life that comes between" (9). The emphasis here, predictably, is on difference: "Like the questions of sexual difference, and of its physical embodiment, the issue of racial distinction and integrity will necessarily be neglected by a project concerned to foster the notion of a universal and unchanging human identity, and a common, reachable 'human nature,' palpable beneath the cultural veil" (12).

Hawkes encourages "the abandonment of any sense of a 'final' meaning that must necessarily be dug out of [the plays]" (13). They are, after all, different as they collide with and inform different zeitgeists. "Shakespeare can still engage modern audiences without [their] needing to locate a phantom quality of 'transcendency' in the plays, or to construct ghostly entities vaguely promoted by the plays 'themselves' " (14).

Writing in 1939, L. C. Knights said, "Historians frequently resort to literature for descriptions of the social scene, but in doing so they reduce literature to the level of documentation and ignore the qualities which, as literature, it embodies" (1933, 214 n. 1). The play is to be read as one document in the flow of the discourse about this or that in early modern England. This is the apolitical thrust of the American wing of the historicist movement. The play is to be seen in its relationship to authority, either upholding the hierarchical values of the patrons of the players (King James, for example) or subverting those values, or doing both through the interrogation of kingship that *Henry V* represents. This is the more politically edged, leftist attack of British cultural materialism, represented here under the "colonialist" category.

The concept of "history of ideas" came under attack years ago because the "ideas" were those of authority. Even ideas once considered subversive had been absorbed into a flow controlled by those who wrote (and therefore "controlled") history.

Gary Taylor provides an anecdotal account of the New Historicist method, which itself invariably begins with an anecdote. Stephen Greenblatt, says Taylor, "recounts and analyzes a 1552 sermon by Hugh Latimer, Dudley Carleton's description of an abortive execution in 1603, William Strachey's narrative of a troubled expedition to Virginia in 1610, and H. M. Stanley's recollection of a perilous encounter with Moa tribesmen in central Africa in May 1877. He also talks about *The Tempest*" (1991, 347). The execution is halted by a pardon from the king. It "dramatizes the king's mercy" (349). "In the same way," says Taylor, paraphrasing Greenblatt, "Prospero's chief magical device is to harrow others with anxiety, to create in them a state of 'managed insecurity.' Shakespeare himself creates a corresponding insecurity in the audience. Will the characters on the ship drown? Will Antonio murder Alonso? Will Caliban murder Prospero?" No—though one doubts that we are that insecure about these questions. Everything becomes a tragicomedy: "Deaths are threatened but do not materialize" (350). "Greenblatt's narrative and critical method treats all these materials equally, as comparable examples of 'discourse.' . . . The ceremonies of the church, of the state, of the theatre, all speak the same language" (350) and serve the same purposes. "Greenblatt's historicism subjects a whole new continent of texts to the technologies of an imperialist literary criticism and critical theory. Greenblatt's lecture not only discusses but itself enacts the display of power" (351).

Greenblatt suggests that "in *The Tempest*, as in *Measure for Measure*, Shakespeare once again conceived of the playwright as a princely creator of anxiety" (1988, 141). Anxiety is "a strategy for shaping the inner lives of others and for fashioning their behavior" (143). It is to ask the phrase "in effect" to do much of the critic's work to say that "Prospero's art has in effect created the conspiracy as well as the defense against the conspiracy" (145). The unexamined assumption becomes the premise for the conclusion. We agree that Prospero does defend himself, but it does not follow that he fomented the threat. "Prospero's magic is the romance equivalent of martial law" (157). Prospero can— as can martial law—prohibit action. His magic can provide opportunity for action, as in his scholarly neglect of his political role, his leaving Antonio and Sebastian awake, and his putting glistering garments on the line, but Prospero cannot dictate human action any more than he can reach in and click the "virtue" switch inside an evil soul. Greenblatt claims that what Shakespeare derived from Strachey's letter is "its central concern with the public management of anxiety" (149). No doubt Prospero creates anxiety, but it is not for its own sake, or merely for political advantage, as Greenblatt argues. It has a spiritual goal.

In his balanced Norton introduction (1997), Greenblatt asks questions about survival, the ways emergency reveals character, the relationship between theory and practicality, the nature of willing and forced obedience, conspiracy, providence, relationships with natives or with disgruntled colonists, and superiority and inferiority (3052). He wisely grounds the discussion of the New World within these large questions, to be worked out in different ways in different places over time, as opposed to narrowing them to specific moments or locations, where limited "answers" to the questions confine the play and make it mean things it does not mean (as New Historicism and cultural materialism tend to do).

In an article derived from Greenblatt that demonstrates the weaknesses of the New Historicist approach, Curt Breight suggests that rulers like Elizabeth and James liked to keep the threat of assassination alive and indeed encouraged it, the better to fortify their own positions. Certainly that is true. Henry V goes on at length to the Cambridge Conspirators about the archetypal depth of regicide, a daring excursion given his father's translation of kingship from a hereditary to a competitive office. *Macbeth* can be said to be a response to the effort to blow James to the moon (see Wills 1995 and Coursen 1996). Breight says that "conspiracy is often a fiction, or a construct, or a real yet wholly containable piece of social theatre" (1990, 1); "the ruler must simultaneously appear vulnerable to assassination while being, as nearly as possible, invulnerable" (20). He goes on to say that "it is arguable that Prospero [has set up the] conspiracy" of Antonio and Sebastian (16). What is indisputable is that the selective slumbering of the King's party—only Antonio and Sebastian are left awake—is Prospero's doing. It follows that he creates an opportunity for Antonio to entice Sebastian to regicide. It may be, then, that "Shakespeare's audience undoubtedly viewed the stage-managed assassination attempt and its frustration with cynical detachment" (16). That is to attribute a blanket response to the audience—hardly an "undoubted" result—and to suggest that regicide, however manipulated by its potential victims—was not feared by most subjects, that is, that the entire Blackfriars audience or that in Whitehall with the King viewed the King's fear of assassination and his manipulation of that fear with a secret sneer.

Caliban, meanwhile, "is temporarily freed from log-toting duties [to become part of] a wholly containable plot" (19). It is arguable that the arrival ashore of Stephano and Trinculo is not part of Prospero's overall plan and that Ariel, the intelligencer, is the source of Prospero's information. It is necessary for Breight, however, to say that Caliban is set up, because Caliban and his stinking accessories become object lessons for the aristocrats at the end. "Prospero exploits these conspirators as negative *exempla*—as mirrors for the aristocrats [whereby]

Prospero instructs his aristocratic enemies in the new politics of his own superiority and invulnerability" (23). These "few odd lads" (5.1.255) carry a heavy weight. It would be helpful for Breight's thesis were those aristocrats to exclaim, "Yea, I am chastened, and see the error of / My ways in light of these exempla here." They do not. Sebastian and Antonio exchange cynical comments. Antonio, the calculator, figures Caliban's market value. Furthermore, Prospero is busy weeping for Gonzalo and embracing his old enemy, Alonso. If Prospero is displaying power in the final scene, it is the result of the power he has given up, and it culminates in the tableau of that surrender, Ferdinand and Miranda playing at chess.

The heart of Breight's case depends on our not knowing the play. The same is true of Kott, who has Prospero say, "My ending is despair," leaving out the crucial "Unless I be reliev'd by prayer" (Epilogue 15–16). The qualification torpedoes Kott below the waterline. Breight quotes the speech Prospero gives to Ariel up to the threat of "Ling'ring perdition . . . shall step by step attend you and your ways" (3.3.77–79). Ariel goes on to tell them that "to guard" themselves from these "wraths," they must achieve "heart-sorrow / And a clear life ensuing" (3.3.79–82). Breight goes so far as to italicize "ling'ring perdition." He then claims that "retrospective criticism cannot ignore this passage. At this moment the spectator has no reason to anticipate 'mercy.' Rather the audience begins to lick its collective lips in anticipation of blood" (18). The same would be true were the Communion exhortation to stop after "wherinsoever ye shall perceyve your selves to have offended eyther by wil, worde, or deede, there bewayle your owne synfull lives," as *Queen Elizabeth's Prayer Book: 1559* says (1911, 99). A process is at work, however: "Confess yourselves to almighty God, with ful purpose of amendement of life" (1911, 99). Why this exhortation? Alonso and his party have just been denied a version of Communion service. It cannot be enjoyed until "ye shall reconcyle youre selves unto [your neighbours], ready to make restitucion and satisfaction according to the uttermost of your powers for all injuries and wronges done by you to any other. . . . For otherwyse the receiving of the holy Communion doth nothing else, but encrease your dampnation" (1911, 99).

Having interrupted Ariel at a point where it fits his thesis, Breight goes on to claim that "Prospero . . . encourages his enemies to play the Romans and kill themselves" (18). Alonso comes close to despair, as opposed to a "heart-sorrow" that would yield to positive rhythms, but—and on this the play is clear—he is held in suspension by Prospero's "charm" (5.1.17) and thus cannot commit the suicide that Breight claims Prospero encourages.

Prospero is, no doubt, out to regain his dukedom and to create a larger polity through the marriage of his daughter and Prince Ferdinand. Prospero promises to use his knowledge of Antonio and Sebastian's conspiracy if he needs it. His aim has been that "they be . . . penitent" (5.1.28). That failing, they can be controlled by their guilt, if not by inward contrition. Any gestures or words to the contrary (even to Ariel, even in soliloquy), Breight claims, are merely evidence of "a characteristic of state power . . . to mask subjugation of the body with a show of benevolence" (28). Prospero's acknowledgment of Caliban—"this thing of darkness" (5.1.275)—does not fit Breight's thesis. The thesis can be applied to Antonio and Sebastian if we grant that they are puppets of Prospero, as opposed to Sebastian's being a swamp ready to drain in the direction that Antonio channels. It is useful to view Prospero as having become, among other things, a Machiavellian politician these many years after bestowing upon Antonio boundless "confidence" (1.2.97). Much of the rest of the case, however, relies on a selective use of the evidence. Breight, for example, claims that "Renaissance spectators probably associated [the Mariner's "roaring, shreiking, howling, jingling chains," 5.1.233] with the seemingly ubiquitous Tudor/Stuart prison," not with "a release from hell" (22). That is possible, but both Laertes and Claudio use "howling" in the context of hell, and Romeo says, "O friar, the damned use that word in hell; / Howling attends it" (*Romeo and Juliet* 3.3.47–48). If the audience has been listening to Shakespeare, their immediate response to the word "howling" will be an association with "hell."

Thomas Cartelli focusses "less on the text's status as a historically determined literary artifact, now open to a variety of interpretations, than on its subordination to what history has made of it" (1987, 105). The "text of *The Tempest* continues to allow Prospero the privilege of the grand closing gesture; continues to privilege that gesture's ambiguity at the expense of Caliban's dispossession" (107), and, therefore, the play "is not only complicit in the history of its subsequent misreadings, but responsible in some measure for the development of the ways in which it is read" (110). No one would deny that a text is in some measure responsible for the ways in which it is read. Conrad's *Heart of Darkness*, Ngugi Wa Thiong'o's *A Grain of Wheat*, and *The Tempest* each suggest a different way of being read. Prospero does not say, "Exterminate all the brutes," as Joseph Conrad's Kurtz does. Nor is Prospero investigated for killing Mau Mau prisoners, as Ngugi's British colonialist administrator is. Richard Levin writes of "refuting the ending" (1979), that is, denying what the play ostensibly shows. Does it, for example, show the "triumph" of magic, as Stephen Orgel says (1987, 54), or "the lengths to which the play has to go to achieve a legitimate ending [which involves] the quelling of a fundamental disquiet concerning . . . the projects of colonialist discourse," as Francis Barker and Peter Hulme say (1985, 202)? R. V. Young, in responding to Cartelli, says that "from a New Historicist perspective, what counts as civilized behavior is a matter of 'ideological construct' anyway; so it is difficult to determine on what basis Shakespeare or Prospero or even Hitler might be condemned" (1995, 12). Young neglects to mention that we did have to create a new rationale to confront the crimes of the Nazi regime and to try its surviving functionaries (see Bradley F. Smith 1981). The important difference, though, between Conrad, Ngugi, and Shakespeare is that the latter wrote plays. Plays are interrogated by critics, of course, but they are designed to be performed, that is, to be interrogated by actors within a continuum that includes an audience. The question is, how much of the anxiety or subversion of manifest content can be incorporated into a production and conveyed to an audience? Heavily conceptualized productions of the play too often bury it in contemporary "meanings," as I shall suggest in chapter 6.

Donna Hamilton sees the play as a mirror for magistrates, specifically as an elegant series of instructions for Shakespeare's patron and early auditor of the play, King James. Hamilton examines the Parliament of 1610 and the struggle between James's vision of unlimited royal authority and the Parliament's effort to define limits: "Students see [the language of Caliban and Ariel] not only as poetic but as made up of contemporary political discourse" (1992, 69). Hamilton suggests that "some of the central values of the play—such as order by way of restraint and discipline—match rather well the values that the Commons were urging James to adopt as his own" (70). "What is especially interesting about Shakespeare's representation of these values, however, is that in the play they are the *ruler's* values. . . . the ruler himself is made to represent the value of reining in an acquisitive and appetitive nature" (70). Hamilton describes Shakespeare's challenge: "But to structure the compliment [to James] so that the values emphasized—restraint and discipline—could also be understood as the opposite of unlimited power, transcendent rule, and extravagant expenditure gives the play the capacity not only to compliment the king but also to side with those who thought he should temper his position" (70).

Louise Schleiner views the play, and Prospero's interruption of the Wedding Masque, as part of a very specific political allegory in which James is urged to be the wise colonist at home: "I believe that Shakespeare was urging for the kingdom and king a renewal of a much older contract [than the early-sixteenth-century effort at constitutionalism], a quasi-feudal one whereby the king out of moral strength was to practice good 'husbanding' of his wife/nation's resources; the king should step from the vastly gratifying but unsustainable role of puppeteering magician to that of self-disciplined human ruler. . . . it was time now for his revels to end and himself to return to active, responsible government" (1992, 494–95). I doubt that Shakespeare is advocating any form of feudalism. He had shown Bolingbroke resorting to a neofeudalism in *Richard II*, but that was because Bolingbroke had cooperated with Richard to erase all other modes of rule (Coursen 1984).

David Scott Kastan knows that he belabors the obvious when he says that "the play is obviously set in the Old World; the tempest is called up as the Italian nobles are returning from Africa to Italy" (1998, 93). He goes on to say that "if the play has a relation to the New World colonial activity, it is not writ deep into its texture" (94). He makes the compelling cultural point that "imagination of the past now enthralls us as once we were enthralled by the imagination of the future, and this desire seems worthily motivated by the felt need to rescue the play from the banality of the moral claims made for it in the name of its putative timelessness and transcendence" (95). One recalls—though it was too early for Kastan—the trylon and perisphere of the New York World's Fair of 1939–40, with its pools, heroic statuary, and gleaming art deco pavilions, and the pin for visitors: "I have seen the future." The "Americanization of *The Tempest* may itself be an act of cultural imperialism," Kastan says (95). He points out the disinheriting of Antonio's unseen or at least unheard son (96) and links the play to King "James's fantasy of European peace and coherence" (96). James was well known for his wish to unite his own island under the title of Britain. Kastan cites Rudolf II, deposed by the Hapsburg archdukes because he "is interested only in wizards, alkymists, Kabbalists, and the like, sparing no expense to find all kinds of treasure, learn secrets, and use scandalous ways of harming his enemies" and to maintain a "whole library of magic books" (R.J.W. Evans 1973, 196). The play insists, says Kastan, on the "priority of arts of rule over the rules of magical art" (1998, 99). It must be understood in the context of "England's deep involvements in Europe," of which colonial activity was an aspect (100). Kastan's essay provides a useful corrective—not merely another topical allegory but a set of facts and inferences that have a claim on our attention more compelling than that of the discourse of colonialism. Kastan isolates some of the many circulating documents of which *The Tempest* is the most significant, partly because of its interrogation of the excesses of empire and partly because it continues to circulate in our culture.

COLONIALIST CRITICISM

The colonialist approach is sometimes strident, occasionally compelling, and often silly. Shakespeare exposes colonialism at its worst in Trinculo's and Stephano's exploitative and imperialist assumptions. The New World is either a way to wealth in the old or the site for an extension of tyranny. Is Prospero merely a subtler, more plausible variation on this stance? Is the play, like *The Taming of the Shrew*, to be expunged because it does not fit current standards of political correctness? Historical revisionism on the basis of an "enlightened politics" can resemble eighteenth-century adaptation on the basis of artistic taste.

Leah S. Marcus argues that "insofar as we have attempted to define the shadowy historical person behind the giant name, we have identified a playwright who used topicality not to limit, select, and shape his audiences in ideological terms but to disperse ideology prismatically so that his plays . . . would take on different colorations in different settings and times" (1988, 218). Shakespeare explores colonialism in *The Tempest*, but it is a borderland of his concern here across which his illumination shines on occasion, not with a steady glare of interrogation.

Inga-Stina Ewbank shrewdly warns that "if your own country has not, in recent centuries, wielded imperial power, you are that much less likely to hear [the colonialist critic] through the reverberations of a post-colonial conscience" (1991, 110). Some critics view the colonial problem as a product of inevitability. Jan Kott describes a clash between linguistic codes—historical experience and Virgilian myth. Both contemporary plantation and mythic golden age are repeated in the play, not purgatively but as an expression of the "most bitter . . . lost hopes of the Renaissance" (1976, 435). Caliban merely repeats Brutus's "Freedom." It is a motto for anarchy. Shakespeare's attitude is "sardonic." He "had no illusions" (435). Stanley Wells says that "we are shown the totally irreconcilable situation that arises when civilizations clash" (1995, 365). That is true, but more true of *Antony and Cleopatra*, I think, than of *The Tempest*. David Fromkin describes the only model of political power that both Prospero and the audience of *The Tempest* knew: "Arbitrary rule, the divinity of kings, the hereditary principle: these were among the burdens of the human race for almost the whole of its political history, burdens that therefore seemed to be unchangeable" (1999, 133).

While agreeing with the case the New Historicists and cultural materialists have made, Ben Ross Schneider, Jr., says, "The play is too large to look at through the knothole of colonialist discourse. In doing so these critics unconsciously silence other kinds of discourse . . . Arthurian legend, Jungian archetypes, Freudian psychoses, regeneration rituals, vegetation cults, Plato's three parts of the soul, good angels/bad angels, chess, Italy, drama theory, Shakespeare's life, magic, the ethics of magic, and who knows what else?" (1995, 140).

Francis Barker and Peter Hulme argue that it is the critics—the New Critics—who lend respectability to the play. The "play's unity is constructed only by shearing off some of its 'surface' complexities and explaining them away as irrelevant survivals or unfortunate academicisms" (1985, 196). The discourse of colonialism becomes the only relevant ground of inquiry. A "discourse" involves the "field of linguistic strategies operating within particular areas of social practice" (Paul Brown 1985, 69 n. 3).

The discourse of colonialism is not of recent origin, as some critics would have us believe. Skottowe, in 1824, raised the issue of the consistency of Caliban's characterization: "Of explaining to the 'poisonous slave,' his indisputable right to the dominion of the island under the double claim of inheritance and possession, his able master will not even be suspected" (Furness 1892, 381). In 1863, Charles Cowden-Clark condemned Prospero: "By nature he is a selfish aristocrat. When he was Duke of Milan he gave himself up to his favourite indulgence of study and retired leisure. When master of the Magic Island he is stern and domineering, lording it over his sprite subjects and ruling them with a wand of rigour. He comes there and takes possession of the territory with all the coolness of a usurper; he assumes despotic sway, and stops only short of absolute unmitigated tyranny" (Furness 1892, 367). In 1873, Daniel Wilson argued that Caliban is "no degraded savage," but is kept by Prospero like "some caged wild beast pining in cruel captivity" (Furness 1892, 382).

In 1875, William Watkiss Lloyd dealt with the assumptions and the realities of colonialization: "the imaginary and actual characteristics of man in the state of nature, the complications with the indigenae, the resort, penally or otherwise, to compelled labour, the reappearance on new soil of the vices of the older world" (2). In 1888, Richard G. Moulton discussed colonialism as a shadow of the Victorian belief in progress: "The wrongs [inflicted upon] the savage, and his dispossession by the white man . . . the early and pleasant relations between the two [involving] an interchange of good offices, education on the one side, on the other reverence and gifts of natural riches [are followed by] a moral gulf, [then by] the forced domination of the white man [s]o that the gift of civilization is turned into a curse" (250–51). The "old ideology . . . idealized the colonizer," says Russ McDonald (1991, 27). That Prospero was universally praised by previous generations of critics is often the invention of those who wish to denigrate him. Dr. Garnet, writing in the Irving edition of 1890 and quoted in the New Variorum edition, said of Prospero that "his errors have been the product of his own nature; he has . . . been too bookish. . . . It is what one continually sees in men of great parts and long experience, intimately persuaded that no one can do anything so well as themselves" (1890, in Furness 1892, 370).

Frederick S. Boas, writing in 1912, took a pro-colonist line when he said of Prospero that "unlike Marlowe's Faustus, he had not used his power for personal ends. He had worked a beneficent revolution on the island, freeing Ariel from his captivity, and seeking to educate Caliban to a higher level. The history of the intercourse between the civilized man and the savage in most epochs is epitomized in the relations of Prospero and the son of Sycorax. . . . The 'native' is always apt to be demoralized in the transition from his instinctive barbarism to a civilization he imperfectly comprehends" (532–33). Boas went on to make Shakespeare the epitome of the colonizer. Indeed, as Boas reaches for his peroration, Shakespeare becomes like Henry V, the personification of everything to which an English male could aspire: "To conquer and colonize is instinctive in the veins of the sea-king's sons, but it was an unparalleled grace of fortune that predestined the mightiest Teutonic 'organizer of victory' to the creative, not the active sphere. The glories of the Armada and of Waterloo may be repeated, but when shall be born a second *Hamlet* or *Othello*? . . . 'Here was a Caesar!' " (539). These words come only a few years before the butchery along the lines of wire that stitched across the Somme.

William Sidney Lee, one of the first critics to call Caliban an American Indian, adopts a paternalistic stance: "Every explorer shared Prospero's pity for the aborigines' inability to make themselves intelligible . . . and offered instruction in civilised speech [to] a creature stumbling over the first stepping-stones which lead from savagery to civilization" (1907, 326, 328).

We hear distant echoes of the colonizing attitude even after World War Two. For G. Wilson Knight, colonizing involved the "will to raise savage peoples from superstition and blood-sacrifice, taboos and witchcraft and the attendant fears and slaveries, to a more enlightened existence" (1947, 255). In 1962, Robert Speaight said, "Prospero derives his title from the intrinsic superiority over savages, and Caliban is very properly reduced to his natural status of slavery. There is no room for sentiment here, though there may be room for pity" (168). If slavery is a natural status, why should it be pitied? A response like Speaight's gives credence to a strong rebuttal: "Allegorical and Neoplatonic overlay masks some of the most damaging prejudices of Western civilization" (Leininger 1980a, 122).

Terence Hawkes compares Shakespeare's activity to that of "a colonist [who] acts essentially as a dramatist. He imposes the 'shape' of his own culture, embodied in his speech, on the new world, and makes that world recognizable, habitable, 'natural,' able to speak his language . . . his language expands the boundaries of our culture, and makes the new territory over in his own image. His 'raids on the inarticulate' open up new worlds for the imagination" (1974, 228). Similarly, C. L. Barber and Richard Wheeler see *The Tempest* as a version of colonialization that asks, "What would the series of events reveal about the redeemability and unredeemability of human nature?" (1986, 339).

David Scott Kastan summarizes the colonialist critique: "No longer is *The Tempest* a play of social reconciliation and moral renewal, of benevolent artistry, and providential design; it now appears as a telling document of the first phase of English imperialism . . . even as an 'instrument of imperialism' itself" (1998, 92). The play performs "the necessary act of colonialist legitimation by naturalizing domination as the activity of 'providence divine' " (92). "Prospero's art . . . has become the colonizer's technology of domination and control" (92).

Two major essays exemplify the colonialist approach. Barker and Hulme (1985) move away from "contextual background—which previously had served merely to highlight the profile of the individual text—[to] the notion of *intertextuality*, according to which . . . no text is intelligible except in its differential relations with other texts" (192). English colonialism provides the "dominant discursive con-texts" for the play (198). Prospero is an unreliable narrator, somewhat like Browning's Duke of Ferrara. To accept Prospero's vision is to ignore the ways in which the play undercuts his narrative. "As part of this [strategy], Prospero reduces Caliban to a role in the supporting sub-plot, as instigator of a plot that is programmed to fail, thereby forging an equivalent between Antonio's initial *putsch* and Caliban's revolt. This allows Prospero to annul the memory of his failure to prevent his expulsion from the dukedom, by repeating it as a mutiny that he will, this time, forestall" (196). Among the assumptions here are that Caliban is set up—a necessary premise for the anti-Prospero school—and that Prospero does forget ("annul the memory of") the previous coup d'état. No evidence exists for the former assumption, and strong evidence suggests that Prospero hardly forgets or erases what Antonio did. He does annul the results.

The text reveals, through Caliban, its "own anxiety about the threat posed to its decorum by its New World materials" (198). That is another way of saying that the ending is qualified by Caliban as it is by that Old World representative, Antonio. It takes no cultural materialist come from the nave to tell us that the ending is heavily qualified. Prospero's Epilogue extends the qualifications to us, though in the context of our souls and their eternity, as opposed to England and its colonies. This "anxiety and the drive to closure it necessitates" have been ignored by "critics, who have tended to listen exclusively to Prospero's voice:

after all, he speaks their language" (200). Kermode is apparently an exception. "It has been left to those who have suffered colonial usurpation to discover and map the traces of that complexity by reading in full Caliban's refractory place in both Prospero's play and *The Tempest*" (201). We need the victim's point of view, and that has merit in redressing the overemphasis on white, male domination. The thesis swings out to balance a too-Prosperocentric approach. John Andrews suggests that Barker and Hulme "appear to be persuaded that, notwithstanding its sympathy to an anti-colonialist view of the political situation it depicts, *The Tempest* is finally complicit in the colonizing enterprise that was gathering momentum as Shakespeare's career drew to a close" (1994, 215). Whether its application to *The Tempest* is valid or not, the thesis itself is persuasive: "Capitalist societies have always presupposed the naturalness and universality of their own structures and modes of perception, so, at least for the foreseeable future, critiques will need to include an *historical* moment, countering capitalism's self-universalization by reasserting the rootedness of texts in the contingency of history" (194).

Paul Brown claims that "a sustained historical and theoretical analysis of the play's involvement in the colonialist project has yet to be undertaken" (1985, 48). The play is "an intervention," even if it is a "pleasurable narrative" (48). Brown uses the story of John Rolfe and Pocahontas (1614) to show that the site of contestation becomes the site of authorization. The anecdote stands, as in this criticism, for the type. Masterlessness and savagism "constitute a powerful discourse" (50–51)—actually two discourses, class discourse and race discourse (51). Stephano and Trinculo's "alliance with the savage Caliban provides an antitype of order . . . a threat [to] the ruling classes" (53). They are indeed, but do they justify the erasure of hierarchy or hierarchy? The play demonstrates the "capacity to reorient masterlessness and savagism into service without recourse to the naked exercise of coercive power" (54). Brown claims that Gonzalo's utopian discourse "rehearses the standard formula by which the colonized is denigrated (56). Perhaps, but Brown does not recognize the immediate puncturing of Gonzalo's conception, nor does he remark Gonzalo's later praise of those he takes to be the islanders. He does not notice that Gonzalo's ideal of "chaste productivity" is reenunciated by the Masque and in Prospero's injunctions to Ferdinand.

The constant assertion of this critique is that Prospero must "produce . . . a disruptive other . . . to assert the superiority of the coloniser" (58). In other words, Caliban is invited to try to rape Miranda so that Prospero can subjugate him. Caliban becomes "a linguistic subject of the master language" (61). "Whatever Caliban does with this gift [of language] announces his capture by it" (61). This has to include his cursing, though Brown does not say so. Were Caliban unable to curse, he would not be pinched for it. Prospero is reduced by Caliban "to the raucous registers of the other" (61). How, one might ask, if Caliban is captured by language, can he capture Prospero with it?

Prospero is "strong father," "rescuer and taskmaster," "coloniser whose refused offer of civilization forces him to strict discipline," "surrogate providence who corrects errant aristocrats and punishes plebeian revolt," and "master." He manifests, though, a "division between liberal and stately arts" which should be "united in the princely magus" (59). He admits the latter shortcoming in his opening narrative. Prospero "mystifies [a] colonialist regime . . . by producing it as a result of charitable acts (by the sea, the wind, and the honest courtier, Gonzalo)" (60). "The most apparent distinction between black and white regimes would seem to be that the latter is simply more powerful and more flexible" (61). Goals, however clearly stated—penitence followed by clarity of life— being suspect, are irrelevant. All that Prospero does is ultimately self-serving: "Disruption was produced to create a series of problems precisely in order to effect their resolution" (59). Prospero insists that the others "recognize them-selves as subjects of his discourse, as beneficiaries of his civil largesse" (59). As Caliban and Ariel know, "Beneath the apparent voluntarism of the white, male regime lies the threat of precisely this [Sycoraxian] coercion" (61). Such an approach excludes any spiritual activity in the characters. Any statement about spiritual activity becomes merely an acquiescence to a threat, either ex-press or implicit.

Prospero's acknowledgment of "this thing of darkness," Caliban, "designates the monster as his property, an object for his own utility." It is "an ironic identification *with* the other" (68), as opposed to a recognition of Prospero's own dark qualities and of something within him that has resisted nurture. It is part of the play's "*political* unconscious" (69; Brown's emphasis). One must ask, who is not aware? Shakespeare, apparently. As Russ McDonald says, this critical approach asserts that "*The Tempest* cannot be aware of its own partici-pation in the language of oppression and colonial power" (1991, 17).

McDonald attacks the colonialist approach as "tendentious in conception and narrow in scope . . . censorious and shrill" in tone (16). "The new orthodoxy, which exalts the colonized, is as narrow as the old, which idealizes and excuses the colonizer" (27). The "new orthodoxy [is] as one-sided as that which it has sought to replace" (17). Anthony Dawson adds that these critics may "expose the hidden biases of traditional criticism," but only on the basis of their own "ideological assumptions" (1988a, 71).

It may be, as Bruce Erlich suggests, that Shakespeare's "insights exceeded his sympathies" as he wrote *The Tempest* (1977, 63). As Richard Marienstras says, however, the colonialist critique "reinforces a single ideological system. The same can certainly not be said of . . . *The Tempest*" (1985, 169). For the colonialist critic, "Caliban is the hero of the piece, with Shakespeare a dubious accomplice in his oppression and exploitation," says Brian Vickers (1993, 245). "If modern critics want to denounce colonialism," Vickers continues, "this is the wrong play" (246).

The canceling alternatives that William Rockett ascribes to colonization apply as well to critical response to Prospero: " 'The plantation of the island' [was] of great importance for those in the seventeenth century who were aware of the spiritual implications of the New World. [It had] one of two effects: it could hold the prospect of renewal and virtue on the one hand or, on the other, of renewed corruption and vice" (1973, 84).

In a somewhat schizophrenic essay, Ben Ross Schneider, Jr., shows that the colonialist approach to Prospero's repentance "requires an elaborate exercise in looking the other way" (1995, 124). The colonialist critics "simply erase the climax of the play" (124). The play is "an egregious hypocrite" (125). "The colonialist critics have," he goes on to say, "laid to rest forever the idealist interpretation of Prospero, and definitively located the mythos of colonialism in his treatment of Caliban" (140). So, while their attack has been successful, the "new historicists . . . marginalize not only a large field of pertinent contemporary discourse, but also *The Tempest* itself" (121). "By too assiduously implementing the colonialist frame [they] forestall any attempt to answer the question ['What difference did *The Tempest* make to which fields of discourse?'] in terms of a full range of possibilities" (121). "All critiques proceed in much the same fashion to dismantle a presumed 'authorized version' of the play that idealizes and romanticizes Prospero as a noble regenerator of fallen humanity" (122). That is true. Most critical critiques of any school begin with a refutation of previous analyses, the better to raze the ground for the establishment of the "right" answer. The "political approach closes the door in advance on any nonpolitical explanation" (123). Is Caliban "an innocent victim of colonial exploitation or a criminal deservedly punished for a crime"? Does Prospero "bring . . . up the matter of the rape to divert attention from Caliban's rightful claim to the island"? Do "colonists always excuse their barbarity by attributing sub-human characteristics to the native population" (123)? These are questions to be asked, not just answered.

An early objection to the colonialist approach was launched by the bracing literalist E. E. Stoll: "There is not a word in *The Tempest* about America or Virginia, colonies or colonizing, Indians or tomahawks, maize, mocking-birds, or tobacco. Nothing but the Bermudas [as an example] of faraway places, like Tokio or Mandalay" (1927, 494). That is not quite true, of course. Trinculo mentions an "Indian" (2.2.34).

Meredith Anne Skura's cogent attack on the colonialist thesis says that the "similarities [between *The Tempest* and the literature of colonialism are] taken to be so compelling that the differences are ignored" (49). Caliban, for example, does not fall for "trinkets and trash" (49), as the American Indian or any savage is supposed to do. "Savages are [to be] entertaine[d] with Trifles and Gingles," as the stereotype has it (Bacon 1887, 142). Prospero's admission of kinship to Caliban is "too brief to counter [his] underlying colonialism" (49), says the colonialist critic. "Sycorax arrived and promptly enslaved [Ariel], thus herself becoming the first colonist, the one who established the habits of dominance and erasure before Prospero ever set foot on the island" (50). Some contrast exists, then, between Sycorax and Prospero.

The discourse of colonialism "destroys the evidence of the play as a unique cultural artifact, a unique voice in the discourse" (51). If New Critics "isolate text from contexts" (52), the colonialists bury the text in contexts. Colonialism, Skura says, was not "already encoded . . . in 1611" (53). She challenges the stereotypes that revisionists place in the discourse. In 1611, "what the New World seems to have meant for the majority of Englishmen was a sense of possibility and a set of conflicting fantasies about the wonders to be found there" (57). The play "contains the 'colonial' encounter firmly within the framing story of [the] family story" (66). "Shakespeare had been for several years concerned with the aging, loss, mortality, and death that recur in so much of what we know he was writing and reading at the time. . . . both the play and its context deal with the end of the individual self, the subject and the body in which it is located" (67). The play is "a story in which 'a merciful God,' a loving and fatherly protector rescues a whole shipload of people from certain death" (68). Shakespeare "was not merely reproducing a preexistent discourse; he was crossing it with other discourses, changing, enlarging, skewing, and questioning it" (69).

Skura may underestimate the amount of material on voyages and explorations already circulating in England prior to the "Bermuda Pamphlets." For a splendid summary and evaluation of the colonialist argument up to the late 1970s that puts the discourse into perspectives that help with the play as play, see Charles Frey (1979, 29–41). Frey demonstrates that narratives of voyages and discoveries formed a huge "linguistic and narrative force-field" (33). Frey sees the play as Leo Marx does, a sui generis "crossing of history and romance" (Marx 1967, 39). Furthermore, for Skura, "Shakespeare's 'others'—Aaron the Moor, Othello, Shylock, Cleopatra, and Caliban—have a deep structural likeness to one another. . . . these barbarous others carry a taint that no virtue can wash away," says Richard Helgerson (1996, 213). It is necessary in certain of today's discourses to label Caliban and Cleopatra "the other," and the label certainly deepens the psychological impact of such characters on "normality." But what is Caliban? The question can be answered only in production, as I think Shakespeare intended it to be. Cleopatra, historically, was Greek.

Perhaps the ultimate last gasp of "colonialist" criticism is that of Barbara Fuchs (1997, 45–62). "The general absence of Ireland from discussions of colonialism in the play is troubling," she says (46)—very much so if it is the critic's wish to discuss the topic. Hamlet does not deal with it in any depth either, allusions to Saint Patrick notwithstanding. The Chorus to Henry V 5 (30–34) shows that Shakespeare was familiar with the ongoing "Irish problem." The allusion would seem to be hegemonic in the extreme, even if we treat the Chorus as an "unreliable narrator." Fuchs argues that "English domination of Ireland might take cover in the text under precisely such details" as the relationship between Caliban's cloak and a similar Irish garment (48; Fuchs's emphasis). Caliban's "gaberdine" might more easily link him with Shylock (who also wears a "gaberdine" [1.3.108]) as a Fiedlerian "Outsider."

Fuchs performs other wonders by suggesting that "the description of Claribel's forced marriage recalls grim accounts of Christians captured by Barbary Coast pirates" (59). How? "Presumably," she says, "the king of Tunis would support his royal consort's claims to a European throne" (60). All of this represents the "containment of a historical empire, Carthage" (60). The issue that Antonio raises by overemphasizing the distance of Tunis from Milan is Milanese succession. Historically, Carthage, far from posing any threat to the Italian boot, had already been sacked and burned by Rome. It is true, as Fuchs suggests, that *The Tempest* must be "viewed from the perspective of multiple contexts" (62). The play does not, however, incorporate her contextualization. Paul Brown points vaguely to a "general analogy . . . between Ireland and Prospero's island" (1985, 57). Also remaining unproven is Dympna Callaghan's suggestion that Ireland "might be understood as the sublimated context for colonial relations in *The Tempest*" (qtd. in Vaughan and Vaughan 1999, 53–54). (See also Andrew Hatfield, "The Natural and the Dead: Elizabethan Perceptions of Ireland" [Marquerlot and Willems 1996, 32–54].)

A distant allusion to Ireland might lie in the disappearing banquet of 3.3. As narrated by Alexander Eliot (1997, 171–73), King Finn of Fena, on a hunting trip in Limerick, meets the sorcerer Midac. Finn answers Midac's riddle—the answer is "the river Boyne." Finn and his followers blindly accept Midac's invitation to dine with him at his Palace of the Quicken Tree. There, hospitality turns untoward. "We were invited to a feast," Finn cries. "Where is it?" The king and his party end up trapped on the clay floor of the forest, victims of an overconfidence for which no answer, easy or otherwise, exists. They are in for "ling'ring perdition." The application to failure in Ireland, which has become a trap for England, is clear, assuming the allusion is being made.

Leslie Fiedler asserts that "the whole history of imperialist America [is] prophetically revealed to us in brief parable: from the initial act of expropriation through the Indian wars to the setting up of reservations, and from the beginnings of black slavery of fugitive white slaves to the first revolts and evasions" (1972, 238). "And it prophesies, finally, like some inspired piece of science fiction before its time, the revolt against the printed page" (134). *Henry VI, Part II* had done that through Jack Cade and his mob. Fiedler sees Shakespeare mixing "savage man" and Indian because "the age had not been able to decide in fact what Indians were" (233). The play makes clear that Caliban is not an American Indian, regardless of his being taken as one.

In a brilliant essay, Leo Marx (1967) argues that the play's spectrum of possibilities—contradictory versions of the American landscape from a second Eden to a savage wilderness—emerges from European travel narratives. The play involves a dialectic between the ability to transform fallen nature and the inevitable limits of that process. Against the "image of a new earthly paradise" (38), the garden of abundance, was the contrary conception of the " 'hideous wilderness' [wherein] the New World is a place of hellish darkness . . . arous[ing] the fear of malevolent forces in the cosmos, and of the cannibalistic and bestial traits of man. It is associated with the wild men of medieval legend"

(41). "Prospero's situation is in many ways the typical situation of voyagers in newly discovered lands . . . the remote setting, the strong sense of place and its hold on the mind, the hero's struggle with raw nature on the one hand and the corruption within his own civilization on the other, and, finally, his impulse to effect a general reconciliation between the forces of civilization and nature" (35).

The concept of garden expressed "aspirations still considered utopian . . . toward abundance, leisure, freedom, and a greater harmony of existence" (43). But William Bradford, in 1620, "saw deprivation and suffering in American nature, [not] abundance and joy," says Marx (41–42)—dour Puritan eyes saw what they knew to be a fallen world. This "hideous wilderness expresses a need to mobilize energy, postpone immediate pleasures, and rehearse the perils and purposes of the community" (43). "America was neither Eden nor a howling desert. These are poetic metaphors, imaginative constructions which heighten meaning far beyond the limits of fact. And yet, like all effective metaphors, each has a basis in fact" (43), so the New World is like the play. The play is written to demonstrate variable responses within its fiction and invite them to its fiction. Formal and final cause mirror each other. As the island absorbs point of view, so does the play. A "most striking fact about the New World," says Marx, "was its baffling hospitality to radically opposed interpretations" (45).

Prospero "forc[es] his old enemies to re-enact his own passage from civilization into nature," says Marx (51). His inclination "to trust in primal nature (as indicated by his original attitude toward Caliban) now has been checked by his experience of the hideous wilderness, by what he knows of . . . his own aggressive impulses and, of course, by what he has come to accept as the truth about Caliban" (65). Marx goes on to show how the "New World" motifs of the play develop in different ways in writers like Jefferson, Thoreau, Melville, Twain, James, and Fitzgerald.

Ania Loomba offers the intriguing paradox that "Prospero's gift of language . . . initiates the resistance of the slave" (1996; Hawkes 1996, 173). Language gives the slave the ability to articulate a resistance to the white man's "inherit[ing] here" and insisting that the natives learn the "inheriting" language, but only to a point that allows them to obey commands. Slaves in this country could be killed for learning to read, though Frederick Douglass and Paul Robeson's father slipped the surly bonds of illiteracy. It is probably true that language itself is subversive, that to make distinctions it must offer contrasts that, in turn, permit the position of the oppressed to be articulated. Caliban has learned bigger and less, greatest and least, king and slave. His purposes, "endow'd / With words that made them known," became revolutionary. Like many revolutions, however, the "new order" would have proved more "sore" than the old. It should be pointed out that Caliban also learned a language that permits him to express the melodic poetry of his own island. Loomba weakens her case by gendering Caliban's resistance as feminine. That will not work within the play as given, or within Prospero's psychology as inferred. Loomba could have avoided this psychological naïveté by adducing Sycorax.

Walter Cohen claims that "*The Tempest* uncovers, perhaps despite itself, the racist and imperialist bases of English nationalism" (1985, 401). Paul Brown calls *The Tempest* an "intervention [in the] form of a powerful and pleasurable narrative which seeks at once to harmonise disjunctions, to transcend irreconcilable contradictions and to mystify the political conditions which demand colonialist discourse. Yet the narrative ultimately fails to deliver that containment and instead may be seen to foreground precisely those problems which it works to efface or overcome" (1985, 48). In other words, the play is an elegant piece of propaganda crafted to conceal its approval of the vicious nature of colonialization, a concealment successful until this generation of critics uncovered it. We are asked to accept the critic's superiority to the work of art. This "deliberately anti-aesthetic" approach (McDonald 1991, 17) denies art except as a "pleasurable" deception. McDonald refutes the play's unwitting complicity with the colonialist impulse: "The sophisticated effects of form and style bespeak a degree of self-consciousness considerably greater than most recent political readings can admit, a self-awareness that comprehends the issues of politics and power central to the colonialist argument" (26).

The attack on *The Tempest* by way of colonialism offers a useful corrective to oversentimentalized approaches to the play. Like *Henry V*, the script can be said to contain a tough-minded critique of its manifest content. As Orgel says, "Shakespeare, as he does so often, dramatizes both sides of the debate" (1987, 35).

RELIGIOUS CRITICISM

While *The Tempest* may suggest Aeneas seeking his new world in an old world, and while it does show Prospero seeking to regain his old world and to widen it in the next generation, it also reflects the religious issues of its time, not in any doctrinal way but in picking up and reprojecting the great themes and patterns of the Bible and of Christian tradition and ritual. R. Chris Hassel, Jr., relates the play's Christian content precisely to the shift in paradigms that the moment represented: "As these last plays return to the comic-Christian sense of human life as an insubstantial pageant with a benevolent, forgiving auditor, so they urge upon their Renaissance audience a comforting old response to the new scientific rationalism that may be threatening their composure. . . . Such an attitude gives a profound wholeness to Shakespeare's dramatic canon" (1980, 222).

Karol Berger suggests that the play's disappearing banquet "contains . . . reminiscences of the Eucharistic ritual in which God sends down his Holy Spirit (whom the Christian iconography often represents as the dove) to bless the sacrificial offering" (1977, 226–27). G. K. Hunter calls the banquet "a type . . .

of the commonest of all symbolic banquets: the Communion table" (Battenhouse 1994, 264). Later, Prospero will tell Alonso, "Let us not burthen our remembrance' with / A heaviness that's gone" (5.1.199–200). Alonso has responded like the sinners who confess during the Communion service: "The remembraunce of [our sins] is grevous unto us: the burthen of theim is intollerable" (*Queen Elizabeth's Prayer Book: 1559*, 100). Among the priest's responses immediately after the general confession are the "comfortable wordes," which include "Come unto me all that travaile and be heavy laden, and I shal refreshe you." The sinners have, of course, suffered a storm, which, in Alonso's case, has also been psychological. Such torment is promised by the Prayer Book's "A Commination against Sinners": "It is a fearfull thing to falle into the handes of the lyvinge God: he shal pour doune raine upon the synners, Snares, fyre, and brimstone, storme and tempeste, thys shalbe their portion to drincke," and by its paraphrase of Psalm 11.6: "Upon the wicked he shal raine snares, fyer, and brimstone, & stormie tempest: this is the portion of their cup" (quotations and citations are from the Geneva Bible [1560], except where the Bishops' Bible [1572] is indicated).

E. J. Devereux says that "heart-sorrow" is one of the "traditional requirements for sacramental Penance in Catholic theology and repentance in reformed theology" (1968, in Battenhouse 1994, 256). Shakespeare provides archetypes as opposed to narrow, doctrinal formats. The play's "imagery . . . has run from Baptism, with which spiritual life begins, through Communion, Penance, and Matrimony, through finally to . . . prayers for one who can no longer help himself" (257). D. P. Walker underlines the significance of the Mass as archetype, arguing that it is the basic influence underlying Renaissance magic (1958, 36). Its configuration in the Renaissance imagination, then, goes deep. Its reconfiguration in a play—Hamlet forcing wine down the throat of a dying Claudius, Banquo's Ghost denying the table to Macbeth—would echo profoundly, if perhaps unconsciously, in a spectator.

Many moments of the play call biblical phrases to mind. Alonso's hearing Prospero's name in the storm calls up Jeremiah 31.35: "Thus saith the Lord which giveth the sunne for a light to the day, and the courses of the moone and of the starres for a light to the night, which breaketh the sea, when the waves thereof roare: his Name is the Lorde of hostes."

Prospero's "revels" speech inevitably echoes the Bible: "He shal flee away as a dreame, & thei shal not finde him, and shal passe away as a vision of the night" (Job 20.8). "For a thousand yeres in thy sight *are* as yesterdaie when it is past, and *as* a watche in the night. Thou hast overflowed them: they are *as* a slepe" (Psalm 90.4–5). "Lift up your eyes to the heavens, and loke upon the earth beneth: for the heavens shal vanish away like smoke, and the earth shal wax olde like a garment, and they that dwell therein, shal perish in like maner" (Isaiah 51.6). "For the hope of the unthankeful shal melt as the winter yce, and flowe away as unprofitable waters" (Solomon 16.29). "Seest thou these great buyldings? there shal not be left on stone upon a stone, that shal not be thrownen downe" (Mark 13.2). It is "cast downe" in Matthew (24.2). "He behelde the citie, and wept for it. . . . 'For the dayes shal come upon thee . . . And shal make thee eaven with the grounde and . . . not leave in thee a stone upon a stone' " (Luke 19.41–44). "All these things must be dissolved" (2 Peter 3.11).

Perhaps the ultimate gloss on Prospero's "revels" speech is found in Revelation: The seventh angel who comes "downe from heaven, clothed with a cloud, and the raine bowe upon his head," swears "by him that liveth for evermore . . . that time shulde be no more," and that "even the mysterie of God shalbe finished" (10.1, 6, 7). That takes us into a time we cannot know, for knowledge will not exist, nor anything to respond to, nor anyone to respond.

Prospero's comforting of Miranda in 1.2 may echo Matthew: "And the ship was now in the middes of the sea, and was tossed with waves; for it was a contrarie winde" (14.24). Christ walks to the ship and calms Peter and the disciples. "Be of good comfort . . . be not afraied" (27). A famous biblical episode depicts the pacification of a storm: "And behold, there arose a great tempest in the sea, in so muche as the ship was covered with waves. . . . Then he arose & rebuked the windes & sea & there followed a great caulme. But the men merveiled saiyng: what maner of man is this, that bothe wyndes and sea obeye hym" (Matthew 8.24–27, Bishops' Bible).

Prospero's breaking of his staff finds an analogue in God's breaking of "Beautie" in Zechariah: "And I toke my staff, even Beautie, and brake it, that I might disanul my covenant which I had made with all people" (11.10). Prospero disannuls his covenant with whatever powers, white or black, he has deployed.

Martin Lings equates the opening storm to Purgatory, correctly, given the play's movement toward contrition and forgiveness: "The greater part of Purgatory is concentrated in the tempest itself at the opening of the play. Having passed through this storm, Everyman has reached the enchanted island which is no less than a setting for the sacred precinct that marks the end of the soul's quest . . . the outskirts of Paradise. . . . even Caliban is aware of it" (1966, 112).

It is worth noting, however, in light of too-facile allegories, that storms were also precursors of the end of the world: "There shalbe signes in the Sonne, & in the moon, and in the Starres, & in the yearth, the people shalbe at their wittes ende, through dispayre. The sea, and the water shal roare, and mennes hartes shall fayle them for fear, and for looking after those thynges which shal come in a cloud, with power and great glory. When those thinges begin to come to pass, then looke up, and lift up your headdes, for youre redempcion draweth nygh" (Luke 21.25–28, Bishops' Bible). "And there folowed voyces, thundringes, and lightnynges: and there was a great earthquake, and as was not since men were upon the earth" (Revelation 16.18, Bishops' Bible).

Voices are like the ocean, of course, and God is storm, as in Jeremiah: "Their voice roareth like the sea" (6.23). "He giveth by *his* voyce the multitude of waters in the heavens, and he causeth the cloudes to ascend from the ends of the earth: he turneth lightnings to rain, and bringeth forthe the winde out of his treasures" (10.13).

Along with storms, healing music can also be heard in the Bible: "And so when the *evil* spirit of God came upon Saul, David toke an harpe and plaied with his hand, & Saul was refreshed, & was eased: for the evil spirit departed from him" (I Samuel 16.23). Perversely, the Geneva gloss argues the punishing intent even of the soothing strings: "God wolde that Saul shulde receive this benefite as at Davids hand that his condemnations might be the more evident, for his cruel hate toward him."

One of Caliban's options for killing Prospero has a biblical analogue: "Then Jael Hebers wife toke a nayle of the tent, and toke an hammer in her hand, and went softly unto him [Sisera], and smote the nayle into his temples, and fastened it into the grounde, (for he was fast a slepe, and wearie) and so he dyed" (Judges 4.21).

Stephen Greenblatt says of Prospero's "thing of darkness" that "perhaps . . . the word 'acknowledge' implies some moral responsibility, as when the Lord, in the King James translation of Jeremiah, exhorts men to 'acknowledge thine iniquity, that thou has transgressed against the Lord thy God' " (in Bloom 1988, 67). The lines in the Geneva version of Jeremiah 3.13, when God chastises Israel, read differently, but are still appropriate: "But knowe thine iniquitie: for thou hast rebelled against the Lord thy God & hast scatered thy waies to the strange gods under everie grene tre, but ye wolde not obeye my voyce, saith the Lord."

Both Howard Felperin (1972) and D'Orsay Pearson (1974) argue that Prospero's traffic with spirits is potentially damnable. He must repent and abandon the Faustus in himself. Samuel Johnson says, "This power was called the *Black Art* or *Knowledge of Enchantment.* . . . Thus *Prospero* repents of his art" (1951, 530–31). According to Johnson, Prospero must repent. Of Prospero's harsh "forgiveness" of Antonio, Robert G. Hunter says, "As a man, Prospero forgives even the unregenerate, for the justice of man should be tempered with as much mercy as man would hope to find on the Latter Day" (1965, 267).

Prospero's opening storm is stronger than the pagan god of the sea, Neptune, as Ben Jonson's Scrivener notes in the Induction to *Bartholomew Fair*: "He [the playwright Jonson] is loth to make Nature afraid in his *playes*, like those that beget *Tales, Tempests*, and such like *Drolleries*" (Spencer 1933, 416). Prospero is a "type of Christ" in the Old Testament sense, a dispatcher of pagan gods, as in Samson's defeat of Dagon in the Book of Judges (a process dramatized in *Samson Agonistes*), Elijah's victory over Baal (I Kings) and Christ's defeat of rebel angels in *Paradise Lost* and *Paradise Regained* and of pagan gods in "The Morning of Christ's Nativity." Prospero defeats Setebos and, in abandoning his magic and freeing Ariel, returns to the conventional dispensation, as his Epilogue suggests. There, in lines 19–20, J. W. Cunliffe finds "an allusion to the verse of the Lord's Prayer 'Forgive us our trespasses' " (1935, 933). "Mercy itself [is] the Almighty," says William Sidney Walker (1860, 9). Prospero also echoes the Homily of Common Prayer and Sacraments of the late sixteenth century: "For the prayer of them that humble themselves shall pearce through the clouds, and till it draw nigh unto God" (1623, 142). "[T]he weighty allusion to the Lord's Prayer," says Kermode, "lends force to some of the many allegorical interpretations" (1964, 134n).

Perhaps the most allegorical reading of the play is Colin Still's: Prospero is God, Ariel, the angel of God, Caliban, the devil, and Miranda, the celestial bride (1921, rev. 1936). Another allegorical reading places Miranda and Milton's *Comus* within the "tradition that would read the Lady's chastity as Christian charity" (Grant 1979, 82). Grant cites Augustine's *Confessions* in reference to Ferdinand: "Yes, the very pleasures of human life men acquire by difficulties. . . . It is also ordered, that the affianced bride should not at once be given, lest as a husband he should hold cheap whom, as betrothed, he sighed not after" (8.3.7; Grant 1979, 83). Grant associates "wonder" with "admired Miranda," contrasts her with concupiscent Venus, and suggests that Prospero's charity nurtures Miranda (82–85).

George Slover argues that in responding to Gonzalo "and remembering Gonzalo's charity . . . only there does Prospero find the virtue which makes possible completion of 'the rarer action' " (1978, in Battenhouse 1994, 259). That strikes me as exactly right. Prospero surrenders concept for feeling, at last. He has known of providence, heavenly messengers, and auspicious stars. When he weeps in response to Gonzalo's tears, they know him. Slover says, "Finally, the analogical construction [that is, an analogue of Christ, as in a four-level reading of any verse of the Bible] of the event is proposed to and ratified by an act of faith, and it 'becomes' history [is transformed to and, since it is analogic, is becoming to, suitable to], becomes luminous with the will of God. It is this sacramental mode which Shakespeare, in creating *The Tempest*, seems to have absorbed from the Bermuda literature" (261). "Not nature alone but the events of history are sacramental," says Slover. "The deepest meaning of the Virginia plantation lies in its re-enactment of the apostolic action" (258–59): "to propagate the Gospell of Jesus Christ" (page 26 of the *True Declaration of the state of the Colonie in Virginia*).

James Walter (1983) says that "Shakespeare reincarnates" Augustine's "allegorical figures by incorporating them into a mimetic image of life" (in Battenhouse 1994, 272). The island's "landscape [insists that those who arrive there] experience their spiritual conditions in a physical way . . . like Dante's damned and redeemed souls" (272). Antonio would "make a new society based on a 'new man' " (273). He is, like Richard III or Iago, alienated from past modes of inheritance and other continuities. He is one who would rise in spite of barriers through intelligence and quick wits. "As the still legitimate ruler of Milan, Prospero is . . . wisely merciful as he rightfully attempts not simply to punish the criminals but to restore them to good faith and conscience" (274). At the end, in the Epilogue, Shakespeare is asking his spectators "not immediately to pray but to *imagine* prayer and openness to grace as a possible means to human freedom from guilt and sin. Making this plea is as close as he can come to the stance of a prophet and still remain a poet" (278). "By interpreting the play in their consequent thought and through their deeds of love, the audience win a freedom that is identical with Prospero's freedom to renew every traveller to his isle" (279). Prospero may have the freedom, but he lacks the power. Antonio and the spectator must avail themselves of the opportunity. Harry Berger, Jr., argues that Prospero's Epilogue imposes a profound obligation on each spectator: "Only when the prayer for mercy is accepted does the possibility arise of stopping, at least for a moment, the vengeful exchanges of history, of breaking the vicious circle of human violence" (1969, 237).

William Watkiss Lloyd equates Prospero and Joseph, "victim through youthful inexperience of fraternal jealousy and animosity, excited by his own incautiousness, but becoming, through trials, the experienced governor and man of the world, controlling his passions and affections, and in calm wisdom subjecting his oppressive kindred to that discipline of trouble and perplexity that best awakes the dormant conscience, and, at last, when full signs appear of renewed hearts, opening his own, declaring his name, and with full forgiveness reuniting the ties of family and home" (1875, 5–6). The story of Joseph also features a significant outer garment, many tears from its protagonist, and long life at the end of Genesis.

That Ariel as spy does not merely equate to an Elizabethan-Jacobean system of secret police is suggested by the Geneva gloss to Zechariah, who "compareth God to a King, who hathe his postes and messengers abroad, by whome he still worketh his purpose and bringeth his matters to passe" (1.8). "Ariel" is a name in Isaiah (Bishops' Bible, 29), in which the following verse appears: the altar of Jerusalem "shall be visited of the Lord of hostes with thundre, and shaking, and a great noyse, a whirlwinde, and a tempest, and a flame of a devouring fyre" (Geneva Bible, 29.6). In Job, we find, "He shalbe about to fil his belly, *but* God shal send upon him his fearce wrath, & shal cause to raine upon him, *even* upon his meat" (20.23). Kermode quotes the Authorized (King James, 1611) version: "When he is about to fill his belly, God shall cast the fury of his wrath upon him. . . . The heaven shall reveal his iniquity; and the earth shall rise up against him" (20.23, 27; Kermode 1964, 85n). Thus Kermode misses the Harpy-like words of the Geneva version, "*even* upon his meat" (the Authorized version has "and shall rain it upon him while he is eating"). Furthermore, as James Black points out, "The dates of [the Authorized Bible] and the play make this exercise tricky" (1991, 37 n. 8). James's scholars began their work in 1607, but the results published in 1611 postdate or, at best, coincide with *The Tempest.*

Isaiah 29 also employs the figure of the hollow banquet: "And it shalbe like as an hungrie man dreameth, and beholde, he eateth: and when he awaketh, his soule is emptie: or like as a thirstie man dreameth, / and lo, he is drinking, and when he awaketh, beholde, he is fainte, and his soule longeth" (8). The gloss to verse 24 explains that "except God give understanding, & knowledge, man can not but stil erre, and murmure against him." The equation between food and spirit is reiterated in the Geneva gloss to Zechariah 7.6: "Did ye not eat, and drinke for your owne commoditie, & necessitie? and so likewise ye did absteine according to your owne fantasies, and not after the prescript of my Lawe?"

The theological point is that if faith is not present, the consumer will be empty: "And truely as the bodily meat cannot feede the outward man, unlesse it be let into a stomacke to bee digested, which is healthsome and sound: No more can the inward man be fed, except his meate bee received into his soule and heart, sound and whole in faith. . . . It is well knowne that the meat we seeke for in this Supper, is Spirituall food, the nourishment of our soul, a heavenly refection, and not earthly, an invisible meat, and not bodily, a ghostly substance, and not carnall, so that to think that without faith wee may enjoy the eating and drinking thereof, or that that is the fruition of it, is but to dreame a grosse carnall feeding, basely objecting and binding our selves to the elements and creatures," says Part 1 of the late-sixteenth-century Sermon concerning the Sacraments (1623, 200–201). Part 2 describes the psychology of Communion: "Weighest thine owne conscience, which is sometime thine inward accuser" (204). This "Table received no unholy, uncleane, or sinfull ghests" (205). Therefore, "If thou have defrauded [thy neighbor,] now restore to him" (204). The homily goes on to link this feast with the one the Harpies defile in Book 3 of *The Aeneid*: "We ought to purge our owne soule from all uncleanesse, iniquitie, and wickednesse, lest when we receive the mysticall bread . . . we eate it in an uncleane place, that is . . . foule defiled and polluted with sinne" (204). To partake unworthily, of course, "doth nothing els, but encrease your dampnation" (*Queen Elizabeth's Prayer Book: 1559*, 99).

Francis Neilson (1956, 168) suggests that the scene in which Stephano and Trinculo steal the garments from the line and exit pursued by hounds (4.1.255ff.) is a parody of Psalm 22. This is the Psalm that Christ was reciting from the cross—often mistaken for a cry of existential despair—because it is a precise prediction of his crucifixion ("My God, my God, why hast thou forsaken me? . . . they perced mine hands and my fete. I maie tel all my bones"). The psalm talks of the "roaring" of the oppressed individual "compassed" by "dogges," says, "They parte my garments among them, and cast lottes upon my vesture," and seeks escape from "the power of the dog." In the Geneva gloss to verse 12 of the psalm it is David-Christ's enemies who are "so fat, proude, and cruel, that they were rather beastes than men."

Given the play's sense of beginnings and its emergence from the "Paradise" of Ferdinand's rapture, it is not surprising that Genesis is the book of the Bible perhaps most often adduced in response to it. Harold Bloom remarks "Prospero's Jehovah-like reflections upon his fallen creature," Caliban (1988, 6). Northrop Frye says that "the Masque has about it the freshness of Noah's new world, after the tempest had receded and the rainbow promised that seedtime and harvest should not cease" (1959, 18). Noah, instructed to build an ark to avoid God's wrath, is delivered at the end to safety. God says to him, "I have set my bowe in the cloude, and it shalbe for a signe of the covenant betwene me and the earth. And when I shal cover the earth with a cloude, and the bowe shall be seen in the cloude, Then wil I remember my covenant, which is betwene me and you, & betwene every living thing in all flesh, & there shalbe no more waters of a flood to destroy all flesh" (Genesis 9.13–15). The Geneva gloss says, "Hereby we se that signes or sacraments not to be separate from the worde." Unlike things, God's word partakes of essence. In a Platonic sense, God is the only form; everything is immanent in his word. It is what it is, and is not subject to a formula controlled by a priestly caste. The problem, of course, is that a direct sign from God to Noah needs no interpretation and therefore encourages mysticism, a personal relationship with God that requires no intermediary.

Bruno Bettelheim makes a shrewd point about the "psychology" of Genesis: "The story of Cain and Abel shows . . . no sympathy . . . for the agonies of sibling rivalry—only a warning that acting upon it has devastating consequences" (1976, 231). William Rockett relates Ferdinand's work to "commentaries on Genesis [that] illuminate a specifically Christian nature of Shakespeare's thematic use of labor since, for the Renaissance, the Christian utopia, Eden, was a pattern of spiritual cultivation" (1973, 78). Howard Felperin suggests that Prospero is trying to purge the Caliban in Ferdinand (1972, 262–66). Karen Flagstad suggests that Prospero struggles with the "god/beast antithesis which preoccupied Bruno" (1984, 211). It is, she says, "as though Prospero were grooming the lovers as unfallen counterparts of Adam and Eve" (211). The bearing of logs achieves the "purgation of whatever in Ferdinand might be fallen, tainted" (212). It follows that Prospero's hope for the next generation erases the original narrative of sin and death: "Fallen human nature, as a given, precludes utopia/Paradise regained; conversely a utopian brave new world precludes fallen human nature. To enact utopia is to reenact Genesis [and] to nullify a fall which was originally the consequence of partaking from a forbidden Tree of Knowledge" (213).

Frye summarizes the case for a Christian interpretation of *The Tempest*. Its comic action parallels "the central myth of Christianity . . . the comic framework of the Bible, where man loses a peaceable kingdom, staggers through the long nightmare of tyranny and injustice that is human history, and eventually regains his original vision. Within this myth is the corresponding comedy of the Christian life. We first encounter the law in its harsh tyrannical form of an external barrier to action, a series of negative commands, and we are eventually set free of this law, not by breaking it, but by internalizing it: it becomes an inner condition of behavior, not an external antagonist as it is to the criminal" (1965, 133). *King Lear* reverses the figures in the allegory, insisting that the crucifixion follow the resurrection. That works even if we are not habituated to the allegory but have only been educated by events and characters in the immediate fiction of performance. The story told by the Bible and later by Milton is at work deep in the underlying rhythms of *The Tempest*, but so are other stories, of pagan voyages across the depths of prehistory and of new worlds just coming into view.

POSTMODERNISM

"Postmodernism" involves not so much a definition but a set of tendencies—possibly of literature itself, certainly of some productions and of many critics. Postmodernism is in some ways a codification of response to Shakespeare. The plays invariably "signify" in different ways to different people. The same production of a script will elicit radically varying responses. When Ihab Hassan (1986, 1987), then, says that postmodern literary theory rejects a determinate meaning of the text, he is making a claim that directors of the plays have known for a long time. There can be no definitive production of any one of Shakespeare's plays, only an interpretation. Indeed, in the face of indeterminacy, Hassan insists that a "rereader" participates in the creation of a text. For Shakespeare, this rereader is actor, director, member of an audience, and, insofar as his or her work contributes to how the plays work as plays, critic.

I do not believe that Shakespeare wrote according to postmodernist tenets. His plays are unified around principles of analogy and contrast, as *The Tempest* demonstrates. Productions show, however, that questions of "meaning"—Prospero as tyrannical colonizer, Prospero as benevolent humanist, Prospero as controlling god, Caliban as irredeemable monster, or Caliban as sympathetic victim, and so on—are open and subject to the emphasis that a given production provides. One can agree that a critic must, as Hassan says, "deconstruct, displace, decenter, demystify the [apparent] logocentric . . . order of things" (1987, 445) in Shakespeare's plays without agreeing that they are themselves unorganized or unsynthesized fragments. The nature of the synthesis, however, is forever debatable. Different ages and different cultures will find different meanings within the multiplicity of options the plays offer. Often, even opposite meanings will be valid at the same time and place, so remarkably open to imaginative interaction are these scripts.

Terence Hawkes's introduction to *Alternative to Shakespeares II* (1996) claims Shakespeare for postmodernism. There are great strengths in that stance because it permits the script to reshape itself against the friction of a zeitgeist, but there are also weaknesses. One is that a postmodernist production can become an incoherent mishmash that denies any interpretation of the script. If postmodernism comes to mean that the script no longer need be subject to a point of view, then the play is lost at its most basic level, that is, a script designed to be interrogated by performance. No performance delivers "the truth," as I will argue in the chapter on performance, but it must deliver "a truth." Harold Bloom, as his 1998 book shows, dislikes postmodernist modes: "You can New Historicize Caliban if you wish, but a discourse on Caliban and the Bermudas trade is about as helpful as a new-Marxist analysis of Falstaff and surplus value, or a Lacanian-feminist exegesis of the difference between Rosalind and Celia" (1988, 5).

Let us admit that Prospero's art is shadowed, as the human personality inevitably is. He cannot project his art without a shadow, any more than a scientist can construct a hypothesis without some element of the indeterminacy principle entering into his construct. To label the play as blatantly sexist, colonialist, or racist is to ignore other things that are there (as disguise, it seems), and to deny the play any theatrical possibilities, unless as an advocate for impostors, an impostor itself, covertly espousing all that is worst in people and society. What Shakespeare is saying is that here are some issues that complicate Gonzalo's obviously exclusive and hyperbolic assertion that "all of us [found] ourselves / When no man was his own" (5.1.211–12). The complications provide avenues for exploration as the play moves from age to age.

6

THE PLAY IN PERFORMANCE

THE TEMPEST ON STAGE

Like many of Shakespeare's plays, *The Tempest* as play has suffered its revisions and eclipses. Herbert E. Green, writing in 1913, said, *"The Tempest* is undramatic and is seldom performed today" (xix). In 1916, Percy MacKaye produced *Caliban by the Yellow Sands*, a masque depicting the education of Caliban into "that serener plane of pity and love, reason and disciplined love" (as MacKaye called Prospero and Miranda). Caliban becomes the object of the "Americanization movement" that Thomas Cartelli says was "moving into high gear in 1916" as it encountered immigration (1998). Also in gear were the machine guns of the western front. Writing in 1940, Hazelton Spencer said, "Long extremely popular in the theatre, it failed to survive the rise of nineteenth-century realism and materialism. With the recent collapse of confidence in the machine as civilization's greatest achievement and in the lavish use of mechanical accessories as essential to the effective staging of Shakespeare, the time is ripe for a great revival of *The Tempest"* (373). Unfortunately, the machinery of World War Two was already rolling. In 1945, however, the great Margaret Webster mounted a production in New York City with the black actor Canada Lee as Caliban. The production, however, "did not advance a view about colonialism" (Barnet 1998, 187).

We know from the Revels Accounts (Kermode 1964, 150) that the play was performed on Hallowmas Eve, 1 November 1611, before King James at Whitehall. John Dryden, some fifty-eight years later, tells us that "the Play itself had formerly been acted with success in the *Black-Fryers"* (Furness 1892, 390), that

1904 poster, His Majesty's Theatre, London.

Poster for the 1974 Amherst College production of *The Tempest*.
Courtesy of Kirby Memorial Theater, Amherst College

is, in Shakespeare's indoor Blackfriars Theatre. E. K. Chambers (1923), Bernard Beckerman (1962), and G. E. Bentley (1941, 1948) do not record that production. Sylvan Barnet argues that "nothing specified in *The Tempest*['s complete and specific First Folio stage directions] was beyond the facilities available at the Globe" (218). (On the implications of the original production at Whitehall, including the confrontation of monster-king Caliban with James I, see Demaray 1998.)

According to Ernest Law, the Banqueting House at Whitehall "must have afforded full scope for scenic illusion and the presentation of 'tableaux' on a scale and in a setting of unprecedented splendour . . . suitable for the presentation of such a play as *The Tempest*, with its frequent spectacular effects—storms with thunder and lightning and rain, spirit appearances and 'monstrous shapes,' phantom banquets, 'marvellous sweet music' " (1920, 6). Law goes on to say that the Revels Accounts for 1611 listed "a special provision of 'a curtain of silk for the Musick House at Whitehall'—silk because, while effectively screening the musicians and singers from view, it would have offered but little obstruction" to the heard melodies from unseen musicians that resound throughout the play. That is a good point because unseen musicians are written into the script, so their presence/absence at the original production would have reinforced meanings in the play itself, lending, as Roger Poole suggests, "a surrounding impression, a spiritual presence" (1988, 55).

Keith Sturgess provides what could be a valuable hint for modern directors: "Only a full sympathy towards the Renaissance belief in the ethical, religious and therapeutic effects of music will release all the significance of what Shakespeare is doing in this music-theatre" (1987, in Vaughan and Vaughan 1998, 117). Michael Goldman makes a similar point: "The producer searching for keys to a production of *The Tempest* must begin with the atmosphere. . . . The quality of the enchantment is central. . . . The play's events are less important than the way they are felt: how they are received by the characters, how they appear to us, and how they are related to the arts of theatrical illusion in general" (1972, 137). David William, who saw more productions in his time than most of us, indicts "producers [who] offer a visual accompaniment that more often than not distracts from the action rather than illuminating it" (1960, 133). This is a tendency of a postmodernism that no longer believes in thematic unity, but if Aristotle is to be adduced, we should notice that he places spectacle far down on his list of dramatic attributes.

Robert Weimann, one of the most important critics of our times, suggests that the *locus* of the Shakespeare script is conservative; politically it will uphold the authority and rights of rule, and linguistically it will reflect an inevitable early-modern diction and syntax. Its *platea*, however—the interpretation of a performance, its space and mounting—can be radical (1988). We find "meaning" in production by examining the inherited script, the script as represented in production, and the space between *locus* and *platea*. Each area is subject to interpretation. The "space between" for any given production will always be subject to debate and disagreement.

Weimann's thesis was severely applied immediately after the Restoration of the Monarchy by the Dryden-Davenant version of 1667, to which Samuel Pepys refers constantly in his diary for 1667–1669. The acting edition opens with this description: "a thick Cloudy Sky, a very Rocky Coast, and a Tempestuous Sea in perpetual Agitation. This Tempest (supposed to be raised by Magic) has many dreadful Objects in it, as several Spirits in horrid shapes flying down amongst the Sailors, then rising and crossing in the Air. And when the Ship is sinking, the whole House is darkened, and a shower of Fire falls upon 'em . . . accompanied with Lightning, and several Claps of Thunder, to the end of the Storm" (Furness 1892, 392).

Miranda and her sister, Dorinda, have never seen a man. Prospero has kept his ward, Hippolito, hidden on the island from infancy to young manhood. Hippolito asks what he should fear.

[Pro.] But here are creatures which I named not to thee,
Who share man's sovereignty by nature's laws,
And oft depose him from it.

Hip. What are these creatures, sir?

Pro. Those dangerous enemies of men, called women.

Hip. Women! I never heard of them before—
What are women like?

Pro. Imagine something between young men and angels;
Fatally beauteous, and have killing eyes;
Their voices charm beyond the nightingale's;
They are all enchantment: those, who once behold them,
Are made their slaves forever.

The themes of enchantment and slavery are made a subcategory under misogyny. One suddenly appreciates Shakespeare's Ferdinand, hardly a fascinating character, but not ignorant. Man, in this environment, is equally nasty, as Prospero explains to Miranda and Dorinda: "No woman can come near them, but she feels a pain, full nine months." This cryptic warning is lost on the two women. The "symmetry" is extended to give Caliban a sister, Sycorax, and Ariel a female spirit called Milcha, who is chased by two newly hatched sailors.

Subsequent respondents do not celebrate Dryden's revision. Charles Lamb calls it "a vile mixture" (1811, 13). In it, says Sir Walter Scott, "the wild and savage character of Caliban is sunk into low and vulgar buffoonery" (qtd. in Hazelton Spencer 1940, 377). It represents a "marked coarsening and vulgarization of the original," says Palmer (1968, 18), and, in its time, it produced not laughter but "cheap sniggers" (18).

One amusing byproduct of the production is the note provided for the New Variorum edition of 1892 by Commander F. N. Green, U.S.N. He suggests that the ship in Dryden's version would have disintegrated under the command of these sailors: "The scud never goes against the wind. . . . There is no such thing as a 'Seere-Capstorm,' and there has never been such a thing. . . . The orders contained in the preceding seven lines are incoherent and unintelligible. . . . the words and phrases put into the mouth of the Boatswain are manifestly used by a person who did not at all understand them" (Furness 1892, 392–94).

The play continued, however, to invite spectacular treatment. Thomas Shadwell's production at Dorset Gardens in 1674 featured an "Ariel flying from the sun toward the Pit . . . a tempestuous sea in continual agitation" (original stage directions, Royal Shakespeare Company 1994, 13). Shadwell's opera had a chorus of devils and a ballet of winds. In 1695, Henry Purcell added his music. The program for Charles Kean's version over 150 years later, at the Princess's Theatre in 1857, boasted that "the scenic appliances of the play are of a more extensive and complicated nature than has ever been attempted in any theatre in Europe, requiring the aid of one hundred and forty operatives nightly, who, unseen by the audience, are engaged in working the machinery and carrying out the various effects" (Royal Shakespeare Company 1994, 13). Of this production, Lewis Carroll exclaimed: "The most marvellous [thing] was the shipwreck in the first scene, where (to all appearance) a real ship is heaving on huge waves, and is finally wrecked under a cliff that reaches up to the roof. The machinery that works this must be something wonderful" (qtd. in Peter Reynolds 1988, 9–10).

While the Dryden version was "produced at the Theatre Royal, Drury Lane, almost every year from 1701 to 1756" (Barnet 1987, 220), David Garrick restored Shakespeare's play in 1756, cutting only 442 lines and adding only 14. The latter number, given Garrick's inventiveness, shows remarkable restraint. In 1838, Charles Macready, to whom we all owe a great debt, restored Shakespeare's text for good (as he did with *King Lear*), with himself as Prospero and Helen Faucit as Miranda. William Poel's "Elizabethan" staging in 1897 encouraged George Bernard Shaw to say that "the best scenery you can get will only destroy the illusion created by the poetry" (qtd. in Styan 1977, 59). Poel argued that these big sets destroyed the continuity of Shakespeare's staging. As Shaw said, " 'See that singers' gallery up there! Well, let's pretend that it's the ship.' But how could we agree to such a pretence with a stage ship? . . . we could say, 'Take that thing away: if our imagination is to create a ship, it must not be contradicted by something that apes a ship so vilely as to fill us with denial and repudiation at its imposture.' The singing gallery makes no attempt to impose on us: it disarms criticism by unaffected submission to the facts of the case, and throws itself honestly on our fancy, with instant success" (qtd. in Barnet 1987, 222–23). Poel, then, believed that the audience must be asked to use its imagination to complete the dramatic continuum. Keith Sturgess agrees, saying that "the magic island should not be scenically realised. . . . It is a symbolic landscape . . . Utopia . . . Garden of Eden . . . desert place . . . empire and possession [and] prison" according to who interprets it (1987, in Vaughan and Vaughan 1998, 113).

The contrast between spectacular and spare productions continues, causing J. C. Trewin to divide productions into the categories of "spangled or plain" (1978, 274). Defending the spangled approach, Sylvan Barnet says that "the Victorian and Edwardian producers could with some reason believe they were fulfilling Shakespeare's intention when they provided as much splendor and magic as the theater . . . could produce. When electricity was introduced, in the third quarter of the nineteenth century, even more wonderful illusions became possible." Barnet argues that "Shakespeare had himself sought to provide both realism and marvelous spectacles" (1987, 221).

For the plain, Bernard Beckerman argues that "*The Tempest* glows in austerity. The less spectacle it has, the more wondrous it seems. It is easy to be seduced into giving form to the mysteries of the island, but that is a temptation to be resisted" (1976, 57). Writing of an Atlanta production of 1980, Charles Lower says, "Often *The Tempest* draws forth the most massive symbolic stage settings, this production showed how successfully the play can be done unpretentiously, intimately. The values were clear . . . because unobtrusively so" (1982, 237). A rationale for the plain approach is that, as Carol McGinnis Kay says, "This play is molded out of so many diverse elements—comedy, romance, magic, masque, politics, and so forth—that a harmonious production is a rarity." The results can be, as she says, an "uncoordinated collection of slapstick comedy, flower-covered lovers, and tedium" (1976, 66). Stephen Booth replies that "doing everything right in a Shakespeare production consists in doing everything—putting all Shakespeare's ideationally incompatible signals out on a stage and trusting the play to control them. *The Tempest*, like Prospero, keeps telling its audience how to respond, and, again like Prospero, makes the undeniably appropriate responses undeniably impossible. If ever there was a play that demands directorial interpretation, it is *The Tempest*." But then Booth says, "The trick is in resisting the demand. [For example,] the play presents a Caliban not readily summed up in critical essays or neat theatrical interpretations, a linear Caliban who evokes different kinds of responses from moment to moment" (1983, 95). "The spangled," says Trewin, "can get in Shakespeare's way, nudging him along unwisely. The plain trusts him; how far the director himself may be trusted we are likely to guess from the opening scene. . . . do we hear the words as the ship is splitting during a wreck?" (1978, 268). Trewin comes out in favor of the words, as do I.

It is imperative to note that the experience of theater is not the same as that of film or television. We enter into an unwritten contract when we go to the theater, what Coleridge calls "a willing suspension of disbelief for the moment that constitutes dramatic faith" (Harbage 1959, 17). Harbage also cites "a sort of temporary half-faith" and "a kind of negative belief" (17) as Coleridgian efforts to express the nature of our agreement in going to a play. Harbage cites Lord Kames ("lulled into a dream of reality") and S. W. Schlegel ("a waking dream to which we voluntarily surrender," 17–18). This approach to the experience of a play—a conscious yielding to the "truth" of the fiction—counters Samuel Johnson's denial of an imaginative communion with the drama: "The truth is that the spectators are always in their senses, and know, from the first act to the last, that the stage is only a stage, and that the players are only players. They come to hear a certain number of lines recited with just gesture and elegant modulation" (qtd. in Harbage 1959, 18). *The Tempest* might be an alienating experience if it were conducted under these premises.

Even as the play was beginning to become Shakespeare's version again, Charles Lamb's antitheatricalism inveighed against it as a performable text: "It is one thing to read of an enchanter, and to believe the wondrous tale while we are reading it; but to have a conjuror brought before us in his conjuring-gown, with the spirits about him, which none but himself and some hundred of favoured spectators before the curtain are supposed to see, involved such a quantity of the *hateful incredible*, that all our reverence for the author cannot hinder us from perceiving such gross attempts to be in the highest degree childish and ineffectual. . . . That which in comedy, or plays of familiar life, adds so much to the life of the imitation, in plays that appeal to the higher faculties, positively destroys the illusion which it is introduced to aid" (D. Nichol Smith 1916, 218; Lamb's emphasis). Lamb can only see Thomas Dekker's *The Shoemaker's Holiday* as stageworthy and refuses to engage in "the willing suspension of disbelief for the moment that constitutes dramatic faith" that his contemporary Coleridge advocates. Lamb belonged to a group that still exists: those who prefer the study to the theater and who believe that production is a form of degradation: "[B]y the inherent fault of stage representation," Lamb says, "how are these things sullied and turned from their very nature by being exposed to a large assembly" (D. Nichol Smith 1916, 220).

One result of the rediscovery of the Shakespeare text in the nineteenth century was an increasing interest in Caliban. Frank Benson played the role at Stratford-upon-Avon in the late 1890s as a missing link, pursuing the thesis of Daniel Wilson (1873, in Furness 1892, 381–83). Benson chittered, showed his teeth, and swung from branches. The Beerbohm Tree production of 1904, in which Tree played Caliban, featured an amazingly realistic shipwreck. At the end, according to the playbill, "the ship is seen on the horizon, Caliban stretching his arms towards it in mute despair. The night falls, and Caliban is left on the lonely rock. He is a King once more" (qtd. in Barnet 1987, 222). According to Hirst, Caliban shaded "his eyes to catch a final glimpse of the boat transporting a civilization he humbly worshipped" (1984a, 45).

A further recovery of Shakespeare's text was accomplished by the great Harley Granville-Barker, as Russell Jackson reports: "Granville-Barker placed well-known and accomplished actors in central roles, but the texts were not rewritten to favour them. . . . Granville-Barker's Shakespeare, dubbed 'Post-Impressionist' by some critics, responded to a general movement in the visual arts towards stylization, abstract values of colour and space, and the rediscovery of 'primitive' forms and methods" (Jackson and Bate 1996, 126).

The great Prospero of modern times has been John Gielgud, whom many saw reprising the role in Peter Greenaway's *Prospero's Books*. Robert Speaight treats Peter Hall's 1974 production, with Gielgud, in detail. It was, says Speaight, "by a long way the best I have seen" (1974, 393). The "balance between the natural and the supernatural, the formal and the familiar, had never been so surely struck" (394). John Bury's set placed "Prospero's cave on one side and Caliban's on the other—thus establishing the dialectic of passion and reason, civilization and savagery, which is the basic conflict of the play" (394). Caliban himself (Dennis Quilley) was "bisected"—deformed monster on one side, noble savage on the other (Hirst 1984a, 48). The Masque, however, suffered from "dreary modern music, where the note of festivity was sadly missing" (Speaight 1974, 393). "Prospero's mind as [Gielgud] read it was forever beating, and renunciation, like forgiveness, came hard to him" (394). Of Stephen Williams's Ariel, Speaight says, "We realized, as we rarely do, that Ariel is stronger than Prospero" (394). My own memory of Prospero's speech of renunciation is that, as Gielgud gave it, loneliness pooled coldly around him with the words. He was giving up something he knew even as he knew he had to give it up. Was his voice singing above the trials of lesser humans, or was he a detached being hardly noticing humanity—a cold and lonely Mona Lisa? He gave us that choice. The emphatic way he shook his right hand on "I'll *break* my staff" seemed to snap the staff. He exited, leaving a full moon behind. Now it was in charge. Harold Hobson said of Gielgud's delivery of the "revels" speech that Prospero was "a man who looks into the future and sees . . . the destruction of the great globe itself with a shuddering fear" (qtd. in Hirst 1984a, 55).

Sylvan Barnet says that an earlier manifestation, Gielgud in Peter Brook's 1957 production, was "a haunted figure out of El Greco, a man filled with anguish, struggling to rise above the 'high wrongs' he had endured. He finally conquered his passions, and, at the end, armed with a sword, set out for Milan, not as one who would live in easy retirement, but as one who would continue to struggle against evil" (1987, 225). He was, then, a tortured, mannerist portrait of a man on a rack, a suffering, still-militant, saint. Hirst provides a variation on that interpretation: the 1957 "Prospero has absolutely no intention of pardoning the deceiver when he initiates the project" (1984a, 57). "A man bent first and foremost on revenge, [he] is gradually convinced that hatred and vengeance are useless" (57). Brook's ship returned to Naples "with Prospero triumphantly at the helm" (57).

Gielgud's Prospero was accused of being too much the virtuoso—his "vocal skills were something of a hindrance in the role. . . . careful organization of vocal effects [made] it difficult to believe in any spontaneous reaction to events," says Hirst (1984a, 58)—and of overwhelming the play, as Harold Hobson said: his Prospero was "detached . . . blessedly making the rest of the production irrelevant" (qtd. in Hirst 1984a, 59). Hirst says that Hall originally wanted Laurence Olivier for the role (59).

In discussing Inigo Jones, who designed Jonson's masques in the early seventeenth century, Peter Hall suggests what he tries to do when he directs this play, with its prominent masquelike qualities: "Jones's designs demonstrate the shifting contradictions of life with the ease of poetry. And if they are done well and seriously, they can have the same effect today. Spectacle is the chief instrument of the masque, as music is of the opera. It excites wonder. Out of that wonder, comes meaning" (qtd. in Hirst 1984a, 66). That may be, assuming that the poetry itself is not ignored. With Gielgud as Prospero, of course, the poetry will be heard.

Other notable Prosperos of this century have been Charles Laughton's "serene, majestic octogenarian" opposite Elsa Lanchester's Ariel in 1934, in contrast to Derek Jacobi's "vigorous middle-aged portrayal" of 1982 (Pringle 1998, 13). Jacobi's was a Prospero who "found it hard to exchange the role of omnipotent magus for that of a mortal duke" (Beyenburg 1995, 203). Jacobi's Prospero, according to Jay L. Halio, was "not only younger, but angrier than he is usually played. . . . Still smouldering with resentment after many years of exile, [he] awaits his opportunity . . . to take revenge" until he is dissuaded by Ariel (1988, 42). John Wood's was a "retiring, almost reluctant Prospero" in Nicholas Hytner's 1988 Royal Shakespeare production (Pringle 1998, 13). Michael Bryant "yearn[ed] for God's forgiveness" (Beyenburg 1995, 203), while Tom Fleming, for Cheek by Jowl, summoned the storm as an "improvisation exercise" (Beyenburg 1995, 203). Alec McCowen gave Simon Beale's Ariel a pinecone in the 1993–94 RSC production. Ariel "seemed to realise with horror that it came from the very pine in which he had been imprisoned" (204). In John Barton's 1970 RSC production, Ian Richardson's Prospero reached for Ben Kingsley's Ariel and touched only air. Ariel had fulfilled his vision—and Prospero's. "Max von Sydow was tempted to smash Antonio's face with his staff before he decided to forgive him" (208).

Writing of a production in 1975, Robert Speaight says, "No two plays of Shakespeare have invited more frequent failure on that stage than *The Tempest* and *Macbeth*, the first because it seems not to be theatrical" (1976, 15). Paul Schofield in Peter Hall's production at the National Theatre (1975) "present[ed] Prospero as an active protagonist, wrestling with the problems of his own 'beating mind' as well as redeeming, so far as he was able to, the world around him." Thus Schofield "gave an unaccustomed tension to both the character and the play . . . and the performance was sustained throughout by an inward struggle and excitement which made nonsense of the all too common conclusion that Prospero is something of a bore" (15).

"Difference" may be a tenet of postmodernism, but the plays as plays, that is, as productions, have been, for a long time now, breaking the scripts down into production units that emphasize difference. They have to do that. Furthermore, as soon as a script is subjected to an initial read-through, the play as transcendent embodiment of truth disappears into whatever the skill and craft of actors bring to the spoken lines. If the production then communicates "truths" to its audience—and it should—it does so from its very specific dynamics and attack, and in very different ways with different spectators.

We have discovered that we do not have to alter the words or the actions. Within remarkably plastic limits, they become what our shifting of tone, emphasis, and design want them to be. We can discover in them rather than invent different versions, as the seventeenth and eighteenth centuries did, although artistic variations on this suggestive script continue to be written. Like music, but unlike more static forms of art, Shakespeare permits us to inhabit the work of art in imaginative collaboration with the original. The play, as the Vaughans say, is "almost an invitation to complete a story that seems naggingly unfinished" (1999, 75).

It is worth noting that theater is live. As Margaret Spillane says, in words very appropriate for *The Tempest*:

Actual human bodies are on display before us, bodies trained to communicate the consequences of desire or authoritarianism or avarice or rapture. As with all liturgies, theater's gestures are meant to reverberate backward and forward in time, encompassing human history and human potential. But because this epiphany can occur only through the agency of finite, corruptible flesh—which is different today than from yesterday or tomorrow—theater is also about a present moment that cannot be repeated. . . . every performance is a singular event. (1999, 7)

Furthermore, as Matthew Gurewitsch says in his discussion of modern American drama, in "a classic . . . the material lend[s] itself to reinterpretation in the light of changing circumstances" (1999, 25). Few of Shakespeare's scripts demonstrate that principle as consistently as *The Tempest*.

Four essays provide background for any discussion of the play on stage and invite us to play their generalizations against our own experience of *The Tempest* in production: Keith Sturgess uses his sense of the original Blackfriars production as a guide for how the play should be shaped for any performance, while Ralph Berry and Anthony Dawson summarize their sense of the script's progress through the late 1980s, and Lois Potter moves from there. I will deal with more recent stage productions at the end of this section, particularly to suggest variations on the script since these essays were written.

Sturgess (1987, in Vaughan and Vaughan 1998) takes the play through its specific manifestation as a Blackfriars production. He says of it, "An experiment in metatheatre, the whole play explores the baffling territory marked out by 'magic,' 'illusion' and 'trick'. . . . [D]esign, not narrative, is *The Tempest*'s major impulse and its structure is architectural, not dynamic" (107). "The scenery of the first scene is . . . largely acoustical" (115). The "play structurally makes much of abrupt transitions" (115). Our apprehension of the play depends on the "Elizabethan emphasis on costume denoting the man and his function" (113). Trinculo "becomes the comic butt of the true wit of the play, Ariel" (111). "What Shakespeare created [in Caliban] was not some version of the noble savage . . . but a genuine grotesque, half man half beast, something outside nature" (121). On "the modern stage we create a sentimentalised version far from the original" (121). At "its most profound moments [this play is] a kind of nonverbal theatre" (123). "We would turn it into our own—as 'cruel' theatre, or psychological theatre, or political theatre. Shakespeare tells us what it is—'an insubstantial pageant,' given significance by an indulgent audience" (128).

The play has the "unified and elegant shape of Keats's urn" (129). If we think of the upcoming wedding, of people coming to a ceremony on one side of the urn and lovers always being near their goal of union on the other side, we can say that the play leaves us in anticipation, at a point of the suspension of truth and beauty just before their fusion. Shakespeare wisely leaves that oxymoron to our imaginations or to a teasing out of thought. Sturgess in going back to the origins of the play's performance, like Peter Hall in discussing Inigo Jones's designs, would tend to agree with Richard Hornby that "ceremonies always embody some change [and] accompany the major turning points of personal life—birth, puberty, marriage, death," but ceremony "is never plot oriented" (Hornby 1986, 53). For Sturgess and Hall, *The Tempest* tends toward ceremony.

Ralph Berry says that *The Tempest* "remain[s] in the inner repertory of Shakespeare, that part of the canon most charged with meaning today" (1993, 127). "Meanings have changed gradually . . . yet our sense of the play in performance has changed greatly" (127). The twentieth century has seen "a sustained movement to bring [Caliban] within the ambit of civilized society" (128). For the Victorians he was "a figure of loathing and expulsion, a monster against whom society's recourse was exclusion" (128). Nowadays "all start from the premise that Caliban has a case, which must be given a hearing, and that some prospect of his readmission into society must be entertained" (128), under one of two categories: "Caliban must fit into the history of the white man" or Caliban must be an "outcast" (129). Directors "have become bored with Caliban as a victim of colonial oppression. [That] cliche [or] stereotype [serves as a] constriction on the play" (128). Caliban in the Declan Donnellan (Cheek by Jowl) production was "very attractive and consequently very dangerous" (131).

Ariel, says Berry, has an "ambiguous but charged relationship with his master," often with a "homoerotic tinge" (133). Ariel is "almost invariably" male (133), a tendency begun in this century by Leslie French in the 1930 Harcourt Williams production. Prospero is "unfailingly angry, disturbed, bitter" (135). "The actor can always make a 'point' by relating a line to a sudden or prolonged gust of anger" (135). "Anger is fashionable. It has long been banished from the Deadly Sins" (135). "The audience can be left to relate to this field of energy in terms of its own perceptions and preoccupations" (136). This appeals to "multiple response," and there is no need for inner motivation. Members of the audience, it is assumed, have plenty of anger to use as a source of interpretation. The play also emerges from the assumption that "authority in general was socially sanctioned, a generation and more back, in ways that have now disappeared" (137). One "is going to look rather odd portraying authority in the mode of de Gaulle" (137). Ariel's "final gesture is often to disappear without indicating goodbye to Prospero. That is his reward and his revenge" (139). Prospero's Epilogue, Berry notes, is the first time he says "please" (139). Regardless of how the *episteme* may have altered both performance and perception, Berry reemphasizes an ancient truth: "Our experience of [*The Tempest*] will suggest fragments of a great allegory" (138).

Anthony Dawson suggests the range of options available in interpreting the script, its characters, and its performative segments. The play offers a "host of problems—so many in fact that it is a wonder that it is done as often as it is" (1988b, 231). It is often "an excuse for operatic and scenic variety" (231). Dawson quotes Peter Brook to the effect that "usually it only serves to put generations of school children off theatre for life" (231). Since "the Second World War," Dawson says, "the play has been overloaded with allegorical and symbolic meanings" (231–32). "But . . . the play does invite allegorical treatment; it is conceived in symbolic terms" (232). John Barton saw "Prospero as played out, weary and disillusioned," whereas Jonathan Miller "emphasi[zed] colonization, thus calling Prospero's benevolence into question" (232). Recent approaches "either de-emphasize [magic] as much as possible and approach the play realistically, underlining magic's ultimate inadequacy; or build an approach to the play around the centrality of magic, but a magic that manifests itself directly and unspectacularly" (233). Dawson describes a science-fiction "antiphysics" Ariel and company as "spiritual beings unbound by physical laws and appearing to humans as vibrations or shimmerings," making it "possible to believe that [Ariel] actually was invisible" (233). "The text, in fact, makes it fairly clear that Caliban will be delighted to have his island again," Dawson says (234). Caliban may make the claim, but is he to sue for grace in isolation afterwards? "The central figure, however, is certainly Prospero, and other directorial decisions will follow from the initial decision about how to read the enigmatic magician" and how to deal with "the arrogance . . . of his power" (235).

Dawson asks a central question: "How does one find a style [for the Masque] that fits credibly with the overall conception, whether the emphasis is on colonialism, magic, symbolic representation and renewal, or weary and resigned futility?" (237). Dawson would like to see "a little bit of stolen passion" (238) between Ferdinand and Miranda. Like most teenagers, they do behave differently and say pleasing things when the parents are around so that they can just, please, be alone. Of the "revels" speech, Dawson says, "The disillusioned, weary, or even bitter Prosperos will necessarily adopt a different accent from the more traditional, benevolent ones" (239). "If the current popular weariness, disillusion and cynicism tend sometimes to be exaggerated, the old benevolence was often sentimental" (239). In Robin Phillips's 1976 production at Stratford, Ontario, "Hesitation and doubt accompanied [Prospero's] signal to forgive," as opposed to "the older way . . . Prospero simply confirming in his benevolent way the intention he has had all along" (240). "Shakespeare is fully aware, and wants us also to be aware, of the boundaries of both Prospero's magic and the ephemeral magic of the theatre" (241).

Lois Potter (1992) has seen few "traditional sentimental" productions. She recalls "not Prospero's forgiveness but his aged bitterness" (in Gielgud) and the "tyrannical colonialism" of 1970 and 1988 (Graham Crowden and Max von Sydow), the "deeply sinful nature of his dabbling in magic" (Michael Bryant), "comic human fallibility" (John Wood for Hytner, 1988), a "revenge fantasy" (Bill Wallis for Michael Bogdanov), and a "director forcing actors to improvise according to his changing moods" (Timothy Wright in Declan Donnellan's Cheek by Jowl production)—all interpretations showing "distrust of any unproblematically presented authority figure" (450). "British directors," she says, "will often deal with speeches that are either verbally or ideologically difficult by using nonverbal signals to clarify or subvert the apparent meaning" (451). Demands for Miranda's attention are Prospero's "way of underlining the most important facts in" his opening narrative (452). Caliban's "Be my god," she says, is not necessarily funny. A production can be "more sympathetic with the desire to worship than the desire to ridicule" (454). At the end of a production in which Antonio and Prospero were reconciled—an embrace after "Please you, draw near"—she says, "I suddenly glimpsed something of what tragicomedy might have meant when it burst onto the European stage in the late sixteenth century—not the sentimental drama of wish-fulfillment that it sometimes seems to us but an attempt to bring a classical kind of drama within the range of contemporary audience experience and beliefs. One might describe this dramaturgy as post-classicism. The cynical productions I referred to earlier can be seen, equally, as the rejection of conventional interpretations by a post-Christian society. But it seems to me debatable whether such productions speak any longer for their societies, in the United States at least, [where] we have seen in recent years the attempt to unite the capitalist emphasis on freedom with the socialist desire for social justice" (454–55).

Few modern practitioners agree with Robert Speaight that *The Tempest* is an "almost inaccessible play" (1973, 286). Too few of them, however, grasp the truth that Hallett Smith articulates: "*The Tempest* is primarily a play for the theatre. . . . The hero is a man who puts on shows. And the play is full of music" (1974, 1606). Directors tend to search for ways in which they can be seen as clever. Thus in recent times, *The Tempest* has often become merely an allegory of the times. Jan Kott's antiromantic reading of *The Tempest* took over almost from the moment of the publication of *Shakespeare, Our Contemporary* in 1964. Kott claims that Caliban is the "rightful lord [of the island], at least in the feudal sense" (173). "The island," Kott says, "is a stage on which the history of the world is being acted and reenacted. History itself is madness" (180). "Prospero is the producer of the morality play; but the morality play has exposed the reasons of his failure; it repeats history, without being able to alter it" (187). "When the morality play is over, Prospero's magic power must also end. Only bitter wisdom remains" (191).

This dark view certainly has colored productions that have been staged since Kott's reduction of Shakespeare to the visions of modern, existentialist playwrights. The major metaphor for *The Tempest* becomes the collision between the self-styled superior civilization and a heart of darkness. In 1970, Jonathan Miller, ever one to be trendy, raised the issue of colonialism in a production at the Mermaid Theatre in London. Caliban was the uneducated field hand, "a detribalized, broken-down, shuffling, disinherited being" (Ronald Bryden, qtd. in Hirst 1984a, 50), Ariel the clever house slave. Both were played by black actors. "Ariel has read the works of Regis Debray" (theorist of the Black Power movement in the 1960s), says Ralph Berry; "Caliban just knows that you do it with a machete" (1993, 134). "Graham Crowden play[ed] Prospero as a tough local governor" (Hirst 1984a, 43). Underlying the production, Miller said, "is the tragic destruction consequent upon a white assault on a tribal culture" (paraphrased in Barnet 1987, 224).

Suddenly we are in that postcolonialist space that we recognize, if only when we go to see this play in the theater. Many productions of the play since the late 1960s were variations on the theme of colonial oppression. Of a 1971 Stratford, Connecticut, production, Errol Hill, an African American, says, "I have always made common cause with Caliban, being myself one of the dispossessed ex-colonials. . . . Caliban does have a legitimate grouse. He is forced to serve a foreign master in his own land" (1971, 373). Of a 1974 New York Festival production, M. E. Comtois says, "The clowns came out of the Third world: Jame Sanchez played a Puerto Rican Caliban, and Randy Kim, a Hawaiian, played Trinculo in white-face" (1974, 407).

Joseph Papp was on to multiculturalism long before it became trendy. In fact, Papp can be credited with promoting it in the theater and thus with encouraging awareness in other sectors as well. Of a 1976 Great Lakes Festival production, Lester Barber says, "Ariel was played by a black actress, and an atmosphere of black primitivism was deliberately stressed with the use of conga drum music" (1977, 223). Of a 1978 production in Scotland, Graham Barlow and Priscilla Seltzer say, "All the submission implied in colonization—all the rigors of learning rules imposed by an alien culture—were contained in the simple gesture of Caliban drawing on a pair of grubby serving gloves. Similarly the problems attendant on civilizing natives were cynically expressed when . . . Sebastian made a brief re-entry and thrust, as if in afterthought, a large crucifix into the hands of a bewildered Caliban" (1979, 161). Of a 1980 production in Edinburgh, Barlow and Seltzer say, "The comedy in the scenes with Stephano and Trinculo was never allowed to obscure our insight into the intricacies of colonization. Matthew Francis's Caliban, eschewing the grotesque, showed the pains and confusion of the half-educated savage" (1980, 162). Of a 1980 production in West Germany, Werner Habicht says, "Caliban . . . was a black slave who, though curbed by his bondage, had moments when he seemed to be discovering his true nature. . . . When the civilized company was ready to depart at the end, however, he was left on the island dressed in an Uncle Tom costume—a dubious emblem of Prospero's colonizing achievement" (1981, 414).

By the early 1980s, some reaction had set in. Of a Champlain Festival production of 1983, Kenneth Rothwell says, "This was not a *Tempest* for the disciples of Jan Kott. The darker elements of bondage and suppression that mark Prospero's domination of Caliban and Ariel were simply not in evidence. The island's atmosphere remained more benign than malign" (1983, 471). Of a 1982 Stratford, Ontario, production, Ralph Berry says, "Nowadays, directors have gone off Caliban: I suspect that they are bored with symbols of colonial oppression" (1983, 95). If so, the script moves on in time to explore what Stephen Orgel calls its "endlessly malleable" quality and "the history," which Orgel says, "is assumed to be speaking through it" (1987, 76).

A Southbank documentary on Peter Hall's production of 1988 and the two others in Hall's 1988 trilogy, *Cymbeline* and *The Winter's Tale*, appeared in Great Britain in 1988 and subsequently on Bravo Channel in the United States. It features interviews with Hall and rehearsals and depicts the struggles of the actors in a repertory company. Tim Pigott-Smith, for example, did Iachimo, Leontes, and Trinculo and dramatizes the tensions inherent in getting ready to go on with these complicated scripts. Of Prospero, Hall says, "He is in a struggle with himself. He is a man on an island allowed to play God. He performs black magic. The play is blasphemous, which is why it is so elliptical. He hates Caliban because Caliban represents Prospero's own fear of lust and sensuality" (Southbank 1988). Hall claims that Prospero does not intend to bring Trinculo and Stephano ashore and that their plot with Caliban is a surprise. This documentary is vivid and useful as it relates to how the script is interpreted for purposes of performance.

This production is treated at length by Roger Warren (1998). The opening dialogue should not be "drowned in noisy confusion" (153). Hall is quoted as saying, "Prospero has done the *wrong* thing. He was born to rule. Instead he indulged himself in introspection, and so was worthily deposed" (155). "These late plays are concerned with seizing the moment when people are ready" (paraphrase of Hall, Warren 1998, 156). The "fusion of past and present [places] tremendous pressure on Prospero" (156). He betrays a "shifty sense of guilt" in "transported and rapt" (157). Hall says that "Prospero has great trouble in organizing this creature," Ariel, and that their relationship incorporates "tense acrimony and . . . affectionate cooperation" (159). Prospero, says Hall, "may be reacting . . . against the dark side of himself" (160), that is, the shadow, the personality developed by Prospero's repression of his body politic. That becomes an evil or threatening quality likely to emerge in excessive efforts to control others.

Prospero "sees in Caliban the dark, potentially violent and uncontrolled side of himself" (178). In Caliban "the distinction between the civilized man and the brute wore very thin," says Hall (Warren 1998, 161). The "island is multifaceted, and . . . how it appears depends upon who is looking at it" (paraphrase of Hall, Warren 1998, 165). Prospero is "testing his brother," Warren says (166), providing an opportunity. He cannot motivate Antonio any more than he can reform him. Sebastian's "most high miracle" arrives with an "ironical snarl" (168) as he recognizes that he is more steps away from a throne than he had thought. In the play, Prospero is "undergoing a purgatorial crisis" (169). Stephano, Trinculo, and Caliban undergo a "physical ordeal, [the] court . . . a spiritual one" (170). The "process they are undergoing parallels" Prospero's (181).

Music in the play, says Warren, "is at first frightening, then soothing, then deceptive" (172). In the Hall production, the spirits appeared with Ariel, so that Prospero spoke to "elves of hills." They disappeared after the "heavenly music." Warren notes that "not a single positive achievement [is] mentioned" in the "elves of groves" renunciation speech, but that is inevitable if Prospero is surrendering something he perceives to be both dangerous and damnable. Prospero "has challenged God's authority in raising the dead. . . . God has much to forgive him for" (183). The scene is transformed by "heavenly music," but Bryant had to wait for it. The court party became "people gradually emerging from the influence of a magic power [as opposed to the replacement] of one magic spell with another" (184). The "change is not achieved all at once" (185). Michael Billington, writing in *The Guardian* for 21 May 1988, said that "the conjuration of heavenly music . . . becomes the urgent plea from a man who has been dabbling in satanism" (qtd. in Warren 1998, 187). Bryant was "straining under the psychological burden of each act of magic," an approach that contrasted with the concept of "all-powerful patriarch and magus," said Gary Jay Williams (1993, 238).

A look at other productions, some major, some minor, will vivify the issues involved when actors encounter the script and illustrate the remarkable range of interpretation not only possible but inevitable, given the impact of these words on the imaginations of those trying to bring them alive in front of an audience. Most productions try to subvert what they take to be the dominant interpretation of the play, and some are subversive even when they are trying to play it "straight."

Bernard Knox spoke in the mid-1950s, of "a recent production of the Yale Dramatic Association [that] presented *The Tempest* as 'science fiction'; the shipwreck scene took place in a spaceship, and the action which occurs away from Prospero's cell was seen [by him] on a giant television screen. . . . Shakespeare [too] has substituted for the normal laws of the operation of matter a new set of laws invented for the occasion" (1955, in Barnet 1987, 164). With space invaders "in the air" in the 1950s, it was inevitable that *Forbidden Planet* was about to appear. I will discuss that film later.

In writing of *Return to Forbidden Planet*, the Vaughans report that "while the colonialist theme so prominent in *Tempest* interpretations during the 1960s and 70s still lingers, Shakespeare's most spectacular play is now more often the inspiration for visual display and fantasy than for political didacticism" (1992, 17). That "he can still be lampooned as the epitome of high culture in a popular farce is another sign of his staying power. . . . it confirms Shakespeare's cultural versatility and persistence" (1992, 16).

The Vaughans provide samples of Aimé Césaire's *Une Tempête*, translated by Richard Miller and performed by the Ube Repertory Company in 1992: Boatswain: "Shove it! If you want to save your skins, you'd better get back to those first-class cabins of yours" (1992, 17); Caliban: "I respect the earth because I know that it is alive. . . . The Europeans think the earth is dead and tread upon it with the steps of a conqueror" (17). Having said, "What an idiot I am! How could I ever have thought I could create the Revolution with swollen guts and fat faces," Caliban "determines to fight Prospero to the death, alone" (17). "Prospero stays with Caliban and gradually rots away" (17). Caliban will win in this battle of attrition—he is on nature's side. Nature spelled backwards is nabilac.

Peter Holland says that Brook's *La Tempête* (originally staged in Paris, and which Holland saw in Glasgow in 1991) was an "inversion of colonist readings" with "an African Prospero [and] a white German Caliban," a "thrilling" effort to "resist politicalisation in favour of theatricality" (1997, 266). But, says Holland, it demonstrated "its own colonialism [in] its own annexation of other cultures for its aesthetic ends" (267).

This production, Dennis Kennedy says, employed "a few witty metonyms" (1993, 283): bamboo sticks for the sinking ship, a cage for Ferdinand, Ariel with a ship on his head, Gonzalo surrounded by miniature castles—sand castles for his Utopia, one assumes. David Bennent, a white illegitimate son of colonials, "threw off any easy view of European domination of the magic island [and] upset the standard political interpretation" (284). The production aimed at "the theme of freedom as a universal desire" (285). "Shakespeare wrote for . . . architectural scenography: the theatre building itself provided the design for the production of his plays" (25), what Kennedy calls "a medieval scenography," as opposed to that of Inigo Jones and Restoration playhouses.

Mladen Engelsfeld reports a wonderfully appropriate version of the play: "During the summer [the Histrion Actors Company of Zagreb, Croatia] hire a ship in which they travel along the richly indented Croatian coast giving performances in the remotest islands and in faraway hamlets for people who have never seen or heard of a theatre" (1982, 505).

One knows how much one can trust the director when he or she sees an astrolabe. It was not until the late eighteenth century, after all, that Captain James Cook invented the sextant and made longitude available to the sailor. The astrolabe measured only latitude, the distance north or south of the equator on the basis of the noontime sun. Later in this production, Robert Strane's for Asolo Theater (Sarasota, Florida) in 1980, the breakup of the Wedding Masque was designed to remind us of the passengers and crew leaping from their seemingly doomed ship in the first scene of the play. The production reinforced the various "unities" of the script, telling us that everything we witnessed was a moment within a single great event.

William French's review of a Lime Kiln (Virginia) *Tempest*, with a black Prospero, and Miranda, Alonso, Antonio, Sebastian, Gonzalo, Ariel, Caliban, Stephano, and Trinculo played by white actors, says that "the inversion of racial casting coupled with a benign Prospero neatly subverted both old and new approaches to the script." The location became an African kingdom, says French, and the theater—"an amphitheatre with vine-covered limestone walls that rise forty feet above the main playing area to a display of lush foliage—was ideally suited to represent a tropical island" (1992, 42).

Liviu Ciulei says that "the actors . . . must know what universe they populate, what their surroundings are" (qtd. in Kennedy 1993, 290). Ciulei directed a powerful surreal *Midsummer Night's Dream* and a Bismarckian *Hamlet* that realized a superb contrast between a grim court world and a bright Elizabethan "Gonzago." His *Tempest* of 1981 in Minneapolis was "eclectic" (Kennedy 1993,

291). "Ciulei presented an image of time's paradox: instruments of art, mercantilism, and violence confused and simultaneous, all of equal value, all of equal meaning (291), with "a strong inclination toward the distance, coolness, and irony of proscenium images" (292). Kennedy says that "postmodern design is apt to rely on visual quotation and dislocation, methods that ask the spectator to assume a skeptical or even sardonic relationship to the ocular: the signifier is drained of its conventional signification" (293). This "non-pictorialism" incorporated an abandoned rowboat, an empty suit of armor, a clock without hands, the Mona Lisa (obviously not knowing what to make of the set she was part of, but smiling nonetheless), an antique typewriter, an old cash register, the trunk of a Greek statue, a horse's head, a sewing machine, a rifle, a stuffed chicken, a lute, and a globe.

Michael Fitzgerald's Prospero in Silviu Purcarete's 1995 version for Nottingham was "unambiguously Mozart," Peter Holland reports (1997, 230). "Caliban [at the end] sat playing the melody [the opening of Act 4 of Mozart's *Marriage of Figaro*] on a violin, at first as hideous scratchings but metamorphosing magically and movingly into beauty" (231). "Prospero's confrontation was not with his enemies but with the fact of death" (231); the play is, for Purcarete, "about time before death" (qtd., 231). One assumes that Purcarete was pointing at the poignant fact that Mozart was planning to write music based on *The Tempest* just before he died.

In Leon Schiller's production in Lodz (1947), Prospero stood in front of a map and spoke "Our revels" as prologue. He pointed to a ship on the map, and the storm began. The audience saw the ship through a circle in a drop. The framing showed that the tempest was "Prospero's artifice, and suggested a tension in his character between the creator and the colonist" (Kennedy 1993, 189), that is, one assumes, between a godlike creature above mankind and one who attempts to work primarily as a human on the human level. In this production, in pantomime, Caliban bowed to Prospero, who laid his hand on Caliban's head. But "this tacked-on resolution was more likely to reveal the contradictions in the text than Shakespeare's own ending" (190).

A Marxist version of Friedo Solter (1974) exposed the "ambivalence and inner contradictions of Prospero as colonizer" (Kennedy 1993, 208). He "had to use force to maintain his dominance but was racked with doubt . . . far from the wise magus who implied Shakespeare as ethereal poet, transfigured and apotheosized" (208). "Any revolution about private ownership must occur in the mind before it can occur in the land" (Karl Marx, qtd. in Kennedy 1993, 209). The "production read [the] text with Marxist eyes . . . as an incipient plea for the rights of the other" (210). The liberation of Ariel and Caliban, "represented as fleshly mortal men[,] became the rightful conclusion to a comic action" (210–11).

Giorgio Strehler's production in Milan (Piccolo Teatro, 1978) used a female Ariel (Giulia Lazzarini). The "meeting of Ferdinand and Miranda," Kennedy reports, "took place without effects. . . . we watched two young people fall in love, heedless of the political and historical forces that had brought them together: a vision close to what Shakespeare's audience probably saw" (310). Strehler "made the theme of his version the exploration of the nature and power of the stage" (Hirst 1984a, 61). According to Strehler, the play "is the most poignant lament over the failure of a marvelous humane project, a project which has not succeeded" (qtd. in Hirst 1984a, 62). The court fled the Harpies in this production, leaving robes and Alonso his crown. These objects became the glittering apparel with which Stephano and Trinculo approach Prospero's cell later (64).

The play's eclecticism was captured in Yukio Ninagawa's Tokyo version in 1990, described by Kennedy. It had "multiracial casting," with "the African and Asian instrumentalists in full view" (1993, 57). "The noble characters performed in a style suggestive of the noh, especially in moments like the disappearing banquet scene, while Caliban and the servants used the devices of the comic kyogen plays that are often seen between noh performances" (60). "There was no one source culture for [this] *Tempest* but rather a number of them: Japanese theatre and theatre history, a Swedish film, Western music, Stanislavskian acting, and of course . . . a speculative or symbolic Shakespeare" (62). "While deconstructive directors often force their audiences to reassess attitudes to Shakespeare, intercultural performances do something more. By foregrounding Shakespeare's foreignness, they urge audiences to reassess attitudes about the integrity of culture. These productions . . . are about Shakespeare *in* culture" (63). As Shakespeare invades or collides with other cultures, he shows those cultures what they are and are not.

A refutation of Keith Sturgess's assertion that *The Tempest* "has always been staged in a spectacularly visual way" (1987, in Vaughan and Vaughan 1998, 111) was the 1993 A Center for Theater Research (ACTER) production. Jane Arden as Ariel became the figurehead of the King's ship, suggesting her control of the storm and its ultimately benevolent objective. This beautiful apparition, whoever she was and whatever she represented, could not be an instrument of evil, so that even in the first scene we sensed positive powers at work. All of this was done without any effort at the spectacular. That production did the play with only five actors. John Ford recalls "the ingenious yet self-effacing way the actors solved the logistical problems of tripling, quadrupling . . . through movements and blocking that helped create a world. . . . in that wide gap of time between one character and another, [they] would not exit the stage but fall into a trance. When that actor suddenly metamorphosed into a new consciousness, it was as if the very language he spoke had awakened him. The stage was filled with dreamers and wakers" (1999, 1–2). As Ford suggests, the players insisted that we become coproducers of their imaginative construct.

Of Ian McKellen in the 1999 West Yorkshire Playhouse production, Benedict Nightingale says, "You don't doubt that Prospero has spent 12 years on the island, but you also wonder why he hasn't used his magic to improve his standard of living." He is "life-battered, weather-beaten . . . wryly disillusioned." He "still feels anger at his foes, but doesn't need Ariel to tell him he must show pity to them" (1999, 36).

Robert Brustein, artistic director of the American Repertory Theatre, points out that "*The Tempest* has always lent itself to considerable reinterpretation. Stimulated by New World ideas, George C. Wolfe's recent New York Shakespeare Festival production was an essay on the kind of racial divisions caused when a colonial master imposes his will on a native Caribbean population. Our director, Ron Daniels—a native Brazilian himself expatriated for much of his life in England and America—has imagined the play as representing the synthesis of a variety of cultures into *La Raz Cosmica*, the Cosmic or fifth race. This may explain why the masque scene . . . involving Juno, Ceres, and Iris, has been recast with characters named Americas, Europe, and Africa, the three major continents (and races) of the world" (1995, 1).

Regardless of concepts, however, Brustein rightly says that "productions of *The Tempest* ultimately stand or fall on how well they deliver the characters and the story—a story of sin and forgiveness, of revenge softened by reconciliation, of drunken ribaldry, of magic and enchantment that test the human capacity for amazement" (1995, 1). Fortunately, some productions are able to escape from under their heavy overlay of "interpretation" and to tell different stories movingly.

Sam Mendes's *Tempest* for the Royal Shakespeare Company (1993–94) had less negative design—sets that get in the way of the actors or that try to tell the audience what the play means—to overcome than other productions of that RSC London-Stratford season. Even then, however, Alec McCowen, who played Prospero, suggested that there is nothing that even a lead actor can do against the tyranny of design: "I spend quite a bit of time standing up a ladder at the back of the set, watching the action I've planned unroll—people tell me it's a marvelous image, but sometimes I do find myself wondering quite what I'm *doing*, trying to climb a ladder in this long, heavy robe. Sometimes designer's take actors' lives in their hands!" (qtd. in Elgin 1993, 14; McCowen's emphasis).

The production began with Ariel swinging a lantern, which summoned wind, storm, and the pitching decks of a ship. "By watching an actor make a tempest we are invited to think about actors making *The Tempest*," says Robert Smallwood (1996, 176). The lines emerged clearly—unlike the opening scene of Ashland's 1994 version, where sound effects obliterated the Conradian contrast between the perceptions of mariners and landlubbers. McCowen's Prospero stood above it all, behind a scrim. Ariel stood midcenter, and the Boatswain was down front, shouting orders. A hierarchy descended toward us, the audience. We were the sea and, at the end, of course, the ultimate authority to which Prospero prays. The opening neatly articulated the issues of theater and the issues beyond theater by placing characters on stage so that they told us who we were. And we "are in turn simply another group of players in a larger play, and . . . the physical theater in which [we] sit is not final reality but simply another stage on which a longer play is being enacted before an unseen audience" (Kernan 1974b, 1).

The production, then, removed the script from postmodernism, with its suggestion that the attitudes of art are almost (but not quite) nihilistic, and put it back within premises that argue that plays create a community of response that shares a single experience even if the evaluation of that experience breaks down into myriad, singular responses. Prospero became a storyteller, with Miranda sitting to his left watching the various characters appear as Prospero named them from behind an upstage screen. This was, says Russell Jackson, "the only play in the main house [Stratford] to be presented with direct appeal to the text's own theatricality, sustained by its opportunities for metatheatrical devices and ideas" (1994a, 345).

Both Stephano and Trinculo were Prospero "offshoots," the former an uncontrolled megalomaniac—"a mad parody of Prospero himself" (Billington 1994, 26)—the latter a failed ventriloquist from Yorkshire with a lookalike puppet. The payoff with the puppet, of course, was when Ariel said, "Thou liest," and poor Trinculo thought that his wooden head had come alive, as in various modern versions, from Pinocchio's wish to be a real boy, echoed in *The Tempest* by Cupid, to more malign manifestations. Trinculo emblematized the equivocal nature of "illusion" and the fragility of "theater." The tricksiness did not necessarily evoke a parallel psychological response, particularly from James Hayes's impassive Antonio. David Troughton's Caliban, however, a Boris Karloff imitation, was afraid of Trinculo's puppet, as if it were another of Prospero's spirits sent to torment him. The central concept was developed in Prospero's cardboard pop-up, picture-book theater, which became a life-sized proscenium for the puppet-show masque. This was a very "theatrical" and "stagey" sequence, but was a splendid way to integrate the Masque, which is often difficult to present, with the idea of theater that dominated the play. In the Masque, of course, Cupid must be dissuaded from his venereal attack on the betrothed couple, and in this Masque, the "sunburnt sicklemen of August" turned out to be Caliban and party, having hidden within illusion as a cover for their ambush. We watched a simultaneous creation and stripping away of fictive layers that demonstrated at once the "reality" of theater—the action behind the mimesis— and the nothingness there as well: not even "a rack" of elegant but insubstantial cloud "behind." For Paul Taylor, however, "Prospero's eventual image of life and theatre dissolving into one another" was undercut by "Mendes' playfully illusionistic approach," in which "all the island's a stage from the outset," and thus the final "perception is pre-empted" (1994, 38).

A bit of staginess that did not work was Ariel's dispersing of the banquet. Rather than a "sea-nymph," he appeared as Banquo's Ghost, blood-boltered, to remind the "men of sin" of their crimes through a physical manifestation of them. This allusion to the denial of a eucharistic feast to "notorious evil-livers," as the Communion rubrics have it, which also pertains to the "solemn supper" in *Macbeth*, was valid enough ideationally, but finally only proved the old adage that "you can't play a concept." The Antonio-Sebastian conspiracy, meanwhile, was very much underplayed, indeed, lazily performed as if it were a function of almost suicidal boredom. Sebastian made a point, however, at the end when he took the crown that Stephano had appropriated from the various items that Prospero had put out to deflect Caliban and confederates. "Or stole it, rather," Sebastian said. Again, the production's constant contrast between "reality" and "stage property" was underlined.

Simon Beale's Ariel was a stiff, angry-eyed, pajama-clad Mao holding within this shape a yearning for freedom—a state beyond the "freedom/service" paradox that the play keeps asserting. It was "the best Ariel" that Michael Billington had "seen in a lifetime's theatregoing" (1994, 26). Benedict Nightingale, in a review that concentrated on Beale's Ariel, wondered, however, "If you had been jammed in a tree by a witch for 12 years, would you be quite so rude to your rescuer on your very last day of employment? . . . would you act like that if your rescuer was . . . McCowen's . . . benign [Prospero]?" (1994, 34). But Ariel's "smouldering impassivity" (Farley 1994, 13) could also be attributed to Prospero's threats to do worse to Ariel than Sycorax had done. When reminding Ariel of the torment he had freed him from, Prospero handed Ariel a pinecone. At Stratford, Ariel spat in Prospero's face at the end, perhaps making some point about colonization. In London, no spitting happened. It would have been against whatever the ending was saying. "My Ariel chick!"—are you still here? Prospero asked, in lines rearranged for this emphasis. "To the elements—be free!" I have set you free—go! Ariel, having yearned for the moment, seemed reluctant to accept it. He had not received much reassurance in his quest for "love," and he had come close to being human in talking of "*your* affections" to Prospero, so he vacated a kind of emotional vacuum for whatever vacuum he would henceforth inhabit. He looked back as if on a zone like a dream or a memory from childhood—an uncompleted space that must remain incomplete. It was a moving ending that then asked us, through Prospero, to respond to it.

"Prosperos today," says Ralph Berry, "are, and have long been, unfailingly angry, disturbed, bitter" (1993, 135). It was a relief, then, to escape from the John Wood version of Prospero to one who might be considered "old fashioned"—calm, controlling, even underplayed, and speaking the lines with a sense that they are "high poetry"—in Alec McCowen. Prospero was decentered, the fragility of theater was placed in the forefront, and thus Prospero became a kind of Ronald Colman explaining Shangri-la to Jane Wyatt. The joy of watching this Prospero may have stemmed from his refusal to "tap . . . one of the mysterious themes of our time, the legitimization of anger" (Berry 1993, 136), certainly a theme that Kent in Shakespeare's time also tapped (cf. *King Lear* 2.2.68). For critics, however, conditioned by the recent trend, this Prospero was inadequate: "Having abdicated the driving forces of rage and revenge for a kind of melancholy irony, McCowen finds it hard to exert real authority over this band of exiled misfits and the result is a *Tempest* with no real eye of the storm" (Morley 1994, 17). It is doubtful that Prospero has revenge in mind at all, except as an option he had discarded at some point during his twelve years on the island (cf. Coursen 1969, 1976, 1986). Peter Holland found McCowen a "grumpy Victorian father, neither magus nor duke" (1997, 171). Holland attributed the problem to the transition from the Swan at Stratford to the Barbican in London (where I saw it), which had not been "fully accomplished" (175). "Prospero has been voice-coached out of existence" (Billen 1994, 2). The "stress on Prospero as meta-theatrical manipulator, frequently seen atop a ladder, diminishes his own sense of buried grievance" (Billington 1994, 26). The "play needs to be alive with Prospero's sense of grievance and hunger for revenge. This McCowen does not manage" (de Jongh 1994, 31). "This Prospero is so much master of himself that he robs the play of half its tension" (Macaulay 1994, 38). "McCowen's tetchy Prospero is . . . dispiritingly low-key" (Hanks 1994, 1). "He seems to need reminding that it was this detached attitude that precipitated his exile in the first place" (Farley 1994, 13). Paul Taylor called McCowen's "dapper, donnish" Prospero "damagingly under-driven" (1994, 38). Sara Abdulla, however, found McCowen to be "a generous and attractive Prospero," infused with "warmth and humanity," with "no room in his reading for the customary megalomaniac: indeed his omniscience seems a wholly acceptable consequence of his superior moral fibre in comparison to the rest of the island's inhabitants" (1994, 39). Indeed, the extreme position that critics would wish upon Prospero was inhabited by Mark Lockyear's Stephano. Charles Spencer found that it was "the undertow of sadness that makes this *Tempest* so moving. . . . McCowen's . . . dry pedantry and sense of repressed grief [are] deeply affecting. [At the end] Prospero seems an old and broken man, courteously begging release from the heartache of this cruel and unfathomable world. It's a chilling moment, as if Shakespeare himself were finally admitting both bafflement and defeat" (1994, 23). Perhaps, but we, the audience, were the sea from which Prospero had come, and the gods to whom he prayed at the end, and it was we who had to "fathom" his meaning in our response. This was a Prospero who asked for "final cause"— our willingness to complete his fiction, to make it whatever "reality" we could or would—and that was the powerful point of his understated Duke.

One of the few problems with this production was Mark Lewis Jones's sappy, falsetto Ferdinand, lucky to be compared to Caliban at all. As I had in watching Troughton's Cloten opposite David O'Hara's incomprehensible Posthumus a few years earlier in RSC's *Cymbeline*, I was rooting for his Caliban against this Ferdinand, but to no avail. The alacrity with which Miranda at the end began inspecting "such people" as inhabited this "brave *new* world" got a big laugh, perhaps because Ferdinand suddenly had competition that might prove insurmountable. "With [Jones] as her benchmark of mankind, we can well understand Miranda's wide-eyed joy when she beholds the other men on the island" (Abdulla 1994, 39). "A chap who quacked around like [Ferdinand] would leave a Miranda as spirited as Sarah Woodward wondering if she hadn't made a mistake spurning Caliban's advances" (Nightingale 1994, 34).

It is tempting to argue that Prospero was engaged in the psycho-game that

William Watterson describes. Having "enjoyed the . . . satisfaction of enslaving Caliban's rowdy masculinity" (forthcoming), Prospero "welcomes the arrival of Ferdinand since it gives him another opportunity for compensatory dominance and filial subjugation. . . . Ferdinand draws his sword against the patriarch only to be disarmed by the latter with a stick. Prospero then makes the young man's 'weapon drop.' . . . Prospero's symbolic emasculation of his son-in-law is the kind of petty sadism born of homosexual envy," or perhaps, of Prospero's repressed incestuous desire. At least, Prospero gained in this Ferdinand an adoring foot-licker, not only in Prospero's power but forever in Prospero's debt.

The George Wolfe version, which moved from Central Park to the Broadhurst Theatre on 44th Street in 1995, received some rave reviews. I come down on the side of those who did not like it. I am just not a postmodernist. Yet, for reasons I will deal with, this will remain for me the greatest *Tempest* I have ever seen.

John Simon, in one of his total pans, claimed that the transplanting of the play "to some Central American or Caribbean salsa-spouting locale makes for instant disorientation" (1995, 97). That assumes another orientation to begin with, of course. "In the first moment of the play, the actors of the ensemble crash through the map of Renaissance Europe, like an angry child demanding our attention," said Karin Coonrod in a program note (1995, 40). We were meant to believe that Eurocentric assumptions were being smashed. Fine. Iconoclastic—cartoclastic—forces were at work. But would we get more than an angry child's interpretation here? What troubled me was the bewildering mixture of styles that characterizes postmodernism on stage these days. We got Kabuki, where the actors are supposed to be invisible, an approach that worked well once, as four black-clad actors carrying long poles closed Ariel in with the threat of oak in which Prospero will peg the spirit if it more murmurest. But this was part of what Pia Lindstrom called "a mishmash of styles" (1995), including blue streamers for the storm, which was given to us twice, once in word and again in mime, stilt-walkers for the Wedding Masque, puppets styled after Bunraku for the banquet, a shadow-mime behind a scrim as Caliban and confederates were chased by Mountain and the other dogs, a little touch of *Prospero's Books*, in that a mariner quoted from a copy of *The Tempest* during the first storm sequence, and a live percussion section that sometimes drowned out the words of the play—MacIntyre Dixon's excellent Gonzalo being the chief victim. I kept looking for Carmen Miranda. Clive Barnes called it "spectacle rather than poetry, glitz rather than passion" (1995, 23). Irene Backalenick labelled it "a Mardi Gras atmosphere that effectively demolishes the text . . . a circus—and a poor man's circus at that" (1995, 24). John Lahr claimed that "we leave the theatre remembering the sound of drums and the spectacle of gargantuan Brazilian saint-goddesses, but not one vivid line of poetry" (1995, 121). This "racing, tumbling production sometimes tends to wear you out," said Clifford A. Ridley. "It also comes perilously close to upstaging the play" (1995, 39). "Where's the play?" asked Dennis Cunningham (1995). Linda Winer said that "this magic island has surprisingly little enchantment: lots of spirits but almost no sense of the spiritual" (1995, 39). "Wolfe," said Robert Feldberg, "was trying to deconstruct the play and make it more magical at the same time, and neither approach clicked" (1995, 17).

Coonrod asked, "What kind of a Shakespeare production is this that smashes through Europe? This is not the stuff of psychological theater. This is bigger. It's a piece of spatial poetry that at once exposes the deep pain of cultural silence and celebrates the angry explosion of that silence" (1995, 40). But it is not to insist upon a "Eurocentric" reading to suggest that the visual and auditory cacophony of this production silenced whatever the play may be saying, tossing it into space, no doubt, but space without a magnetic field.

Add to this conceptual incoherence the fact that the usually sure-fire comic scenes failed here, and the problems deepened. Teagle F. Bougere delivered an impressively dignified Caliban, and Ross Lehman was amusingly out of the play as Trinculo. But Mario Cantone's Stephano was a fugitive from a terrible television show, full of that big-city "in-group" subtext for which Joseph Papp's productions were infamous. People from outside of the city are bewildered by all of that, particularly when the material in the play itself can be very funny if performed. This, said Feldberg, was "the kind of thing that killed vaudeville" (1995).

For me, Carrie Preston's Miranda was another problem. She was hardly "the usual sleeping-beauty" (Tretick 1995, 18). Rather, she was a "jittery" (Greg Evans 1995, 79) girl who had even begun to eye the handsome African American Caliban as someone she might invite to violate her honor. One could understand, given her frantic father, how she had gotten that way, but "where," as Brad Leithauser asked, "has she acquired her repertoire of salacious smirks, hotfooted flouncings, pouting moues?" (1995, 119). Some teenage behavior resides in a master gene, perhaps, but this Miranda had been prowling the malls. She "plays," said Christopher Rawson, "like a half-witted Peter Pan" (1995, D9) and was "too hoydenish," as Irene Backalenick said (1995, 24). She was "a maid," no doubt, but "no wonder" (1.2.429–30). Why did Ferdinand call her one? Because the word is in the script.

The soul of Wolfe's *Tempest* was Patrick Stewart's Prospero. The role is primary to the play, of course, but Stewart worked against the deafening frenzy of the production by delivering a quirky, nuanced magician who could convince us that he had to struggle with revenge even after deciding intellectually that "not a hair" of his enemies would perish and even after prompting the love at first sight of Miranda and Ferdinand. If the rest of the production had a rationale, it was that the unintegrated importations from many cultures reflected Prospero's turmoil. Stewart began as a jumpy and very troubled man, speaking, as John Simon said, in "short-winded, staccato word clusters separated by pauses" (1995, 98). These were not the stately cadences of the great man recapitulating history, as in Alec McCowen's strong Prospero for RSC in 1994, but the outpourings of someone who had long repressed his story and who drew his breath in pain

1996 advertisement for the New York Shakespeare Festival.

even to tell it now. His admonitions to Miranda were, for him, necessary pauses within an agonizing experience. He lay his forehead against hers as he asked what she could see in "the dark backward and abysm of time" (1.2.50) in a remarkable image of taking her back where he had gone in his agonized recollection. Prospero forgot the name of his benefactor and paused until it came back to him. That set up a key moment much later.

Stewart is a remarkably intelligent actor. He knows where his character is going—Prospero is heading toward Act 5, which is almost all his—but he knows that the actor must show us how the character gets there. Stewart convinced us that Prospero, although confused and angry early on, had found his way to clarification at the end. As Gonzalo began his too-inclusive speech about everyone finding himself "when no man was his own" (5.1.213), Prospero whispered "Gonzalo" to Miranda. Prospero had to "recall" the Gonzalo in himself, as he had done only moments before when he saw his old friend weeping at the distress of the King and his company. "Holy Gonzalo, honorable man, / Mine eyes e'en sociable to this show of thine, / Fall fellowly drops" (5.1.62–64). Prospero's passion had to find compassion. Before that moment, Prospero had paused for a long time, his staff threatening to descend upon a cringing Ariel, who had dared to say, "Mine would, sir, were I human." Prospero's paralysis at this moment echoed those that he had induced in Ferdinand earlier, and, through Ariel, in the "three men of sin" after the banquet vanishes. It was a moment made more powerful by its silence, one of the few still moments within the vortex of this production. The male power to thrust and hurt had to be suspended and replaced with something else. The frozen image asked, literally, whether Prospero would crush his own spirit—Ariel and his own soul. That Ariel was played by a young and beautiful Afro-American woman (Aunjanue Ellis) made the situation even more threatening than it was merely by dint of Prospero's poised staff. Stewart very quietly said, "And mine shall."

On the word "abjure" in Prospero's speech about giving up his magic, Stewart fell on his back in the sand, and the island shook and flashed as Prospero's psyche released its negative energies. Having made the decision—this time with heart and not just with mind—he could weep at yet another of the many analogues of pity presented to him in the play. As his tears flowed at the sight of Gonzalo's tears, the sea from which he had escaped emerged from within him. Then, Prospero, having bedecked himself in his ducal garments, took his hat off and presented himself to Caliban, whom he had enslaved so painfully. "This thing of darkness [long pause] I acknowledge mine." Caliban held a murderous club in his hand. Caliban hesitated, dropped the club, and leaped off to join Ariel, having freed himself by not deploying the club, as Prospero had by not smashing Ariel with his staff. The lines about decking Prospero's cell and about Caliban's seeking "for grace" were cut to facilitate this linking of the two slaves in some zone free of bondage. Both young and attractive Afro-Americans, free of Prospero at last, exited together to explore whatever allegory their union would come to represent. It was the first time that I have seen Caliban paired up. The pairing of the former slaves created a kind of parallel world, existing out of sight and out of history, to the marriage of Ferdinand and Miranda.

In 1982, Derek Jacobi directed his "every third thought shall be my grave" to Antonio, as if to say, I will be constantly on guard against your treachery. This was, of course, to extend the political theme beyond the play's ending. Stewart's "every third thought" was spoken to Gonzalo and seemed to say, "I will think less of death now than I have done." That reading was splendidly consistent with the coming to humanity that Stewart charted for us.

At the very end, as the actor removed his finery—linking it with the trash that

Stephano and Trinculo had filched from the line—Stewart gestured to the wings on "Now I want . . ." and paused. The setting rose to the flies. The lights came up.

Through the Wedding Masque, Prospero had glimpsed masked evil coming toward Ferdinand and Miranda. His dismissal of the sprites was grim and disturbing, but it neatly set up his dismissal of illusion at the very end of the play. We were in the brick and catwalk world of a bare theater. Prospero's magic had been theatrical. Had it been anything more? The question had to be answered by the gods to whom the actor prayed—the audience out there. The answer, of course, was yes—if we had attended to Prospero in spite of the sound and fury of so much of the rest of the production. The erasure of theatrical premises was hardly a new device, but Stewart's sheer presence made it very convincing.

This Prospero becomes one of the great ones of our times, to be contrasted with the other great one, Gielgud's icy and alienated version in the 1974 Peter Hall production. Stewart built on several previous performances: his splendid Enobarbus for Trevor Nunn in the early 1970s, where a finely detailed struggle between reason and emotion led to the wrong decision, his remarkable Shylock at the Other Place in 1977, where his refusal to play stereotype led to a subtle characterization that permitted the final act to evoke the depths of the script's potential comedy, even as the comic closure excluded Shylock, and his Oberon for John Barton in the late 1970s, where the character's menace melted somewhat when he got his way about the Indian Boy. All of this and much more went into this magnificent Prospero.

Sand is the site of *The Tempest* these days. The American Repertory Theatre version added a giant compass, about forty degrees worth, to the dunes. The compass was all that remained, it seemed, from some race of giants that had crashed the face of their enterprise into these yellow sands. We were not meant to muse about this event. It was a given, as much a part of the play's prehistory as Prospero's narrative. The problem with this large object curling down like a crumbled roller coaster from a scaffolding up left to a giant fragment down center was that it blocked the stage in the middle. The primary playing area was down left, although Ferdinand and Miranda played down right at moments. Prospero stood up right during much of the final scene—maestro of the genre of romance. But any fluid movement across the stage was prevented by the decay of that colossal wreck.

Director Ron Daniels put the built-in disadvantage of this set to some use by making the spot at the bottom of the compass the site of power. Since this script features at least eight characters who are, would be, or talk of being rulers, their moment in the sun of power or their basking in dreams of power often occurred in the elevated space down center.

The primacy of this position was signalled by the Boatswain in the first scene, who stood in front of the curtain while two mariners tugged at sheets on either side of the stage. The King and his party entered from behind the curtain to quarrel with the Boatswain and to be shaken as the ship shuddered before a new blast of storm. The problem here was that the Boatswain either had a cold or had not done his vocal warmups, so that the Conradian contrast between the inexorable rules of the sea and the Machiavellian ways of the court was not well drawn.

Prospero stood on the compass, his right foot on his staff, for much of his exposition to Miranda. His was the commanding voice, of course, although his sense that Miranda was not attending to his story was a product of his own pain in telling it. Caliban's cave was at the base of the shattered compass, suggesting the things of darkness that lie beneath man's inventions—the Jungian shadow that is invariably a product of repression. Caliban came out and spoke of being his own king from the central position but was chased by Prospero, who got the "any print of goodness" speech that the First Folio assigns to Miranda. Gonzalo described his Utopia from there, and Sebastian and Antonio prepared to kill King and courtier there. Caliban inhabited that space for a moment as he began to become the leader of the anti-Prospero conspiracy. There, Prospero drew the magic circle—in blood, it seemed, from his staff—into which the three men of sin, Alonso, Antonio, and Sebastian, collapsed in the final scene. The payoff for this emphasis on a single area occurred when Prospero summoned Ariel at the end. Ariel did not come. We were left to infer that Ariel had freed himself and that Prospero's boast that calm seas and auspicious gales would help them to catch the royal fleet far off might go unfulfilled. Prospero's power was fleeing. His Epilogue, in which he broke his staff and flung the halves away, was delivered from that same central place, now a zone from which power had fled—unless our good hands and our indulgence flowed forward. We had been where the sea and the storm were. We now became a many-handed god to whom Prospero prayed.

The acting was uneven. Paul Freeman (Prospero) is an actor of what used to be called "the old school" that went out with the solos of Donald Wolfit and the tremulous recitations of Maurice Evans. Freeman's Claudius for the New Shakespeare Company in 1994 sounded as if it had been imported intact from an old repertory company and simply dumped like a broken record into a production trying to emerge from very different concepts of dramaturgy and acting styles. As Prospero, he ranted and raved and glinted opaquely out at the audience, a berserk colonizer out of Conrad stumping around the sand like Robinson Crusoe, leaving no "r" untrilled. Miranda (Jessalyn Gilsig) was infected by this frenzy and could have been termed hysterical were that word not sexist and therefore politically incorrect. Benjamin Evett's calm and clearly spoken Ariel began to help the script make sense, but he was hampered by the necessity of exhaling some of his lines through a seashell and singing some of his songs in a falsetto, which perhaps said something of androgyny but obscured the words. The words to the songs in Shakespeare are never merely background noise, but the distinction has become lost since the deaths of Cole Porter and Ira Gershwin.

Remo Airaldi, a wonderful Quickly in the *Henry IV* plays, was a pudgy Antonio who laughed too much, signalling his own shallowness. He made no objection when Prospero reclaimed Milan, as Nestor Serrano had in the Wolfe production in New York. Charles Levin's Stephano was costumed like a soldier out of Hakluyt's *Voyages* and therefore ready to be fanned by his wine into a convincing parody of tyranny. Jack Willis's Caliban was merely a confused islander, no monster. He wore one of Prospero's discarded ruffs along with presumably aboriginal beads, a necklace of bone, and some sort of tribal marking on his forehead. In the New York production, Bougere's Caliban wore an old pair of Prospero's breeches. Each Caliban was clad in the white man's discards, suggesting that neither had his own identity. Willis was best when he tried to simulate the sense of humor that he thought human beings possessed, his "ha, ha, ha" being labored and artificial. Thomas Darrah, a versatile actor for the American Repertory Theatre (ART), was particularly good as Trinculo in charting the alienation that Stephano's drink induces in him. After the three anti-Prosperoites fell into the filthy pool, Darrah did wonderful things with his now-detumescent clown-fool's cap. Here we got none of the campy, queeny business that made the New York sequences incomprehensible to all but those "in" on the topical and ephemeral subtext that those actors were playing. Scott Ripley's Ferdinand was endearingly bemused as he spoke of loving and being loved for the first time, regardless of his claims of "prior experience."

Daniels and designer John Conklin tried to overcome the static quality of their roller coaster with amusing stage spectacles that told us that we had little to fear for any of the creatures wandering the sands. For "Full fathom five," giant tropical fishes were swung from poles by sprites in a silver-blue sea, even as Alonso's bier ascended from the briny in front of a bewildered Ferdinand. Ariel rose on a wire from the same space with Harpy wings to indict the three men of sin in an amplified voice accompanied by an impressive Bach-like postlude—the "organ" for which Alonso calls. The Wedding Masque presented three spirits—the Americas, Europe, and Africa—under giant parasols that echoed the earlier fish. The deities bore gifts à la *Prospero's Books* or the Magi to Ferdinand and Miranda. We were asked to join in with the "Chant for Omulu" in a moment too close to "An Evening at the Pops" for comfort.

This was a trendy effort, according to Shawn Rene Graham's program note, to show that "for this global society of ours to become a true union of all cultures, the old cultures should not be thought of as dying, but living in new forms" (1995, 8). That, however, is to use the play to say something that it probably is not saying. What do we do with Caliban at the end? Wolfe's production freed him and seemed even to give him, in Ariel, the mate for which he has wished. Here, the question was simply ignored. The Masque, meanwhile, tells the story of the deflection of Cupid's threat to the young couple into Cupid's determination to be "a boy right out." The Masque, then, sublimates whatever Ferdinand's lust might wish to do prior to ceremonial confirmation of that impulse. The Masque also predicts Prospero's transition from god to man. Not so here. But it was brief, and Prospero's stopping of it was sudden and dramatic. To Freeman's credit, he read the "revels" speech quietly. It was "in context," for a change, as opposed to just another rip-roaring recitation of a famous speech. Freeman paused before he asked Ariel, "Dost thou think so, spirit?" and again after Ariel spoke of being "human." This was not the spiritual wrestling to which Stewart subjected his Prospero, but a reconsideration of original intentions. Yes, Freeman's Prospero said, that is what I meant when I first raised the storm. The pauses here permitted us to recognize that he had never intended revenge, regardless of Freeman's fury and sound.

Two aspects of the production confused me. Some productions of *The Tempest* show the sun moving across the sky, suggesting the time within which these events are occurring. Prospero brings Miranda up to date. The narrative can continue now after twelve years. The King and his party are forced to pull their own roles in these events up from the depths of their repression of them. Here we got what seemed to be a full moon, a time of high tides and madness. Stephano pointed at it when he claimed to have been "the man in the moon" (although Antonio's previous line about the man in the moon was cut here). At times, as when Trinculo entered, this moon was erased by storm clouds, and before the banquet scene by an eclipse. After the intermission, however, this moon seemed to have become a sun, setting toward its green flash. If this was meant to "provoke thought on the audience member's relationship to the environment[, as] both Conklin and Daniels wish to instill" (*American Repertory Theatre News* 1995, 3), I suppose it worked. I felt like Kate on the road to Padua.

Miranda and Ferdinand played at chess in front of a huge, tilted landscape in an ornate frame—classic columns and elegant elms spoke of a place other than this island. Was this an artifact that Gonzalo had provided in his survival kit? Was it a signal of the golden age of artistic flowering and patronage that Ferdinand and Miranda will bring to a unified Naples-Milan? It was a beautiful image, but it was isolated and not prepared for by anything that had gone before. Perhaps that was the point. The painting might have borne some relationship to the giant compass. Perhaps it signalled a vision beyond mere technology.

In 1998, Ferdinand's "patient log man" created a controversial image in Adrian Noble's *The Tempest* for the Royal Shakespeare Company at Stratford-upon-Avon. Evroy Deer has a Caribbean accent as yet not tuned to the rhythms of the RSC, and certainly at odds with Ferdinand's courtly tongue. It was unsettling to see the only African actor in the cast thrust into the role of slave. Or perhaps the unsettling aspect was to hear his scripted acquiescence to the role. Michael Billington "looked in vain for an exploration of the play's colonial politics" (1998, sect. 2, 2). Prospero as slave master was right there in front of his eyes.

I appreciated Adrian Noble's effort to do something with the inflexible Stratford main house. To create a thrust stage would be to eliminate so many seats in the balcony that significant revenue would be lost at each performance. Noble has raked his stage, has thrust it as far forward as he can, and has built a ramp down the left-hand aisle (stage right). The payoff for *The Tempest* was to have Prospero, Miranda, and Ferdinand come down into the audience to observe the Masque. This removed a plane of fiction, or a level of mediation, but it permitted the Masque to come right at the audience. The Masque is more of an independent production within the play than is "Nine Worthies" or "Pyramus and Thisbe," to which the aristocratic audience responds, or "Gonzago," which may capture Claudius but certainly entraps Hamlet. Noble's treatment also made the issues of the Masque—Cupid's conversion from anarchic glee to humanity, for example—potentially available to us, if, as here, the poetry was spoken clearly. We heard a narrative that has its resonance in the play outside the Masque. This approach, as John Gross says, made Prospero "a bit like God in the Old Testament" (1998, 12), but in placing Prospero within our community, it conferred godlike status on us, the audience, as well. It is to us, the audience as god, that Prospero prays at the end, even as he defines the reciprocal nature of prayer: "As you from crimes would pardon'd be, / Let your indulgence set me free."

Chip Egan's *Tempest* at Clemson University in 1999, part of the splendid Clemson Shakespeare Festival, was played on a scaffolding at the center of Clemson's black-box theater. Thus the opening storm occurred on two levels. Above, the mariners toiled. Below, the King's party huddled and occasionally went up to scold the sailors. It turned out that these were spirit-swabbies who had already put the real mariners to sleep and were functioning under Ariel's command. They saluted Ariel and left wheel and rope once the ship itself had been abandoned. Ferdinand got the line Ariel imputes to him ("Hell is empty, / And all the devils are here!" [1.2.214–15]) so that we could identify him later. Egan surrendered the poetry of the Masque for an amateur hour. None of the spirits had ever played a goddess, and none had had time to memorize the lines. Cues were missed, lines amusingly misspoken. John Keebler was a reluctant Juno in drag and blew his entrance. Ceres' "I know her by her gait" (4.1.102) was a desperate improvisation to cover Juno's delay. The Masque can be tedious and is often cut. At its best it images a "natural Utopia" that balances against the contradictory vision enunciated earlier by Gonzalo. Egan's approach gave his audience a change of pace, a kind of antimasque in front of all the solemnity of Act 5. The audience also enjoyed Libby King's befuddled and ineffectual Trinculo. "The devil take your fingers" was a superbly inept curse, as Trinculo recognized while trying to reach for a more devastating response. Lisa Mercer's agile Ariel swung on the scaffolding and continued the countertrend back to the female Ariel of the nineteenth century. B. W. Gonzalez at Ashland in 1994, Aunjanue Ellis at New York's Public Theater in 1995–96, and Hannah Matis at Brunswick High School in 1999 were also splendid in a role played mostly by men since the 1930s. R. W. Smith played Caliban as an intelligent, if drunken, undergraduate and was a clumsy and nonthreatening counterpart to Ariel in this fast-paced and well-spaced version.

A sparkling production by Pamela Leddy at Brunswick, Maine, High School in 1999 showed what can happen with some shifts in gender. A female "Sebastine," bitingly delivered by Shannon Dougherty, was obviously having a desultory affair with Robert Vigus's Antonio. Once he convinced her to join him in the assassination plot—a neat reversal of the Macbeth/Lady Macbeth

Alex Petroff (left) and Hannah Mattis (right) in the 1999 Brunswick (ME) High School performance of *The Tempest*. Copyright © The Pierce Studio, 14 Pleasant Street, Brunswick, ME 04011

dynamics—they represented a union more profoundly threatening to Prospero's plans for Miranda and Ferdinand than a merely political alliance. Meanwhile, Elizabeth Steiner's fetching "Stephana" flirted with John Bronson's Caliban, then pushed him away—she was the Audrey of the island—and ceded him Miranda without regret. The relationship contrasted splendidly with the more formal and controlled courtship of Ferdinand and Miranda.

Kurt T. Von Rosador says that "the pursuit of essences and inner-textual functions is, to put it politely, an unprofitable one" (1991, 1). Assuming that a director wants coherence in his production, he might emphasize a theme around which to center his action. If he or she were editing the script—not as necessary with a short play like *The Tempest* as with a *Hamlet* or a *Richard III*—the director might profit from an essay like Reuben Brower's, which shows how the poetry of the script reinforces its meanings at various moments and links its disparities of tone and style. That is not to deny the multitude of documents and

1999 Brunswick (ME) High School performance (left to right): Grant Tremblag as Trinculo, John Bronson as Caliban, Elizabeth Steiner as Stephano. Copyright © The Pierce Studio, 14 Pleasant Street, Brunswick, ME 04011

events circulating in the culture at the time the play was written, but it is to insist that efficient cause (Shakespeare) knew what he was doing when he created formal cause (the play). Implicit in much recent criticism is the suggestion that this play and others would have emerged simply from the friction engendered by circulating documents. Furthermore, at least one director of the play has found that "discussions of *The Tempest* in terms of colonialism, or slavery . . . never seemed to me to be anything but peripheral, at least to production in the theatre" (Shrimpton 1976, 65). What he does find valuable are precisely the thematic aspects that configure dramatic action: "penitence and reconciliation . . . revenge and forgiveness" (65). If we assume that these are plays meant to be produced by actors, much of what is written about them is irrelevant.

BRUNSWICK HIGH SCHOOL PLAYERS
PRESENT
THE TEMPEST

BY
WILLIAM
SHAKESPEARE

MARCH 24,
25, 26 & 27
—7:30 PM—

CROOKER THEATER

TICKETS: *Students & Seniors:* $4 in advance/$5 at the door
Adults: $5 in advance/$6 at the door

INFORMATION: 798-5500

Roger Warren says that "theatrical interpretation of Shakespeare is a continuing process. Each new production makes its own discoveries" (1991, 243). Kennedy agrees: "One way to imagine the scenographic history of the century for Shakespeare is to see it as a series of attempts to make a home for the otherness of the texts" (1993, 310). *The Tempest* is a play of great "otherness," and it is an otherness that changes as history decides what "the other" is and is not.

THE TEMPEST ON FILM AND TELEVISION

To conflate film and television, not to ask students to make distinctions between the media, to ignore the ways in which a given production deviates, by addition or subtraction, from an inherited script, or to neglect to ask what a script is is to smudge distinctions just when they should be focussed tightly, and to deny students a crucial aspect of their education: that is, how do the media work? The question can be answered by asking another: what happens when Shakespeare is translated to television or film? To say that "video is excellent for teaching Shakespeare . . . because . . . students come to us with thousands of hours of TV and movie watching under their belts" (LoMonico 1994, 219–20) is to miss the point. Perhaps under their belts, but can they describe the experience analytically, explain the difference between a light-sensitive medium and a cathode-ray tube being bombarded with electrons, begin to explore the differences between what can happen on a large movie screen and a much smaller television set, or talk intelligently about the differences in expectation between watching a show at home on television and going to a cinema complex to see a film? Being a frequent flyer does not mean that one knows how to fly the airplane.

What we observe on the screen—film or television—and not on a printed page is a relationship between word and image.

A written text on the right-hand side of any script page which makes complete sense in itself is a bad text. What are the pictures there for? . . . The words, except in exceptional circumstances, need to follow the pictures. . . . Pictures have their own grammar, their own logic . . . and cannot easily be kept waiting. . . . To such a picture you could speak no more than about 25 words. . . . [L]anguage seems to play a secondary role in television. (Hearst 1978, 4–5)

As Peter Hall suggests, in Shakespeare, "what is meant is said. Even his stage action is verbalized before or after the event. This is bad screen writing. A good film script relies on contrasting visual images. What is spoken is of secondary importance. And so potent is the camera in convincing us that we are peering at reality, that dialogue is best underwritten or elliptical" (1969, 37). The great Russian filmmaker Grigori Kozintsev agrees, calling "half of the text of any play a diffused remark that the author wrote in order to acquaint actors as thoroughly as possible with the heart of the action to be played" (1966, 215).

In other words, actors and directors collaborate with the original work. This is particularly true of film.

To use "*film* as a blanket term for all formats," as Jo McMurtry does in her very useful book *Shakespeare Films in the Classroom*, is to mislead the student by "leveling . . . the distinctions . . . between productions conceived for the 'big' screen and for television, or between productions that interpret the plays visually, eliminating much of the language in the interest of images and productions that essentially record stage performances," as Hardy Cook says. "These are distinctions that I find very useful," Cook says (1994, 77).

I have written at length on this topic (Coursen 1997b). My point here is that the cassette tends to erase distinctions that we must make before we can evaluate the success or failure of a Shakespeare script as translated to different media. The conceptual space—its field of depth, its use of light, its conventions, and our expectations of it—defines what can and cannot happen within it.

When no television version of a particular script is good, it helps to ask why. It also helps to sort out elements that do work on television and to ask why. Negative examples are often more useful than positive ones.

With the exception of the 1992 animated version, none of the available television versions of *The Tempest*—the 1960 Schaefer, with Maurice Evans, the BBC production of 1980, directed by John Gorrie, with Michael Hordern, the 1983 Bard, directed by William Woodman, with Efrem Zimbalist, Jr., or the NBC "Deep South" version of late 1998—is particularly successful. The reasons lie not only in the productions but in the nature of the medium. Television is not a good vehicle for this script. As Caryn James suggests in a recent review of a PBS analysis of television (1996, 25–27), the tube shows real people snarling at each other over their pizza. It has evolved, then, from its early days as "kitchen table drama" to a depiction of the frustrations and crude solipsisms of the lower middle class that occur in the same zone. *The Tempest*, with its magician, its prince and princess, its dynastic conspiracies, its monster and its spirit, and its possible examination of the deep shadow that colonialism casts, is not likely to extend a medium that trivializes and domesticates its trivial and domestic material. Add to that the structural limits of television, which are also imaginative limits—lack of physical depth tends to mean lack of artistic depth—and you do not have a fit between script and medium.

Jack Gould notes that the play "poses a severe traffic problem" for the small screen and that close-ups are not helpful in a play that "requires [the] fanciful, not [the] factual" (1960, 63). Television lacks the magnitude for the play's larger effects, even as its capacity for intimacy proves no advantage. Close-ups invite "psychological" interpretations perhaps less appropriate to this script than for others. Prospero's soliloquies and major speeches, for example, tend to be grand announcements or pronouncements.

The farcical byplay among Caliban, Stephano, and Trinculo, abetted in the Schaefer production by an Ariel voluntarily concealed in a tree, as opposed to imprisoned, is well framed for television. Ariel must seem to be hidden, of course, since television is a realistic medium that does not ask us to suspend our disbelief. The Bard version, which is a televised stage play, keeps Ariel in full view of us. We are asked to assume his invisibility to Trinculo and Stephano.

Contrasting versions of Act 3, Scene 2, will be useful in class. The generic question is a good one to ask. We are to some extent conditioned to farce by television, *I Love Lucy* being one of the supreme examples. The scene's scope is small, requiring only four characters, and therefore the predictable camera work can occur without our noticing it. The close-up, two-shot, and reaction shot are inevitable here. We are granted superior knowledge in that we know that Ariel is there. We need comprehend only the situation, that is, that none of the other characters can see Ariel. No imaginative work is involved, nor any thinking. Even those who complain about the difficulties of Shakespeare's language can probably translate "Thou liest!" into "You are lying!" We can probably infer that no harm will come to anyone. It is a practical joke. The context tells us that Trinculo is in no real danger, that Stephano is posing as a tyrant. Scale and "degree of difficulty" are calibrated precisely to those limited things that television can do.

The Schaefer production is pleasant but lightweight. The play is shaped, shortened, and simplified for commercial television and its presumed audience. The opening storm is brief (one minute), narrated, and unconvincing. We are introduced to characters who roll and rock "near a mysterious and uninhabited island." Two of the inhabitants, Prospero and Ariel, talk about the storm before Miranda makes her plea and before Prospero brings her up-to-date. Prospero's narrative is accompanied by a crystal ball in which the disembodied characters of the story swim. The Caliban-Stephano-Trinculo meeting precedes the Antonio-Sebastian conspiracy, a transposition intended to permit Richard Burton and the others to hold the audience.

Well charted by the actors are the wine-induced descents into the stereotypes of paranoia, megalomania, and compulsiveness. Tom Poston's vulnerable Trinculo, Ronald Radd's queasy and cowardly Stephano, and Burton's sonorous Caliban—with finlike ears, armadillo shoulders, and a brush of tail—work well together. All are "obviously having a good time" (V. Vaughan 1984, 3).

Antonio is a pot-bellied villain, Sebastian a fop in peach, pink, and pearls who does not realize that he is heir of Naples until Antonio points it out to him. The "living drollery" are squat and dancing rocks. No banquet appears or, it follows, disappears. Ariel does appear and gets one of his wings tangled in a bush. The Wedding Masque is miniaturized and lasts for one minute. Prospero's "No more!" expresses disapproval, not just dismissal.

Maurice Evans's Prospero is of the crinkly, "father-knows-best" model. The role suits the actor's tendency toward recitation. Roddy McDowell's Ariel has stiff, sticklike spangles gleaming from his head, as if he has just slid from the frost-baked earth. Ariel admires Lee Remick's dewy Miranda and wishes he were human. Having an experiential sense of what punishment is, he pities

Caliban. McDowell makes one hilarious entrance from above, to Stephano and Trinculo. Released too soon, he plummets to the floor and seems lucky to escape a broken leg. Another moment one misses in today's more sophisticated productions occurs in the last scene, when Alonso's ornate collar brushes a camera lens.

The production accepts Margaret Webster's suggestion and ends with the "revels" speech. Evans moves forward as the camera dollies back. The rest of the characters grow indistinct on a diminishing promontory. This is a good production for 1960, but except for the Caliban underplot and a few moments in the Antonio-Sebastian conspiracy, the effect is bland.

The BBC version is not as bad as critics claim. "Everything goes wrong here" (Charney 1980, 290). "Horrendous . . . a lead-footed production" (Cecil Smith 1980, 4). "Stiff, aimed at the archives, and one can certainly see it gathering a lot of dust there in the years to come" (Stanley Reynolds 1980, 9). Certainly the critics have something to complain about, as would students were we to sit them down in front of this production and then put ourselves in the false position of trying to defend it.

The opening scene is filmed, as opposed to taped, yet it presents no sense of emergency. Masts and sheets appear under the opening credits, but the rain falls straight down, as if the ship were safely moored in a windless harbor. Film, if carefully scaled, works on television, but BBC wastes four minutes and forty seconds of film here. As in other productions, most of the words are inaudible, so that the point that "authority" and "the name of king" are useless in the face of "these roarers" is lost. To lose the lines to the storm is invariably a mistake.

The production tends to fall between stage, which can incorporate long speeches, and film, which demands visual equivalents for the language and which uses the camera as an aspect of the art form. Even in an oral medium like television, Prospero's expositions are tedious, though Pippa Guard does what she can as listener. She delivers the "abhorred slave" speech, as the First Folio says she should, and surprises and frightens Prospero. Having seen Hordern in Clifford Williams's tame 1978 RSC production, I thought that a muted Prospero might work on television, a medium that rewards underplaying. "What has been very interesting," Hordern says, "is that instead of trying to reach the back of the gallery with your most innermost thoughts, you have only to cover the distance between you and the camera, which may be only 18 inches away" (qtd. in Fenwick 1980, 26). The result is the irascible-schoolmaster model. His stupid students are right in front of him. When he is not angry, Hordern delivers a "droningly grandfatherish" Mr. Badger (Charney 1980, 290), slightly warmed by the mild affection he feels for his daughter.

Caliban's is the complaint of the aborigine, who, having instructed the colonist on the local environment, is consigned to its slums. None of the television productions touch on the ideological implications that materialist critics discern in the script. This Caliban (Warren Clarke) is a shaggy, pot-bellied bum awaiting introduction to his first six-pack. He contrasts with David Dixon's frail Ariel, with his boy-soprano voice. Each contrasts with Christopher Guard's tall, dark, and virile Ferdinand.

Director Gorrie's concentration on body types runs into disaster with the group of virtually naked men who, prancing to the lascivious pleasings of a pipe, form the "living drollery" of the banquet scene (3.3). It is, as Cecil Smith says, "quite embarrassing in a professional production" (1980). Almost as embarrassing is the Masque, meant to resemble a morris dance (Fenwick 1980, 22). It is remarkably awkward. Spirits step on other spirits' lines. Spirits cast heavy shadows, and those naked boys return as pale sicklemen bent on having an orgy with nymphs peeled from a Victorian mural.

For all the lapses in taste that make students laugh and teachers cringe, the production sometimes places characters effectively within the frame. Television's dimensions prevent much movement within its space, but relationship and emphasis can be established with placement. As Miranda and Ferdinand exchange the sight of first love, Prospero, camera right, tells us that he must prevent "too light winning." Antonio and Sebastian plot in a two-shot that frames Alonso and party, the target of the conspiracy. Trinculo's lines about Caliban (2.2.144–73) are delivered as sour asides. This technique grants the jester surprising "interiority." The main-plot and subplot conspiracies are splendidly orchestrated. Nigel Hawthorne's Stephano is particularly good when he tries to concentrate through his stupor on Caliban's plot to kill Prospero. Clarke's "Be not afeard" is excellent. He expresses a sense of selfhood symbiotically interfused with his island. One senses the source of his grievance against Prospero. Since the banquet disappears beneath Ariel's enclosing wings, Prospero's "A grace it had devouring" has a visual antecedent. At the end, Miranda's "How beauteous mankind is" is directed at Antonio. It is a wonderfully ironic instant, neatly setting up Prospero's bitter " 'Tis new to thee."

The Bard production begins as Prospero's head dreams up the storm. Or are we to take the entire play as Prospero's dream (as *The Taming of the Shrew*, with the Induction, can be viewed as Sly's fantasy of male supremacy)? This production is set on a Globe-like stage, with Tudor facades on the sides, a long balcony between, and an inner stage underneath the balcony. The ship is the balcony, a placement that gives the storm an oddly linear quality accentuated by the two long streamers of blue, pulled up and down by spirits, that simulate wind and wave. One problem with having Prospero in charge from the outset is that the storm lacks even a theatrical sense of danger, though the sound effects do drown the lines. Another is that Prospero's calming of Miranda is irrelevantly ex post facto.

Zimbalist is a naturalistic television actor, notable as an FBI officer in a long-running series of the 1970s. Perhaps as a carryover from this role, he is mildly ingratiating—the public servant pretending to be concerned for the public. Instead of the modulation that can occur at the beginning of Act 5, a softening into an insight informed by its compassionate equivalent, Zimbalist's Prospero is blandly consistent. J. E. Taylor's Miranda is not helped by having her hair pulled back to sharpen her severe bone structure. Prospero's luxuriant mane would have looked better on Taylor. William Hootkins plays Caliban with sullen and understated precision. The scene between Caliban, Stephano, Trinculo, and Ariel (3.2) is excellent. Ariel is in full view, but we accept his invisibility. A lithe dancer, Duane Black, as Ariel, would have been excellent in live performance. The entire production would have picked up a useful energy had it been played in front of a live audience.

The Tudor facade keeps forcing us to unsuspend the disbelief that the stage-like setting and the front-on camera work encourage. Its presence also blurs the nature-nurture, savage-civilized tension in the script. Our own imaginations are seldom pulled into the transaction, partly because Woodman does not vary his lighting. With no contrast in visual tones, the production is duller than it needs to be. Woodman does have an event occur off-camera now and then. The banquet is replaced by skulls, but we are looking at Prospero when the substitution occurs. Thus issues that could be a problem on a stage are not a problem here. Still, the production does not work out a consistent compromise between the premises of stage and of television camera. The production itself could be more imaginatively conceived, as when the living drollery become the dog-faced creatures that chase Caliban and confederates. This "doubling" gives us a brief glimpse of the plasticity of Prospero's and Shakespeare's "bare island."

A documentary "Page to Stage" cassette produced by the Stratford, Ontario, Festival is based on John Hirsch's 1982 production. Narrator Nicholas Pennell tells us that the script "distills the imagery of [Shakespeare's] life work." That, I believe, is accurate, though I think that whoever wrote Pennell's script means themes, not imagery. Is it helpful, however, to ask, as Pennell does, whether "Prospero's desire for revenge motivates him towards positive action because he is an innately good person"? Is it accurate to claim that, at the end of the play, "justice prevails and the natural order is restored"? That seems Gonzalo-like, too all-embracing and, for any production, smothering as well.

From what we see of the production, one of its high points is Pennell's Stephano, "a masterly miniature," as Ralph Berry says, with the "brutality of sentiment" of Iago (1983, 96). From the brief glimpse we get, it seems that Pennell is creating a parody of Ian McKellen's superb Macbeth. Caliban (Miles Potter), however, is incredibly grotesque, a creature incapable, one must assume, of copulating with a human, a gray and weed-bearded thing covered with rocks and shells, having emerged from the bottom of a tidal pool.

The production employs the multitiered Stratford Main Stage splendidly. The storm finds the Boatswain on the upper stage, wrestling with a huge wheel. Antonio enters from a trap in the main platform below. The audience confronts a full-scale storm, one that television permits us to appreciate, if not experience. We do, though, lose some of the lines. The Masque represents an actual wedding, Miranda in white gown, Juno presiding from the upper stage. Here, physical levels become conceptual planes. A quasi-Shakespearean stage can create a sense of the script's integration as a design for a specific space. Most modern stages cannot do this, and television seldom tries. Jane Howell used a unit playground set for her brilliant *Henry VI* sequence for BBC. Desmond Davis, in his excellent BBC *Measure for Measure*, deployed the same set with a different paint job for his convent and brothel.

The weaknesses of the Stratford *Tempest* would seem to reside in Sherry Flett's Miranda, who sought not for Ferdinand, but for Congreve or Sheridan, and, chiefly, in Len Cariou's Prospero. His "revels" speech is read in a panic, an acceptable interpretation even if it runs against the poetry, but badly overdone here. Cariou's delivery is often singsongy, as if he has been told to "go for the music." But here it is disinterested and oddly stressed ("As you from *crimes* would pardoned be," as opposed to parking tickets). He gives his fellow actors nothing on stage even as he carries on an unrequited love affair with the audience. Ralph Berry says that "all that emerged was that Prospero was in a foul mood. . . . For Miranda to say 'Never till this day / Saw I him touch'd with anger so distemper'd' suggested that she hadn't been paying attention: he was like that all the time" (1983, 95). Regardless of the production, the tape has the great virtue of showing how the Stratford stage can make visual—and thus imaginative—sense of this complicated script.

Television has a linear movement and lacks the frame that held a metaphoric cosmos in front of Shakespeare's audience within the "great globe itself" (4.1.153). Television can incorporate splendid "spots of time," but the good moments are not integrated into a sense of "the whole." No frame exists within which to include the large and the small, the soliloquy and the spectacle, and to relate them to each other. With postmodernism now in control of production, television's inadequacies should be strengths, since any mishmash of styles passes as production these days. Unfortunately—or fortunately—BBC either exhausted the possibilities of or discouraged further television productions of Shakespeare. Only the occasional televised stage play occurs these days.

Television is also limited in its ability to produce special effects. The twisters in *The Wizard of Oz* or the final cataclysm in *Forbidden Planet*, products of the great MGM special-effects expert Arnold Gillespie, do not work well in miniature. Schaefer's special effects in his *Tempest* are better than they were for his 1954 *Macbeth*. In that early color production, Banquo's head bounced through the Banquet Scene like a runaway, bright-orange bowling ball. The effects in *The Tempest* are almost as silly, particularly for a latter-day audience that knows that television does not try to do such things. At one point, Prospero tries to waft Ariel from his arm, but the timing is off, and it looks as if Prospero is trying to shoo a clever and irritating insect. Except for an Ariel who leaps into space and vaporizes, Gorrie eschews special effects. "We felt," says his producer, Cedric Messina, "it wasn't fair to the play to do too much. If you make an electronic night's dream, you are asking for trouble" (Fenwick 1980, 17). That is a wise decision, but it leaves Gorrie with his heavy Doré set and the blank wash of studio land, not a "real place where magic things happen" (Fenwick 1980, 17). Television "style," with its emphasis on "reality," is not a site for the strange or miraculous.

"Magic" on television is, to borrow a phrase from Robert Frost, "a diminished thing," where Kirk and Scotty "beam up," where the explosion of a tiny spacecraft cannot threaten domestic space from twenty-one diagonal inches as it can when it shatters on a large screen in a darkened cinema. Television is a "fourth-wall" medium that asks little of us. Color does much of the imagining for us. The stage asks us to suspend belief. Film forces us to believe in the twister tugging at Dorothy as she struggles with that storm door, or in the biplanes buzzing around King Kong as he straddles a pretelevision Empire State Building with Fay Wray in his paw, or in the flames behind Rhett and Scarlett as they flee Atlanta (and part of the old *King Kong* set adds to the conflagration). Film has the width and depth within which to create its effects. Television tends to psychologize the supernatural, rendering it "natural" and rendering special effects "questionable, even laughable" (Dessen 1986, 8; Coursen 1989). Thus directors who attempt to translate the other worldly or the supernatural in Shakespeare to television are likely to be defeated when they try to calibrate that material to a resistant medium.

The half-hour animated version (1992), edited by Leon Garfield, directed by Stanislav Sololov, and designed by Elena Livanova, is a good précis of this very short script. Animation is a good mode for what Hazelton Spencer calls Shakespeare's "ocean-girt Never-never Land" (1940, 376). It is done with puppets made and manipulated by Soviet craftspersons, as opposed to the celluloid animation used for several of the other productions of this series or the painting on glass employed so powerfully for *Hamlet*. The background is narrated by Martin Jarvis, thus eliminating the need for Prospero's long exposition. "On a misty, forgotten island [lives] Prospero the mighty enchanter." The production achieves necessary condensation by identifying Prospero's enemies on the ship, just before Prospero summons the storm. But, unlike other productions in this series, the narrated portion gives way to the play's language. Ferdinand gets his line "Hell is empty, / And all the devils are here!" The Wedding Masque is also cut. Thus Prospero's "Our revels now are ended" comes strangely, since no Wedding Masque has been presented. It is as if, having just given Miranda away, he is suddenly reclaiming her. Prospero's " 'Tis new to thee" is also cut. Ariel is an androgynous sprite, feminized by the voice of Ellen Hoard. Caliban is a squat, vaguely human monster who scuttles around like a crab. He has no grievance, it seems, but he is a threat, at one point attempting to wrest Prospero's magic staff away. Caliban has a blue band across his eyes—an inheritance from Sycorax, who is not mentioned in this version. The island features splendid music by the Mosfilm Symphony, directed by Vladimir Rylov, and, in addition to Ariel's observant scouting, Easter Island faces that look on and report directly to Prospero's cell. Ariel makes an impressive Harpy, and one also notices a unicorn munching the foliage. Many famous lines are there, though not the one about "strange bedfellows" or Ariel's promise of "clear life ensuing." As in cartoons, all the characters are reduced to stereotypes. At the end, Caliban capers happily on the yellow sands as the King's ship sails away, and Prospero breaks his staff and dumps the pieces and his book into the drink.

As in all the animated versions, the lines are very well spoken, if in those British accents that serve to offend merchandisers hawking American versions of the plays. This makes for an excellent introduction to the play for younger students and a good assignment for more experienced students, the basic question being, What does the animated version tell about the script, and what does it not?

The NBC version, which premiered on 13 December 1998, was strange. The play's thematic links with the American Civil War emerge from the "freedom-bondage" concept that runs through the play and describes in different ways the conflicts of Caliban and Ariel. Here, though, we had an irrelevant Gator Man (J. Pyper-Furgeson) who wanted his bog back. Ariel (Harold Perineau) was a combination Caliban and Ariel. He could become a crow, but he also did a lot of domestic chores. He was an unfreed slave who learned about the Emancipation Proclamation two years after it had been issued and who wanted to join Grant's army on its way to Vicksburg.

The production looked like a story of voodoo dropped upon a Civil War reenactment or perhaps like a nightmare of Mr. Hightower, Faulkner's minister in *Light in August*, whose sermons keep rumbling off in the dust of one of Stuart's cavalry columns. A specific 1865 made U. S. Grant a subhero, thus introducing a host of issues the script does not raise and blurring questions for which the script does invite the exploration of production. A specific time period is seldom a good environment for a Shakespeare script. A detailed set tends not to work in a medium with a limited field of depth. Here, it did not matter. The special effects, "from the same masters who dazzled in the 1999 spring mini-series, 'Merlin' " (Williams 1998, 2), were tame and tiny, as they must be in a medium that simply lacks the scale for the spectacular. We learn all we need to learn when we are told that "the teleplay is by veteran TV writer James Henerson, whose work [includes] 'I Dream of Jeanie' and 'Bewitched' " (Bobbin 1998, 2).

The major problem with the production was its lack of believability. Television is a soap-opera medium that explores in tedious detail the reasons for meaningless actions. The sudden lynching of Gideon Prosper—who was, after all, the chief landowner of the area—was as improbable as his deliverance from the rope. His motivation to stay in his swamp grew more and more implausible as pressure was brought to bear on him to develop a conscience. Why did he object to his daughter's elopement with her handsome Union officer? Since his swamp was right around the bend from his old plantation, Prosper could have gone after his brother at any time. His excitement at hearing that his brother had come near was thus incomprehensible. After Prosper's storm, Miranda (Katherine Heigl), little homemaker that she was, got herself off-camera by saying that she was going to check on the house. We remained breathless until she returned to tell us that nothing of the vine-wound, bark-covered Tarzan treehouse had been damaged. At another moment, after Gideon was plugged through the chestbone by his brother (John Glover, who was a terrible shot until asked to shoot offhand from a rocking boat), I thought we were going to be asked to clap our hands and say that we believed in "dat ole black magic."

At the end, rewards were handed out. The production answered the still-vexed question of Caliban by showing that Gator Man got his swamp back because he had courage. It is a wonder that Gideon did not hand the cowardly crock a Purple Heart. As Prospero, Miranda, and Fred left the island, Gator Man stood on the deck of his new home. No one waved goodbye. What did work was Anthony's sneering refusal to accept his brother Gideon's hand at the end even though a firing squad awaited him. But we wondered, given this blank Prospero and Anthony's perfidy (far beyond anything committed by the play's Antonio), why the hand had been offered in the first place. Since the action was heavily influenced by the voodoo priestess appearing as a face out of flames, the sudden advent of a "Christian" set of values was not prepared for. *The Tempest* is more pagan or cabalistic, more Cornelius Agrippa and Giordano Bruno than Richard Hooker, but it does have a strong Christian rhythm. How could it not? "After all," as Bonamy Dobree, writing of the final plays, says, Shakespeare "belonged to a Christian country; he had been brought up on the Bible: so its ideas, its familiar phrases, would naturally occur to him" (1961, 148).

The production reminded us of our dispensation by constantly intersecting itself, at what the directors must have thought were moments of unbearable suspense, with vast deserts of commercial breaks. Many of them were for what must be the worst television shows imaginable. At other moments, since there were only a dozen shopping days until Christmas, the mosquito-buzzing swampland of the lower Mississippi was juxtaposed against snowflakes, balsam trees, colored lightbulbs, and other clichés of a white, middle-class Christmas.

Freeing the slaves was necessary and overdue, but only a secondary reason for the American Civil War. I assume that we were meant to infer the knowledge that the "brave new world" of Reconstruction became a version of the old world very quickly. What on earth is Executive Producer Bonnie Raskin talking about when she says, "We loved the banishment and the isolation, in this case, in terms of North versus South" (qtd. in Williams 1998, 2)? That statement signals incoherence at the heart of the project.

I asked myself (a) whether the production would have been successful without any knowledge of *The Tempest*, and (b) whether this production enhanced our sense of the source. In each case, I answered no. The production itself was tedious, elongated beyond its intrinsic content, and centered on a mere Scrooge. Its connections with the original were so tenuous or simplified that it distorted rather than illuminated. Unlike other works of art—painting and sculpture, for example—the scripts of Shakespeare insist that we reanimate them within our own time and space. This production simply deserted its originating source and provided emptiness in its place.

The Tempest has produced four filmic offshoots. I do not recommend Peter Greenaway's *Prospero's Books* for use in the teaching of *The Tempest*. It adds absolutely nothing to our understanding of the play. It does nothing with Caliban and ends with the most stultifyingly conventional closure possible. For reasons not worth asking about, it includes a numbing twelve-minute parody of *Home Shopping Network*. It incorporates long and pointless tracking shots, and its imposition of high-definition television on film undermines its claim to be film. The definition of a television picture does not affect content, does not make a Warhol a Rembrandt or a Rockwell a Raphael. Greenaway aims at the perfection of a cliché. That is a stupid effort, for all of the sophistication of the surface. The books themselves are often interesting, but are totally irrelevant to *The Tempest* and thus to the narrative. The books do not interact with the story. Something escaping from one of those books and getting into the film might have been interesting. I have dealt with *Prospero's Books* elsewhere (Coursen 1993, 163–76) and have tracked down many of Greenaway's allusions to suggest their irrelevance to any purpose other than to demonstrate his intellectual superiority and the abysmal ignorance of anyone seeing his film. As the Vaughans say of the film, "The eye is bombarded in this film with a wide array of violent and sexual images, many of them apparently gratuitous. Nothing links them to the rest of the montage to provide coherence or thematic integrity. . . . Shakespeare is exploited . . . to create self-conscious 'high art,' an effort that largely fails" (1992, 17).

Douglas Lanier (1996) defends the film from a postmodernist stance. Lanier's argument is complicated, but it goes to the heart of the purposes of this volume, so I will deal with it here in some detail. Lanier argues that "Shakespeare can take the stage only insofar as the actors are not made to stand before the judgement of his book" (188)—meaning, I assume, the tyranny of the inherited text. I do not think that anyone is arguing otherwise nowadays, except when an actor is robbed of the book, as Terrence Rafferty rightly claims Laurence Fishburne was in the 1996 film *Othello*: "What [director Oliver] Parker sacrifices is the volcanic flow of language that conveys the hero's pride, confusion and anguish, and without it Othello is nothing" (1995, 109). Furthermore, as Laurie Osborne argues, Lanier's argument that "modern performances of Shakespeare [are seen as] supplemental, fleeting theatrical variations, of varying authenticity on a prior, originary book" (1996, 188) is increasingly not the case. One reason is that, as Lanier says, we may be recognizing at last "that Shakespeare anticipated and approved both textual and performative variations" (1996, 190).

Whether Orgel is right in his hypothesis that "Shakespeare habitually began with more than he needed" (1988, 7), options have always existed, particularly for plays unlike *The Tempest* where different texts have come from Shakespeare's time—the Quarto 1 placement of Hamlet's "To be or not to be," earlier than in Quarto 2 or the First Folio, Quarto's trial of Goneril and Regan in the hovel, almost invariably incorporated into First Folio–based productions, or the Hecate material in *Macbeth*, which is usually cut. The nature of film insists that much of the language itself be excised. As Lanier says, "The cinema has more readily taken up the challenge of textual authority than the theatre, perhaps because filming Shakespeare entails more consciously translating the work from one medium (and cultural register) to another" (1996, 191). The issue of translation also involves expectation, a segment of Aristotle's fourth cause, that is, response to the work of art. We tend to get more of the language in a stage production than in a film. We may object to the editing of a script for stage or film, but we accept the fact of editing, particularly for film.

Lanier's argument serves what he perceives to be the need to "(re)graft [Shakespeare] on to performative media or textual documents (re)conceived as performance scores or unique artifacts," so that "he and the cultural capital he represents can be uncoupled from the decline of the book in an increasingly post-literate society" (191). But Shakespeare as book is really an ex post factor development. True, quartos were published during his lifetime, and the 1623 First Folio appeared shortly after his death, but it was the publishing explosion of the eighteenth century that made "Shakespeare" into text. The plays, as we know, were being radically translated into Restoration and eighteenth-century paradigms and performance spaces. At any rate, *Prospero's Books* is an odd choice of example of Shakespeare's being "uncoupled" from the book. Whatever Shakespeare may be, he is chained to Greenaway's books in the film.

Lanier cites the prompter in Laurence Olivier's film of *Henry V*—a caricature of Shakespeare—to demonstrate the "textual ideal that casts its shadow over the performance we are seeing" (192). But that film escapes from its early moments in a model London and replica Globe Theatre and becomes a film, perhaps best exemplified by the long tracking shot of the French charge at Agincourt, an event neither depicted nor described in the text. At the end, we return suddenly to Henry V-Burbage-Olivier next to his boy-actor Katherine, but the film meanwhile has moved far from both its textual and theatrical premises. The prompter's shadow is cast only over the opening stage performance. His erasure emphasizes the performance of the actor playing Henry. That actor may begin as Burbage, but he quickly becomes Olivier. Furthermore, since the film was produced during World War Two, just before another invasion of France, it is better examined as a piece of propaganda than as one of textual authority. A cultural-materialist argument, of course, would say that the entire project served the dominant ideology for which the story of the patriot king is canonical. If that is so, the text is manipulated toward a dominant cultural authority, as in the cutting from the film of the cutting of the throats of the French prisoners, a topic recently discussed in the context of Douglas Hughes's 1996 production in New York City (see Weschler 1996 and, on Olivier's erasure of the episode, Patterson 1994).

"In *Prospero's Books* Greenaway recasts *The Tempest* within a filmic vocabulary that constantly acknowledges its competition with Shakespearean textuality while remaining faithful . . . to the play's received text" (Lanier 1996, 194). What we see is Prospero (Gielgud) writing the text quite literally with a quill pen. As Lanier says, "The written text [is] kept obsessively before the viewer" (1996, 195). This is to deny film its own identity and its ability to escape from written word to the plasticity of image. The constant presence of the text cannot be said to be at once "faithful to it while dismantling its received monumentality and authority" (196). With Gielgud reading it? Greenaway is credited with doing many clever things with books that come alive, but it is an old device. Some of us recall the many 1940s musicals that began with an etching of Olde New York that suddenly moved as a jolly policeman stole an apple from a fruit stand and a struggling but upright songwriter banged out a song on an ancient but upright piano. Shakespeare's script is simply hijacked as a vehicle for Greenaway's self-proclaimed genius. *Prospero's Books* is simply not a good film. At times, of course, it is not a film at all.

It may be that "by eschewing the characterology of the realist stage and cinema, Greenaway is free to treat the text as a collection of verbal images that he can defamiliarize by (re)literalizing them as arresting visual tableaux . . . static though visually sumptuous dumb shows that emblematize the text's imagery" (Lanier 1996, 195). But, as I have argued, these tableaux do not derive from the text and are far more static than sumptuous (1993). The exception is the one Lanier makes the rule: "Gonzalo's famous set-speech outlining his ideal island commonweal, we observe, is culled from the Book of Utopias. Through such allusions Greenaway makes visible *The Tempest*'s intertextuality, its status as a collection of discourses culled from a variety of prior sources rather than a unified freestanding artwork" (197). Perhaps, but Gonzalo's discourse refutes itself, as Antonio and Sebastian deftly show, and the play surrounding the discourse hardly supports any vision of Utopia. The play forms a disjunctive analogy to this example of intertextuality, a point that Greenaway's ingenuity fails to discern. The "Alphabetical Inventory of the Dead" is *not* a source of *The Tempest*. "The Book of Revenge"—another of this Prospero's books—is one that Shakespeare's character has read and long since discarded. That Prospero has not yet experienced his rejection of the revenge thesis emotionally is probably true, but Greenaway's smothering concept does not permit Gielgud to chart that progress.

"[T]he *act* of writing and imagining," Lanier says, "is false to the very bodily processes that bring it into being [and therefore the bodies of *Prospero's Books*] are patently *not* in the service of thematics, a fact that explains why many have labeled the production's nudity gratuitous" (199–200). In other words, the many naked bodies parading around Prospero's palace were meant to show the irrelevance of writing and imagining even as the film is being simultaneously written and imagined. The bodies are just there, naked, as in a locker room. Meanwhile, the text of *The Tempest* itself is saved from drowning at the end by "the barbaric man-fish Caliban, here a wry surrogate for the *enfant terrible* director himself

. . . a desecrater of books who nevertheless saves them from oblivion" (202). "In the end, Greenaway's film is itself destined to become a cinematic 'text' to be 'read' according to interpretive protocols of close reading with many of the same assumptions about 'textual' monumentality" (202). The film, then, serves the tenets of a creed outworn—the New Criticism. For all of its facile inventiveness and its claim to be on the edge of the future, it is deeply anachronistic conceptually and trapped in time insofar as it deploys the modernist medium of television.

This film does not serve the old mythology, nor does any film, in spite of Lanier's assertion that "video and film have encouraged us to assimilate . . . performances to the condition of texts, stable artifacts, rather than contingent, unstable, ephemeral experiences" (203). Olivier's *Henry V* must be seen in its historical context. Olivier's Othello mimics stereotypic "black" mannerisms consciously before an enthralled Venetian Senate in a performance that is likely to be read as racist more than a quarter-century later. Peter Brook's *Lear* (1970) emerges from his despair about the Vietnam War, but it also captures vividly the element of existential despair in the script and thus is not confined in its Kottian premises—*Lear* is a script framed for existentialist approaches—even though it is helpful to understand them as the generative force behind the film. It is also helpful to contrast the minimalist Brook film with the 70-mm Kozintsev version (1971), hugely panoramic and inclusive, while Brook's camera is intentionally exclusive and often decentered. But Kozintsev's film is of its time, both in its sense of the tide of the proletariat beneath the parapets of absolute power and in its sheer size. Twenty-five years later the film might well have been scaled to the cassette. The 1936 *Romeo and Juliet*, with the famously superannuated Leslie Howard and Norma Shearer, can be viewed and even enjoyed against the zeitgeist of 1936—its songs, its films, and its Great Depression (see my response, Coursen 1996).

What Lanier calls a "technological revolution—the VCR— . . . subtly reestablishing . . . a new monolithic and stable 'text'—the ideal performance, recorded on tape, edited and reshaped in post-production, available for re-viewing" (1996, 203–4), is itself, in its specific manifestations, subject to history and the product of a past that recedes rapidly and, as rapidly, "dates" its productions. I doubt that "the 'videotext' [will] encourage us to elide the very historicity and materiality we have sought to recover with the return to performance" (204). If anything, the videotext, implicated as it is in technology, presents itself as a historicized commodity almost immediately—particularly in that copyright warning here in these colonies from one of our occupying powers, the FBI. It is true, of course, that we can restudy a production on cassette as we cannot with a stage production, unless the stage production itself is available on tape. Then, however, it is no longer a stage production, having been removed from the space and the dimensions in which it occurred.

While reading Lanier's essay, I agreed that the concept of character may be a socially determined construct, but I kept asking, it is still something an actor must work with, is it not? Derek Jacobi suggests how in discussing the role of Hamlet: "The personality of the actor playing the role . . . is the determining factor. You don't actually have to play the character, you play the situation in which Hamlet finds himself and your own personality, your own outlook, takes over" (Unger 1980, 19). I have a strong sense that something like what Jacobi describes is what Shakespeare had in mind when he wrote the part. He had actors in mind. They complete the script by interacting with it. They must do that within any of the conceptual spaces to which Shakespeare is translated.

Peter S. Donaldson also tries to justify *Prospero's Books*. If, however, "Prospero conjures with words he himself has written, the words of *The Tempest*" (1997, 169), it follows that he wrote his own wronging those twelve years before so that he could right it now, or, as Donaldson has it, so that he can "control female sexuality and 'appropriate' the birth-giving powers of the maternal body" (169). Why was his lengthy and punishing strategy—he himself says that he regretted it as he navigated in that rowboat—necessary? And why did it take Prospero so long to write in the shipwreck that allows him to right the earlier wrong? The answer, obviously, is that he finally tires of his self-flagellation and invents an opportunity to shift the aim of his sadism to Alonso, while at the same time controlling the process of gestation that brought him into this vale of tears.

Donaldson equates the advent of artificial intelligence with the Renaissance magic that wafted Friar Bacon, Marjorie Jourdain, John Faustus, and John Dee across forbidden borderlands. As one would expect from the founder of MIT's Interactive Archive, Donaldson has some brilliant things to say about Greenaway's appropriation of "representational technology" (172) in the film. In defending *Prospero's Books*, however, Donaldson must agree with Greenaway that Prospero has to overcome his wish for revenge. I believe that what Prospero must do is to replace his intellectual decision not to take revenge—one he makes clear very early to Miranda and Ariel—with the emotional equivalent, which presents itself to him as he views Gonzalo and feels his own tears, the salinity of an inner sea, coming out of him.

To defend Greenaway, Donaldson must explore elements that are not in the film. "The filmscript's treatment of the erotic union of [Ferdinand and Miranda] would, if it had been realized in the film, have made an impressive central scene" (181). "Though, in fact, she never appears in the finished film, this figure of 'The Juggler' is worth discussing precisely because, in her melding of the erotic and the creative, she is so unlike the almost endless succession of naked creatures. . . . She represents a spontaneous and unruly sexuality that is absent from the film" (182). Donaldson cannily designs another film. I agree with him that the film he has in mind would have been superior to the one we got. That *Prospero's Books* is a happy hunting ground for postmodernist critics says something about its fundamental failure as a film. I have to admit, however, that

Donaldson mitigates some of my own vivid objections to Greenaway's travesty (see my chapter " 'Tis Nudity," in Coursen 1993, 163–76, where I, too, make a plea for concupiscence [168]).

However the plays came into being—it seems that no one wrote them, or if they were written down, the writing was without intention—they were not shaped under postmodernist premises. While Richard Levin demolished thematic approaches to the plays two decades ago (1979), a director probably still should seek some unifying principle within a script in a collaborative effort with an assumed playwright who, like Hooker's host, coexists at the moment of reception. I think that this principle is particularly true in film, where weaknesses are often "thematic," as in the 1995 *Othello*, which exchanges images and bodies for the few clarifying lines that would have helped us understand why in the film, as opposed to the original story, some of these events are occurring. Multiple signification is not the same thing as nonsignification. Lia M. Hotchkiss (1998) examines *Prospero's Books* from the standpoint of Derrida's search for the invisible origins of graphic representation (1993) and Lacan's "relationship to a signifier" (1982). Hotchkiss's conclusion is that the film shows that "theater is the loved and hated double as well as the aggressively mourned lost object" (20).

The Derek Jarman film (1980) is not commercially available. It was made, says John Collick, "in the context of various transgressive movements within 1970s sub-culture," including punk rock, and it "often deliberately challenges orthodox perceptions of Shakespeare" (1989, 103). Of it, eminent critic Samuel Crowl says, "The film is decidedly Jarman's recreation of the text in his own, highly individualized cinematic style . . . more Jarman's *Tempest* than Shakespeare's." Crowl finds "Elizabeth Welch's wonderful rendition of Harold Arlen's *Stormy Weather* . . . inspired. Its refrain of 'Keeps rainin' all the time' became a wonderful modern equivalent for Festes's corrective to *Twelfth Night*'s midsummer madness: 'the rain it raineth every day.' This moment worked because it created a witty resonance with all those other moments in the comedies where, in the midst of the festive celebration of love and romance, Shakespeare carefully places reminders that holiday is not every day" (1980, 7). Russell Jackson says of the film that "the world we enter is not so much an island whose magical properties are drawn on by a magus, as the realm of a magus who has withdrawn into a house which his magic has since made special" (1994b, 107–8). Vincent Canby, however, calls the film "very nearly unbearable" and Welch's song "a bravura effect gone feeble" (1980, C20).

Because Jarman believes "that the problem with Shakespeare film settings is that they are often too realistic and fight with the descriptive power of the verse, he chose a more abstract approach. . . . He used the burnt-out, half-ruined eighteenth-century wing of the crumbling [Stoneleigh Abbey. . . . He] sees the significance of magic as deeply political. Shakespeare, strongly influenced by [John] Dee, was he feels, making a statement about the superiority of Renaissance values—learning, rediscovery of the art, scientific exploration—over the reactionary attitude which dominated the new century when James I came to the throne" (Hirst 1984a, 54). "Jarman's Prospero is virtually omnipotent. He does not reject his magic" (55).

Catherine Belsey describes Jarman's techniques and their intention: "The blue filter, the use of distorting lenses, mirrors, firelight, foreground the film's own devices. [Jarman] produces formal discontinuities which repudiate coherence in favor of a series of brilliant visual moments. The consequence is a fragmentation of meaning which enhances plurality" (1983, 157).

Walter Coppedge effectively revalues Jarman's film version of *The Tempest* after the trashing it received in 1980. Jarman, he says, is not merely a member of the "radical counterculture," but shares with others "an awareness of English culture . . . a love for landscapes and nature . . . for those who witness to wholeness (Blake) and the holiness of the heart's affections (the romantics). [These] attitudes [are] altogether traditional" (1998, 12). In responding to Vincent Canby's complaint that the film was "a fingernail scratch along a blackboard . . . a limbo, or a house party of undergraduates who like to play dressup" (Canby 1980, C20), Coppedge deploys Jack Jorgens's taxonomy (theatrical, realistic, and filmic). Jarman inhabits the third category. Coppedge says that "Jarman seems to be the first filmmaker to detemporize the classics. . . . If the point is to get away from the limitations of time . . . then Jarman's audacious use of props is as logically justifiable as the anachronism of dress" (Coppedge 1998, 12). Coppedge provides an excellent description of how the film functions. Jarman's flashbacks, for example, "break up long expository dialogue which, without transposition or illustration, have no cinematic potential" (14). The final song, "Stormy Weather," involves "the glorious irony of the juxtaposition [that] becomes obvious as the pleasure of the performance mounts. The words of the song through their negation affirm: there is a sun up in the sky" (14). Coppedge's article insists that Jarman's film be viewed again and given an opportunity to work in its own terms. When and if the film becomes commercially available, it will be valuable to let students see the film and then ask them to mediate between Canby and Coppedge.

Pauline Kael calls Fred Wilcox's *Forbidden Planet* (1956) "the best of the science fiction interstellar productions of the 50s" (videocassette cover); more sophisticated students today find its depiction of 2300 A.D. merely amusing. Ariel is Robby the Robot, a character who "has a quiet dignity about him" (McCarten 1956, 92). Altaira (Anne Francis), the Miranda counterpart, loses her virginity symbolically. Her symbiotic relationship with her environment fades as her contact with the space visitors grows. She is here a product of "the male gaze" (Mulvey 1985, 57). Perhaps the film's most interesting theme is its suggestion that the person who attempts to control nature represses in nature powerful and destructive forces, here known as "Id." The extension of Freudian or, for that matter, Jungian psychodynamics from individual psychic to planetary dimensions gives the film an unexpectedly strong and convincingly apocalyptic ending. "It makes King Kong look like an organ grinder's monkey," says *Time*

("Review" 9 April 1956). Merrell Knighten suggests that the Prospero analogue, Dr. Morbius (Walter Pidgeon), "has made his Caliban": it is himself, of course, who "in his initiation into forbidden knowledge" becomes "this thing of darkness" (1994, 36–37). Knighten suggests Marlowe's *Dr. Faustus* as a possible further source of the film: "Precisely in the manner of his cautionary model Faustus, Morbius rejects his Id-beast too late and dies at its hands" (37).

Paul Mazursky's *Tempest* (1982) is a slow and underwritten contrast between the world of Manhattan upper-crust careerists and that of a sexless Aegean island, which does have some horny inhabitants. It has its king, duke, jester, islander, mariners, prince, and princess, the last played luminously by Molly Ringwald in her screen debut. Students will respond to Ringwald's line, "We're studying *Macbeth* in school. It's unbelievably boring!" Allusions to the source abound. "It's a paradise here! You're learning things here you'd never learn anywhere else," says John Cassavetes, the Prospero figure, to Ringwald. "I was boss here before you showed up," says Raul Julia, Kalibanos, to Cassavetes. "I'm a monkey, just like you," says Cassavetes to Kalibanos. "Anyway, I'm a virgin," says Ringwald to Freddie (Sam Robards). We are asked to believe that Cassavetes achieves magical powers through celibacy, which, in turn, is the product of a mild and unconvincing midlife crisis out of Gail Sheehy's *Passages*, as critic Richard Combs notes (1983, 179). Lucianne Buchanan plays Dolores, a hilarious and apparent afterthought of the screenwriters, and the film ends with a vocal from the great Dinah Washington.

These offshoots are not in a class with Akira Kurosawa's *Throne of Blood*, but each will chase the student back to the original, and each argues, however marginally, Shakespeare's continued power to generate further imaginative efforts. *Forbidden Planet* invites futuristic conceptions of other scripts, while Mazunsky's *Tempest* raises the issue of translating Shakespeare into a contemporary mode. These make good assignments because they point out the limitations of adaptations of the inherited scripts. Any production, of course, is a translation.

To involve students in the issues of translating Shakespeare to film or television is to get them to ask some good questions: What are the difficulties of this script as television? As film? To what extent do one's expectations of a light-sensitive or a magnetic medium condition what can occur there? How does zeitgeist affect the work and our response to it? At the risk of sounding like T. S. Eliot, I suggest that each new production alters our perception of all previous productions. Kenneth Branagh's 1989 *Henry V* permitted us to see Olivier's 1944 version as we had never done before. A film or television version is "fixed" in time; we learn about that time as it deals with Shakespeare and about our own as we respond to an artifact from the past. We thus move out of the biased formulations, either positive or pejorative, that are likely to produce a too-immediate reaction and into the zone where we can create contexts for evaluation.

Perhaps the greatest contribution of film and video to learning is that the productions insist that students notice detail. If the student selects a short segment from three *Tempest*s, for example, she or he has no choice but to enter into a detailed analysis. We contribute to a student's growth when we move the student from the swamp of generalities to the foothold of specifics.

In 1940, Hazelton Spencer hoped that "some day an enlightened director will set sail from the California shore and make a wonderful motion picture of [*The Tempest*]" (378). Perhaps on Alcatraz, perhaps on Santa Catalina—it has not happened yet.

EPILOGVE,
ſpoken by _Proſpero._

NOw my Charmes are all ore-throwñe,
   And what ſtrength I haue's mine owne.
Which is moſt faint : now 'tis true
I muſt be heere confinde by you,
Or ſent to Naples, Let me not
Since I haue my Dukedome got,
And pardon'd the deceiuer, dwell
In this bare Iſland, by your Spell,
But releaſe me from my bands
with the helpe of your good hands :
Gentle breath of yours, my Sailes
Muſt fill, or elſe my proiect failes,
Which was to pleaſe : Now I want
Spirits to enforce : Art to inchant,
And my ending is deſpaire,
Vnleſſe I be relieu'd by praier
Which pierces ſo, that it aſſaults
Mercy it ſelfe, and frees all faults.
  As you from crimes would pardon'd be,
  Let your Indulgence ſet me free.   **Exit.**

The Scene, an vn-inhabited Iſland

Names of the Actors.

Alonſo, K. of Naples:
Sebaſtian his Brother.
Proſpero, the right Duke of Millaine.
Anthonio his brother, the vſurping Duke of Millaine.
Ferdinand, Son to the King of Naples.
Gonzalo, an honeſt old Councellor.
Adrian, & _Franciſco_, Lords.
Caliban, a ſaluage and deformed ſlaue.
Trinculo, a Ieſter.
Stephano, a drunken Butler.
Maſter of a Ship.
Boate-Swaine.
Marriners.
Miranda, daughter to _Proſpero._
Ariell, an ayrie ſpirit.
Iris
Ceres
Iuno   } Spirits.
Nymphes
Reapers

FINIS.

The last page of _The Tempest_, First Folio, 1623.

BIBLIOGRAPHICAL ESSAY

The best modern editions of *The Tempest* are those of Kermode (1964), Orgel (1987), and the Vaughans (1999). Kermode is masterful in his summary of the scholarship of the first half of the twentieth century, Orgel very strong on the political currents that converge in the play, and the Vaughans excellent on the ways in which the play has been appropriated by various cultures for a range of purposes.

On the sources of the play, Bullough's *The Narrative and Dramatic Sources of Shakespeare*, volume 8 (1975), is the book. Kermode also has a lengthy discussion of possible sources. Charles Frey (1979) shows the materials of which the play is an amalgamation, from the travel narratives that so excited the Renaissance imagination to their close relative, the romance.

Leslie Fiedler (1972) looks at "the stranger"—the Othello, Shylock, or Caliban—who invades the white, aristocratic space of Shakespeare's plays. Now known as "the other" or as "the transgressive force," this character has become central to Shakespearean criticism since Fiedler's powerful book. Leo Marx (1967) looks at the play as a generator of the contradictions in visions of America: a paradise, another chance at a perfect world, or a wilderness, full of a savagery that makes "civilization" both preferable and necessary. I find Marx's sparkling book useful for both Shakespeare and the rich vein of nineteenth-century American literature that culminates in James and Fitzgerald. Meredith Ann Skura (1989) and Russ McDonald (1991) both cast skeptical eyes on overconfident readings of the play, Skura undercutting "colonialist" approaches and McDonald demonstrating that the poetry of the play is designed at once to attract and to discourage definitive interpretations. Of the many recent reappraisals of the play, Greenblatt (1990) is probably the best. He is worth reading for the depth and subtlety of the argument. Often, the New Historicists and the cultural materialists seem to rephrase what has already been said of the play, recasting the criticism into an aggressive political stance (particularly the cultural materialists, the British branch of this mode of historicism).

Harry Berger, Jr. (1969) craftily qualifies simplistic notions of characterization in the play. His is an article that would place high on any "short list" of *Tempest* criticism, as would Reuben Brower's superb New Critical analysis (1951). To read Brower is to understand why his mode of criticism has to give way to other approaches. He perfects it.

The works of Walter Clyde Curry (1937) and Robert H. West (1968) are splendid scholarly explorations of the background of *The Tempest* and other Shakespeare plays. One of the best essays on the intellectual ferment of the English Renaissance is Alvin Kernan's introduction to *The Alchemist* (1974a).

Of the introductions to the play, those of Van Doren (1939), Frye (1959), Bevington (1980), Righter (1968), Mowat and Werstine (1994), and Greenblatt (1997) strike me as the most useful, though none should be seen as "complete," nor does any of them claim to be. Useful summaries of criticism are included in Daniell (1989), Andrews (1994), and Barnet (1987 and 1998), often with generous quotation from the critics themselves.

On productions of *The Tempest*, Hirst (1984a) and Ralph Berry (1993) are useful. For production, John Russell Brown's Applause edition (1996) should prove invaluable.

The essays in Battenhouse (1994) on the Christian dimension of the play (250–79) strike me as very persuasive examples of that genre and likely to be overlooked in an increasingly secular critical atmosphere.

One way to chart the changes and the constants in response to the play is to examine the several anthologies of essays available. They include D. J. Palmer (1968), Hallett Smith (1969), Harold Bloom (1988), Linda Cookson and Bryan Loughrey (1988), and Alden T. Vaughan and Virginia Mason Vaughan (1998). Maurice Hunt's Collection (1992) is designed for college teachers, but is full of insightful essays that will help teachers on any level, and college students as well. Each of these anthologies should be on the desk of the teacher who teaches *The Tempest* regularly. Each contains a wealth of possibilities for student response.

I had intended to include a section on the "afterlife" of the play and the issues the play bequeaths to us, looking at Milton's *Comus* and "On the Morning of Christ's Nativity," Coleridge's theory of imagination, Browning's "Caliban on Setebos," some of Hawthorne's romances, Meredith's *The Ordeal of Richard Feverel*, James's *The American* and *The Ambassadors*, Conrad's *Heart of Darkness*, Verne's *The Mysterious Island*, some of Orwell's essays and his *Burmese Days*, Achebe's *The Center Cannot Hold*, T. S. Eliot, Auden's "The Sea and the Mirror" in *For the Time Being*, Fitzgerald's *The Great Gatsby*, Huxley's *Brave New World*, and modern African-American literature (where the log-carrier becomes the tender of the furnace, in Wright and Ellison), and to examine some of the material that Jonathan Bate (1995), Thomas Cartelli (1987), Peter Erickson (1991), Inga-Stina Ewbank (1991), Martin Scofield (1991), Michael Scott (1989), Susan Snyder (1983), Alden and Virginia Mason Vaughan (1988, 1999), and J. N. Wysong (1968) have written on the play's lingering presence. I had also hoped to touch on the play's manifestations in music and ballet: Berlioz's "Fantaisie" (circa 1830), Tchaikovsky's "The Tempest" (1873), "La Tempête" (Paris ballet, 1834), "Miranda" (London, 1838), "La Tempesta" (Turin, 1869), and more recent ballets by Arne Norheim, Rudolph Nureyev, and Michael Smuin's San Francisco Ballet, which performed its brilliant version of *The Tempest* on 1 April 1981 on PBS. Space limitations preclude these discussions. They become "Topics for Further Study." The play is, and will continue to be, as Bate says, "a vehicle through which later cultures can reflect on pressing contemporary concerns" (1995, 162) and from which new works of art can emerge into ages otherwise powerless to be born.

WORKS CITED

Abdulla, Sara. 1994. *"The Tempest." What's On*, 20 July, 39.

Abenheimer, Karl M. 1946. "Shakespeare's *Tempest*: A Psychological Analysis." *Psychoanalytic Review* 33: 399–415.

Abram, David. 1997. *The Spell of the Sensuous*. New York: Vintage Books.

Adams, Richard. 1988. *"The Tempest* and the Theme of Social Organisation." In Cookson and Loughrey 1988, 68–77.

Adelman, Janet. 1992. *Suffocating Mothers: Fantasies of Maternal Origin in Shakespeare's Plays: "Hamlet" to "The Tempest."* London: Routledge, 1992.

Aercke, Kristiaan P. 1992. " 'An Odd Angle of the Isle': Teaching the Courtly Art of *The Tempest*." In Hunt 1992, 146–52.

Agrippa, Henry Cornelius. 1651. *Three Bokes of Occult Philosophie*. London: n.p.

Allen, Don Cameron. 1960. *Image and Meaning: Metaphoric Traditions in Renaissance Poetry*. Baltimore: Johns Hopkins Press.

American Repertory Theatre News. 1995. 15(2).

Anacreon. 1554. "The Insect." Trans. anon. Manuscripts, British Museum. London, England.

Andrews, John F., ed. 1994. *The Tempest*. Rutland, VT: Tuttle.

Asimov, Isaac. 1978. *Asimov's Guide to Shakespeare*. New York: Avenel.

Auden, W. H. 1944. *For the Time Being*. New York: Random House.

———. 1962. *The Dyer's Hand and Other Essays*. New York: Random House.

Backalenick, Irene. 1995. "Icons, Comedies, Classics on Broadway." *Westport News* (CT), 17 November, 17.

Bacon, Sir Francis. 1887. *Bacon's Essays*, Ed. W. Aldis Wright. New York: Macmillan.

———. 1900. *The Essays of Francis Bacon*. Ed. George E. Woodberry. New York: Century.

————. 1904. *The Physical and Metaphysical Works of Lord Bacon.* Ed. Joseph Devey. London: George Bell.

Barber, C. L., and Richard Wheeler. 1986. *The Whole Journey: Shakespeare's Power of Development.* Berkeley: University of California Press.

Barber, Lester. 1977. "Great Lakes Shakespeare Festival." *Shakespeare Quarterly* 28: 223–24.

————. 1980. "Great Lakes Shakespeare Festival." *Shakespeare Quarterly* 31: 232–36.

Barker, Francis, and Peter Hulme. 1985. "Nymphs and Reapers Heavily Vanish." In *Alternative Shakespeares*, ed. John Drakakis. London: Methuen, 191–205.

Barlow, Graham, and Priscilla Seltzer. 1979. "Shakespeare in Scotland." *Shakespeare Quarterly* 30: 160–63.

————. 1980. "Shakespeare in Scotland." *Shakespeare Quarterly* 31: 161–63.

Barnes, Clive. 1995. "Taking B'way by Storm." *New York Post,* 2 November, 27.

Barnet, Sylvan, ed. 1987, 1998. *The Tempest.* New York: Signet.

Barton, Anne Righter, ed. 1968. *The Tempest.* London: New Penguin.

————. 1980. "Leontes and the Spider: Language and Speaker in the Last Plays." In *Shakespeare's Styles: Essays in Honour of Kenneth Muir,* ed. Philip Edwards, G. K. Hunter, and Inga-Stina Ewbank. Cambridge: Cambridge University Press, 131–50.

Bate, Jonathan. 1989. *Shakespeare and the English Romantic Imagination.* Oxford: Oxford University Press.

————. 1993. *Shakespeare and Ovid.* Oxford: Clarendon Press. Excerpted as "From Myth to Drama," in *Critical Essays on Shakespeare's "The Tempest,"* ed. Alden Vaughan and Virginia Mason Vaughan. New York: G. K. Hall, 1998, 39–59.

————. 1995. "Caliban and Ariel Write Back." *Shakespeare Survey* 48: 155–62.

Bate, Jonathan and Russell Jackson. 1996. *Shakespeare: An Illustrated Stage History.* Oxford: Oxford University Press.

Battenhouse, Roy W., ed. 1994. *Shakespeare: The Christian Dimension.* Bloomington: Indiana University Press.

Baugh, Albert C. 1957. *A History of the English Language.* 2nd ed. New York: Appleton, Century, Crofts.

Beckerman, Bernard. 1962. *Shakespeare at the Globe, 1599–1609.* New York: Macmillan.

————. 1976. *"Tempest* in a Loft." *Shakespeare Quarterly* 27: 56–57.

Belsey, Catherine. 1983. "Shakespeare and Film: A Question of Perspective." *Literature/Film Quarterly* 11: 152–57.

Bentley, G. E. 1941–68. *The Jacobean and Caroline Stage.* Vol. 1. Oxford: Oxford University Press.

————. 1948. "Shakespeare at the Blackfriars Theatre." *Shakespeare Survey* 1: 38–50.

Benveniste, Emile. 1974. *Problemes de linguistique generale.* Vol. 2. Paris: Sorbonne.

Berger, Harry, Jr. 1969. "Miraculous Harp: A Reading of Shakespeare's *Tempest.*" *Shakespeare Studies* 5: 253–83.

————. 1987. "Bodies and Texts." *Representations* 17: 144–66.

Berger, John. 1985. *The Sense of Sight.* New York: Pantheon.

Berger, Karol. 1977. "Prospero's Art." *Shakespeare Studies* 10: 211–39.

Bergeron, David. 1985. *Shakespeare's Romances and the Royal Family.* Lawrence: University Press of Kansas.

————. 1991. *Royal Family, Royal Lovers.* Columbia: University of Missouri Press.

Bernheimer, Richard. 1952. *Wild Men in the Middle Ages: A Study in Art, Sentiment, and Demonology*. Cambridge, MA: Harvard University Press.

Berry, Francis. 1965. *The Shakespeare Inset: Word and Picture*. London: Routledge and Kegan Paul.

Berry, Lloyd E., ed. 1969. *The Geneva Bible, a Facsimile of the 1560 Edition*. With an introduction by Lloyd E. Berry. Madison: University of Wisconsin Press.

Berry, Ralph. 1983. "Stratford Festival Canada, 1982." *Shakespeare Quarterly* 34: 93–98.

———. 1993. "Within the Bermuda Triangle: Reflections on Recent *Tempest*s." In *Shakespeare in Performance*. New York: St. Martin's, 127–39.

Bettelheim, Bruno. 1976. *The Uses of Enchantment*. New York: Knopf.

Bevington, David, ed. 1980. *The Complete Works of Shakespeare*. Glenview, IL: Scott, Foresman.

Beyenburg, Romana. 1995. "*The Tempest*." In *Shakespeare in Performance*, ed. Keith Parsons and Pamela Mason. London: Salamander, 202–8.

Billen, Andrew. 1994. "*The Tempest*." *Independent on Sunday*, 17 July, sec. 6, p. 2.

Billington, Michael. 1994. "*The Tempest*." *Guardian*, 15 July, 26.

———. 1998. "Review of *The Tempest*." *Guardian*, 27 February, sec. 2, p. 2.

Black, James. 1991. "The Latter End of Prospero's Commonwealth." *Shakespeare Survey* 43: 29–41.

Bloom, Harold, ed. 1988. *William Shakespeare's The Tempest: Modern Critical Interpretations*. New York: Chelsea.

———. 1998. *Shakespeare*. New York: Riverhead Books.

Blos, Peter. 1962. *On Adolescence*. New York: Free Press.

Boas, Frederick S. 1912. *Shakespeare and His Predecessors*. New York: Scribner's.

Boas, Frederick S., and A. O. Lovejoy. 1935. *A Documentary History of Primitivism and Related Ideas*. Baltimore: Johns Hopkins Press.

Bobbin, Jay. 1998. "Shakespeare's 'Tempest' Brews Anew on NBC." *TV Week*, 13–19 December, 2.

Bodkin, Maud. 1934. *Archetypal Patterns in Poetry*. London: Oxford University Press.

Bono, Barbara J. 1984. *Literary Transvaluation: From Vergilian Epic to Shakespearean Tragicomedy*. Berkeley: University of California Press.

Boose, Lynda E., and Richard Burt, eds. 1997. *Shakespeare, The Movie*. New York: Routledge.

Booth, Stephen. 1983. *Indefinition in Tragedy*. New Haven, CT: Yale University Press.

Booty, John E., ed. 1976. *The Book of Common Prayer*. Charlottesville: University Press of Virginia.

Boughner, D. C. 1970. "Jonsonian Structure in *The Tempest*." *Shakespeare Quarterly* 21: 3–10.

Bowers, Fredson. 1955. "Hamlet as Minister and Scourge." *PMLA* 70: 40–49.

Bowling, L. E. 1951. "The Theme of Natural Order in *The Tempest*." *College English* 12: 33–37.

Bradley, A. C. 1904. *Shakespearean Tragedy*. London: Macmillan.

Breight, Curt. 1990. "Treason Doth Never Prosper." *Shakespeare Quarterly* 41: 1–28.

Bristol, Michael. 1990. *Shakespeare's America, America's Shakespeare*. London: Routledge.

Brockbank, Philip. 1966. "*The Tempest*: Conventions of Art and Empire." In *Later Shake-*

speare, ed. John Russell Brown and Bernard Harris. Stratford-upon-Avon Studies 8. New York: St. Martin's 183–201.

———, ed. 1985. *Players of Shakespeare*. Cambridge: Cambridge University Press.

Brook, Peter. 1972. *The Empty Space*. London: Penguin.

Brower, Reuben. 1951. *The Fields of Light*. New York: Oxford University Press.

Brown, John Russell. 1969. *Shakespeare: The Tempest*. London: Edward Arnold.

———, ed. 1996. *The Tempest*. New York: Applause.

Brown, Paul. 1985. "This Thing of Darkness I Acknowledge Mine." In *Political Shakespeare: New Essays in Cultural Materialism*, ed. Jonathan Dollimore and Alan Sinfield. Manchester: Manchester University Press, 48–71.

Browne, E. Martin. 1958. *Religious Drama 2*. Selected and introduced by E. Martin Browne. New York: Meridian.

Browne, Thomas. 1885. *Religio Medici*. Ed. W. A. Greenhill. London: Macmillan.

Bruno, Giordano. 1964. *The Expulsion of the Triumphant Beast*. Trans. Arthur D. Imerti. New Brunswick, NJ: Rutgers University Press.

Brustein, Robert. 1995. "To Our Friends." *Tempest* program, American Repertory Theatre.

Bullough, Geoffrey. 1975. *Narrative and Dramatic Sources of Shakespeare*. Vol. 8. New York: Columbia University Press.

Bulman, James C., ed. 1996. *Shakespeare, Theory, and Performance*. New York: Routledge.

Burgess, William. 1903. *The Bible in Shakespeare*. New York: Thomas Y. Crowell.

Camus, Albert. 1955. *The Myth of Sisyphus and Other Essays*. Trans. Justin O'Brien. New York: Alfred A. Knopf.

Canby, Vincent. 1980. "Jarman's *Tempest*." *New York Times*, 22 September, C20.

Cantor, Paul A. 1981. "Prospero's Republic: The Politics of Shakespeare's *The Tempest*." In *Shakespeare as Political Thinker*, ed. John Alvis and Thomas West. Durham: Carolina Academic Press, 239–55.

Cartelli, Thomas. 1987. "Prospero in Africa: *The Tempest* as Colonialist Text and Pretext." In *Shakespeare Reproduced: The Text in History and Ideology*, ed. Jean E. Howard and Marion O'Connor. London: Methuen, 99–115.

———. 1998. Commentary. Conference on Undergraduate Shakespeare, Susquehanna University, Selinsgrove, Pennsylvania, November.

Chambers, Edmund K. 1923. *The Elizabethan Stage*. Vols. 1–2. Oxford: Clarendon Press.

———. 1925. "The Integrity of *The Tempest*." *Review of English Studies* 1: 129–50.

———. 1930. *William Shakespeare: A Study of Facts and Problems*. Vols. 1–2. Oxford: Clarendon Press.

Charney, Maurice. 1980. "Shakespearean Anglophilia." *Shakespeare Quarterly* 31: 287–92.

———. 1993. *All of Shakespeare*. New York: Columbia University Press.

Chaucer, Geoffrey. 1947. *The Canterbury Tales*. Ed. Edwin J. Howard and Gordon D. Wilson. New York: Prentice-Hall.

Chickering, Howell. 1994. "Hearing Ariel's Songs." *Journal of Medieval and Renaissance Studies* 24: 131–72.

Childress, Diana. 1974. "Are Shakespeare's Plays Really Romances?" In *Shakespeare's Late Plays*, ed. Richard C. Tobias and Paul G. Zolbrod. Athens: Ohio University Press, 44–55.

Chute, Marchette. 1949. *Shakespeare of London*. New York: Dutton.

Ciardi, John, trans. 1954. *The Inferno,* by Dante Alighieri. New York: Mentor.

Cohen, Walter. 1985. *Drama of a Nation: Public Theater in Renaissance England and Spain.* Ithaca, NY: Cornell University Press.

Coleridge, S. T. 1836. *Literary Remains of Samuel Taylor Coleridge.* London: n.p.

Coletti, Theresa. 1974. "Music and *The Tempest.*" In Tobias and Zolbrod 1974, 185–99.

Collick, John. 1989. *Shakespeare, Cinema, and Society.* Manchester: Manchester University Press.

Collins, J. Churlton. 1908. "Poetry and Symbolism: A Study of *The Tempest.*" *Contemporary Review* 23: 111–39.

Combs, Richard. 1983. "Mid-Life Crisis *Tempest.*" *TLS,* 25 February, 179.

Comtois, M. E. 1974. "New York Shakespeare Festival: Lincoln Center, 1973–74." *Shakespeare Quarterly* 25: 405–9.

Cook, Hardy. 1994. "Table of Contents." *Shakespeare Bulletin* 12: 77.

Cookson, Linda, and Bryan Loughrey, eds. 1988. *Critical Essays on "The Tempest."* Essex: Longman.

Coonrod, Karin. 1995. "The Visceral Poetry of George C. Wolfe's *Tempest.*" *Tempest* program. Playbill (12 December).

Coppedge, Walter. 1998. "Jarman's *The Tempest.*" *Creative Screenwriting* 5: 12–14.

Cotta, John. 1616. *The Triall of Witch-craft:* London.

Couliano, I. P. 1987. *Eros and Magic in the Renaissance.* Chicago: University of Chicago Press.

Coursen, H. R. 1969. "Prospero and the Drama of the Soul." *Shakespeare Studies* 4: 316–32.

———. 1976. *Christian Ritual and the World of Shakespeare's Tragedies.* Lewisburg, PA: Bucknell University Press.

———. 1984. *The Leasing Out of England.* Lanham, MD: University Press of America.

———. 1986. *The Compensatory Psyche: A Jungian Approach to Shakespeare.* Lanham, MD: University Press of America.

———. 1989. "Television, Medium, and Performance: Special Effects on Television." *Shakespeare on Film Newsletter* 14(1): 8.

———. 1992. *Shakespearean Performance as Interpretation.* Cranbury, NJ: Associated University Presses.

———. 1993. *Watching Shakespeare on Television.* Cranbury, NJ: Fairleigh Dickinson University Press.

———. 1996. *Shakespeare in Production: Whose History?* Athens: Ohio University Press.

———. 1997a. *Macbeth: A Guide to the Play.* Westport, CT: Greenwood Press.

———. 1997b. *Teaching Shakespeare with Film and Television.* Westport, CT: Greenwood Press.

———. 1999. *Shakespeare: The Two Traditions.* Cranbury, NJ: Associated University Presses.

Craig, Hardin. 1936. *The Enchanted Glass.* New York: Oxford University Press.

———. 1962. *The Literature of the English Renaissance, 1485–1660.* New York: Collier.

Crawley, Robert Ralston. 1926. "Shakspere's Use of the Voyagers in *The Tempest.*" *PMLA* 41: 688–726.

Croce, Benedetto. 1920. *Aristo, Shakespeare, and Corneille.* Trans. Douglas Ainslee. London: George Allen and Unwin.

Crossley, J. 1851. *John Dee: Discourse Apologeticall and Autobiographical Tracts*. Manchester: n.p.

Crowl, Samuel. 1980. "Stormy Weather: A New *Tempest* on Film." *Shakespeare on Film Newsletter* 5(1): 1, 5, 7.

Culliford, S. G. 1965. *William Strachey, 1572–1621*. Charlottesville: University Press of Virginia.

Cunliffe, J. W., Tucker Brooke, and H. N. McCracken, eds. 1935. *Shakespeare's Principal Plays*. New York: Appleton-Century.

Cunningham, Dennis. 1995. "Review." WCBS, 2 November.

Curry, Walter Clyde. 1937. *Shakespeare's Philosophical Patterns*. Baton Rouge: Louisiana State University Press.

Cutts, John P. 1955. "Robert Johnson: King's Musician in His Majesty's Public Entertainments." *Music and Letters* 36(2): 110–25.

———. 1968. *Rich and Strange: A Study of Shakespeare's Last Plays*. Pullman: Washington State University Press.

Daniell, David. 1989. *"The Tempest": The Critics Debate*. Atlantic Highlands, NJ: Humanities Press International.

Davidson, Frank. 1963. *"The Tempest*: An Interpretation." *Journal of English and Germanic Philology* 62: 501–17. In Palmer 1968, 212–31.

Davis, Charles. 1998. "Reconstructing Knowledge: Francis Bacon and Scientific Ethos." *Boston Book Review*, July/August, 22.

Dawson, Anthony B. 1988a. *"Tempest* in a Teapot: Critics, Evaluation, Ideology." In *Bad Shakespeare*, ed. Maurice Charney. Cranbury, NJ: Associated University Presses, 61–73.

———. 1988b. *Watching Shakespeare: A Playgoers' Guide*. London: Macmillan.

de Grazia, Margreta. 1981. *"The Tempest*: Gratuitous Movement or Action without Kibes and Pinches." *Shakespeare Studies* 14: 249–65.

de Jongh, Nicholas. 1994. *"The Tempest."* *Evening Standard*, 14 July, 31.

Demaray, John G. 1998. *Shakespeare and the Spectacles of Strangeness: "The Tempest" and the Transformation of Renaissance Theatrical Forms*. Pittsburgh: Duquesne University Press.

Derrida, Jacques. 1993. *Memoirs of the Blind: The Self-Portrait and Other Ruins*. Trans. Pascale-Anne Brault and Michael Naas. Chicago: University of Chicago Press.

Dessen, Alan. 1986. "The Supernatural on Television." *Shakespeare on Film Newsletter* 11(1): 1, 8.

Devereux, E. J. 1968. "Sacramental Imagery in *The Tempest*." In Battenhouse 1994, 254–57.

Devlin, Diana. 1988. "Caliban—Monster, Servant, King." In Cookson and Loughrey 1988, 20–28.

Devlin, Keith. 1988. *The Language of Mathematics*. New York: Freeman.

Dobree, Bonamy. 1961. "The Last Plays." In *The Living Shakespeare*, ed. Robert Gittings. New York: Fawcett, 147–60.

Doebler, John. 1974. *Shakespeare's Speaking Pictures*. Albuquerque: University of New Mexico Press.

Donaldson, Peter S. 1997. " 'Prospero's Books.' " In *Shakespeare, the Movie*, ed. Lynda E. Boose and Richard Burt. New York: Routledge, 169–85.

Doolittle, Hilda (H.D.). 1949. *By Avon River*. New York: Macmillan.

Doran, Madeleine. 1964. *Endeavors of Art*. Madison: University of Wisconsin Press.

Dowden, Edward. 1875. *Shakspere: A Critical Study of His Mind and Art*. London: Henry S. King.

Driscoll, James P. 1983. "The Shakespearean 'Metastance.' " In *Identity in Shakespearean Drama*. Cranbury, NJ: Associated University Presses. In Bloom 1988, 85–98.

Dubrow, Heather. 1999. "Shakespeare's Colonialist *Tempest*." In *Shakespearean International Yearbook*. Brookfield, VT: Ashgate.

Durant, Will. 1926. *The Story of Philosophy*. New York: Simon and Schuster.

Durband, Alan, ed. 1984. *The Tempest*. London: Barron's.

Eden, Richard. 1577. *History of Travayle in the West and East Indies*. London: Wm. Powell.

Edwards, Philip. 1960. "The Danger Not the Death: The Art of John Fletcher." In *Jacobean Theatre*, ed. John Russell Brown and Bernard Harris. London: Edward Arnold.

Egan, Robert. 1972. " 'This Rough Magic': Perspectives of Art and Morality in *The Tempest*." *Shakespeare Quarterly* 23: 171–82.

———. 1975. *Drama within Drama: Shakespeare's Sense of His Art in "King Lear," "The Winter's Tale," and "The Tempest."* New York: Columbia University Press.

Elgin, Kathy, 1993. "The Man behind Elgar's Moustache." *RSC Magazine*, Autumn, 13–15.

Eliot, Alexander. 1997. *The Timeless Myths*. New York: Meridian.

Ellis-Fermor, Una. 1964. *The Jacobean Drama: An Interpretation*. New York: Vintage.

Elyot, Thomas. 1907. *The Boke Named the Governor*. London: Everyman, Dent.

Empson, William. 1960. *Some Versions of Pastoral*. New York: New Directions.

Engelsfeld, Mladen. 1982. "*The Tempest* along the Croatian Coast in 1980 and 1981." *Shakespeare Quarterly* 33: 505–6.

Erickson, Peter. 1991. *Rewriting Shakespeare, Rewriting Ourselves*. Berkeley: University of California Press.

Erlich, Bruce. 1977. "Shakespeare's Colonial Metaphor: On the Social Function of Theatre in *The Tempest*." *Science and Society* 41: 43–77.

Evans, B. Ifor. 1940. *A Short History of English Literature*. Harmondsworth: Penguin.

Evans, Bertrand. 1960. *Shakespeare's Comedies*. Oxford: Clarendon Press.

Evans, G. B. 1974. *The Riverside Shakespeare*. Boston: Houghton Mifflin.

Evans, Greg. 1995. "*The Tempest*." *Variety*, 6–12 November, 78–79.

Evans, R.J.W. 1973. *Rudolf II and His World*. Oxford: Clarendon Press.

Ewbank, Inga-Stina. 1991. "*The Tempest* and After." *Shakespeare Survey* 43: 109–19.

Fain, John Tyree. 1968. "Some Notes on Ariel's Song." *Shakespeare Quarterly* 19: 329–32.

Falconer, A. F. 1964. *Shakespeare and the Sea*. n.p. Excerpted in Orgel 1987, 207–8.

Farley, Barbara S. 1994. "*The Tempest*." *Shakespeare Bulletin* 12(1): 13.

Farnham, Willard. 1936. *The Medieval Heritage of Elizabethan Tragedy*. Berkeley: University of California Press.

Feldberg, Robert. 1995. "Patrick Stewart's Prospero Encore." *Record*, 2 November, 31.

Felperin, Howard, 1972. *Shakespearean Romance*. Princeton: Princeton University Press.

Fenwick, Henry. 1980. "The Production." In *The Tempest*. London: BBC.

Fiedler, Leslie. 1949. "The Defense of the Illusion and the Creation of Myth." In *English Institute Essays: 1948*. New York: Columbia University Press, 71–82.

———. 1972. *The Stranger in Shakespeare*. New York: Stein and Day.

Fineman, Joel. 1977. "Fratricide and Cuckoldry: Shakespeare and His Sense of Difference." *Psychoanalytic Review* 64: 409–53.

Fitts, L. T. 1975. "The Vocabulary of the Environment in *The Tempest.*" *Shakespeare
Quarterly* 23: 42–47.

Flagstad, Karen. 1986. " 'Making This Place Paradise': Prospero and the Problem of
Caliban in *The Tempest.*" *Shakespeare Studies* 18: 205–33.

Ford, John. 1999. "Chip Egan's *Tempest.*" *Upstart Crow* 19: 141–43.

Frank, Mike. 1974. "Shakespeare's Existential Comedy." In Tobias and Zolbrod 1974,
142–65.

French, William W. 1992. *"The Tempest."* *Shakespeare Bulletin* 10(1): 40–42.

Frey, Charles. 1979. *"The Tempest* and the New World." *Shakespeare Quarterly* 30: 29–
41.

Fromkin, David. 1999. *The Way of the World: From the Dawn of Civilizations to the
Eve of the Twenty-first Century.* New York: Knopf.

Frye, Northrop. 1957. *Anatomy of Criticism.* Princeton: Princeton University Press.

———. 1959. *The Tempest.* New York: Penguin.

———. 1965. *A Natural Perspective: The Development of Shakespearean Comedy and
Romance.* New York: Harcourt, Brace and World.

———. 1976. *The Secular Scripture: A Study of the Structure of Romance.* Cambridge,
MA: Harvard University Press.

———. 1986. *Northrop Frye on Shakespeare.* Ed. Robert Sandler. New Haven, CT:
Yale University Press.

Frye, R. M. 1982. *Shakespeare: The Art of the Dramatist.* Rev. ed. London: George
Allen and Unwin.

Fuchs, Barbara. 1997. "Conquering Islands: Contextualizing *The Tempest.*" *Shakespeare
Quarterly* 48: 45–62.

Furness, Horace Howard. 1892. *The Tempest.* Philadelphia: Lippincott.

Furnivall, F. J., ed. 1877. *The Leopold Shakespeare.* London: Cassell, Pether and Galpin.

Garber, Marjorie. 1974. *Dream in Shakespeare: From Metaphor to Metamorphosis.* New
Haven, CT: Yale University Press.

———. 1980. "The Eye of the Storm: Structure and Myth in Shakespeare's *Tempest.*"
Hebrew University Studies in Literature 8. In Bloom 1988, 43–60.

Garner, Stanton B., Jr. 1979. *"The Tempest:* Language and Society." *Shakespeare Survey*
32: 177–87.

Garnett, Richard, and Edmund Gosse. 1904. *English Literature: An Illustrated Record.*
4 vols. London: Macmillan.

Gatti, Hilary. 1989. *The Renaissance Drama of Knowledge: Giordano Bruno in England.*
London: Routledge.

Geertz, Clifford. 1973. *The Interpretation of Cultures.* New York: Basic Books.

Gibson, Rex, ed. 1995. *The Tempest.* Cambridge: Cambridge University Press.

Gill, Roma, ed. 1998. *The Tempest.* Oxford: Oxford University Press.

Gillies, John. 1994. *Shakespeare and the Geography of Difference.* Cambridge: Cambridge University Press.

Gilman, Ernest B. 1980. " 'All Eyes': Prospero's Inverted Masque." *Renaissance Quarterly* 33: 214–30.

Goddard, Harold. 1951. *The Meaning of Shakespeare.* Chicago: University of Chicago
Press.

Golding, Arthur. 1567. *Shakespeare's Ovid, Being Arthur Golding's Translation of the Metamorphoses*. Ed. W.H.D. Rouse. 1961. New York: Norton.

Goldman, Michael. 1972. *Shakespeare and the Energies of Drama*. Princeton: Princeton University Press.

Gordon, George. 1944. *Shakespearian Comedy and Other Studies*. Oxford: Oxford University Press.

Gorrie, John, dir. 1980. *The Tempest*. Video production. BBC-TV.

Gottfried, Martin. 1995. " 'The Tempest' Stirs Up a Storm Indoors." *New York Law Journal*, 3 November.

Gould, Jack. 1960. "Review." *New York Times*, 4 February, 63.

Graham, Shawn Renee. 1995. "Program Note." *The Tempest*. American Repertory Theatre. Cambridge, MA.

Grant, Patrick. 1979. *Images and Ideas in Literature of the English Renaissance*. Amherst: University of Massachusetts Press. Excerpted as "*The Tempest* and the Magic of Charity" in Battenhouse 1994, 267–70.

Green, Herbert E. 1913. *The Tempest*. The Tudor Shakespeare. New York: Macmillan.

Greenaway, Peter, dir. 1991. *Prospero's Books*. Film. Miramax Films.

Greenblatt, Stephen. 1988. *Shakespearean Negotiations: The Circulation of Social Energy in Renaissance England*. Berkeley: University of California Press. Excerpted in Barnet 1998, 156–79.

———. 1990. *Learning to Curse: Essays in Early Modern Culture*. London: Routledge.

———. 1997. "Introduction to *The Tempest*." In *The Norton Shakespeare*. New York: Norton, 3047–53.

Greenblatt, Stephen, Walter Cohen, Jean E. Howard, and Katherine E. Maus, eds. 1997. *The Norton Shakespeare*. New York: W.W. Norton.

Greene, Gayle. 1990. "Margaret Laurence's *Diviners* and Shakespeare's *Tempest*." In *Women's Re-Visions of Shakespeare*, ed. Marianne Novy. Urbana: University of Illinois Press, 165–82.

Greene, Robert. 1952. *Friar Bacon and Friar Bungay*. In *An Anthology of English Drama before Shakespeare*, ed. Robert Heilman. New York: Rinehart.

Greer, Germaine. 1986. *Shakespeare*. Oxford: Oxford University Press.

Griffin, Alice V. 1951. *Pageantry on the Shakespearean Stage*. New Haven, CT: College and University Press.

Griffiths, Trevor R. 1983. " 'This Island's Mine': Caliban and Colonialism." *Yearbook of English Studies* 13: 159–80.

Gross, John. 1998. "Review of *The Tempest*." *Sunday Telegraph*, 1 March, sec. 5, p. 12.

Grudin, Robert. 1979. *Mighty Opposites: Shakespeare and Renaissance Contrariety*. Berkeley: University of California Press.

Guarini, Giambattista. 1601. *A Compendium of Tragi-comic Poetry*. London: n.p.

Gurewitsch, Matthew. 1999. "Land of Lesser Giants in the Annals of Drama." *New York Times*, 4 April, sec. 2, pp. 1, 25.

Gurr, Andrew. 1996. "Industrious Ariel and Idle Caliban." In Maquerlot and Willems 1996, 193–208.

Habicht, Werner. 1981. "Shakespeare in West Germany." *Shakespeare Quarterly* 32: 412–15.

Hakluyt, Sir Richard. 1927. *A Selection of the Principal Voyages: Traffiques and Discoveries of the English Nation*. New York: Knopf.

Halio, Jay L. 1988. *Understanding Shakespeare's Plays in Performance*. Manchester: Manchester University Press.

———. 1996. "Review." *Shakespeare Quarterly* 47: 221–22.

Hall, Kim F. 1995. *Things of Darkness: Economies of Race and Gender in Early Modern England*. Ithaca, NY: Cornell University Press.

Hall, Peter. 1969. "Shakespeare's *Dream*." *Times*, 26 January, 37.

Halliday, F. E. 1954. *The Poetry of Shakespeare's Plays*. New York: Barnes and Noble.

Hamilton, Donna B. 1989. "Defiguring Virgil in *The Tempest*." *Style* 23: 352–73. In Vaughan and Vaughan, 1998, 17–38.

———. 1990. *Virgil and "The Tempest": The Politics of Imitation*. Columbus: Ohio State University Press.

———. 1992. "Shakespeare's Romances and Jacobean Political Discourse." In Hunt 1992, 64–71.

Hankins, John E. 1947. "Caliban: The Bestial Man." *PMLA* 71.

Hanks, Robert. 1994. "*The Tempest*." *Independent on Sunday*, 17 July, sec. 6, p. 1.

Harbage, Alfred, ed. 1946. *The Tempest*. New York: Appleton-Century-Crofts.

———. 1959. "Introduction." In *Coleridge's Writings on Shakespeare*, Ed. Terence Hawkes. New York: Capricorn.

———. 1963. *William Shakespeare: A Reader's Guide*. New York: Noonday.

Hardman, Christopher. 1988. "Dramatic Pattern and Expectation in *The Tempest*." In Cookson and Loughrey 1988, 30–39.

Harrison, Gilbert B. 1954. *Introducing Shakespeare*. Rev. ed. Harmondsworth: Penguin.

———. 1963. "*The Tempest*." In *Stratford Papers 1962*, ed. Berners W. Jackson. Toronto: University of Toronto Press, 228–41.

Hartwig, Joan. 1972. *Shakespeare's Tragicomic Vision*. Baton Rouge: Louisiana State University Press.

———. 1983. *Shakespeare's Analogical Scene: Parody as Structural Syntax*. Lincoln: University of Nebraska Press.

Hassan, Ihab. 1986. "Pluralism in Postmodern Perspective." *Critical Inquiry* 12.

———. 1987. "Making Sense: The Trials of Postmodern Discourse." *New Literary History*.

Hassel, R. Chris, Jr. 1980. *Faith and Folly in Shakespeare's Romantic Comedies*. Athens: University of Georgia Press.

Hatfield, Andrew. 1996. "The Natural and the Dead." In Maquerlot and Willems 1996, 32–54.

Hawkes, Terence, ed. 1959. *Coleridge's Writings on Shakespeare*. New York: Capricorn.

———. 1974. *Shakespeare's Talking Animals: Language and Drama in Society*. Totowa, NJ: Rowman and Littlefield.

———. 1992. *Meaning by Shakespeare*. London: Routledge.

———, ed. 1996. *Alternative Shakespeares II*. London: Routledge.

Hawking, Stephen. 1988. *A Brief History of Time*. New York: Bantam Books.

Hawkins, Sherman. 1967. "The Two Worlds of Shakespearean Comedy." *Shakespeare Studies* 3: 62–80.

Hawthorne, Nathaniel. 1991. *The Scarlet Letter*. Ed. Ross C. Murfin. Boston: Bedford Books.

Haydn, Hiram. 1950. *The Counter-Renaissance*. New York: Charles Scribner's Sons.

Hearst, Stephen. 1978. "It Ain't Necessarily So." *New Review* 5: 1–13.

Hebel, J. William, Hoyt H. Hudson, Francis R. Johnson, A. Wigfall Green, and Robert Hoopes. 1953. *Tudor Poetry and Prose*. New York: Appleton-Century-Crofts.

Heilman, Robert, ed. 1952. *An Anthology of English Drama before Shakespeare*. New York: Rinehart.

Helgerson, Richard. 1996. "Review." *Shakespeare Quarterly* 47: 212–14.

Heninger, S. K. 1974. *Touches of Sweet Harmony: Pythagorean Cosmology and Renaissance Poetics*. San Marino, CA: Huntington Library.

Hennedy, John F. 1985. "*The Tempest* and the Counter-Renaissance." *Studies in the Humanities* 12 (December): 90–105.

Herold, Niels. 1997. "Yet More New Uses of Adversity in Teaching *The Tempest*." *Shakespeare and the Classroom* 5: 57–59.

Hill, Errol. 1971. "The 1971 Season at Stratford, Connecticut." *Shakespeare Quarterly* 22: 371–76.

———. 1984. *Shakespeare in Sable: A History of Black Shakespearean Actors*. Amherst: University of Massachusetts Press.

Hillman, Richard. 1983. "Chaucer's Franklin's Magician and *The Tempest*: An Influence beyond Appearances?" *Shakespeare Quarterly* 34: 426–32.

———. 1985–86. "*The Tempest* as Romance and Anti-Romance." *University of Toronto Quarterly* 55: 141–60.

Hirst, David. 1984a. *The Tempest: Text and Performance*. London: Macmillan.

———. 1984b. *Tragicomedy*. London: Methuen.

Holland, Peter. 1997. *English Shakespeares: Shakespeare on the English Stage in the 1990s*. Cambridge: Cambridge University Press.

Holloway, Brian. 1999. "Review." *Shakespeare and Renaissance Association of West Virginia Papers* 22: 84–88.

Holquist, Michael. 1968. "How to Play Utopia." *Yale French Studies* 41: 106–23.

Homan, Sidney R. 1973. "*The Tempest* and Shakespeare's Last Plays: The Aesthetic Dimension." *Shakespeare Quarterly* 24: 69–76.

Hooker, Richard. 1593. *Of the Lawes of Ecclesiaticall Politie*. London: John Windet.

———. 1907. *Of the Laws of Ecclesiastical Polity*. Vol. 5. New York: Everyman's Library.

Hornby, Richard. 1986. *Drama, Metadrama, and Perception*. Lewisburg, PA: Bucknell University Press.

Horowitz, David. 1965. *Shakespeare: An Existential View*. New York: Hill and Wang.

Hotchkiss, Lia M. 1998. "The Incorporation of Word as Image in *Prospero's Books*." *Post Script* 17(2): 8–25.

Howard, E. J., and G. D. Wilson, eds. 1937. *The Canterbury Tales*. New York: Prentice-Hall.

Howard-Hill, Trevor H. 1972. *Ralph Crane and Some Shakespeare First Folio Comedies*. Charlottesville: University Press of Virginia.

Hunt, Maurice, ed. 1992. *Approaches to Teaching "The Tempest" and Other Late Romances*. New York: Modern Language Association.

Hunter, Robert G. 1965. *Shakespeare and the Comedy of Forgiveness*. New York: Columbia University Press.

———. 1976. *Shakespeare and the Mystery of God's Judgments*. Athens: University of Georgia Press.

Hunter, William B., Jr., ed. 1963. *The Complete Poetry of Ben Jonson*. Garden City, NY: Doubleday.

Iselin, Pierre. 1995. " 'My Music for Nothing': Musical Negotiations in *The Tempest.*" *Shakespeare Survey* 48: 135–45.

Jackson, Russell. 1994a. "Shakespeare at Stratford-upon-Avon." *Shakespeare Quarterly* 45: 322–48.

———. 1994b. "Shakespeare's Comedies on Film." In *Shakespeare and the Moving Image*, ed. Anthony Davies and Stanley Wells. Cambridge: Cambridge University Press. 99–120.

James I, King of England. 1918. *The Political Works of James I.* Ed. C. H. McIlwain. Cambridge, MA: Harvard University Press.

James VI, King of Scotland. 1597. *King James, the First: Daemonologie (1597) in Forme of a Dialogue.* Edinburgh. Ed. G. B. Harrison. 1924. London: Bodley Head.

James, Caryn. 1996. "Television, the Medium That Defies Sharp Focus." *New York Times*, 7 July, 25, 27.

James, D. G. 1937. *Skepticism and Poetry.* London: Allen and Unwin.

———. 1951. *The Dream of Learning.* Oxford: Clarendon Press.

———. 1967. *The Dream of Prospero.* Oxford: Clarendon Press.

James, Henry. 1907. "Introduction." In *Complete Works of Shakespeare.* Vol. 16. London: Renaissance.

James, William. 1965. "The Dilemma of Determinism." In *A Modern Introduction to Philosophy*, rev. ed., ed. Paul Edwards and Arthur Pap. New York: Macmillan, 25–37.

Jarman, Derek. 1984. *Dancing Ledge.* London: Quartet.

Johnson, Francis R. 1937. *Astronomical Thought in Renaissance England.* Baltimore: Johns Hopkins Press.

Johnson, Samuel. 1951. *Johnson: Prose and Poetry.* Ed. Mona Wilson. Cambridge, MA: Harvard University Press.

Jonson, Ben. 1933. *Bartholomew Fair.* In *Elizabethan Plays*, ed. Hazelton Spencer. Boston: Heath.

———. 1963. *The Complete Poetry of Ben Jonson.* Ed. William B. Hunter, Jr. Garden City, NY: Doubleday Anchor.

———. 1974. *The Alchemist.* Ed. Alvin Kernan. New Haven, CT: Yale University Press.

Jowett, John. 1983. "New Created Creatures: Ralph Crane and the Stage Directions in *The Tempest.*" *Shakespeare Survey* 36: 107–20.

Judson, A. C., ed. *Seventeenth Century Lyrics.* Chicago: University of Chicago Press.

Kahn, Coppelia. 1980. "The Providential Tempest and the Shakespearean Family." In *Representing Shakespeare: New Psychoanalytic Essays*, ed. Murray M. Schwartz and Coppelia Kahn. Baltimore, Johns Hopkins University Press, 217–43. Also in *Man's Estate.* Berkeley: University of California Press, 1981, 193–225.

Kamps, Ivo, ed. 1991. *Shakespeare Left and Right.* London: Routledge.

Kastan, David Scott. 1998. " 'The Duke of Milan / And His Brave Son': Dynastic Politics in *The Tempest.*" In Vaughan and Vaughan 1998, 91–103.

Kaufmann, Walter. 1960. *From Shakespeare to Existentialism.* Garden City, NY: Doubleday.

Kay, Carol McGinnis. 1976. "The Alabama Shakespeare Festival, 1975." *Shakespeare Quarterly* 27: 66–71.

Keats, John. 1817. Letter to George and Tom Keats, December 1817. In *The Letters of John Keats*, ed. Hyder E. Rollins. Cambridge, MA: Harvard University Press, 1958.

————. 1962. *Selected Poetry and Letters of John Keats*. Ed. Richard M. Fogel. New York: Holt, Rinehart, and Winston.

Kennedy, Dennis. 1993. *Looking at Shakespeare: A Visual History of Twentieth-Century Performance*. Cambridge: Cambridge University Press.

Kermode, Frank, ed. 1964. *The Tempest*. New York: Random House.

Kernan, Alvin. 1974a. "Introduction." In *The Alchemist*, by Ben Jonson. New Haven, CT: Yale University Press.

————. 1974b. "This Goodly Frame, The Stage: The Interior Theater of Imagination in English Renaissance Drama." *Shakespeare Quarterly* 25: 1–5.

————. 1979. *The Playwright as Magician*. New Haven, CT: Yale University Press.

Keyishian, Harry. 1995. *The Shapes of Revenge: Victimization, Vengeance, and Vindictiveness in Shakespeare*. Atlantic Highlands, NJ: Humanities Press International.

King, Thomas J. 1992. *Casting Shakespeare's Plays: London Actors and Their Roles, 1590–1642*. Cambridge: Cambridge University Press.

Kinney, Arthur F. 1992. "Teaching *The Tempest* as the Art of 'If.' " In Hunt 1992, 153–59.

Kirsch, Arthur. 1994. "Montaigne and *The Tempest*." In *Cultural Exchange between European Nations during the Renaissance*, ed. Gunnar Sorelius and Michael Srigley. Uppsala: Uppsala University Press, 111–21.

Kittredge, George Lyman, ed. 1939. *The Tempest*. Boston: Ginn and Co.

Knight, G. Wilson. 1932. *The Shakespearian Tempest*. Humphrey Milford: Oxford University Press.

————. 1947. *The Crown of Life*. London: Methuen.

Knighten, Merrell. 1994. "The Triple Paternity of *Forbidden Planet*." *Shakespeare Bulletin* 12(3): 36–37.

Knights, L. C. 1933. "How Many Children Had Lady Macbeth?" In Knights 1964, 15–54.

————. 1939. "The University Teaching of English and History: A Plea for Correlation." In Knights 1964, 206–19.

————. 1964. *Explorations*. New York: New York University Press.

————. 1974. "*The Tempest*." In Tobias and Zolbrod 1974, 15–31.

Knox, Bernard. 1955. "*The Tempest* and the Ancient Comic Tradition." In *English Stage Comedy*, ed. W. K. Wimsatt, Jr. New York: Columbia University Press, 52–73. In Barnet 1987, 163–81.

Kott, Jan. 1964. *Shakespeare, Our Contemporary*. Garden City, NY: Doubleday.

————. 1976. "*The Aeneid* and *The Tempest*." *Arion* 3: 424–51.

————. 1987. "*The Tempest* or Repetition." In *The Bottom Translation: Marlowe and Shakespeare and the Carnival Tradition*. Trans. Daniela Miedzyrzecka and Lillian Vallee. Evanston: Northwestern University Press.

Kozintsev, Grigori. 1966. *Shakespeare: Time and Conscience*. London: Dennis Dobson.

Lacan, Jacques. 1982. "Desire and Interpretation of Desire in *Hamlet*." In *Literature and Psychoanalysis*, ed. Shoshana Felman. Baltimore: Johns Hopkins Press, 11–52.

Lahr, John. 1995. "Big and Bad Wolfe." *New Yorker*, 14 May, 121.

Lamb, Charles. 1986. "*The Tempest*." *Tales from Shakespeare*. New York: Signet.

————. 1811. *Of the Tragedies of Shakespeare, Considered with Reference to Their Fitness for Stage Representation*. London.

Langbaum, Robert. 1987. "Introduction." In *The Tempest*. New York: Signet.

Lanier, Douglas. 1996. "Drowning the Book: *Prospero's Books* and the Textual Shakespeare." In *Shakespeare, Theory, and Performance*, ed. James C. Bulman. London: Routledge, 187–209.

La Primaudaye, Pierre de. 1586. *The French Academie*. London: n.p.

Latham, Jacqueline E. M. 1975. "*The Tempest* and King James's *Daemonologie*." *Shakespeare Survey* 28: 117–23.

———. 1979. "The Magic Banquet in *The Tempest*." *Shakespeare Studies* 12 (1979): 215–28.

Law, Ernest. 1920. *Shakespeare's "Tempest" as Originally Produced at Court*. London: Shakespeare Association.

Lawrence, W. J. 1920. "The Masque in *The Tempest*." *Fortnightly Review*, n.s. 108 (June): 941–46.

Lea, Kathleen M. 1934. *Italian Popular Comedy*. Oxford: Clarendon Press.

Lee, John Allan. 1974. "The Styles of Loving." *Psychology Today*. Reprinted in *Reading, Writing, and the Humanities*, ed. Jo Ray McCuen and Anthony C. Winkler. San Diego: Harcourt Brace Jovanovich, 1991, 300–311.

Lee, William Sidney. 1907. "The American Indian in Elizabethan England." *Scribner's* 42: 313–30.

Leech, Clifford. 1950. *Shakespeare's Tragedies*. London: Chatto and Windus.

———. 1958. "The Structure of the Last Plays." *Shakespeare Survey* 11: 25–27.

Leininger, Lorrie. 1980a. "Cracking the Code of *The Tempest*." *Bucknell Review* 25: 121–31.

———. 1980b. "The Miranda Trap: Sexism and Racism in Shakespeare's *Tempest*." In *The Woman's Part: Feminist Criticism of Shakespeare*, ed. Carolyn R. S. Lenz, Gayle Greene, and Carol T. Neely. Urbana: University of Illinois Press, 285–94. Reprinted in Barnet 1998, 146–55.

Leithauser, Brad. 1995. "They Blew It." *Time*, 20 November, 119.

Leonardo da Vinci. 1994. Qtd. in *The Tempest*. Stratford-upon-Avon: Royal Shakespeare Company, 15.

Levin, Harry, 1969a. *The Myth of the Golden Age in the Renaissance*. Bloomington: Indiana University Press.

———. 1969b. "Two Magian Comedies: *The Tempest* and *The Alchemist*." *Shakespeare Survey* 22: 47–58.

Levin, Richard. 1977. "Refuting Shakespeare's Endings." Part 2. *Modern Philology* 75 (November): 132–58.

———. 1979. *New Readings vs. Old Plays: Recent Trends in the Reinterpretation of Renaissance Drama*. Chicago: University of Chicago Press.

Lindstrom, Pia. 1995. "Review." WABC, 2 November.

Lings, Martin. 1966. *Shakespeare in the Light of Sacred Art*. London: George Allen and Unwin.

Lloyd, William Watkiss. 1875. *Critical Essays on the Plays of Shakespeare*. London: n.p.

LoMonico, Michael. 1994. "Teaching Shakespeare with Video." In *Shakespeare Set Free*, ed. Peggy O'Brien. New York: Washington Square Press, 217–20.

Loomba, Ania. 1989. *Gender, Race, Renaissance Drama*. Manchester: Manchester University Press.

———. 1996. "Shakespeare and Cultural Difference." In Hawkes 1996, 164–91.

Lorimer, David. 1995. "Newtonian Time Lord: On the Physics of Ilya Prigogine." *Times Higher Education Supplement*, 30 June, 18.

Loughrey, Bryan, and Neil Taylor. 1982. "Ferdinand and Miranda at Chess." *Shakespeare Survey* 35: 113–18.

Lovejoy, A. O. 1936. *The Great Chain of Being*. Cambridge, MA: Harvard University Press.

———. 1948. *Essays in the History of Ideas*. Baltimore: Johns Hopkins Press.

Lower, Charles. 1981. "Shakespeare in Atlanta." *Shakespeare Quarterly* 32: 236–37.

Luce, Morton, ed. 1901. *The Tempest*. London: Methuen.

Lyly, John. 1911. *Endymion, The Man in the Moon*. In *The Chief Elizabethan Dramatists*, ed. William Allan Neilson. Boston: Houghton Mifflin.

Macauley, Alistair. 1994. "*The Tempest*." *Financial Times*, 14 July, 38.

MacDonald, Michael. 1985. "Science, Magic, and Folklore." In *William Shakespeare: His World, His Work, His Influence*, vol. 1, ed. John F. Andrews. New York: Scribner's 175–94.

Machiavelli, Niccolo. 1940. *Discoursi*. Trans. Christian E. Detmold. New York: Modern Library.

MacKaye, Percy. 1916. *Caliban by the Yellow Sands*. Garden City, NY: Doubleday, Page, and Company.

Maguin, Jean-Marie. 1995. "*The Tempest* and Cultural Exchange." *Shakespeare Survey* 48: 147–54.

Maguire, Nancy Klein, ed. 1987. *Renaissance Tragicomedy: Explorations in Genre and Politics*. New York: AMS Press.

Malone, Edmond. 1808. *An Account of the Incidents from Which the Title and Part of the Story of Shakespeare's Tempest Were Derived*. London: C. and R. Baldwin.

Mandel, Jerome. 1973. "Dream and Imagination in Shakespeare." *Shakespeare Quarterly* 24: 61–68.

Manly, John M. 1897. *Specimens of the Pre-Shakespearean Drama*. Vol. 2. Boston: Ginn and Co.

Mannoni, Octave. 1964. *Prospero and Caliban: The Psychology of Colonialization*. Trans. Pamela Powesland. New York: Praeger.

Maquerlot, Jean-Pierre, and Michele Willems, eds. 1996. *Travel and Drama in Shakespeare's Time*. Cambridge: Cambridge University Press.

Marcus, Leah S. 1988. *Puzzling Shakespeare: Local Reading and Its Discontents*. Berkeley: University of California Press.

Marienstras, Richard. 1985. *New Perspectives on the Shakespearean World*. Trans. Janet Lloyd. Cambridge: Cambridge University Press.

Markham, Clements R. 1894. *The Letters of Amerigo Vespucci and Other Documents*. Trans. with notes and an introduction by Clements R. Markham. London: Hakluyt Society.

Marlowe, Christopher. 1980. *Doctor Faustus*. Ed. Sylvan Barnet. New York: Signet.

Marsh, D.R.C. 1962. *The Recurring Miracle: A Study of Cymbeline and the Last Plays*. Lincoln: University of Nebraska Press.

Marx, Leo. 1967. "Shakespeare's American Fable." In *The Machine in the Garden: Technology and the Pastoral Ideal in America*. New York: Oxford University Press, Chapter 2.

Mazursky, Paul, dir. 1982. *The Tempest*. Film: Columbia Pictures.

McCarten, John. 1956. "The Current Cinema: Big Brains in the Beyond" (review of *Forbidden Planet*). *New Yorker*, 12 May, 92.

McCurdy, Harold G. 1953. *The Personality of Shakespeare.* New Haven, CT: Yale University Press.

McDonald, Russ. 1991. "Reading *The Tempest.*" *Shakespeare Survey* 43: 15–28.

McGuire, Philip. 1985. *Speechless Dialect: Shakespeare's Open Silences.* Berkeley: University of California Press.

———. 1994. *Shakespeare: The Jacobean Plays.* New York: St. Martin's.

McLuskie, Kathleen. 1985. "The Patriarchal Bard: Feminist Criticism and Shakespeare." In *Political Shakespeare*, ed. Jonathan Dollimore and Alan Sinfield. Manchester: Manchester University Press, 88–108.

McMurtry, Jo. 1994. *Shakespeare Films in the Classroom.* Hamden, CT: Archon.

Mebane, John S. 1989. *Renaissance Magic and the Return of the Golden Age: The Occult Tradition and Marlowe, Jonson, and Shakespeare.* Lincoln: University of Nebraska Press.

Mico, Stephen. 1982. "*The Tempest.*" *English Literary History* 49: 1–17.

Milano, Paolo. 1949. *The Portable Dante.* New York: Book Society.

Miola, Robert. 1986. "Vergil in Shakespeare: From Allusion to Imitation." In *Vergil at 2000: Commemorative Essays on the Poet and His Influence*, ed. J. D. Bernard. New York: AMS Press.

Montaigne, Michael. 1904. *The Essayes of Michael Lord Montaigne.* Trans. John Florio. World's Classics. London: Frowde.

———. 1950. *Essays.* New York: Modern Library.

Mooney, Michael E. 1992. "Defining the Dramaturgy of the Late Romances." In Hunt 1992, 49–56.

Morley, Sheridan. 1994. "*The Tempest.*" *Spectator*, 23 July, 17.

Morse, William. 1992. "A Metacritical and Historical Approach to *The Winter's Tale* and *The Tempest.*" In Hunt 1992, 133–38.

Moseley, Charles. 1988. "Masque Spectacle in *The Tempest.*" In Cookson and Loughrey 1988, 114–25.

Moulton, Richard G. 1901. *Shakespeare as a Dramatic Artist.* 3rd ed. Oxford: Clarendon Press. The *Tempest* chapters were added in the second edition of 1888.

Mowat, Barbara A. 1976. *The Dramaturgy of Shakespeare's Romances.* Athens: University of Georgia Press.

———. 1981. "Prospero, Agrippa, and Hocus Pocus." *English Literary Renaissance* 11: 281–303. In Vaughan and Vaughan 1998, 193–213.

Mowat, Barbara A., and Paul Werstine, eds. 1994. *The Tempest.* New York: Washington Square.

Muir, Kenneth. 1961. *Last Periods of Shakespeare, Racine, Ibsen.* Detroit: Wayne State University Press.

———. 1965. *Shakespeare: The Comedies.* Englewood Cliffs, NJ: Prentice-Hall.

Mulvey, Laura. 1985. "Visual Pleasure and Narrative Cinema." In *Film Theory and Criticism*, ed. Gerald Mast and Marshall Cohen. New York: Oxford University Press.

Murry, J. Middleton. 1936. *Shakespeare.* London: Jonathan Cape. "Shakespeare's Dream" in Palmer 1968, 109–21.

Neilson, Francis. 1956. *Shakespeare and "The Tempest."* Rindge, NH: Richard R. Smith.

Nevo, Ruth. 1987. *Shakespeare's Other Language.* London: Methuen.

Newell, W. W. 1913. "The Sources of Shakespeare's *Tempest.*" *Journal of American Folklore* 16: 234–57.

Nicholson, Marjorie Hope. 1935. "The 'New Astronomy' and English Literary Imagination." *Studies in Philology* 32: 428–62.

Nicoll, Allardyce. 1938. *Stuart Masques and the Renaissance Stage.* New York: Harcourt, Brace, and Company.

Nietzsche, Friedrich. 1905. *Thus Spake Zarathustra.* New York: Boni and Liveright.

Nightingale, Benedict. 1994. *"The Tempest." The Times,* 14, July, 34.

———. 1999. "Lively under the Plastic." *The Times,* 11 February, 36.

Nilan, Mary. 1972. *"The Tempest* at the Turn of the Century." *Shakespeare Survey* 25: 113–23.

Norton, Thomas, and Thomas Sackville. 1897. *Gorboduc.* In *Specimens of the Pre-Shakespearean Drama,* vol. 2, ed. John M. Manly. Boston: Ginn and Co.

Nosworthy, J. M. 1948. "The Narrative Sources of *The Tempest." Review of English Studies* 24: 281–94.

Nuttall, Anthony D. 1967. *Two Concepts of Allegory.* London: Routledge and Kegan Paul.

Oates, Joyce Carol. 1973. *The Edge of Impossibility: Tragic Forms in Literature.* New York: Fawcett.

Orgel, Stephen. 1975. *The Illusion of Power: Political Theatre in Renaissance England.* Berkeley: University of California Press.

———. 1984. "Prospero's Wife." *Representations* 8. In Bloom 1988, 99–112.

———. ed. 1987. *The Tempest.* New York: Oxford University Press.

———. 1988. "The Authentic Shakespeare." *Representations* 21: 1–25.

Ornstein, Robert. 1960. *The Moral Vision of Jacobean Tragedy.* Madison: University of Wisconsin Press.

Osborne, Laurie E. 1996. "Rethinking the Performance Editions: Theatrical and Textual Productions of Shakespeare." In *Shakespeare, Theory, and Performance,* ed. James C. Bulman. London: Routledge, 168–86.

Palmer, D. J. 1968. *Shakespeare: The Tempest: A Casebook.* London: Macmillan.

Panofsky, Erwin. 1962. *Studies in Iconology.* New York: Harper.

Paris, Bernard J. 1989. *"The Tempest:* Shakespeare's Ideal Solution." In *Shakespeare's Personality,* ed. Norman Holland, Sidney Homan, and Bernard J. Paris, Berkeley: University of California Press, 206–25.

Paris, Jean. 1960. *Shakespeare.* Trans. Richard Seaver. New York: Grove Press.

Parker, Matthew, et al. 1572. *The holie Byble [The Bishops' Bible].* Canterbury: n.p.

Parsons, Keith, and Pamela Mason, eds. 1995. *Shakespeare in Performance.* London: Salamander.

Patrick, Julian. 1983. *"The Tempest* as Supplement." In *Centre and Labyrinth: Essays in Honor of Northrop Frye,* ed. Eleanor Cook, Chaviva Hosek, Jay Macpherson, Patricia Parker, and Julian Patrick. Toronto: University of Toronto Press. In Bloom 1988, 69–84.

Patterson, Annabel. 1994. " 'A Political Thriller': The Life and Times of Henry V." In *Teaching with Shakespeare: Critics in the Classroom,* ed. Bruce McIver and Ruth Stevenson. Cranbury, NJ: Associated University Presses, 222–53.

Pearlman, E. 1992. "The Invention of Richard of Gloucester." *Shakespeare Quarterly* 43: 410–29.

Pearson, D'Orsay. 1974. " 'Unless I Be Reliev'd by Prayer': *The Tempest* in Perspective." *Shakespeare Studies* 7: 253–82.

Pechter, Edward. 1987. "New Historicism and Its Discontents." *PMLA* 102: 292–303.

Perkins, William. 1603. *The Works*. Cambridge: n.p.

Peterson, Douglas L. 1973. *Time, Tide, and Tempest: A Study of Shakespeare's Romances*. San Marino, CA: Huntington Library.

———. 1992. "The Utopias of *The Tempest*." In Hunt 1992, 139–45.

Pettet, E. C. 1949. *Shakespeare and the Romance Tradition*. London: Staples.

Phillips, James E. 1964. "*The Tempest* and the Renaissance Idea of Man." *Shakespeare Quarterly* 15: 147–59.

Pinciss, Gerald M., and Roger Lockyer, eds. 1989. *Shakespeare's World: Background Readings in the English Renaissance*. New York: Continuum.

Pitcher, John. 1984. "A Theatre of the Future: *The Aeneid* and *The Tempest*." *Essays in Criticism* 34: 193–215.

Plato. 1956. *Phaedrus*. Trans. W. C. Helmbold and W. G. Rabinowitz. Indianapolis: Bobbs-Merrill.

Poole, Roger. 1988. "Music in *The Tempest*." In Cookson and Loughrey 1988, 53–66.

Portantiere, Michael. 1995. "Stars in Our Eyes." *Staten Island Register*, 21 November, 17.

Potter, George R., ed. 1928. *Elizabethan Verse and Prose (Non-dramatic)*. New York: Holt.

Potter, Lois. 1992. "A Brave New *Tempest*." *Shakespeare Quarterly* 43: 450–55.

Price, George R. 1962. *Reading Shakespeare's Plays*. Great Neck, NY: Barron's Educational Series.

Pringle, Marian. 1998. "*The Tempest*: A Stage History." *The Tempest*. Program, Royal Shakespeare Company, Stratford.

Procter, William C. n.d. *Shakespeare and Scripture*. London: H. R. Allenson.

Prosser, Eleanor. 1965. "Shakespeare, Montaigne, and the Rarer Action." *Shakespeare Studies* 1: 261–64.

Purkiss, Diane. 1996. *The Witch in History*. London: Routledge.

Pyles, Thomas. 1964. *The Origins and Development of the English Language*. New York: Harcourt, Brace and World.

Queen Elizabeth's Prayer Book: 1559. Edinburgh: John Grant, 1911.

Quiller-Couch, Sir Arthur. 1921. "*The Tempest*." In Hallett Smith 1969, 12–19.

Quiller-Couch, Sir Arthur, and John Dover Wilson, eds. 1994. *The Tempest*. Hertfordshire: Wordsworth.

Rabkin, Norman. 1981. *Shakespeare and the Problem of Meaning*. Chicago: University of Chicago Press.

Rafferty, Terrence. 1995. "Mad Love." *New Yorker*, 2 October, 109.

Raskin, Bonnie, exec. prod. 1998. *The Tempest*. Television production, 13 December.

Rawson, Christopher. 1995. "Broadway's Brave Old World." *Pittsburgh Post-Gazette*, 28 November, 31.

"Review of *Forbidden Planet*." 1956. *Time*, 9 April, 73.

Reynolds, Peter. 1988. "*The Tempest*—Act I, Scene 1: A Dramatic Analysis." In Cookson and Loughrey 1988, 9–18.

Reynolds, Stanley. 1980. "*The Tempest*." *The Times*, 28 February, 9.

Richards, I. A. 1960. *Coleridge on Imagination*. Bloomington: Indiana University Press.

Richmond, Hugh M. 1992. "Teaching *The Tempest* and the Late Plays by Performance." In Hunt 1992, 124–32.

Rickey, Mary Ellen. 1965. "Prospero's Living Drolleries." *Renaissance Papers 1964*: 35–42.

Rickey, Mary Ellen, and Thomas B. Stroup, eds. 1968. *Certaine Sermons or Homilies*. Facsimile. Gainesville, FL: Scholars' Facsimiles and Reprints.

Ridley, Clifford. 1995. "The Latest Prospero: A Postmodern Conjurer Who Is Also Very Angry." *Philadelphia Inquirer*, 7 November, 39.

Righter, Anne. 1967. *Shakespeare and the Idea of the Play*. London: Chatto and Windus.

———. 1968. "Introduction." In *The Tempest*. London: Penguin.

Roberts, Jeanne Addison. 1978. " 'Wife' or 'Wise': *The Tempest* 4.1.123." *University of Virginia Studies in Bibliography* 31: 203–8.

———. 1980. "Ralph Crane and the Text of *The Tempest*." *Shakespeare Studies* 13: 213–33.

———. 1991. *The Shakespearean Wild: Geography, Genus, and Gender*. Lincoln: University of Nebraska Press.

Robertson, D. W. 1962. *A Preface to Chaucer*. Princeton: Princeton University Press.

Rockett, William. 1973. "Labor and Virtue in *The Tempest*." *Shakespeare Quarterly* 24: 77–84.

Rose, Mark. 1972. *Shakespearean Design*. Cambridge, MA: Belknap Press.

Rose, Martial, ed. 1963. *The Wakefield Mystery Plays*. Garden City, NY: Doubleday Anchor.

Rothwell, Kenneth S. 1983. "The Champlain Shakespeare Festival, 1983." *Shakespeare Quarterly* 34: 470–72.

Rothwell, Kenneth S., and Annabelle Henkin Melzer. 1990. *Shakespeare on Screen*. New York: Neal-Schuman.

Rowse, A. L., ed. 1984. *Macbeth*. Lanham, MD: University Press of America.

Royal Shakespeare Company. 1994. *The Tempest*. Program. Stratford-upon-Avon.

Salingar, Leo. 1996. "The New World in *The Tempest*." In Maquerlot and Willems 1996, 209–22.

Sanford, James, trans. 1569. *Henrie Cornelius Agrippa: Of the Vanitie and Uncertaintie of Artes and Sciences*. London.

Schaefer, George, dir. 1960. *The Tempest*. Video production. NBC.

Schleiner, Louise. 1992. "Review." *Shakespeare Quarterly* 43: 494–95.

Schmidgall, Gary. 1981. *Shakespeare and the Courtly Aesthetic*. Berkeley: University of California Press.

Schneider, Ben Ross, Jr. 1995. " 'Are We Being Historical Yet?': Colonialist Interpretations of Shakespeare's *Tempest*." *Shakespeare Studies* 23: 120–45.

Schoenbaum, Samuel. 1977. *William Shakespeare: A Compact Documentary Life*. Oxford: Clarendon Press.

Scofield, Martin. 1991. "Poetry's Sea-Changes: T. S. Eliot and *The Tempest*." *Shakespeare Survey* 43: 121–29.

Scott, Michael. 1989. *Shakespeare and the Modern Dramatist*. New York: St. Martin's.

Sewell, Arthur. 1961. *Character and Society in Shakespeare*. Oxford: Clarendon Press.

Seznec, Jean. 1961. *The Survival of the Pagan Gods: The Mythological Tradition and Its Place in Renaissance Humanism and Art*. New York: Harper Torchbooks.

Shrimpton, Nicholas. 1976. "Directing *The Tempest*." *Shakespeare Survey* 29: 63–67.

Siddal, Stephen. 1988. "*The Tempest*: Confinement and Release." In Cookson and Loughrey 1988, 79–88.

Sider, John William. 1973. "The Serious Elements of Shakespeare's Comedies." *Shakespeare Quarterly* 24: 1–11.

Sidney, Sir Philip. 1926. *The Defence of Poesie.* In *The Complete Works*, vol. 3, ed. Albert Feuillerat. Cambridge: Cambridge University Press.

Simon, John. 1995. "Shakespeare: The Next Generation." *New York*, 13 November, 97–99.

Sisson, C. J. 1958. "The Magic of Prospero." *Shakespeare Survey* II: 70–77.

Sitwell, Edith. 1961. *A Notebook on William Shakespeare.* Boston: Beacon.

Skura, Meredith Anne. 1989. "Discourse and the Individual: The Case of Colonialism in *The Tempest.*" *Shakespeare Quarterly* 40: 42–69. In Vaughan and Vaughan 1998, 60–90.

Slights, William W. E. 1992. "Trusting Shakespeare's *Winter's Tale*: Metafiction in the Late Plays." In Hunt 1992, 103–8.

Slover, George. 1978. "Magic, Mystery, and Make-Believe: An Analogical Reading of *The Tempest.*" *Shakespeare Studies* 11: 175–206. Excerpted in Battenhouse 1994, 257–63.

Smallwood, Robert. 1996. "Directors' Shakespeare." In *Shakespeare: An Illustrated Stage History*, ed. Jonathan Bate and Russell Jackson. Oxford: Oxford University Press.

Smith, Bradley F. 1981. *The Road to Nuremberg.* London: André Deutsch.

Smith, Cecil. 1980. "Review." *Los Angeles Times*, 7 May, 4, 8.

Smith, D. Nichol, ed. 1916. *Shakespeare Criticism.* Oxford: Oxford University Press.

Smith, Hallett, ed. 1969. *Twentieth Century Interpretations of "The Tempest."* Englewood Cliffs, NJ: Prentice-Hall.

———. 1974. "Introduction." In *The Tempest, The Riverside Shakespeare*, ed. G. B. Evans. Boston: Houghton Mifflin, 1606–10.

Smith, Irwin. 1970. "Ariel and the Masque in *The Tempest.*" *Shakespeare Quarterly* 21: 213–22.

Smith, Nigel. 1988. "The Italian Job: Magic and Machiavelli in *The Tempest.*" In Cookson and Loughrey 1988, 90–99.

Smuin, Michael, chor. 1981. *The Tempest.* San Francisco Ballet. PBS, 1 April.

Snyder, Susan. 1983. "Auden, Shakespeare, and the Defence of Poetry." *Shakespeare Survey* 36: 29–37.

Southbank Show. 1988. "Peter Hall Directs Shakespeare's Last Plays." Television documentary. Bravo.

Speaight, Robert. 1962. *Nature in Shakespearian Tragedy.* New York: Collier.

———. 1973. *Shakespeare on the Stage.* Boston: Little, Brown.

———. 1974. "Shakespeare in Britain, 1974." *Shakespeare Quarterly* 25: 389–94.

———. 1976. "Shakespeare in Britain, 1975." *Shakespeare Quarterly* 27: 15–23.

Spencer, Charles. 1994. "*The Tempest.*" *Daily Telegraph*, 15 July, 23.

Spencer, Hazelton, ed. 1933. *Elizabethan Plays.* Boston: D.C. Heath.

———. 1940. *The Art and Life of William Shakespeare.* New York: Harcourt, Brace and Company.

Spencer, Theodore. 1961. *Shakespeare and the Nature of Man.* 2nd ed. New York: Macmillan.

Spencer, Edmund. 1936. *The Complete Poetical Works of Spenser.* Ed. R. E. Neil Dodge. Cambridge, MA: Houghton, Mifflin.

———. 1977. *Complete Works.* Ed. R. Morris, London: Macmillan.

Spillane, Margaret. 1999. "Death of a Salesman." *Nation*, 8 March, 7.

Stallybrass, Peter. 1982. "Macbeth and Witchcraft." In *Focus on Macbeth*, ed. John Russell Brown. London: Routledge and Kegan Paul, 191–206.

Stange, G. Robert, ed. 1959. *Coleridge*. New York: Dell.

Stauffer, Donald. 1949. *Shakespeare's World of Images*. New York: Norton.

Stavisky, Aron. 1969. *Shakespeare and the Victorians*. Norman: University of Oklahoma Press.

Steevens, George, ed. 1793. *Mr. William Shakespeare's Comedies, Histories, and Tragedies*. London: n.p.

Steiner, George. 1996. *No Passion Spent: Essays, 1978–1995*. New Haven, CT: Yale University Press.

Still, Colin. 1921. *Shakespeare's Mystery Play: A Study of "The Tempest."* London: Cecil Palmer. Published in revised form in 1936 as *The Timeless Theme*. London: Nicholson and Watson.

Stockholder, Kay. 1992. "Shakespeare's Magic and Its Discontents: Approaching *The Tempest*." In Hunt 1992, 160–67.

Stoll, E. E. 1927. "Certain Fallacies and Irrelevancies in the Literary Scholarship of the Day." *Studies in Philology* 24.

———. 1940. *Shakespeare and Other Masters*. Cambridge, MA: Harvard University Press. An earlier version of his chapter on *The Tempest* is in *PMLA* 47 (1932): 699–726.

Strachey, Lytton. 1922. *Books and Characters*. London: Chatto and Windus.

Sturgess, Keith. 1987. " 'A Quaint Device': *The Tempest* at Blackfriars." In *Jacobean Private Theatre*. London: Routledge and Kegan Paul, 73–96. In Vaughan and Vaughan 1998, 107–29.

Styan, J. L. 1977. *The Shakespeare Revolution: Criticism and Performance in the Twentieth Century*. Cambridge: Cambridge University Press.

———. 1988. "Shakespeare's Fusion of the Arts." *Upstart Crow* 8: 10–27.

Summers, Joseph. 1984. "The Anger of Prospero." In *Dreams of Love and Power*. Oxford: Clarendon Press, 138–61.

Sundelson, David. 1983. *Shakespeare's Restorations of the Father*. New Brunswick, NJ: Rutgers University Press.

Tayler, Edward. 1964. *Nature and Art in Renaissance Literature*. New York: Columbia University Press.

Taylor, Gary. 1991. *Reinventing Shakespeare*. London: Vintage.

Taylor, Mark. 1993. "Prospero's Books and Stephano's Bottle: Colonial Experience in *The Tempest*." *Clio* 22: 101–13.

Taylor, Paul. 1994. *"The Tempest." Independent*, 15 July, 38.

The Tempest. 1984. West Haven, CT: Pocket Classics.

Thompson. Ann. 1991. " 'Miranda, Where's Your Sister?': Reading Shakespeare's *The Tempest*." In Vaughan and Vaughan 1998, 234–43.

Tillyard, E.M.W. 1938. *Shakespeare's Last Plays*. London: Chatto and Windus.

———. 1959. *The Elizabethan World Picture*. New York: Random House.

Timpane, John. 1992. *"The Tempest." Shakespeare Bulletin* 10: 21–22.

Tobias, Richard C., and Paul G. Zolbrod, eds. 1974. *Shakespeare's Late Plays: Essays in Honor of Charles Crow*. Athens: Ohio University Press.

Tobin, J.J.M. 1984. *Shakespeare's Favorite Novel*. Lanham, MD: University Press of America.

Traister, Barbara Howard. 1984. "Prospero: Master of Self Knowledge." In *Heavenly Necromancers: The Magician in English Renaissance Drama*. Columbia: University of Missouri Press. Reprinted in Bloom 1988.

Traversi, Derek. 1949. "*The Tempest.*" *Scrutiny* 16: 127–57.

———. 1955. *Shakespeare: The Last Phase*. New York: Harcourt, Brace.

Tretick, Gordon. 1995. "Trekkie Hero Creates 'Tempest' on Broadway." *Connecticut News*, 4 November, 23.

Trewin, J. C. 1971. *Peter Brook: A Biography*. London: Macdonald.

———. 1978. *Going to Shakespeare*. London: Allen and Unwin.

Tudeau-Clayton, Margaret. 1998. *Jonson, Shakespeare, and Early Modern Virgil*. Cambridge: Cambridge University Press.

Tydeman, William. 1988. "Act I, Scene 2: Prospero's Tale?" In Cookson and Loughrey 1988, 41–51.

Unger, Arthur. 1980. "Derek Jacobi: A Special Kind of Hamlet." *Christian Science Monitor*, 7 November, 19.

Uphaus, R. 1970. "Virtue in Vengeance: Prospero's 'Rarer Action.' " *Bucknell Review* 18: 34–51.

Van Doren, Mark. 1939. *Shakespeare*. Garden City, NY: Doubleday Anchor.

Vaughan, Alden T., and Virginia Mason Vaughan. 1991. *Shakespeare's Caliban: A Cultural History*. Cambridge: Cambridge University Press.

———. 1992. "Tampering with *The Tempest.*" *Shakespeare Bulletin* 10(11): 16–17.

———. 1998. *Critical Essays on Shakespeare's "The Tempest.*" New York: G. K. Hall.

———. 1999. *The Tempest*. New York: Routledge.

Vaughan, Virginia. 1984. "The Forgotten Television *Tempest.*" *Shakespeare on Film Newsletter* 9: 3.

Vespucci, Amerigo. 1894. *The New World*. Trans. anon. London: n.p.

Vickers, Brian. 1993. *Appropriating Shakespeare: Contemporary Critical Quarrels*. New Haven, CT: Yale University Press.

Von Rosador, Kurt T. 1991. "The Power of Magic: From *Endimion* to *The Tempest.*" *Shakespeare Survey* 43: 1–13.

Wain, John. 1964. "In My End Is My Beginning." In *The Living World of Shakespeare: A Playgoer's Guide*. New York: St. Martin's, 225–30.

Walch, Günter. 1996. "Metatheatrical Memory and Transculturalism in *The Tempest.*" In Marquerlot and Willems 1996, 223–38.

Walker, D. P. 1958. *Spiritual and Demonic Magic from Ficino to Campanella*. London: Warburg Institute.

Walker, William Sidney. 1860. *A Critical Examination of the Text of Shakespeare*. Vol. 3. London: John Russell Smith.

Waller, Gary. 1992a. "The Late Plays as Family Romance." In Hunt 1992, 57–63.

———. 1992b. "Review." *Shakespeare Quarterly* 43(1): 102–4.

Walter, James. 1983. "From Tempest to Epilogue." *PMLA* 98: 60–76. In Battenhouse 1994, 271–79.

Warren, Roger. 1990. *Staging Shakespeare's Late Plays*. Oxford: Clarendon Press.

———. 1998. "Rough Magic and Heavenly Music: *The Tempest.*" In Vaughan and Vaughan 1998, 152–89.

Watkins, Walter B. C. 1950. *Shakespeare and Spenser*. Princeton: Princeton University Press.

Watterson, William. "Prospero's Closet." Forthcoming.

Weber, Alfred. 1899. *History of Philosophy*. Trans. Frank Tilly. New York: Charles Scribner's Sons.

Webster, Margaret. 1957. *Shakespeare without Tears*. New York: Premier.

Weimann, Robert. 1974. "Shakespeare and the Study of Metaphor." *New Literary History* 6: 160–76.

———. 1988. "Bi-Fold Authority in Shakespeare's Theater." *Shakespeare Quarterly* 39: 462–71.

Wells, Stanley. 1966. "Shakespeare and Romance." In *Later Shakespeare*, ed. John Russell Brown and Bernard Harris. Stratford-upon-Avon Studies 8. London: Edward Arnold, 49–79.

———. 1973. *Shakespeare*. Oxford: Oxford University Press.

———. 1986. *The Cambridge Companion to Shakespeare Studies*. Cambridge: Cambridge University Press.

———. 1995. *Shakespeare: A Life in Drama*. New York: Norton.

Wells, Stanley, and Gary Taylor. 1997. *William Shakespeare: A Textual Companion*. New York: Norton.

Welsford, Enid. 1927. *The Court Masque*. Cambridge: Cambridge University Press.

Wendell, Barrett. 1894. *William Shakespeare: A Study in Elizabethan Literature*. New York: Charles Scribner's Sons.

Weschler, Lawrence. 1996. "Take No Prisoners." *New Yorker*, 17 June, 50–59.

West, Robert H. 1939. *The Invisible World*. Athens: University of Georgia Press.

———. 1968. *Shakespeare and the Outer Mystery*. Lexington: University of Kentucky Press.

Wharton, Joseph. 1753. "Amazing Wildness of Fancy!" *Adventurer* 93.

White, Hayden. 1972. "The Forms of Wildness: Archaeology of an Idea." In *The Wild Man Within: An Image in Western Thought from the Renaissance to Romanticism*, ed. Edward Dudley and Maximillian Novak. Pittsburgh: University of Pittsburgh Press.

Whitehead, Alfred North. 1925. *Science and the Modern World*. New York: Macmillan.

Whitehead, Sam. 1995. "*The Tempest*." *Time Out*, 8–15 November, 16.

Wilcox, Fred, dir. 1956. *Forbidden Planet*. Film. MGM.

Wilders, John, ed. 1980. *The Tempest*. New York: Mayflower.

William, David. 1960. "*The Tempest* on Stage." In *Jacobean Theatre*, ed. John Russell Brown and Bernard Harris. London: Edward Arnold.

Williams, Gary Jay. 1993. "Review." *Shakespeare Quarterly* 44: 237–38.

Williams, Wendy. 1998. "Fonda Takes on 'The Tempest.'" *Satellite TV Week*, 22–28 November, 2.

Willis, Deborah. 1989. "Shakespeare's *Tempest* and the Discourse of Colonialism." *Studies in English Literature* 29: 277–89.

Wills, Garry. 1995. *Witches and Jesuits*. Oxford: Oxford University Press.

Willson, Robert F., Jr. 1992. "Enframing Style and the Father-Daughter Theme in Early Shakespearean Comedy and Late Romance." In Hunt 1992, 38–48.

Wilson, John Dover. 1932. "The Enchanted Island." In *The Essential Shakespeare*. Cambridge: Cambridge University Press, 131–45. In Hallett Smith, 1969, 34–42.

Wilson, Mona, ed. 1951. *Johnson: Prose and Poetry*. Cambridge, MA: Harvard University Press.

Wilson, Richard. 1997. "Voyage to Tunis: New History and the Old World of *The Tempest*." *English Literary History* 64: 333–57.

Wilson, Robert. 1988. "Prospero—the Changer Changed." In Cookson and Loughrey 1988, 101–12.

Wiltenburg, Robert. 1987. "The *Aeneid* in *The Tempest.*" *Shakespeare Survey* 39: 159–68.

Winer, Linda. 1995. "More Sound and Fury, But Less Enchantment." *Newsday*, 2 November, B9.

Woodman, David. 1974. *White Magic and English Renaissance Drama.* Cranbury, NJ: Associated University Presses.

Woodman, William, dir. 1983. *The Tempest.* Video production. Bard Productions.

Wordsworth, Charles. 1880. *Shakespeare's Knowledge and Use of the Bible.* London: Smith, Elder.

Wright, Eugene. 1992. "Christopher Columbus, William Shakespeare, and the Brave New World." In *The Mutual Encounter of East and West, 1492–1992*, ed. Peter Milward. Tokyo: Sophia University, 111–24.

Wright, Neil H. 1977. "Reality and Illusion as a Philosophical Pattern in *The Tempest.*" *Shakespeare Studies* 10: 241–70.

Wysong, J. N. 1968. "The Influence of Shakespeare's Songs on Housman." *Shakespeare Quarterly* 19: 333–39.

Yates, Frances A. 1964. *Giordano Bruno and the Hermetic Tradition.* Chicago: University of Chicago Press.

———. 1975. *Shakespeare's Last Plays: A New Approach.* London: Routledge and Kegan Paul.

Young, David. 1972. *The Heart's Forest: A Study of Shakespeare's Pastoral Plays.* New Haven, CT: Yale University Press.

Young, R. V. 1996–97. "New Historicism: Literature and the Will to Power." *Intercollegiate Review* 32 (Fall): 3–14.

Zesmer, David A. 1976. *Guide to Shakespeare.* New York: Barnes and Noble.

Zimbardo, Rose A. 1963. "Form and Disorder in *The Tempest.*" *Shakespeare Quarterly* 14: 49–56.

INDEX

Abdulla, Sara, 164
Abenheimer, Karl M., 101
Abram, David, 52
Adrian, 51
The Aeneid, 14–15, 28, 51, 56, 71, 131, 137
Aercke, Kristiaan P., 18, 95
Agrippa, Henry Cornelius, 22, 23, 29, 31, 33, 66, 186
Airaldi, Remo, 170–71
The Alchemist, 32
Allegory, *Tempest* as, 16, 29, 134–35, 153, 154
Allen, Don Cameron, 15, 16, 72
Alonso, 42, 46, 49, 50, 54, 55–56, 86–87, 109; and music, 29; relationship with Antonio, 47, 52, 55–56; relationship with Ferdinand, 51, 60, 90; relationship with Gonzalo, 17, 34, 56; relationship with Prospero, 47, 56, 59, 60–62, 77, 106–7, 118, 132, 191; relationship with Sebastian, 51–52
Alternative Shakespeares II, 81, 83, 139
Anacreon, 12–13
Andrews, John, 5, 105, 125
Antipholus, 32

Antonio, 18, 46, 129, 189; character, 51, 52, 58, 60, 61, 97, 105–6, 108, 112, 118, 135; relationship with Alonso, 47, 52, 55–56; relationship with Prospero, 47, 48, 60, 61, 62, 99, 100, 101, 102, 103, 104, 105–6, 107–8, 116, 117–19, 121, 124, 135–36, 150, 154, 156, 168; relationship with Sebastian, 46, 51–52, 55, 61, 108, 116, 117–19. *See also* Performances, as Antonio
Antony and Cleopatra, 18, 36, 42, 50, 88, 122, 128
Anxiety, 6, 11, 47, 62, 73, 116–17
Appearance and reality, 66, 70, 72, 73–77, 97. *See also* Reason; Science
Applause edition (1996), 6
Apuleius, 38
Aquinas, Thomas, 36
Arden, Jane, 160
Arden edition (1999), 3, 13
Ariel, 6, 30, 66, 120, 135; actions, 9, 13, 15, 29, 56, 57, 58, 60, 61, 62, 95; character, 20, 27, 29, 48, 60, 113–15, 151, 153; and music, 49, 52, 53, 55, 67, 97; relationship with Prospero, 2,

29, 35, 48–49, 50, 55, 56, 58, 60, 62, 69, 94, 99, 102, 106, 107, 108, 109, 113–15, 117, 118, 123, 126, 134, 136, 149, 150, 152, 155, 156, 159, 163, 168, 172, 191; vs. Caliban, 49; compassion of, 59, 60, 107, 113, 115; relationship with Sycorax, 27, 29, 48, 127; sources for, 3, 9, 12–13, 27, 86, 136. *See also* Performances, as Ariel
Ariel (Rodo), 3
Aristotle, 20, 36, 81, 94, 144, 188
Arnold, Matthew, 76, 113
Art, 69, 71, 74–75, 75, 85, 86, 97, 106, 150, 162
As You Like It, 16, 18, 34, 62, 88, 91
Augustine, Saint, 135
Autobiographical criticism, 16, 83–85, 106
Ayrer, Jacob, 14

Backalenick, Irene, 165, 166
Bacon, Sir Francis, 20–21, 25–27, 31, 66, 108, 109, 127
Banquet scene, 55–58, 69, 86–87, 95; vs. Communion Service, 28, 31, 56, 118, 131–32, 137, 162–63; literary analogues to, 15, 32, 33, 36, 56, 129, 136–37; in performance, 160, 161, 162–63, 181
Banquo, 19, 23, 33, 132, 183
Bantam Classic edition (1988), 5
Barber, C. L., 68, 112, 124
Barber, Lester, 155
Barker, Francis, 119, 122, 124–25
Barlow, Graham, 155
Barnes, Clive, 165
Barnet, Sylvan, 6, 143, 146, 149
Barron's "Shakespeare Made Easy" edition (1984), 4–5
Bartholomew Fair, 79, 80, 134
Barton, Anne Righter, 4, 47, 49–50, 76, 97
Barton, John, 150, 153, 169
Basilicon Doron, 13
Bate, Jonathan, 12, 17, 18, 59, 68, 103
BBC edition (1980), 4
Beale, Simon, 150, 163
Beckerman, Bernard, 143, 147

Belsey, Catherine, 87, 193
Bennett, David, 158
Benson, Frank, 148
Bentley, G. E., 143
Benveniste, Emile, 96
Berger, Harry, Jr., 59, 71, 103; on Prospero, 73, 106, 110, 136
Berger, John, 71, 77
Berger, Karol, 29, 68, 75, 131
Bergeron, David, 13
Berkeley, George, 70
Bermuda/"Bermuda Pamphlets," 7, 9, 10–11, 95–96, 116, 117, 127, 128, 135
Berry, Francis, 98
Berry, Ralph, 151, 152, 154, 155, 163, 182, 183
Bettelheim, Bruno, 138
Bevington, David, 5, 57
Biblical allusions: Acts 8.13, 33, 131–40; Acts 8.21, 33; Acts 8.23, 33; Acts 27, 9; Genesis 9.13–15, 137–38; Isaiah 29, 136; Isaiah 51.6, 132; Jeremiah 3.13, 134; Jeremiah 6.23, 133; Jeremiah 10.13, 133; Jeremiah 31.35, 132; Job 20.8, 132; Job 20.23, 136; Job 20.27, 136; Judges 4.21, 134; Luke 4.3, 56; Luke 4.6, 57; Luke 12.25–28, 133; Luke 19.41–44, 133; Mark 13.2, 133; Matthew 4.3, 56–57; Matthew 8.24–27, 133; Matthew 14.24, 133; Matthew 24.2, 133; Matthew 25.31–46, 36; 2 Peter 3.11, 133; Psalm 22, 137; Psalm 90.4–5, 132; Revelation 10.1, 133; Revelation 10.6, 133; Revelation 10.7, 133; Revelation 16.18, 133; 1 Samuel 16.23, 134; 1 Samuel 28.18, 23; Solomon 16.29, 132; Zechariah 1.8, 136; Zechariah 7.6, 136–37; Zechariah 11.10, 133. *See also* Christianity; Communion Service
Billen, Andrew, 164
Billington, Michael, 157, 162, 163, 164, 172
Black, Duane, 182
Black, James, 136
Bloom, Harold, 67, 70, 84, 137, 139

Blos, Peter, 50
Boas, Frederick S., 35, 123
Boatswain, 46, 61, 161, 169–70
Bodkin, Maud, 25
Bogdanov, Michael, 153
Bolingbroke, Henry, 16, 117, 120
Bono, Barbara, 18, 68, 73, 93–94, 95
Booth, Stephen, 11, 147
Bougere, Teagle F., 166, 171
Bowers, Fredson, 94
Bradbrook, M. C., 106
Bradford, William, 130
Bradley, A. C., 72–73, 83, 86
Branagh, Kenneth, 194
Breight, Curt, 117–19
Bronson, John, 174
Brook, Peter, 62, 65, 149, 152–53, 158, 190
Brooke, Tucker, 4
Brooks, Harold F., 57
Brower, Reuben, 6, 73, 86–87, 174–75
Brown, John Russell, 6, 55, 74
Brown, Paul, 54, 102–3, 122, 125–26, 129, 131
Browne, E. Martin, 36
Browne, Thomas, 19
Browning, Robert, 3
Bruno, Giordano, 25, 27, 32, 138, 186
Brustein, Robert, 161
Bryant, Michael, 107, 150, 153, 157
Bryden, Ronald, 154
Buchanan, Lucianne, 194
Bullough, Geoffrey, 11
Burbage, Richard, 32, 110, 188
Burton, J. Anthony, 21
Burton, Richard, 179
Bury, John, 148

Caliban, 6, 27, 62, 66, 81, 133, 135, 145; vs. Ariel, 49; character, 20, 40, 49, 110–13, 122, 128, 139, 148, 151, 152, 153; and language, 49, 96, 97, 103, 112, 120, 130; and music, 29, 51; relationship with Miranda, 49, 88; relationship with Prospero, 15, 34, 35, 41–43, 49, 50, 52–53, 55, 57–58, 61, 69, 72, 73, 99, 100, 102–4, 106, 108, 109, 111, 113–14, 117–18, 119, 122–25, 126, 127, 130, 134, 137, 139–40, 155, 157, 159, 165, 168, 179–80; relationship with Stephano, 35, 53–54, 55, 61, 69, 94, 117–18, 125, 154, 156; relationship with Trinculo, 35, 53, 55, 117–18, 125, 156, 181; sources for, 12, 14, 18, 19, 38, 86. *See also* Performances, as Caliban
Caliban by the Yellow Sands, 141
"Caliban on Setebos," 3
Callaghan, Dympna, 129
Cambridge School edition (1996), 6
Camus, Albert, 114
Canby, Vincent, 192, 193
Canterbury Tales, 37–38
Cantone, Mario, 166
Cariou, Len, 183
Carleton, Dudley, 116
Carroll, Lewis, 146
Cartelli, Thomas, 119, 141
Cassavetes, John, 194
Catholicism, 23
Ceres, 2, 57, 68, 72, 103, 161, 173
Césaire, Aimé, 157
Chambers, E. K., 112, 143
Charney, Maurice, 61, 62, 180
Chastity, 67–68, 88, 95; Prospero on, 37, 38, 57, 86, 102, 103, 135
Chaucer, Geoffrey, 37–38
Chess game, 36, 45, 60–61, 67, 74, 77–78, 172
Christianity, 11, 12, 16; and magic, 23–24; *Tempest* influenced by, 21, 28, 34, 36, 47, 55, 56–57, 62, 66, 68, 69, 70, 74, 75, 91, 100, 131–38, 186. *See also* Biblical allusions; Communion Service
Ciardi, John, 36
Circe, 34, 39, 40, 41
Ciulei, Liviu, 158–59
Claribel, 51–52, 69, 87, 128–29
Clarke, Warren, 180–81
Cleopatra, 36, 42, 128
Cohen, Walter, 131
Coleridge, Samuel Taylor, 6, 17, 66, 147, 148; on Shakespeare, 81, 83, 84, 90
Collick, John, 192

Colonialism, 42, 88; colonialist criticism, 6, 16, 61, 79, 102–4, 113, 116,
   119, 120–31; in productions, 152,
   154–55, 157, 161, 172, 175, 178. *See
   also* Bermuda/"Bermuda Pamphlets";
   New World
Combs, Richard, 194
The Comedy of Errors, 31–32, 34; vs.
   Tempest, 2, 17, 46
Commedia dell'arte, 13
Communion Service, 27, 54, 110; vs.
   banquet scene, 28, 31, 56, 118, 131–
   32, 137, 162–63. *See also* Biblical
   allusions; Christianity
Compassion, 100, 104–5, 109; in Ariel,
   59, 60, 107, 113, 115; in Gonzalo,
   48, 59–60, 135, 168; in Miranda, 47,
   54, 60
Comtois, M. E., 155
Comus, 135
Condell, Henry, 1
Confessions, 135
Conklin, John, 171, 172
Conrad, Joseph, 46, 119
Contemporary Shakespeare edition
   (1984), 5
Cook, Hardy, 178
Coonrod, Karin, 165, 166
Coppedge, Walter, 193
Coriolanus, 18
Cotta, John, 31
Cottam, Martin, 6
Cowden-Clark, Charles, 122
Craig, Hardin, 19
Crane, Stephen, 113
Croce, Benedetto, 71, 108
Crofts Classics edition (1946), 4
Crowden, Graham, 153, 154
Crowl, Samuel, 192
Cultural materialism, 5, 63, 65, 115,
   116, 117, 188. *See also* Historicist
   criticism
Cunliffe, J. W., 134
Cunningham, Dennis, 165
Cupid, 37, 42, 67–68, 95, 162, 171, 173
Curry, Walter Clyde, 21–22, 28–29, 30,
   75; on Ariel, 27; on Caliban, 110; on
   Prospero, 47, 107

Cutts, John, 34
Cymbeline, 18, 49, 156, 164

Daedalus, 34
Daemonologie, 13–14, 31, 39, 40
Daniels, Ron, 161, 169–72
Dante Alighieri, 36, 135
Darrah, Thomas, 171
Darwin, Charles, 110, 111
Davenant, Sir William, 3, 144
Davis, Charles, 26
Davis, Desmond, 183
Dawson, Anthony, 62, 126, 151, 152–
   53
Debray, Regis, 154
*The Decades of the Newe Worlde or
   West India*, 13
Deconstruction, 63, 65
Dee, John, 23–24, 191, 192
Deer, Evroy, 172
De Grazia, Margreta, 41
De Jongh, Nicholas, 164
Dekker, Thomas, 148
Derrida, Jacques, 192
Desdemona, 66, 68
Devereux, E. J., 132
Devlin, Diana, 113
Discorsi, 108
Discovery of the Barmudas, 7, 10
Disenchantment, 34
Dixon, David, 180
Dixon, MacIntyre, 165
Dobree, Bonamy, 186
Dr. Faustus, 31, 32–34, 107, 123, 134,
   194
Donaldson, Peter S., 191
Donne, John, 85
Donnellan, Declan, 152, 153
Doolittle, Hilda, 87
Doré, Gustave, 4
Dougherty, Shannon, 173
Dowden, Edward, 83, 84–85
Dream, 67, 69, 70, 72, 73–76, 92, 96,
   102–3
Driscoll, James, 18
Dryden, John, 3, 19, 110, 141, 143, 144–
   46

Dudley, Sir Robert, 14
Durband, Alan, 4–5

Eden, Richard, 13
Edward the Confessor, 2, 31
Egan, Chip, 173
Egan, Robert, 68, 74–75, 94, 107,
    108–9
Eliot, Alexander, 129
Eliot, T. S., 85, 96
Elizabeth, Princess, 1–2, 87, 88
Elizabeth I, 117
The Elizabethan World Picture, 115
Ellis, Aunjanue, 168, 173
Ellis-Fermor, Una, 70
Endymion, 38–39
Engelsfeld, Mladen, 158
Engstrom, Bonnie, 62
Erlich, Bruce, 126
Eslava, Antonio de, 14
Essentialist criticism, 87, 98
Evans, Bertrand, 17
Evans, B. Ifor, 110
Evans, Gred, 166
Evans, Maurice, 170, 178, 179–80
Everyman, 36
Everyman edition (1994), 3, 5
Evett, Benjamin, 170
Ewbank, Inga-Stina, 121

Face, 32
The Faerie Queene, 38
"Family Romances," 98
Farley, Barbara S., 164
Faucit, Helen, 146
Faustus, 31, 32–34, 107, 123, 134, 191
Feldberg, Robert, 166
Felperin, Howard, 92, 134, 138
Feminist criticism, 87–89
Fenwick, Henry, 4, 184
Ferdinand, 48, 52, 59, 137, 145; during
    Masque, 45, 57; and music, 29; rela-
    tionship with Alonso, 51, 60, 90; re-
    lationship with Miranda, 2, 35, 49–
    50, 53, 54–55, 60–61, 67–68, 69, 74,
    77–78, 86, 88, 90, 95, 101, 102, 118,
    135, 153, 159–60, 166, 168, 169,
    171, 172, 174, 181, 191; relationship

with Prospero, 50, 58, 69, 73, 83, 86,
    101, 102, 125, 138, 165, 166, 174;
    sources for, 14. *See also* Perfor-
    mances, as Ferdinand
Fiedler, Leslie, 75, 129
Fielding, Henry, 100
Film. *See* Productions, film
Fineman, Joel, 101
First Folio edition (1623), 1–2, 3–4, 45,
    47, 143, 170, 180, 188
Fishburne, Laurence, 187
Fitzgerald, Michael, 159
Flagstad, Karen, 57, 68, 104, 138
Fletcher, John, 83, 91
Flett, Sherry, 183
Florio, John, 11
Forbidden Planet, 157, 183, 193–94
Ford, John, 160
Forgiveness/reconciliation, 62, 85, 90,
    94, 109, 124, 154, 161, 175. *See also*
    Revenge
Francisco, 51
Francis, Matthew, 155
Franklin's Tale, 37–38
Frederick V, the Elector Palatine, 1–2,
    87
Freeman, Paul, 170, 171–72
French, Leslie, 152
French, William, 158
Freud, Sigmund, 83, 85, 98–99, 101,
    102–3, 104–5, 122, 193
Frey, Charles, 128
Friar Bacon and Friar Bungay, 39, 191
Fromkin, David, 122
Frost, Robert, 5, 88, 96, 106, 184
Frye, Northrop, 4, 59, 74, 76–77, 106,
    137–38, 138
Fuchs, Barbara, 128–29
Furness, Horace Howard, 2, 3, 122

Garber, Marjorie, 33, 34, 41, 67, 69
Garfield, Leon, 184
Garner, Stanton B., Jr., 97
Garnett, Richard, 13–14, 123
Garrick, David, 146
Gates, Sir Thomas, 7, 10–11, 71
Geertz, Clifford, 111, 115
Generic criticism, 89–96

Genre, 74
Gibson, Rex, 6
Gielgud, John, 148–49, 153, 169, 189
Gill, Roma, 6
Gillespie, Arnold, 183
Gillies, John, 42
Gilsig, Jessalyn, 170
Globe theater, 143
Glover, John, 186
Goddard, Harold, 18
The Golden Ass, 38
Golding, Arthur, 11, 12
Goldman, Michael, 144
Gonzalez, B. W., 173
Gonzalo, 46, 51, 55–56, 88, 96, 140; compassion of, 48, 59–60, 135, 168; relationship with Alonso, 17, 34, 56; relationship with Prospero, 48, 59–60, 109, 118, 126, 135, 168, 191; on Utopia, 11, 52, 57, 77–78, 125, 173, 189. *See also* Performances, as Gonzalo
Gorboduc, 15
Gorgias, 97
Gorrie, John, 178, 180–81, 183–84
Gosse, Edmund, 13–14
Gould, Jack, 178
Graham, Shawn Rene, 171
A Grain of Wheat, 119
Grant, Patrick, 135
Granville-Barker, Harley, 148
Green, F. N., 145
Green, Herbert E., 141
Greenaway, Peter, 148, 187–92
Greenblatt, Stephen, 5, 17, 30, 41; on anxiety, 6, 10–11, 47, 62, 73, 116–17; on Prospero, 10–11, 47, 55, 58, 60, 61, 62, 73, 104, 107, 108, 116–17, 134
Greene, Gayle, 88
Greene, Robert, 39
Greer, Germaine, 27, 71, 109, 114–15
Guard, Christopher, 181
Guard, Pippa, 180
Guarini, Giambattista, 90–91
Guicciardini, Francesco, 66, 105
Gurewitsch, Matthew, 151

Habicht, Werner, 155
Hakluyt, Richard, 9
Halio, Jay L., 47–48, 150
Hall, Peter, 39–40, 107, 148, 149, 152, 155–57, 169, 177
Halliday, F. E., 74, 97
Hamilton, Donna B., 14, 120
Hamlet, 66, 83–84, 158, 184, 187–88, 191; vs. *Tempest*, 16, 17, 52, 76, 94, 100, 106, 119, 128, 132, 173, 174
Hankins, John E., 112
Hanks, Robert, 164
Harbage, Alfred, 4, 46, 48, 49, 58, 147; on Prospero, 50, 70, 74
Hardman, Christopher, 90
Harmony, 62, 65–66, 68, 86–87
Harrison, Gilbert, 55, 112
Hartwig, Joan, 17
Hassan, Ihab, 139
Hassel, R. Chris, Jr., 131
Hawkes, Terence, 81, 83, 85–86, 112, 115, 124, 139
Hawking, Stephen, 26
Hawthorne, Nathaniel, 91–92
Hawthorne, Nigel, 181
Haydn, Hiram, 21, 27, 66
Hayes, Antonio, 162
Hearst, Stephen, 177
Heart of Darkness, 119
Heigl, Katherine, 185–86
Helgerson, Richard, 128
Heminge, John, 1
Henerson, James, 185
Heninger, S. K., 70
Henry V, 66; film versions, 188, 190, 194; vs. *Tempest*, 15, 45–46, 115, 116, 117, 123, 128, 131
Henry VI, 15, 18, 39, 84, 101, 129, 183
Herbert, George, 36
Hierarchy, 115, 116, 125; in nature, 20–22, 29, 111; *Tempest* as challenge to, 12, 22
Hill, Errol, 155
Hillman, Richard, 37, 93
Hirsch, John, 182–83
Hirst, David, 11, 58, 66–67, 148; on Prospero, 47, 59, 73, 94, 107–8, 149
Historicist criticism, 11, 115–21; cul-

tural materialism, 5, 63, 65, 115, 116, 117, 188; New Historicism, 5, 20, 63, 65, 115, 117, 122, 139. *See also* Colonialism, colonialist criticism
History of Italy, 105
Hoard, Ellen, 184
Hobson, Harold, 149
Holland, Peter, 158, 159, 164
Holloway, Brian, 26, 62
Holofernes, 16
Holquist, Michael, 78
Homan, Sidney, 105
Hooker, Richard, 24, 27, 110, 186, 192
Hootkins, William, 182
Horatio, 52
Hordern, Michael, 4, 178, 180
Hornby, Richard, 71, 152
Horney, Karen, 99–100
Horowitz, David, 104–5
Hotchkiss, Lia M., 192
Howard, Leslie, 190
Howell, Jane, 183
Hughes, Douglas, 188
Hulme, Peter, 119, 122, 124–25
Hunter, G. K., 131–32
Hunter, Robert G., 108, 134
Hunter, William B., Jr., 16
Hytner, Nicholas, 150, 153

Iago, 135
Icarus, 34
Intertextuality, 124, 189
Ireland, 128–29
Iris, 57, 161
Irving edition (1890), 123
Iselin, Pierre, 51

Jackson, Russell, 148, 162, 192
Jacobi, Derek, 150, 168, 191
James, Caryn, 178
James, D. G., 75, 114
James, Henry, 84
James, William, 35
James I, 88, 109, 117, 121, 136, 193; on magic and the devil, 13–14, 19, 22, 25, 31, 33, 39, 40, 77; as patron/ spectator, 116, 120, 141
Jamestown, VA, 7

Jarman, Derek, 39–40, 192–93
Jarvis, Martin, 184
Johnson, Samuel, 5, 70, 147; on Caliban, 12–13; on Prospero, 19, 107, 134; on Shakespeare, 81, 96
Jones, Inigo, 149, 152, 158
Jones, Mark Lewis, 164
Jonson, Ben, 16, 32, 34, 79, 81, 134, 149
Jorgens, Jack, 193
Jourdain, Marjorie, 39, 191
Jourdain, Sylvester, 7, 10
Jowett, John, 1
Julia, Raul, 194
Jung, C. G., 83, 98–99, 104, 122, 193
Juno, 57, 68, 72, 95, 103, 161, 173, 182

Kael, Pauline, 193
Kahn, Coppelia, 101–2
Kames, Henry Home, Lord, 147
Kastan, David Scott, 5, 120–21, 124
Kaufmann, Walter, 74
Kay, Carol McGinnis, 147
Kean, Charles, 146
Keats, John, 79, 83, 85, 151
Keebler, John, 173
Kennedy, Dennis, 158, 159–60, 177
Kepler, Johannes, 32
Kermode, Frank, 13, 14, 34, 46, 51, 56, 60–61, 91; on Ariel, 27, 136; on Caliban, 110–11, 125; New Arden edition (1954), 2–3, 45; on Prospero, 12, 29, 62, 108, 135
Kernan, Alvin, 32, 70, 75, 162
Keyishian, Harry, 95
Kim, Randy, 155
King, Libby, 173
King Lear, 26, 188; film versions, 190; vs. *Tempest*, 16, 17, 18, 46, 51, 61, 90, 94, 102, 109, 138, 163
Kingsley, Ben, 150
Kinney, Arthur, 108
Kirk, Robert, 27
Kittredge, George Lyman, 4, 27
Knight, G. Wilson, 17, 18, 52, 85–86, 98, 123
Knighten, Merrell, 194

Knights, L. C., 85–86, 115–16
Knox, Bernard, 6, 35, 157
Kokeritz, Helge, 4
Kott, Jan, 36, 78, 97, 121–22, 155, 190;
    on the *Aeneid*, 14; on Caliban, 154;
    on Prospero, 118
Kozintsev, Grigori, 177–78, 190
Kurosawa, Akira, 194

Lacan, Jacques, 192
Lahr, John, 165
Lamb, Charles, 60, 145, 147–48
Lanchester, Elsa, 149–50
Langbaum, Robert, 6, 16, 68, 70, 91,
    92, 95
Language, 4, 96–98; and Caliban, 49,
    96, 97, 103, 112, 120, 130
Lanier, Douglas, 187–91
La Primaudaye, Pierre de, 22
Latham, J.E.M., 13–14, 33
Latimer, Hugh, 116
Laughton, Charles, 149–50
Law, Ernest, 143–44
Lawrence, W. J., 1–2
Lazzarini, Giulia, 159
Lea, K. M., 13
Lear (film), 190
Leddy, Pamela, 173–74
Lee, Canada, 141
Lee, John Allan, 50
Lee, William Sidney, 123
Leech, Clifford, 85, 110
Lehman, Ross, 166
Leininger, Lorrie Jerrell, 6, 87–88,
    103–4
Leithauser, Brad, 166
Leonardo da Vinci, 9–10
Levin, Charles, 171
Levin, Richard, 63, 67, 119, 192
Lindstrom, Pia, 165
Lings, Martin, 18, 133
Linguistic criticism, 96–98
Livanova, Elena, 184
Lloyd, William Watkiss, 122–23, 136
Lockyear, Mark, 164
Lockyer, Roger, 21, 23
Loomba, Ania, 130–31
Loughrey, Bryan, 77, 95, 107

Love's Labour's Lost, 16, 96, 173
Lower, Charles, 147
Luce, Morton, 110
Lucio, 18
Lust, 37, 38, 57, 67–68, 88, 95, 102,
    171
Lyly, John, 38–39

Macaulay, Alistair, 164
Macbeth, 23, 33, 39, 183, 188; vs. *Tempest*, 2, 11, 17, 18, 19, 28, 31, 52,
    53, 58, 66, 88, 107, 117, 132, 150,
    162, 173–74, 182, 194
Machiavelli, Niccolò, 66, 70, 108
MacKaye, Percy, 141
Macready, Charles, 146
Magic, 17, 18–25, 90, 132, 161; James
    I on, 13–14, 22, 25, 31; Prospero's
    renunciation of, 12, 22, 24, 30–31,
    37, 41, 42, 59–60, 94, 97, 100, 106,
    107, 133, 134, 149, 150, 156–57;
    Prospero's use of, 13, 19, 20, 21, 24,
    29, 30, 31, 32, 33–34, 37, 40–41, 54,
    59, 62, 77, 94, 99, 102, 103, 104,
    105, 108, 109, 116, 118, 121, 153,
    193; during Renaissance, 22, 25, 31,
    132, 191, 192–93; witchcraft, 12, 19,
    34, 38–40, 41, 42
Maguin, Jean-Marie, 112
The Malcontent, 95
Malvolio, 54, 62
Mammon, Sir Epicure, 32
Mandel, Jerome, 30, 74
Mannoni, Dominique Octave, 3
Marcus, Leah S., 121
Margaret of Anjou, 15
Marienstras, Richard, 126
Marlowe, Christopher, 32–33, 123, 194
Marston, John, 95
Marx, Leo, 46, 47, 72, 109, 128, 129–
    30
Marxism, 65, 159
Masque, 1–2, 3, 5, 37, 39, 45, 108; interpretations, 16, 29, 42, 57, 58–59, 67–
    69, 72, 76, 78, 95, 103, 120, 125,
    158–59, 171; in performance, 4, 69,
    148–49, 153, 158, 161, 162, 165,

169, 171, 172–73, 179, 181, 182–83, 184

The Masque of Beauty, 16, 34

The Masque of Queens, 34

Master, 46

Matis, Hannah, 173

Mazursky, Paul, 194

McCowen, Alec, 150, 161, 163–64, 166

McDonald, Russ, 90, 97–98, 123, 126, 131

McDowell, Roddy, 179–80

McGuire, Philip, 47, 62

McKellen, Ian, 160–61, 182

McLuskie, Kathleen, 87

McMurtry, Jo, 178

Measure for Measure, 17, 18, 35–36, 73, 95, 116, 119, 183

Mebane, John, 26

Medea, 12, 39, 40, 59, 107

Mendes, Sam, 161–65

Mercer, Lisa, 173

The Merchant of Venice, 62, 128

Meroe, 38

Messina, Cedric, 183

Metamorphoses, 11, 12, 18, 59, 67

Middle Ages, 35–36

A Midsummer Night's Dream, 16, 18, 45, 85, 95, 158, 173

Milano, Paulo, 36

Miller, Jonathan, 15, 154–55

Miller, Richard, 157

Milton, John, 134, 135, 138

Miranda, 37, 87, 145; character, 41, 42, 47, 54–55, 141; compassion of, 47, 54, 60; during Masque, 45, 57; relationship with Caliban, 49, 88; relationship with Ferdinand, 2, 35, 49–50, 53, 54–55, 60–61, 67–68, 69, 74, 77–78, 86, 88, 90, 95, 101, 102, 118, 135, 153, 159–60, 166, 168, 169, 171, 172, 174, 181, 191; relationship with Prospero, 9, 40–41, 47–48, 49, 50, 61, 88, 90, 98, 99, 101, 102, 104, 106, 133, 154, 166–67, 172, 174, 180, 181, 183, 191. *See also* Performances, as Miranda

Mirrour for Magistrates, 15

"The Monster," 113

Montaigne, Michel de, 11–12, 60, 66

Mooney, Michael, 94, 110

More, Thomas, 78

Morse, William, 25, 30

Moseley, Charles, 67, 92

Moulton, Richard G., 65, 123

Mowat, Barbara, 5–6, 34, 74, 92–93, 107

Mozart, Wolfgang Amadeus, 159

Much Ado about Nothing, 88

Muir, Kenneth, 106

Murry, John Middleton, 73, 105

Music, 134, 150; and Ariel, 49, 52, 53, 55, 67, 97; and Caliban, 29, 51; in productions, 144, 149, 156–57, 159; role in *Tempest*, 3, 29, 36, 49, 50–51, 55–56, 90, 96, 154, 156–57

"The Myth of Sisyphus," 114

Nardo, Anna, 87

Nature, 3, 4, 25–27, 52, 75–76, 193; hierarchy in, 20–22, 29, 111; vs. nurture, 17, 42, 57, 58, 66, 67, 68, 73, 111–12, 129–30, 182; vs. political power, 46; and Prospero, 24, 26, 48, 106

Neely, Carol Thomas, 87

Neilson, Francis, 57, 73, 137

Neoclassical criticism, 79, 81

Neoplatonism, 21–22, 23–24, 28, 29, 32, 47, 51, 124

Nevo, Ruth, 76–77

New Arden edition (1954), 2–3, 45

New Criticism, 6, 63, 65, 85–87, 122, 128, 190

New Folger edition (1994), 5–6

New Historicism, 5, 11, 20, 63, 65, 115, 122

New Penguin edition (1968), 4

New Variorum edition (1892), 2, 3, 123, 145

New World, 3, 39, 117, 127, 128, 129–30, 161; vs. Old World, 15, 40, 120–21, 124. *See also* Bermuda/"Bermuda Pamphlets"; Colonialism

Ngugi Wa Thiong'o, 119

Nietzsche, Friedrich, 67

Nightingale, Benedict, 160–61, 163

Nihilism, 69, 74–75, 162

Ninagawa, Yukio, 160
Noah, 137–38
Noble, Adrian, 172–73
Noches de Invierno, 14
Norton, Thomas, 15
Novum Organum, 25
Nunn, Trevor, 169

Ode to a Grecian Urn, 85, 151
Odysseus, 15
"Of the Caniballes," 11
"Of Cruelty," 12
O'Hara, David, 164
Olivier, Laurence, 188, 190, 194
On the Origin of Species, 110, 111
Order. *See* Hierarchy
Orgel, Stephen, 3, 77, 78, 90, 119, 131,
    155, 187; on Prospero, 13, 31, 101,
    103, 104, 105, 107, 108
Osborne, Laurie, 187
Othello, 66; film versions, 187, 190,
    192; vs. *Tempest*, 16, 68, 128, 135
Ovid, 11, 12, 18, 59, 67
Oxford edition (1987), 3
Oxford school edition (1998), 6

Paine, Henry, 10–11
Palmer, D. J., 21, 90, 91
Papp, Joseph, 5, 155, 166
Parable of the Talents, 16, 32
Paradise Lost, 58
Paris, Bernard J., 99–101
Paris, Jean, 50
Parker, Oliver, 187
Passages, act I: 1.1.4, 46; 1.1.13–14, 46;
    1.1.16–17, 46; 1.1.22–23, 46; 1.1.29–
    30, 46; 1.1.35–37, 46; 1.2.5–6, 47;
    1.2.10–14, 106; 1.2.11, 37; 1.2.15,
    47, 106; 1.2.21, 47; 1.2.30–32, 9;
    1.2.45, 47; 1.2.50, 167; 1.2.93, 105;
    1.2.97, 119; 1.2.128, 58; 1.2.150–51,
    48; 1.2.159, 29, 48; 1.2.162–65, 48;
    1.2.178–80, 48; 1.2.181–84, 92;
    1.2.182, 48; 1.2.196–97, 48; 1.2.198–
    201, 9; 1.2.201, 48; 1.2.204–5, 48;
    1.2.214–15, 48, 173; 1.2.257–58, 104;
    1.2.272–73, 27; 1.2.273, 41; 1.2.318,
    112; 1.2.375, 13; 1.2.424, 14; 1.2.429–

30, 166; 1.2.469–70, 88
Passages, act II: 2.1.46–47, 51; 2.1.60–
    62, 51; 2.1.162, 52; 2.1.197, 52;
    2.1.211, 52; 2.1.272–73, 60; 2.1.307–
    13, 52; 2.1.322, 52; 2.2.1–2, 53;
    2.2.3, 53; 2.2.5, 53; 2.2.9, 53; 2.2.12,
    53; 2.2.14, 53; 2.2.15, 53; 2.2.19, 53;
    2.2.26, 53; 2.2.30–31, 53; 2.2.34–35,
    53, 112; 2.2.40–41, 53; 2.2.45, 53;
    2.2.54, 53; 2.2.58–59, 53; 2.2.67–68,
    53; 2.2.68, 54; 2.2.71, 53; 2.2.98–99,
    53; 2.2.107–8, 53; 2.2.118, 53;
    2.2.127, 54; 2.2.131, 5; 2.2.144–73,
    181; 2.2.157–59, 53; 2.2.165–66, 53,
    54; 2.2.175, 54; 2.2.181, 54; 2.2.188,
    54; 2.2.295–96, 49; 2.2.298, 49;
    2.2.310, 49; 2.2.322, 49; 2.2.339, 49;
    2.2.352–53, 49; 2.2.355–59, 49;
    2.2.365–66, 49; 2.2.374–78, 49;
    2.2.395–96, 49; 2.2.404, 49; 2.2.424–
    25, 49; 2.2.482, 50; 2.2.489, 50;
    2.2.496, 50
Passages, act III: 3.1.2, 54; 3.1.11, 54;
    3.1.30–31, 54; 3.1.38–47, 54; 3.1.55,
    54; 3.1.64, 55; 3.1.66–67, 55; 3.1.75–
    76, 54; 3.1.87–89, 55; 3.1.94, 54;
    3.2.41–42, 55; 3.2.44, 55; 3.2.59, 55;
    3.2.131, 55; 3.2.132, 55; 3.2.133–34,
    42, 51, 55; 3.2.139–41, 55; 3.2.148–
    50, 55; 3.3.18–19, 56; 3.3.31, 60;
    3.3.36–37, 56; 3.3.38, 96; 3.3.50–51,
    56; 3.3.53, 56; 3.3.61, 29; 3.3.77–82,
    56, 118; 3.3.88, 56; 3.3.107, 56;
    3.3.109, 56; 3.3, 15, 28, 31. *See also*
    Banquet scene
Passages, act IV: 4.1.37, 45; 4.1.57–58,
    2; 4.1.60–105, 4; 4.1.101, 42;
    4.1.102, 173; 4.1.105, 103; 4.1.110,
    69, 103; 4.1.119–20, 45, 58; 4.1.123,
    2; 4.1.134–40, 58; 4.1.134, 5;
    4.1.146, 69; 4.1.151, 15, 69; 4.1.153,
    183; 4.1.158–63, 69; 4.1.166, 58;
    4.1.182, 58; 4.1.188–89, 58; 4.1.206,
    58; 4.1.222, 58; 4.1.249–50, 58;
    4.1.267, 58. *See also* Masque; "Rev-
    els" speech
Passages, act V: 5.1.2–3, 59; 5.1.7, 59;
    5.1.17, 118; 5.1.18–20, 59; 5.1.21,
    113; 5.1.26–27, 107; 5.1.28–30, 59;

5.1.28, 107, 118; 5.1.32, 59; 5.1.48–
50, 31, 59; 5.1.77, 108; 5.1.84, 61;
5.1.87, 60; 5.1.92, 60; 5.1.112, 60;
5.1.119, 60; 5.1.124, 90; 5.1.130, 108;
5.1.139, 60; 5.1.149–50, 60; 5.1.170,
77; 5.1.179, 96; 5.1.183–84, 61;
5.1.186–87, 61; 5.1.197–98, 61;
5.1.199–200, 132; 5.1.211–12, 140;
5.1.213, 168; 5.1.222, 61; 5.1.223–
25, 61; 5.1.233, 119; 5.1.243, 61;
5.1.265–66, 61; 5.1.275–76, 61, 119;
5.1.287, 53; 5.1.294–97, 61, 112;
5.1.307, 61–62; 5.1.310–11, 62;
5.1.314–15, 62
Passages, Epilogue, 35, 36–37, 47, 62,
101, 108–9, 110, 118, 124–25, 134,
135–36, 152, 173
Patriarchy, 87, 88–89, 102
Patrick, Julian, 92, 112
Paul, Saint, 9
Pearlman, E., 84
Pearson, D'Orsay, 134
Pelican edition (1958, rev. 1970), 4
Pennell, Nicholas, 182
Pepys, Samuel, 144–45
Performances: as Antonio, 162, 163,
168, 170–71, 172, 173, 179, 181; as
Ariel, 62, 145, 149–50, 152, 154,
155, 159, 160, 161, 162, 163, 165,
168, 170, 171, 173, 178–81, 182,
183, 184–85, 193; of banquet scene,
160, 161, 162–63, 181; as Caliban,
69, 112, 128, 141, 147, 148, 152,
153, 154–55, 158–59, 162, 164, 165,
166, 168, 170, 171, 173, 174, 178,
179, 180–81, 182, 184, 185, 186, 189–
90; as Ferdinand, 159, 164, 169, 171,
172, 173, 181, 184; as Gonzalo, 165,
168, 170; of Masque, 4, 69, 148–49,
153, 158, 161, 162, 165, 169, 171,
172–73, 179, 181, 182–83, 184; as
Miranda, 148, 159, 164, 166, 169,
170, 174, 179, 180, 181–82, 183, 193;
as Prospero, 62, 107, 146, 148–49,
150, 153, 157, 159, 160–61, 163–64,
166–69, 170–72, 178, 179–80, 181–
82, 183, 184, 185, 189; of "revels"

speech, 149, 153, 159, 180, 184; as
Sebastian, 155, 156, 163, 170, 173,
179; as Stephano, 69, 154, 155, 156,
162, 164, 166, 171, 172, 174, 178,
179, 180, 181, 182; vs. text, 83, 168,
170, 172, 180, 184, 187–88, 194; as
Trinculo, 69, 151, 155, 156, 162,
166, 171, 172, 173, 178, 179, 180,
182. *See also* Productions, film; Pro-
ductions, stage; Productions, televi-
sion
Pericles, 17, 18, 34, 49, 51
Perineau, Harold, 185
Perkins, William, 23
Peter, Saint, 33
Peterson, Douglas, 109
Phaedrus, 86, 102
Phillips, James E., 20, 109, 122
Phillips, Robin, 60, 153
Pico della Mirandola, 21, 22
Pidgeon, Walter, 194
Pietro Martier D'Anghiera, 13
Pigott-Smith, Tim, 156
Pinciss, Gerald, 21, 23
Plato, 51, 86, 97, 102, 122, 138
Plotinus, 22
Pocket Classics edition, 5
Poel, William, 146
Politics, 120, 121, 144; and Prospero,
66–67, 77–78, 102–3, 109, 116–19,
122
Poole, Roger, 144
Postmodernism, 85, 139–40; in produc-
tions, 139, 144, 150, 159, 162, 165–
69, 183, 187, 191, 192
Poston, Tom, 179
Potter, Lois, 151, 153–54
Potter, Miles, 182
Preston, Carrie, 166
Productions, film, 187–95; *Forbidden
Planet*, 157, 183, 193–94; Jarman
film, 39–40, 192–93; postmodernism
in, 187, 191, 192; *Prospero's Books*,
148, 171, 187–92; vs. stage, 147; vs.
television, 177–78; *Tempest* (1982),
194. *See also* Performances
Productions, stage, 6, 63, 119–20; A

Center for Theater Research (ACTER) (1993), 160; American Repertory Theatre (1995), 161, 169–72; Ashland (1994), 48, 173; Asolo Theater (Sarasota, FL) (1980), 158; at Whitehall/Blackfriars, 117, 141, 143–44, 151; BBC-TV (1980), 4; Beerbohm Tree (1904), 148; Brunswick, Maine, High School, 173–74; Cheek by Jowl, 150, 152, 153; Clemson University (1999), 48, 173; colonialism in, 152, 154–55, 157, 161, 172, 175, 178; Great Lakes Festival, 155; by Hall, 39–40, 107, 148, 149, 150, 155–57, 169; Mermaid Theater (1970), 154, 161; music in, 144, 149, 156–57, 159; National Theatre, 107, 148, 149, 150, 155–57, 169; New York Public Theatre (1995–96), 48, 173; New York Shakespeare Festival (1995), 161, 165–69, 170–72; postmodernism in, 139, 144, 150, 159, 162, 165–69; Royal Shakespeare Company, 62, 69, 107, 150, 153, 161–65, 172–73, 180; spectacular vs. spare, 146–47; storm/shipwreck in, 144–46, 148, 161, 169–70; Stratford, CT (1971), 155; Stratford, ONT (1976), 153; Stratford, ONT (1982), 155, 182–83; *La Tempête*, 62, 158; West Yorkshire (1999), 160–61; by Williams (1930), 152. *See also* Performances

Productions, television, 178–87; animated version (1992), 178, 184–85; Bard production (1983), 178, 179, 181–82; BBC production (1980), 4, 178, 180–81, 183–84; colonialism in, 178; vs. film, 177–78; NBC production (1998), 178, 185–87; "Page to Stage" documentary, 182–83; postmodernism in, 183; Schaefer production (1960), 178–80, 183; vs. stage, 147. *See also* Performances

Prospero, 17, 51, 65, 87, 92, 145; character, 18, 19, 20, 35–36, 42, 47–48, 59–60, 61, 66, 83, 86, 93, 94–95, 98, 99–110, 122, 139, 141, 149, 150, 153, 156, 163; on chastity, 37, 38, 57, 86, 102, 103, 125, 135; as colonizer, 6, 66, 102–3, 122–27, 139, 155, 159; and compassion, 47, 54, 59–60, 100, 104–5, 109, 113, 115, 135, 168; duty as duke neglected by, 13, 15–16, 47, 122; Epilogue of, 5, 35, 36–37, 47, 62, 101, 108–9, 110, 118, 124–25, 134, 135–36, 152, 173; magic renounced by, 12, 22, 24, 30–31, 37, 41, 42, 59–60, 94, 97, 100, 106, 107, 133, 134, 149, 150, 156–57; magic used by, 13, 19, 20, 21, 24, 29, 30, 31, 32, 33–34, 37, 40–41, 54, 59, 62, 77, 94, 99, 102, 103, 104, 105, 108, 109, 116, 118, 121, 153, 193; vs. Medea, 12, 40, 59, 107; and nature, 24, 26, 48, 106; and politics, 66–67, 77–78, 102–3, 109, 116–19, 122; power of, 50, 105, 108, 118, 193; relationship with Alonso, 47, 56, 59, 60–62, 77, 106–7, 118, 132, 191; relationship with Antonio, 47, 48, 60, 61, 62, 99, 100, 101, 102, 103, 104, 105–6, 107–8, 116, 117–19, 121, 124, 135–36, 150, 154, 156, 168; relationship with Ariel, 2, 29, 35, 48–49, 50, 55, 56, 58, 60, 62, 69, 94, 99, 102, 106, 107, 108, 109, 113–15, 117, 118, 123, 126, 134, 136, 149, 150, 152, 155, 156, 159, 163, 168, 172, 191; relationship with Caliban, 15, 34, 35, 41–43, 49, 50, 52–53, 55, 57–58, 61, 69, 72, 73, 94, 99, 100, 102–4, 106, 108, 109, 111, 113, 117–18, 119, 122–25, 126, 127, 130, 134, 137, 139–40, 155, 157, 159, 165, 168, 179–80; relationship with Ferdinand, 50, 58, 69, 73, 83, 86, 101, 102, 125, 138, 165, 166, 174; relationship with Gonzalo, 48, 59–60, 109, 118, 126, 135, 168, 191; relationship with Miranda, 9, 40–41, 47–48, 49, 50, 61, 88, 90, 98, 99, 101, 102, 104, 106, 133, 154, 166–67, 172, 174, 180, 181, 183, 191; "revels" speech, 15, 45, 58–59, 67, 68–77, 132–33; and revenge/forgiveness,

12, 59, 94–95, 99–100, 101–2, 105, 106–8, 109, 124, 149, 150, 153, 154, 161, 163–64, 166, 172, 182, 191; sources for, 13–16, 83, 85, 106; vs. Sycorax, 39–41, 42, 63, 100, 103, 104, 107, 126, 127. *See also* Performances, as Prospero
Prospero and Caliban, 3
Prospero's Books, 148, 165, 171, 187–92
Prosser, Eleanor, 12
Protestantism, 19, 23, 24, 27
Prouty, Charles T., 4
"Providence," 36
Psychological criticism, 61, 98–105, 122, 193
Purcarete, Silviu, 159
Purcell, Henry, 146
Purkiss, Diane, 39, 40–42
Pythagoras, 51

Queen Elizabeth's Prayer Book, 118, 132, 137
Quiller-Couch, Sir Arthur, 5, 14, 85

Radd, Ronald, 179
Rafferty, Terrence, 187
Raskin, Bonnie, 186
Rawson, Christopher, 166
Reason, 66, 68, 70, 109–10, 111–12, 131; vs. passion, 104, 148. *See also* Appearance and reality; Science
Reconciliation. *See* Forgiveness/reconciliation
Religious criticism, 131–40
Remick, Lee, 179
Renaissance, 9–20, 26–27, 28, 30, 32, 47, 55; magic during, 22, 25, 31, 132, 191, 192–93; music during, 144; values during, 67, 68, 122, 131, 138, 192–93
Renan, Ernest, 3
Renewal, 42, 51, 94, 124
Repentence, 107, 118, 132, 134, 175
Return to Forbidden Planet, 157
"Revels" speech, 15, 45, 58–59, 67, 68–77, 132–33; in performance, 149, 153, 159, 180, 184

Revenge, and Prospero, 12, 59, 94–95, 99–100, 101–2, 106–8, 149, 150, 161, 163–64, 166, 172, 182, 191. *See also* Forgiveness/reconciliation
Reynolds, Stanley, 180
Ribner, Irving, 4
Richard II, 16, 17, 18, 109, 120
Richard III, 18, 135, 174
Richardson, Ian, 150
Rickey, Mary Ellen, 36
Ridley, Clifford A., 165
Ringwald, Molly, 194
Ripley, Scott, 171
Robard, Sam, 194
Roberts, Jeanne Addison, 2, 12, 20, 22, 61, 87
Rockett, William, 126–27, 138
Rodo, Jose Enrique, 3
"Roger Malvin's Burial," 91
Roman Catholicism, 23
Romance, *Tempest* as, 90, 91–94, 98–99
Romeo and Juliet, 16, 119, 190
Rose, Mark, 57
Rothwell, Kenneth, 155
Rowe, Nicholas, 81
Rowse, A. L., 5
Rudolf II, 121
Rylance, Mark, 62

Sackville, Thomas, 15
Saint Elmo's fire, 9
Sanchez, Jame, 155
Sandys, George, 59
The Scarlet Letter, 91–92
Schaefer, George, 178–80, 183
Schiller, Leon, 159
Schlegel, S. W., 147
Schleiner, Louise, 120
Schmidgall, Gary, 14
Schneider, Ben Ross, Jr., 122, 127
Schofield, Paul, 150
Die Schöne Sidea, 14
Science, 25–27, 77, 131, 139–40, 192–93. *See also* Appearance and reality; Reason
Scott, Sir Walter, 145
Sebastian, 60, 189; character, 58, 97; relationship with Alonso, 51–52; rela-

tionship with Antonio, 46, 51–52, 55, 61, 108, 116, 117–19. *See also* Performances, as Sebastian

Seltzer, Priscilla, 155

Serrano, Nestor, 170–71

Setebos, 13, 49, 134

Sewell, Arthur, 68, 75

Sexuality, 102, 103, 104. *See also* Chastity; Lust

Shadwell, Thomas, 145–46

Shakespeare, William, 16; Bradley on, 83, 86; Coleridge on, 81, 83, 84, 90; Greenblatt on, 116; Henry James on, 84; Johnson on, 81, 96; Jonson on, 79, 81, 134; Keats on, 79, 83; and Prospero, 83, 85, 106; relationship with Fletcher, 83; Strachey on, 84–85; *Tempest* as fantasy of, 99, 100–101; Wendell on, 79; Wharton on, 81

Shakespeare, Our Contemporary, 36, 154

Shakespeare Films in the Classroom, 178

Shaw, George Bernard, 146

Shearer, Norma, 190

"The Shepheard's Calendar," 69

The Shoemaker's Holliday, 148

Shrimpton, Nicholas, 175

Siddal, Stephen, 60

Sidney, Sir Philip, 25, 89

Signet Classic edition (1998 rev.), 6

Simon, John, 165, 166

Simon Magus, 33

Sitwell, Edith, 110

Skottowe, Augustine, 122

Skura, Meredith Anne, 6, 18, 103, 127–28

Slights, William, 93

Slover, George, 11, 135

Smallwood, Robert, 161

Smith, Cecil, 180, 181

Smith, Hallett, 2, 112, 154

Smith, Irwin, 2

Smith, John, 7

Smith, Nigel, 14, 46–47, 75

Smith, R. W., 173

Sololov, Stanislav, 184

Solter, Friedo, 159

Southampton, Henry Wriothesley, Earl of, 7

Southey, Robert, 81

Speaight, Robert, 73–74, 148–49, 150, 154; on Ariel, 114; on Caliban, 112; on Prospero, 123–24

Spencer, Charles, 164

Spencer, Hazelton, 14, 141, 184, 195

Spencer, Theodore, 109–10

Spenser, Edmund, 38, 52, 69, 70, 96

Spillane, Margaret, 151

Stage directions, 1, 5, 52, 55, 61, 69, 143

Stanley, H. M., 116

"Stanzas from the Great Chartreuse," 113

Steiner, Elizabeth, 174

Steiner, George, 76

Stephano, 58, 121, 137; relationship with Caliban, 35, 53–54, 55, 61, 69, 94, 117–18, 125, 154, 156. *See also* Performances, as Stephano

Stewart, Patrick, 62, 166–69, 172

Still, Colin, 135

Stockholder, Kay, 95, 102, 103, 104, 108

Stoll, E. E., 112, 127

Storm/shipwreck, 7, 9–10, 14–15, 46–48, 133, 180, 181

Strachey, Lytton, 47, 84–85

Strachey, William, 7, 9, 116, 117

Strane, Robert, 158

Strehler, Giorgio, 159–60

Sturgess, Keith, 18, 32, 50–51, 67, 78, 146, 151–52, 160; on music, 50, 144

Styan, J. L., 53

Subtle, 32

Summers, Sir George, 7

Sundelson, David, 102

Sycorax, 13, 49, 87, 131, 184; vs. Prospero, 39–41, 42, 63, 100, 103, 104, 107, 126, 127; relationship with Ariel, 27, 29, 48, 127

The Taming of the Shrew, 88, 121, 181

Taylor, Edward, 111

Taylor, Gary, 116

Taylor, J. E., 181–82

Taylor, Neil, 77, 95, 107
Taylor, Paul, 162, 164
Television. *See* Productions, television
The Tempest: vs. *Aeneid*, 14–15, 28, 51,
56, 71, 131, 137; vs. *Alchemist*, 32;
as allegory, 16, 29, 134–35, 153, 154;
vs. *Antony and Cleopatra*, 18, 36, 42,
50, 88, 122, 128; vs. *As You Like It*,
16, 18, 34, 62, 88, 91; chess game in,
36, 45, 60–61, 67, 74, 77–78, 172;
vs. *Comedy of Errors*, 2, 17, 34, 46;
vs. *Coriolanus*, 18; vs. *Cymbeline*,
18, 49; vs. *Dr. Faustus*, 31, 33–34,
107, 123, 134; duality in, 50, 58, 62,
66, 69, 70, 71, 73, 86, 131; vs. *Faerie Queene*, 38; vs. *Franklin's Tale*,
37–38; vs. *Friar Bacon and Friar
Bungay*, 39; vs. *Golden Ass*, 38; vs.
Hamlet, 16, 17, 52, 76, 94, 100, 106,
119, 128, 132, 173, 174; vs. *Henry
V*, 15, 45–46, 115, 116, 117, 123,
128, 131; vs. *Henry VI*, 15, 18, 129;
hierarchy challenged by, 12, 22; vs.
King Lear, 16, 17, 18, 46, 51, 61, 90,
94, 102, 109, 138, 163; vs. *Love's
Labour's Lost*, 16, 96, 173; vs. *Macbeth*, 2, 11, 17, 18, 19, 28, 31, 52,
53, 58, 66, 88, 107, 117, 132, 150,
162, 173–74, 182, 194; vs. *Malcontent*, 95; vs. *Masque of Beauty*, 34;
vs. *Measure for Measure*, 17, 18, 35–
36, 73, 95, 116, 119; vs. *Merchant of
Venice*, 62, 128; vs. *Midsummer
Night's Dream*, 16, 18, 45, 85, 95,
173; vs. *Much Ado about Nothing*, 88;
vs. *Othello*, 16, 68, 128, 135; vs.
Pericles, 17, 18, 34, 49, 51; vs. *Richard II*, 16, 17, 18, 109, 120; vs. *Richard III*, 18, 135, 174; as romance, 68,
90, 91–94, 98–99; vs. *Romeo and Juliet*, 16, 119; vs. *Taming of the
Shrew*, 88, 121, 181; vs. *Timon of
Athens*, 18, 28; vs. *Titus Andronicus*,
128; as tragicomedy, 90–91, 93–96,
116, 154; vs. *Twelfth Night*, 17, 46,
54, 62, 75; unity in, 57, 65–66, 83,
86, 92, 122, 139, 144, 151, 158, 192;
vs. *Winter's Tale*, 17–18, 46, 49, 79,

81, 90, 92. *See also* Chess game;
Passages; Performances; Productions,
film; Productions, stage; Productions,
television; Storm/shipwreck; *and
specific characters*
Tempest (Mazursky), 194
The Tempest (Renan), 3
La Tempête, 62, 158
Une Tempête, 157
Thacker, David, 62
Thaler, Alwin, 38
Thematic criticism, 84–85
Thompson, Ann, 68, 88
Throne of Blood, 194
Tillyard, E.M.W., 6, 20, 52, 57, 94,
107, 115
Time, 67, 69, 75–76, 77, 86, 92, 98,
106
Timon of Athens, 18, 28
Tinker, Chauncey Brewster, 4
Tintern Abbey, 85
Titus Andronicus, 128
Tobin, J.J.M., 2
Tom Jones, 100
Tragicomedy, *Tempest* as, 90–91, 93–
96, 116
Traister, Barbara Howard, 48, 106
Traversi, Derek, 113–14
Trewin, J. C., 146, 147
Trinculo, 58, 61, 94, 121, 127, 137, 169;
relationship with Caliban, 35, 53, 55,
117–18, 125, 156, 181. *See also* Per-
formances, as Trinculo
Trivet, Nicholas, 94
Troughton, David, 162, 164
*True Declaration of the State of the Co-
lonie in Virginia*, 7, 11, 95–96, 135
True Reportory of the Wracke, 7, 9
Twelfth Night, 17, 46, 54, 62, 75, 192

"Use of Salutary Anxiety," 6
Utopia, 78

Van Doren, Mark, 16
Vaughan, Alden T./Virginia Mason, 31,
32, 81, 83, 90, 92, 150; on Caliban,
110, 111, 112, 113; on chess game,
78; on Masque, 67; New Arden Edi-

tion (1999) of, 3, 13; on Prospero,
    47, 59, 70; on *Tempest* productions,
    157, 179, 187
Venus, 37, 67–68, 95, 135
Vespucci, Amerigo, 11
Vickers, Brian, 111, 113, 126
Victorian criticism, 66, 76, 83, 84, 123,
    152
Vigus, Robert, 173
Vincentio, 18, 73
Virgil, 14–15
Virginia, 7, 10–11, 116, 125, 127, 135
The Virgin Queen, 3
Von Rosador, Kurt T., 30–31, 53, 90,
    174
Von Sydow, Max, 150, 153
Voyages, 9

Wakefield plays, 35
Waldron, F. G., 3
Walker, D. P., 29, 132
Walker, William Sidney, 134
Waller, Gary, 89, 98–99
Wallis, Bill, 153
Walter, James, 48, 67, 68, 75, 135–36
Wandering, 34
Warren, Roger, 55, 156–57, 177
Washington, Dinah, 194
Watterson, William C., 102, 165
Waugh, Patricia, 93
Webster, Margaret, 141, 180
Weimann, Robert, 65, 144
Welch, Elizabeth, 192
Wells, Stanley, 75, 96, 107, 122
Wendell, Barrett, 79
Werstine, Paul, 5–6
West, Robert H., 18–19, 22, 30, 113
Wharton, Joseph, 81, 113
Wheeler, Richard, 68, 112, 124
White, Hayden, 40

Wilcox, Fred, 193–94
Wilders, John, 4, 48, 67
William, David, 49, 144
Williams, Clifford, 180
Williams, Gary Jay, 157
Williams, Harcourt, 152
Williams, Stephen, 149
Williams, Wendy, 185
Willis, Deborah, 112
Willis, Jack, 171
Wills, Garry, 39
Wilson, Daniel, 110, 122, 148
Wilson, John Dover, 5, 46, 52, 84, 85,
    107
Wilson, Richard, 14
Wilson, Robert, 109
Wiltenburg, Robert, 7, 14–15
Winer, Linda, 165–66
The Winter's Tale, 156; vs. *Tempest*, 17–
    18, 46, 49, 79–80, 81, 90, 92
Witchcraft, 12, 19, 34, 38–40, 41, 42
Witch of Endor, 23
The Witch in History, 39
Wittgenstein, Ludwig, 76
Wolfe, George C., 161, 165–69, 170–71
Wolfit, Donald, 170
Wolsey, Cardinal, 39
Wood, John, 150, 153, 163
Woodman, William, 178, 182
Woodward, Sarah, 164
Wordsworth Classics edition (1994), 5
Wordsworth, William, 85
Wright, Neil H., 75, 76–77
Wright, Timothy, 153

Yale Shakespeare edition, 4
Young, R. V., 119

Zesmer, David A., 47, 62
Zimbalist, Efrem, Jr., 178, 181–82
Zimbardo, Rose A., 108

About the Author

H. R. COURSEN teaches at the University of Maine, Augusta. He is the author of more than forty books, including *Macbeth: A Guide to the Play* (Greenwood Press, 1997) and *Teaching Shakespeare with Film and Television: A Guide* (Greenwood Press, 1997), both available from Greenwood Press.

ISBN 0-313-31191-9

90000>

EAN

9 780313 311918

HARDCOVER BAR CODE